Conscientious Objection to Various Compulsions Under British Law

Constance Braithwaite
B.Sc. (Economics), Ph.D.
*Formerly University Lecturer in Social Studies
at Birmingham and Newcastle upon Tyne*

William Sessions Limited
York, England

951034

British Library Cataloguing in Publication Data

Braithwaite, Constance
  Conscientious objection to various
    compulsions under British law.

  1.
I. Title
361.709953

ISBN 1–85072–127–0

Typeset by Woodfield Publishing Services, Fontwell, Sussex.
Printed in Great Britain by The Ebor Press, York.

TO THE MEMORY OF

MY FATHER
WILLIAM CHARLES BRAITHWAITE

MY BROTHER
ALFRED WILLIAM BRAITHWAITE

MY UNCLE
GEOFFREY MORLAND

MY FRIENDS
SOPHIE MESS
PETER URE
PHYLLIS McTAVISH WILLIAM

FOREWORD

This book represents many years of meticulous research and personal debate by my late aunt, Constance Braithwaite. Although she died in 1985, it is apparent that her detailed research takes the book up to about ten years prior to that.

Fortunately, the histories of conscientious objection to oaths, to compulsory vaccination against smallpox and to compulsory military and defence service may be regarded as largely complete by that time. However, in the other two areas – conscientious objection to compulsory religious education and to compulsory medical care of children – history has continued to be made since this book was written.

I have added a short piece to the end of Chapter 1, on oaths and affirmations, (and have also up-dated the relevant portion of Chapter 11) so as to reflect the final developments in this area of the law, which took place in 1978.

With that exception, the original text has been amended only in the few places where it was necessary in order (a) to avoid repetition or (b) to improve clarity or (c) to remove passages which had become too dated.

No attempt has been made to extend the text to cover areas where the issues of conscientious objection discussed in this book may, subsequently, have become of greater significance, or where new issues have emerged.

I am most grateful to my wife, Judith, to my cousin, Anna Kerr, and to my sister, Janet Newell, for their assistance in proof-reading and to Hurlston Design Limited, Birmingham, for donating the cover design.

Geoffrey D. Braithwaite
Literary Executor

INTRODUCTION

When the law imposes upon individuals obligations with which some individuals feel that they cannot conscientiously comply, then, unless special legal provision is made for them, these individuals must choose between disobeying their consciences and disobeying the law. Partly in order to prevent or minimise conscientious law-breaking, Britain made statutory provision for legal conscientious objection in four spheres of law – the law regarding oaths, the law regarding compulsory military service, the law regarding compulsory vaccination against smallpox, and the law regarding religious worship and religious instruction in schools. The history of the compulsions in these four spheres of law, and of both illegal and legal conscientious objection to these compulsions, is described in Part I of this book.

In some other spheres of law there have also been compulsions to which there has been conscientious objection, but in these spheres of law there has never been statutory provision for legal exemption of conscientious objectors. The history of compulsions and of conscientious objection to them in six such spheres of law is also described in Part I of this book. The six types of compulsion described are the following: the compulsion on parents to provide or allow necessary medical care for their children; the three war-time compulsions of industrial conscription, compulsory part-time Civil Defence, and compulsory fire-watching; compulsory payments for military and other Defence purposes; and compulsory payments for religious education. With regard to five of these types of compulsion, all conscientious objection has been illegal objection. With regard to industrial conscription, there were both illegal objectors and objectors whose consciences were satisfied by administrative concessions. Two other types of legal compulsion to which there was illegal conscientious objection – compulsory tithes and compulsory church rates – are not described in this book because I consider these subjects to be now of only historical interest. The book does not describe the histories of general religious freedom or freedom of speech but there is some discussion of these freedoms in their relation to conscientious objection.

It will be noted that the kinds of legal compulsion to which there has been conscientious objection are very diverse – I cannot think of any other subject of enquiry which would involve comparing the law of oaths with the Vaccination Acts. But I have found this very diversity helpful as it assists the enquirer to identify what are the problems of conscientious objection itself, as contrasted with the problems of conflicting views on particular questions. I have found myself in agreement with the views of some conscientious objectors and in disagreement with the views of others and I have had to consider what is the right treatment of objectors holding views which I regard as mistaken or even absurd.

My angle of approach to my subject is the result of three kinds of interest. Firstly, I have had personal experience as a conscientious objector and personal acquaintance with many other objectors. Secondly, as a student and teacher in the field of Social Studies I have been involved in the consideration of general problems of law, ethics and political theory to which I have tried to relate my personal views and experience. Thirdly, as a citizen I am concerned to try to assist in the formation of desirable policies with regard to the attitude of the law and public authorities to conscientious objectors. My personal experience and opinions have influenced the whole book in the sense that the book would not have been written had I not considered that conscientious objection is an important matter. But there is a distinction between the two Parts of the book. In Part I, in which the treatment of the subjects is historical, I have not introduced my personal opinions. In Part II the treatment of the subjects includes evaluation, in addition to analysis and comparison, and in this Part my opinions are freely expressed.

In all the chapters in Part I there are not only histories of conscientious objection but also general histories of the compulsions which were opposed by objectors. There are two reasons for the inclusion of these general histories, in addition to the intrinsic interest of their subjects. Firstly, it is difficult to understand some of the actions of conscientious objectors without knowing, in considerable detail, the nature of the compulsions to which they were objecting. Secondly, in order to understand and evaluate the history of conscientious objection, it is desirable to understand also the reasons for the legal enactment of the various compulsions and the attitudes of those who administered and supported these compulsions. There were usually good reasons and good motives involved on both sides of the particular controversies and this fact gives a special kind of interest to a study of these controversies. The conflict between conceptions of good can be stimulating to the student of history though it was often burdensome and sometimes tragic to the participants.

There is included in this book a considerable number of descriptions given by individual conscientious objectors of their own views and actions. These statements have a flavour which is missing from general descriptions and they exemplify the individual nature of conscientious objection and the variety in the views and standpoints of objectors. Except in examples from the seventeenth and eighteenth centuries, I have usually deliberately omitted the name of the objector with regard to these statements and other references to individual objectors. Many of the names are known to me, but in most cases the name would be one previously unknown to the general reader and to include it would add nothing to his understanding of the subject. I might have deliberately included the cases or names of well known objectors because they were well known but, in my view, such action would have resulted in a serious distortion of my histories. The history of conscientious objection is the history of the decisions of the consciences of ordinary people, most of them unknown to any wide public: anonymity is an appropriate expression of this fact. (In the case of persons acting in a public capacity, for example M.P.s, and of course, in the case of authors, names are included).

I have found it difficult to decide how much background-history to include and I have made certain distinctions with regard to the amount of knowledge assumed to be possessed by the general reader. For example, I have assumed that the reader has a general knowledge of the history of the First and Second World Wars but I have not assumed that he or she has a general knowledge of the history of smallpox and vaccination. Prior to 1752, the year in England began on 25th March, which month accordingly became the year, while January and February formed the eleventh and twelfth months of this preceding year. I have given the year of dates prior to 1752 according to the modern (New Style) calendar. (For example, in Chapter 1, the Fifth Monarchy Rising is described as occurring in January 1661, not as occurring in January 1660 or in January 1660 – 61).

CONTENTS

CHAPTER 2: COMPULSORY VACCINATION AGAINST SMALLPOX

CHAPTER 3: COMPULSIONS FOR MILITARY PURPOSES BEFORE THE TWENTIETH CENTURY

CHAPTER 6: COMPULSORY MILITARY SERVICE 1945 – 1960

CHAPTER 7: OTHER TWENTIETH-CENTURY
COMPULSIONS FOR DEFENCE PURPOSES

CHAPTER 8: RELIGION IN SCHOOLS

PART I

Histories

CHAPTER 1

Oaths and Affirmations

Introduction

The long struggle for religious freedom has resulted in a state of affairs in present-day Great Britain in which, in general, no kind of religious activity is a legal duty of the ordinary citizen, and no legal duty of the ordinary citizen has as a necessary concomitant any religious activity or any statement of religious belief. To this general state of affairs there are two exceptions. One exception, which will be discussed in Chapter 8 of this book, is that the large majority of school-children are obliged by law to attend religious worship and religious instruction at school. The other exception is that certain legal duties, such as giving evidence and serving as a juror, as well as a number of other legal procedures, involve the taking of an oath with a religious reference. In these two exceptional cases present British law avoids direct infringement of religious liberty by providing for rights of conscientious objection.

Nearly two hundred years elapsed between the date of the first legal concessions made to conscientious objectors to oaths, in the Toleration Act of 1689,[1] and the date when the present position was substantially attained, in the Oaths Act of 1888.[2] The taking of oaths was an immemorial tradition and in the seventeenth and eighteenth centuries the occasions when legal oaths were taken were very numerous, considerably more numerous than at present. Many changes in the law allowed affirmations only as alternatives to certain kinds of oaths and the objectors remained under various disabilities until they were allowed to affirm on all occasions when an oath was legally required. The changes in the law were piecemeal not only in this respect but also with regard to the classes of objectors to whom the right of affirmation was allowed: the right was given first to certain classes of religious objectors, it was then

3

extended to all religious objectors, and it was finally extended to atheists and agnostics.

The long history of the controversies about the legal right of affirmation showed on many occasions the presence both of strongly held opinions about the direct question at issue and of strongly held opinions about other aspects of religious toleration. The direct question at issue was what (in addition to any legal penalties for perjury) should be required as the sanction likely to promote truth-speaking or the fulfilment of a promise. Should the sanction be necessarily a religious one, signified by an appeal to God in the wording of an oath, or should the form of words required vary according to what the individual concerned would consider to be most binding on his conscience? But the debates and decisions regarding concessions to objectors to oaths were not influenced only by the conflicting views on this question. The enforcement of oaths could be used as a weapon of religious persecution, and it was so used, for example, against Quakers in the seventeenth century. It could also be used as a weapon of religious discrimination, to exclude from various offices those who refused to take the oath required on assuming those offices, and it was so used, for example, to exclude first Jews and then atheists from Parliament at two periods in the nineteenth century.

It should be explained at this point that this chapter is concerned only with objectors to the form of oaths, that is with objectors who have been willing to make in another form the same statements or promises as have been contained in the oaths to which they have objected. There have also been many cases in which those required to take an oath have objected to the content of the oath, for example, Catholics who objected to the oath of supremacy and, in recent history, certain Irish Nationalists, elected to the British Parliament from Northern Ireland, who objected to the oath of allegiance. In such cases the objection was to the required statement or promise in whatever form it was made: this type of objection is a quite different subject which is not discussed in this book.

The Nature and Forms of Oaths

Oaths provided for by law have been of two kinds, assertory oaths and promissory oaths. In an assertory oath the person taking it swears to the truth of his factual statements: such an oath may take the form of a promise to speak the truth but this form does not make it a promissory oath in the ordinary sense. Current examples of assertory oaths are the oaths taken by witnesses in court and the affidavits made by executors of wills for purposes of taxation. In a promissory oath the person taking it swears to perform some action or course of action or to abstain from some action or course of action. An important current example of a promissory oath is the oath of allegiance; another example is the oath taken by a juror.

What is the essential feature which distinguishes an oath from other forms of assertion or promise? In his book "The Origin and Development of the Moral Ideas" (1908) Edward Westermarck cites considerable evidence that among some primitive peoples the force of the oath was considered to inhere in the oath itself without any connection with religion. "An oath is essentially a conditional self-imprecation, a curse by which a person calls down upon himself some evil in the event of what he says not being true. The efficacy of the oath is originally entirely magical, it is due to the magic power inherent in the cursing words."[3] In some cases an oath has been regarded as potentially dangerous quite apart from any breach of it. Westermarck states that among the Moors "the conditional self-curse is supposed in some degree to pollute the swearer even... though he do not perjure himself... They say that it is bad not only to swear but even to be present when an oath is taken by somebody."[4]

Westermarck gives examples of various methods used in order to charge the oaths with supernatural energy. The swearer may put himself in contact with some object representing the state referred to in the oath, for example, those taking the oath swear upon the lizard's skin "whose scaliness they pray may be their lot if forsworn." Or the swearer may hold a certain object and call on it to inflict on him some injury if perjured, for example, those taking the oath "place the barrel of a gun, or a spear, between their teeth, signifying by this ceremony that, if they do not act up to their agreement, they are prepared to fall by either of the two weapons." Or the swearer may touch or establish contact with a holy object, for example, an old sacred knife or the nose of a bear, which is regarded as an animal endowed with supernatural power.[5]

The oath can also be made efficacious by bringing in the name of a supernatural being to whom an appeal is made, often combining this with some contact with an object associated with that being.

In Westermarck's view, "even though the oath has the form of an appeal to a god, it may nevertheless be of a chiefly magical character, being an imprecation rather than a prayer... but the more the belief in magic was shaken... the more prominent became the religious element in the oath. The fulfilment of the self-imprecation was made dependent upon the free will of the deity appealed to, and was regarded as the punishment for an offence committed by the perjurer against the god himself."[6]

Throughout English history since the conversion of the people to Christianity, oaths taken for legal purposes have usually had a religious reference. Some belief in the magical efficacy of an oath may have existed, and may still exist, in the minds of some people taking oaths, but legally recognised oaths have appealed not to magical but to religious sanctions both in their wording and in the ceremonies connected with them. The following description of the nature of an oath, given by Jeremy Bentham in 1817 – if its sense is taken to cover both assertory and promissory oaths – probably represents fairly well what oaths have meant in recent centuries to many swearers who have regarded them seriously. "By the term oath, taken in its largest sense, is universally understood, a ceremony composed of words and gestures, by means of which the Almighty is engaged eventually to inflict on the taker of the oath, or swearer as he is called, punishment... in the event of his doing something which he, the swearer, at the same time and thereby engages not to do, or omitting to do something which he in like manner engages to do."[7] The appeal to God to judge the oath-breaker is sometimes explicit in the wording of the oath, as in one of the present Scottish forms of oath: "I swear by Almighty God (as I shall answer to God at the great day of Judgment)", and the phrase "So help me God", included in some present English oaths, has often been understood as an appeal to God's judgment. But not all oaths have included words of direct appeal to God as Judge and there have been considerable variations in the religious wording of oaths: the swearer may swear "by" God or "in the name of" God, or may swear "in the presence of" God or in other words call God to witness. The Oxford "New English Dictionary" defines an oath as "a solemn or formal appeal to God (or to a deity or something held in reverence or regard) in witness of the truth of a statement, or the binding character of a promise or undertaking".[8] The Oaths Act of 1888,[9] after

6

stating the initial non-religious wording of the affirmation to be allowed in place of an oath, states that the affirmer shall "then proceed with the words of the oath prescribed by law, omitting any words of imprecation or calling to witness". The way in which oaths have been regarded by swearers taking them seriously must have varied considerably in detail according to the religious views of those concerned. Perhaps the only fact universally true is that all serious swearers have regarded the religious reference of an oath as emphasising the bindingness of their obligation to speak the truth or to fulfil their promises.

The taking of an oath in English law has usually included the touching of an object associated with Christianity; the oath has been a "corporal oath" and has been so described in some legislation. In Anglo-Saxon and medieval times oaths were often sworn on Christian relics or on the cross or the altar; later it became normal for a Christian oath to be taken on the Gospels. For example, the Act of 1559,[10] which prescribed the Elizabethan Oath of Allegiance and Supremacy, stated that the person swearing it "shall make, take and receive a corporal oath upon the evangelist" and the oath itself ends with the words "So help me God, and by the contents of his book." Since that time Christian oaths in England and Wales have normally been taken upon the Gospels (or upon the New Testament or Bible which contains them). The present procedure is described in Section 2 of the Oaths Act of 1909,[11] which states: "Any oath may be administered and taken in the form and manner following: The person taking the oath shall hold the New Testament... in his uplifted hand, and shall say or repeat after the officer administering the oath the words 'I swear by Almighty God that...' followed by the words of the oath prescribed by law." When Catholics ask to use the Douai (Catholic) translation of the New Testament they are allowed to do so if a copy is available. Before 1909 the customary procedure was that the swearer should "kiss the Book" but by the Act of 1909 the procedure just described was substituted.

Fairly recently the wording has been changed in cases when an oath is taken in court by children and young persons and some other persons. Section 28 of the Children and Young persons Act of 1963[12] states: "in relation to any oath administered to and taken by any person before a juvenile court or administered to and taken by any child or young person before any other court, section 2 of the Oaths Act 1909 shall have effect as if the words 'I promise before

Almighty God' were set out in it instead of the words 'I swear by Almighty God that'." (Children are under the age of fourteen and young persons are aged between fourteen and seventeen.)

Since 1885 English law has provided that children of "tender years" may give evidence in court or make depositions without taking an oath. The first provision, in the Criminal Law Amendment Act of 1885,[13] stated a very limited number of occasions when this could be done: the number of occasions was increased under various Acts until the present legal position was established by the Children and Young Persons Act of 1933.[14] Section 38 of this Act states: "Where, in any proceedings against any person for any offence, any child of tender years called as a witness does not in the opinion of the court understand the nature of an oath, his evidence may be received, though not given upon oath, if, in the opinion of the court, he is possessed of sufficient intelligence to justify the reception of the evidence, and understands the duty of speaking the truth." The provision covers depositions. The accused person shall not be convicted unless such evidence is "corroborated by some other material evidence in support thereof implicating him".

In Scotland in the normal oath-taking procedure the Gospels are not used; instead, the person taking the oath raises his right hand. Section 5 of the Oaths Act of 1888[15] allowed the Scottish form of oath to be used in England and Wales. "If any person to whom an oath is administered desires to swear with uplifted hand, in the form and manner in which an oath is usually administered in Scotland, he shall be permitted so to do." In the period before the abolition of the practice of "kissing the Book", a number of English doctors, who regarded this practice as insanitary, claimed the right to take the oath in the Scottish form.

Provision for Non-Christian Religions

In general, English law in the last three centuries has been generous in recognising the validity of oaths taken by religious believers other than Christians. "At common law the form of oath is immaterial, so long as it is binding on the witness's conscience, and it does not matter whether it is Christian or not. In the leading case of Omychund v. Barker (1745)[16] it was laid down that witnesses ought to be sworn according to the peculiar ceremonies of their own religion, or in such a manner as they might declare binding on their conscience."[17] Thus, for example, Muslims take an oath upon the Koran, and some Chinese oaths are taken with ceremonies of breaking a saucer and words stating that, if the swearer does not speak the truth, "as that saucer is broken, so may my soul be broken like it".

In 1838 there was passed "An Act to remove Doubts as to the Validity of Certain Oaths".[18] This Act provided that "in all cases in which an oath may lawfully be and shall have been administered to any person... on any occasion whatever, such person is bound by the oath administered provided the same shall have been administered in such form and with such ceremonies as such person may declare to be binding." The Oaths Act of 1909[19] states in the case of a person who is neither a Christian nor a Jew, the oath shall be administered in any way which is now lawful."

In recent years there have been a number of cases in which difficulties have arisen because there has not been easily available the sacred book or other material necessary for the taking of an oath in the manner of a non-Christian religion. In 1957 a member of the Sikhs, whose sacred book, the Granth Sahib, was very rarely available in this country, was allowed to make an affirmation in court because the book was not available. This man was later prosecuted for perjury and the defence succeeded in its claim that the man could not have committed perjury as he had neither taken an oath nor made an affirmation under the conditions allowed by law.[20] Provision was made in 1955[21] and 1957[22] to allow affirmations instead of oaths in court-martial proceedings when it was not reasonably practicable for a witness to be sworn in the manner of his religion. The Oaths Act, 1961,[23] made this provision general. The Act amended the Oaths Act, 1888,[24] by adding to the circumstances in which a person might be allowed to affirm instead of taking an oath. (For these circumstances see page 41). An affirmation is to be allowed in the case of "a person to whom it is not reasonably practicable to administer an oath in the manner appropriate to his religious belief" and "reasonably practicable" is defined as meaning "reasonably practicable without inconvenience or delay". The Act also states that "a person who may be permitted under this section to make his solemn affirmation may also be required to do so": this is the only kind of case under present British law in which a person can be compelled to affirm instead of taking an oath and is continued under the Oaths Act, 1978. Whilst the Granth is not generally available in courts in rural areas, and the practice there is to ask witnesses of the Sikh faith to affirm, there is a probability that it will be available in towns where immigrants are numerous.

Special legal provision has been made for persons of Jewish religion. The first provision was made shortly after their re-admission to England under the Commonwealth: in 1667 the Court of the King's Bench ruled that Jews might give evidence in a court of law and be sworn on the Old Testament in accordance with their own practice.[25] The Oaths Act, 1909,[26] states: "The person taking the oath shall hold... in the case of a Jew, the Old Testament, in his uplifted hand." As there is no specifically Christian wording in any of the legal English oaths it is unnecessary to provide an alternative wording for Jews.

However, some legal oaths in the past did contain a specifically Christian reference and in the middle of the nineteenth century Jews were prejudiced by the fact that one of the oaths which had to be taken by M.P.s (the oath abjuring the right to the throne of the descendants of the Old Pretender[27]) concluded with the words "upon the true faith of a Christian". In 1858 an Act[28] substituted one oath of allegiance for the three oaths (of allegiance, supremacy and abjuration) previously taken, but the new oath retained the Christian phrase. The same phrase was included in the declarations necessary on taking certain municipal offices. An Act of 1845[29] remedied the matter with regard to the declarations by allowing a Jew to substitute for the declaration prescribed by law one acceptable to his conscience. With regard to the parliamentary oath there was an eleven years' struggle. In 1847 a Jew, Baron Lionel de Rothschild, was elected as one of the M.P.s for the City of London; he declared himself unable, on religious grounds, to take the oath and was therefore excluded from his seat. In the years 1848 to 1857 six Bills, which would have removed the disability of the Christian oath from Jewish M.P.s, were passed by the House of Commons and rejected by the House of Lords. Meanwhile Rothschild had been elected on five occasions, including the original occasion. In 1851 another Jew, David Salomons, was elected as M.P. for Greenwich, refused the oath on the same grounds, and was excluded from his seat. At last in 1858 the House of Lords consented to an Act[30] allowing each House of Parliament to determine by resolution the form of oath to be administered to a Jew, and immediately afterwards Rothschild was allowed to take his seat. In 1859 the House of Commons resolved that any Jew duly elected might swear a special oath, and under this procedure Salomons, re-elected in 1859, took his seat. The matter was finally settled by the Parliamentary Oaths Act of 1866[31] which, in re-wording the oath of allegiance, omitted the phrase "upon the true faith of a Christian".[32]

It seems clear that the legislators who opposed any concession to Jews with regard to the parliamentary oath were concerned not to question the validity of Jewish oaths but to exclude Jews from Parliament. For example, an M.P., Cumming Bruce, opposing one of the bills later defeated in the House of Lords, described it as "a measure to unchristianise the House of Parliament. When it was proposed to admit Jews to the House, they really ought to remember what were the duties and functions of that House. One of the main duties of that House was the inculcation of true religion..."[33] Thus the tolerance shown to Jews in the matter of oaths relating to certain offices had special motives; it was not an exception to the general attitude that the force of an oath is strengthened by its religious sanction but that the religion to which the oath refers need not be Christianity.

Christian Objections to Oaths

Christian thinkers since the time of the early Church have realised that the Christian attitude to oaths is a matter needing serious examination. In particular, two passages in the New Testament seem to forbid all oaths to Christians. The first passage is Christ's reported words in the Sermon on the Mount (Matthew 5. verses 33–37): "Again, ye have heard that it hath been said by them of old time, Thou shalt not forswear thyself, but shalt perform unto the Lord thine oaths: But I say unto you, Swear not at all; neither by heaven, for it is God's throne: Nor by the earth; for it is his footstool: neither by Jerusalem; for it is the city of the great King. Neither shalt thou swear by thy head, because thou canst not make one hair white or black. But let your communication be, Yea, yea; Nay, nay: for whatsoever is more than these cometh of evil." The other passage is in the Epistle of James (chapter 5, verse 12): "But above all things, my brethren, swear not, neither by heaven, neither by the earth, neither by any other oath: but let your yea be yea; and your nay, nay; lest ye fall into condemnation." (These passages are quoted from the Authorised Version. There is no important difference of sense in the passages as translated in the Revised version and in the New English Bible;[34] in the latter the last sentence of the first passage is translated as "Plain 'Yes' or 'No' is all you need to say; anything beyond that comes from the devil.")

Despite these passages, the main body of Christians in most periods of history has not objected to taking oaths for legal purposes. The orthodox position is well expressed in the Thirty-Ninth Article of Religion of the Church of England, which was promulgated in 1553 (probably with the heretical views of the Anabaptists in mind) and has not been subsequently changed. This Article, entitled "Of a Christian man's Oath", states: "As we confess that vain and rash swearing is forbidden Christian men by our Lord Jesus Christ, and James his Apostle, so we judge, that Christian Religion doth not prohibit, but that a man may swear when the Magistrates requireth, in a cause of faith and charity, so it be done according to the Prophet's teaching, in justice, judgment, and truth."

There is considerable discussion of the Christian attitude to oaths in the works of Bishop Jeremy Taylor, written in the middle of the seventeenth century. The following are some of his opinions. He considers that the words of Christ in the Sermon on the Mount, because of their reference to the Third Commandment: "Thou shalt not take the name of the Lord thy God in vain...", do not refer to assertory oaths at all, as these are covered in the Ninth Commandment: "Thou shalt not bear false witness against thy neighbour". With regard to assertory oaths he says: "Since (as St. Paul affirms) 'an oath is the end of all controversy' (Hebrews 6, verse 16) and that the necessity of commonwealths requires that a period should be fixed to questions, as a rule for the nearest certainty for judgment; whatsoever is necessary is not unlawful; and Christ, who came to knit the bonds of government faster by the stricture of more religious ties, cannot be understood to have given precepts to dissolve the instruments of judicature and prudent government." But, though assertory oaths are not forbidden to the Christian, "they may be taken in judgment and righteousness, but never lightly, never extra-judicially".[35] Jeremy Taylor states that Christ himself gave evidence on oath (an argument used also by some other defenders of the Christian Oath). "'I adjure thee by God that thou tell us whether thou be the Christ', said the high-priest to the blessed Jesus, that is, speak upon thy oath; and He then told them fully..." (The reference is to Matthew 26, verses 63 – 64). Christ left the Ninth Commandment "in that condition He found it in the decalogue, without any change or alteration of circumstance... The securing of testimonies was by the sanctity of an oath, and this remains unaltered in Christianity."[36]

With regard to the promissory oaths, Jeremy Taylor states that "Christ seems to forbid all forms of swearing whatsoever" and "many of the fathers have followed the words of Christ in so severe a sense, that their words seem to admit no exception. But here a grain of salt must be taken, lest the letter destroy the spirit. First, it is certain that the holy Jesus forbade a custom of swearing; it being great irreligion to despise and lessen the name of God... by making it common and applicable to trifles and ordinary accidents of our life... Secondly, not only customary swearing is forbidden, but all swearing upon a slight cause... Thirdly, but there are some cases in which the interests of kingdoms and bodies politic, peace and confederacies, require the sanction of promissory oaths; and they whom we are bound to obey, and who may kill us if we do not, require that their interests be secured by an oath: and that in this case, and all that are equal, our blessed Saviour did not forbid oaths, is certain not only by the example of Christians, but of all the world before and since this prohibition, understanding it to be of the nature of such natural bonds and securities without which commonwealths in some cases are not easily combined, and therefore to be a thing necessary and therefore not to be forbidden. . ."[37]

The opinion that Christ's words in the Sermon on the Mount should be understood as forbidding all swearing was held by some medieval heretical sects. The Albigenses, the Waldenses, the schismatic Franciscans, and those of John Huss's followers known as the Bohemian Brethren all objected to oaths. In the fourteenth century John Wycliffe shared this objection, and his followers, the English and Scottish Lollards, continued his protest.[38]

The Christian objection to oaths was continued by some sects originating during the Reformation period: among them were the Hutterian Brothers,[39] the Family of Love, the Anabaptists, and the Mennonites. The Dutch Mennonites, who had great influence on the first English Baptists, were granted the right of affirmation by

William the Silent, Prince of Orange, more than a hundred years before any such right was granted in England. "That the aforesaid petitioners' Yea shall be received by the Magistrates of the aforesaid City instead of an oath; provided, that the transgressors thereof shall be punished as oath-breakers and perjured persons".[40] Thus the English Baptists and Quakers of the seventeenth century were heirs to a tradition of objection to oaths.

In 1675 William Penn, Richard Richardson and eleven other Quakers published, on behalf of their co-religionists, "A Treatise of Oaths containing Several Weighty Reasons why the People called Quakers Refuse to Swear". The following is a much shortened version of the reasons given for objection to all oaths.

(1) "The first is drawn from the cause and ground of oaths, viz. perfidiousness, distrust and falsehood:... he that fears telling untruth, needs not swear, because he will not lie, to prevent which men exact swearing: And he that doth not fear telling untruth, what is his oath worth? He that makes no conscience of that law that forbids lying, will he make any conscience of forswearing?" God "hath taught us to speak the truth, the whole truth, and nothing but the truth, as plainly and readily without an oath, as with an oath, and to abhor lying as much as perjury; so that for us to swear were to take His Holy Name in vain "[41]

(2) To compel the taking of oaths "would gratify distrusts, humour jealousies, and subject truth, and those that love it, to the same checks, curls and preventions, that have been invented against fraud; whereby the honour of a noble profession, the power of a veracious example, and the just difference that ought to be made betwixt trustiness and diffidence, integrity and perfidiousness are utterly lost."[42]

(3) The fear that by complying with the custom of oaths "we should be guilty of rebellion against the discoveries God hath made to our souls in this ancient holy way of truth."[43]

(4) "Oaths have in great measure lost of the reason of their primitive institution, since they have not that awful influence, which was, and only can be a pretence for using them; on the

contrary, they are become the familiar parts of discourse and help to make a great share of the a-la-mode conversation:... the most judicial oaths are commonly administered and taken with so little reverence and devotion (to say nothing of the perjuries, that through ignorance or design are too frequently committed) that we can't but cry out, on the great depravity that is the world!"[44]

(5) "The omnipresence of God rightly understood, shows the uselessness of an oath,... for what need is there of that man's being awed into true evidence by such sort of attestations and imprecations as make the common form of oaths, who knows God to be always present to reside and preside in his soul,..."[45]

(6) "We do not find that oaths answer this part of the end for which they are imposed, viz. to convince those for whose sakes they are taken, of the weight and truth of a man's testimony by force of God's witness joined therewith: for they don't behold God's concurring witness by such an assistance or avenge of that party, as the truth or falsehood of his testimony deserveth; for the judgments of God are secret... and it is an evident sign that God approveth not that sort of invocation, because He doth not answer them that invoke Him, according to their wish; as neither did He in the old law or custom of combatting appear on his side that had the better title or cause,..."[46]

(7) "We look upon it to be no less than a presumptuous tempting of God, to summon Him as a witness not only to our terrene, but trivial businesses;... What! Make God, the Great God of Heaven and Earth our caution in worldly controversies, as if we would bind Him to obtain our own ends?"[47]

(8) Objections to the ceremonies connected with taking an oath. "Swearing by a sign", as in swearing by the contents of the Gospels and kissing the Book, is "Heathenish or Jewish." "...Jew and Gentile, superstition and ceremony, have made up the present form of oaths, which the true Christian-man neither wants, nor we conceive, ought to perform; much less impose where tenderness of conscience is pleaded, and equal caution offered to the law for the integrity of Yea and Nay".[48]

15

(9) "We have both the example and precept of our Lord and Saviour, Jesus Christ, to oppose" the taking of oaths, for "we never read him to have used any further asseveration, than what in English amounts to Verily, Verily or Truly, Truly I say unto you: thus by his example exciting us the more readily to obey his express prohibition of swearing" in the Sermon on the Mount (the passage quoted on page 11). "We are not insensible of the common objection... that he only prohibited vain oaths in communications" but "Christ's prohibition was not a mere repetition of what was forbidden under the Law" and vain swearing was already forbidden by the Third Commandment. "This was the advance he made in his excellent Sermon on the Mount; he wound up things to a higher pitch of sanctity than under the Law, or the childish state of the Jews could receive." This view is supported by "the concurrent testimony of the Apostle James" (in the passage quoted on page 11).[49]

(10) "Besides these express prohibitions, swearing is forbidden by the very nature of Christianity, and unworthy of him that is the Author of it, who came not to implant so imperfect a religion, as that which needed oaths,... The religion he taught, is no less than regeneration and perfections; such veracity as hath not the least wavering; sincerity throughout".[50]

Quakers have maintained a "testimony" against all oaths continuously from the seventeenth century to the present time. In the 1960 edition of "Christian Faith and Practice", issued by the Society of Friends in Great Britain, there are two statements of reasons for objection to oaths. The first refers to and quotes "the express prohibition of Christ and also of the apostle James". The second states: "We regard the taking of oaths as contrary to the teaching of Christ, and as setting up a double standard of truthfulness, whereas sincerity and truth should be practised in all the dealings of life".[51]

Resistance to Oaths in the Seventeenth Century

During the seventeenth century a considerable number of individuals became involved in disobedience to the law because of their objection, on Christian grounds, to all oaths. Such objection was confined, or almost confined, to Christians, other than Catholics, who dissented from the Church of England. (Catholics often suffered because of their refusal to take certain oaths, and, indeed, some of the legislation concerned was especially directed against them, but the objection of Catholics was to the content of certain oaths, not to all swearing.) The denominations mainly concerned in resistance to all oaths were the Baptists and the Quakers. From the time of the founding of the first English Baptist Church in 1612 objection to oaths was a much discussed matter among English Baptists. Throughout the seventeenth century a considerable number of Baptists maintained an objection to oaths and in some periods some Baptists incurred severe penalties on account of their objection. For example, Francis Bampfield, the minister of a parish under the Commonwealth and ejected from his ministry in 1662, was imprisoned for nearly nine years for refusal to take the oath of allegiance. He was later imprisoned again for persistent refusal to take the oath and died in prison.[52] Among the Baptists objection to oaths was a view held by many but not by all members, but among members of the Society of Friends or Quakers the objection seems to have been general from the time of the origin of the Society in 1652.

There were two main reasons why the objector to oaths was so often involved in a criminal offence with consequent punishment. The first reason was the great importance attached by the authorities to two kinds of promissory oath. The existence or fear of civil war or violent rebellion made the oath of allegiance to the supreme authority of the day, whether King or Commonwealth, a matter of great urgency as a test of the loyalty of the subject. Such an oath could legally be required from every adult subject and it often was required. The other important kind of promissory oath was the oath of supremacy, abjuring any claims of the Pope to authority within this country. This oath, either by itself or combined with the oath of allegiance, could also legally be required from every adult subject. Dislike and fear of Catholicism, for both political and religious reasons, led to the frequent enforcement of this oath.

In the period between the Restoration in 1660 and the Revolution of 1688 there was a second reason for the frequent punishment of objectors to oaths. During much of this period there was a fierce persecution of Nonconformists (then known as Dissenters). Although they could be punished under various Acts specifically directed against their activities, it was often found convenient to proceed against those who objected to swearing by tendering to them oaths which they refused to swear and punishing them for this refusal. This fact makes it difficult to determine to what extent the oath-refusers punished during this period were really penalised for this refusal rather than for their other religious views and activities.

Under the Commonwealth, from 1655 onwards, a number of Quakers were imprisoned for refusing the oath of supremacy – there was a widespread idea at the time that Quakers were Jesuits in disguise – or for refusing the oath abjuring the authority of Charles Stuart and promising loyalty to the Commonwealth. George Fox, the founder of the Society of Friends, recorded in his Journal that in 1655 "came out the oath of Abjuration, by which many Friends suffered; and several went to speak to the Protector about it; but he began to harden. And sufferings increasing upon Friends, by reason that envious magistrates made use of that oath as a snare to catch Friends in, who, they knew, could not swear at all, I was moved to write to the Protector."[53]

After the restoration of Charles II in May 1660 Quakers stated their views on swearing to the King and the House of Lords and tried to satisfy the authorities of their loyalty without confirming it by oaths. In the same period the Baptist congregations submitted an engagement which they judged as full as an oath. But any hopes of toleration were crushed by the Fifth Monarchy Rising in January 1661, which re-awakened in the authorities their dread of the extreme Puritan sects. A proclamation prohibited meetings not only of Fifth Monarchy Men but also of Quakers and "Anabaptists" and commanded the Justices of the Peace to tender the oath of allegiance to persons brought before them for assembling at such meetings. During the next few weeks 4,230 Quakers were imprisoned for meeting contrary to the proclamation, for not finding sureties, or for refusing the oath. However, they were all released by May 1661, the authorities having been convinced that they had not been involved in the Rising.[54]

A year later, in May 1662, an Act[55] was passed "for preventing the mischiefs and dangers that may arise by certain persons called Quakers and others refusing to take lawful oaths". This Act made illegal the assembling of five or more Quakers for worship not authorised by law: the same provision was extended to all Nonconformists in the First Conventicle Act of 1664.[56] With regard to oaths the Act of 1662 covered any persons "who maintain that the taking of an oath in any case whatsoever (although before a lawful magistrate) is altogether unlawful and contrary to the Word of God". The Act made it an offence not only "wilfully and obstinately" to refuse to take an oath which could be legally required but also to endeavour to persuade any other person to refuse such an oath or to maintain in printing, writing or otherwise the unlawfulness of all oaths. While the Bill had been before Parliament a number of Quakers had given evidence against it, explaining their principles and practice which were unknown to those members of Parliament who had returned from exile with Charles II. There was some opposition to the Bill but most members regarded Quaker views and practice as dangerous. Because of refusal to take oaths, stated the preamble to the Act, "it often happens that the truth is wholly suppressed and the administration of justice much obstructed." The Act provided for penalties of fines, or alternatively distress on property or imprisonment, for a first or second offence. For a third offence the convicted person must abjure the realm: if he refused to do so he was liable to be transported "to any of His Majesty's plantations beyond the seas". As a person who conscientiously objected to all oaths could not abjure the realm, which involved taking an oath, he became liable to the alternative penalty both under this Act and under any other legislation which compelled this procedure.

With the passing of the Act of 1662 a storm of persecution broke over Quakers in London. But those arrested who were tried for refusing the oaths were not proceeded against under this Act. In the Act's provisions with regard to oath-refusal "the qualifications in this clause frustrated its effect unless the person charged gave evidence against himself".[57] For this and other reasons Quakers proceeded against as oath-refusers seem rarely to have been punished under this Act: instead they were sentenced under an Act of 1609.

The Act of 1609[58] enforced the swearing of a combined oath of allegiance and supremacy: the wording of this oath was contained in "An Act for the Better Discovering and Repressing of Popish Recusants" passed in 1605.[59] The Act of 1609 made it lawful for any two Justices of the Peace, or in many cases for a single Justice, to require the oath from any person of the age of eighteen or above. Refusal of the oath resulted in imprisonment until the next Quarter Sessions or Assizes, when the oath was again to be tendered in open court. If the oath was then refused, married women could be imprisoned until they took the oath. Other refusers were liable to the penalty of *praemunire*. This punishment, originally devised in the fourteenth century, meant that the person found guilty was put out of the King's protection, his estate was forfeited to the crown, and he was imprisoned during life or at the royal pleasure. "The simplicity and severity of a *praemunire* quickly recommended it,... It proved again and again a readier instrument of persecution than the express laws against Quakers and seditious conventicles which were passed by the Cavalier Parliament".[60]

A sentence of *praemunire* involved imprisonment for an indefinite period, ending only with death or the King's pardon. Examples of long continuous imprisonment of praemunired Quakers were the imprisonment of Francis Howgill from 1664 till his death in prison in 1669,[61] the imprisonment of Thomas Taylor for ten and a half years,[62] and the imprisonment of William Dewsbury from the end of 1663 until 1672.[63] In 1672 the King included in one act of pardon the names of 491 Nonconformists, mainly Quakers, and these included 125 praemunired prisoners.[64]

There were a few cases in which refusal to swear led to the imposition of a death sentence on the refusers, though in no case was the sentence carried out. Under an Act dating from the reign of Elizabeth,[65] which was used by the authorities in some cases in their persecution of Nonconformists, a person present at an unlawful conventicle should on conviction conform within three months or forfeit his estate and abjure the realm: if he refused to abjure he should suffer death as a felon. Under this Act twelve Baptists, ten men and two women, were sentenced to death at Aylesbury in 1664 on refusing to conform or abjure the realm: a personal appeal to the King gained a prompt reprieve and subsequent pardon.[66]

The conflict of viewpoint between the authorities and the conscientious objectors to oaths is well exemplified in the account given by the Quaker leader George Fox of what occurred when he refused to take the oath of allegiance and supremacy at the Lancaster Assizes in August 1664. The judge "caused the oath to be read to me, the jury standing by; and when it was read, he asked me whether I would take the oath or not. Then said I, 'Ye have given me a book here to kiss and to swear on, and this book which ye have given me to kiss, says, "Kiss the Son";[67] and the Son says in this book, "Swear not at all"; and so says also the apostle James. Now, I say as the book says, and yet ye imprison me; how chance ye do not imprison the book for saying so?'... Now when the judge still urged me to swear, I told him I never took oath, covenant, or engagement in my life, but my yea or nay was more binding to me than an oath was to many others;... Later in the day, being indicted for not taking the oath and asked to plead, I said 'I am not guilty at all of denying swearing obstinately and wilfully; and as for those things mentioned in the oath, as Jesuitical plots and foreign powers, I utterly deny them in my heart; and if I could take any oath, I should take that; but I never took any oath in my life.

"The judge said I said well; 'but', said he, 'the King is sworn, the Parliament is sworn, I am sworn, the justices are sworn, and the law is preserved by oaths'. I told him they had sufficient experience of men's swearing, and he had seen how the justices and jury had sworn wrongly the other day; and if he had read in the Book of Martyrs[68]... he might see that to deny swearing in obedience to Christ's command was no new thing. He said he wisht the laws were otherwise. I said, 'Our Yea is yea, and our Nay is nay; and if we transgress our yea and our nay, let us suffer as they do, or should do, that swear falsely.' This I told him we had offered to the King, and the King said it was reasonable. After some further discourse, they committed me to prison again, there to lie till the next Assize."[69]

The Toleration Act, 1689

The Act which has usually been known as the Toleration Act[70] was passed in 1689 a few months after the abdication of James II and the accession of William and Mary. Its official title was "An Act exempting their Majesties protestant subjects dissenting from the Church of England, from the penalties of certain laws." "Popish recusants" and "any person that shall deny in his preaching or writing the doctrine of the blessed Trinity" were expressly excluded from any benefits under the Act.

21

The Act left untouched the Corporation Act, 1661,[71] and the Test Act, 1673,[72] which excluded from many offices under the Crown and municipal offices all who did not communicate according to the rites of the Church of England – these Acts were not repealed until 1828.[73] But with regard to those Acts which either enforced attendance at Church of England services or penalised Nonconformist worship, the Toleration Act, while not repealing the Acts, exempted persons who fulfilled certain conditions from the prescribed legal penalties.

One of the conditions of exemption from penalties was that those concerned should take the oath of allegiance and the oath of supremacy in the form prescribed in a recent Act,[74] which substituted these oaths for those formerly in force. (They should also subscribe the declaration against transubstantiation, the Mass, and the invocation of saints which was contained in an Act of 1678.[75]) Because of this condition objectors to oaths would still have been penalised if no special provision had been made for them. But the witness and sufferings of the oath-refusers had made it obvious that any measure of real toleration for Nonconformists must include some provision with regard to oaths: therefore the Toleration Act made the first provision in English history for legal rights of affirmation.

Section 13 of the Act stated: "And whereas there are certain other persons, dissenters from the Church of England who scruple the taking of any oath" such persons should subscribe the declaration against transubstantiation and also a prescribed profession of their Christian belief. Instead of the oaths of allegiance and supremacy they should make a prescribed "declaration of fidelity." The content of the declaration was exactly the same as that of the oaths for which it was a substitute, but instead of the words "I do sincerely promise and swear" and "I do swear" and "So help me God" contained in the oaths, the words in the declaration were, "I do sincerely promise and solemnly declare before God and the world" and "I do solemnly profess and declare." Persons making this declaration instead of taking the oaths had to give evidence that they were Protestant dissenters but the provision was not confined to members of particular sects, so that not only Quakers and Baptists but also any other Nonconformists who objected to oaths were given legal rights of affirmation for the particular purposes of the Act.

Rights of Affirmation for Members of Specified Religious Bodies 1696-1838

In contrast to the provisions of the Toleration Act, the extensions of legal rights of affirmation made over the next century and a half were confined to specified religious bodies, of which the Quakers were the first to be affected.

The Toleration Act gave rights of affirmation only on limited occasions, but Quakers suffered disabilities from their refusal to take oaths on many other occasions. Without taking oaths "they could not sue for their debts, nor carry through their transactions with the customs and the excise, nor defend their titles, nor give evidence: they were, in strict law, unable to prove wills or be admitted to copyholds, or take up their freedom in corporations, and in some places they were kept from voting at elections. Nor could they answer prosecutions in ecclesiastical courts for tithes and church-rates".[76] It was not until 1833 that they were granted rights of affirmation on all occasions, but legislation in 1696 considerably extended their rights.

An Act of 1696,[77] which prohibited those refusing to take the oaths of allegiance and supremacy from voting at elections, provided as an alternative "or being Quakers, shall refuse to subscribe the Declaration of Fidelity". Another Act[78] of the same year provided that every Quaker "who shall be required upon any lawful occasion to take an oath, in any case where by law an oath is required, shall, instead of the usual form, be permitted to make his or her solemn affirmation or declaration". However, the occasions when affirmations were to be permitted were mainly concerned with civil legal procedures, as the Act specifically stated that "no Quaker or reputed Quaker shall by virtue of this Act be qualified or permitted to give evidence in any criminal causes or serve on any juries, or bear any office or place of profit in the government". The Act was not held to include the parliamentary oaths: a Buckinghamshire Quaker, John Archdale, was elected as an M.P. in 1698 but was not allowed to take his seat because unable to take the oaths.[79] The Act provided that the permitted affirmation was to have the same force and effect as an oath and that the penalty for false evidence on affirmation was to be the same as that for perjury. The Act was to remain in force for seven years: it was extended for a further term of years in 1702[80] and an

Act of 1715[81] made the provisions permanent and extended them to Scotland.

The wording of the affirmation in both the Act of 1696 and the Toleration Act had a religious reference: in the Toleration Act the declaration was to be made "before God and the world", in the Act of 1696 the prescribed wording was: "I do declare in the presence of Almighty God, the witness of the truth of what I say". These wordings raised the question as to whether such an affirmation was really distinct from an oath. To many Quakers the plain meaning of the words "was to invoke God as Witness, and this was made the sanction for the truth of the evidence given. The prescribed formula, accordingly, was felt by them to partake of the nature of an oath, though stripped of the accessories and the imprecation; and constituted a sanction for truth-speaking, which obscured that provided by allegiance to Christ".[82] Many other Quakers disagreed with this position and found that they could conscientiously make the prescribed affirmations, and the subject was vigorously debated in the Society of Friends for more than twenty years. In 1715 the Society tried to obtain a plain affirmation with no reference to the name of God: this effort was unsuccessful with regard to the Act of 1715 but was successful seven years later. The sufferings of Quakers unwilling to make the prescribed affirmations had been considerable, by imprisonment in a few cases but more often by loss of property. For example, one Quaker had been fined until he had lost a third of his small property because he could not make the affirmation in excise matters required in his business as a tanner.[83]

In 1722 an Act[84] was passed which, for Quakers, removed all religious references from the wording of the permissible affirmations. Instead the wording of these affirmations was now prescribed as "I do solemnly and sincerely promise and declare" or "I do solemnly, sincerely and truly declare and affirm" or "I do solemnly, sincerely and truly acknowledge, profess, testify and declare". The Act stated that it was evident that Quakers had not abused the liberty and indulgence allowed them by law and that it was reasonable to give them further ease and relief.

In 1749, an Act[85] made it clear that a Quaker's affirmation should be allowed whenever an oath was required or authorised, but affirmations were still not permitted for evidence in criminal cases, service on juries, or any office or place of profit in the government.

In 1749 special provision was made for the Moravian Brethren. This religious body descended from the Bohemian Brethren founded in 1457 by a group of the followers of John Huss. The Bohemian Brethren formed themselves into a community on New Testament principles which included objection to oaths. They spread into Moravia and Poland, were persecuted at intervals during the sixteenth century and in the seventeenth century suffered greatly during the Thirty Years' War. The more recent history of the body known as the United Brethren, the Moravian Brethren, or the Moravian Church dates from 1722. In that and succeeding years groups of refugees from Moravia settled on the estates of Count Zinzendorf at Herrnhut in Saxony. In 1734 a party of Moravian Brethren went to Georgia as colonists and missionaries and it was on this journey that the Brethren first met John and Charles Wesley with whom they had much contact during the following years. They first settled in England in 1738: they formed societies in London and in several counties and in 1754 formed their first settlement, in Yorkshire, on the same lines as the settlement at Herrnhut. In 1822 there were about 3,700[86] members of the Moravian Brethren in Great Britain.

Objection to all oaths was not a tenet held collectively by the Moravian Brethren but a considerable number of their members were objectors: during the Jacobite Rebellion of 1745 this objection exposed some members to trouble in relation to the oath of allegiance.[87] In 1749 four deputies from the Brethren presented a petition to Parliament, asking for their recognition in Britain and in the British colonies in America and for legal concessions with regard to oaths and military service. In the petition the Brethren stated that "they are an ancient Protestant Church, known, countenanced, and relieved in their perplexed circumstances, by the Kings and State of England: That they are a quiet-minded people, whose essential point is, to possess liberty of conscience without restraint". With regard to oaths they asked "that those of them, who conscientiously scruple the taking of an oath, may in all civil cases be exempted from so doing, and that, instead thereof, their affirmation may be accepted".[88] After consideration of the petition by a Committee of the House of Commons a Bill was introduced which became law in the summer of 1749.

With regard to oaths this Act[89] provided that any member of the Moravian Brethren might, instead of an oath, make an affirmation

25

in the words, "I do declare in the presence of Almighty God, the witness of the truth of what I say". Such an affirmation should be legal in any case where an oath was required by law, but no member of the Brethren should by virtue of the Act be qualified to give evidence in a criminal case or to serve on a jury. False affirmation should be treated as perjury.

In 1775 an Act[90] empowered Justices of the Peace to administer oaths or affirmations in any case where any penalty was levied or distress made under any legislation. In 1828 an Act[91] extended the right of affirmation of Quakers and Moravians to evidence in criminal cases. "In any case whatsoever, criminal or civil" an affirmation, with no religious reference in its wording, was to be allowed instead of an oath.

In 1833 the final stage was reached with regard to rights of affirmation for members of these two bodies: they were granted these rights on all occasions. The Quakers and Moravians Act[92] permitted an affirmation instead of an oath "in all places and for all purposes where an oath is or shall be required either by the common law or by any Act of Parliament": the prescribed wording was "I do solemnly, sincerely and truly declare and affirm". Thus Quakers and Moravians were now able to make affirmations both as jurors and instead of the oath of allegiance and other promissory oaths required for the holding of the certain offices. In 1838 rights of affirmation on all occasions were extended to former members who objected to oaths. Under the Act of 1838[93] the person asking to affirm had to state that he or she was a former Quaker or Moravian "and entertaining conscientious objections to the taking of an oath". (To the best of my knowledge, this is the earliest use in legislation of the term "conscientious objection".) The Quakers and Moravians Acts 1833 and 1838, are still in force and include Scotland.

Members of a third religious sect, the Separatists, were given legal rights of affirmation in 1833. In a speech in the House of Commons in favour of the Bill to grant these rights J.A. Murray said "that he was acquainted with many Separatists, and knew them to be a respectable body of persons, who adhered literally to the precept in the Gospel,[94] which recommended that men should not swear." In its preamble the Act[95] stated: "There are in various places in Ireland, and in some parts of England, and elsewhere 'certain dissenters' commonly called Separatists, the members of which class or sect of dissenters, from conscientious scruples, refuse to take an oath in courts of justice and other places, and in consequence thereof are exposed to great losses and inconveniences in their trades and concerns, and are subject to fines and to imprisonment for contempt of court, and the community at large are deprived of the benefit of their testimony."

The Act allowed a Separatist to affirm on any occasion when an oath was legally required. The words of the affirmation included a religious reference and a statement of both individual and collective conscientious objection to oaths. The wording was as follows: "I do, in the presence of Almighty God, solemnly, sincerely and truly affirm and declare that I am a member of the religious sect called Separatists, and that the taking of any oath is contrary to my religious belief, as well as essentially opposed to the tenets of that sect; and I do also in the same manner affirm and declare". This Act, which included Scotland, was repealed[96] soon after the passing of the Oaths Act of 1888.

The Occasions for Oaths and the Statutory Declarations Act, 1835

Before the next stage in the extension of rights of affirmation, legislation in 1835 had greatly decreased the number of kinds of occasion on which legal oaths were necessary. At the time of this legislation oaths were taken for many different purposes and in some cases an individual had to take frequent oaths for the same purpose. In a debate in the House of Lords in 1835 the Duke of Richmond gave some examples of the enforcement of frequent swearing on individuals. "In the Army pay-office there were 86,000 persons, who are obliged to take oaths five times in one year. There were 47,000 who were obliged to take oaths to obtain their half-pay. Some of these oaths were clearly unnecessary, for when a general officer receives his half-pay, he may take it without an oath, but if he has lost an arm he must swear four times a year that he has lost it... Churchwardens were called on every year to appear before the Ordinary, and swear to obey the canons..."[97] In a debate in the House of Lords in 1833 the Bishop of London said that he thought far too many oaths were required and opined that, while assertory oaths were necessary, promissory oaths were unnecessary and produced very bad effects, and that it was very objectionable to administer oaths to young people except when taking evidence.[98]

Jeremy Bentham (1748–1832), the pioneer of the political philosophy of utilitarianism, was a strong critic of the system of oaths existing in his time. He considered that many oaths required at that time should be condemned because they were not taken seriously. "There are some cases in which an oath is invested with great authority and force – that is to say, when it is in harmony with public opinion and enjoys the support of the popular sanction. There are other cases in which it has no such force or authority – that is to say, when it is in conflict with public opinion, or, at any rate, is not supported by it. We may refer to Custom-house oaths, and such as are extracted from the undergraduates of certain Universities." In Bentham's opinion: "Oaths are degraded when applied to trifling matters or when administered in such circumstances that they are violated by a sort of general understanding; and still more so when they are exacted in cases where justice and humanity alike treat their violation as excusable – nay, as almost meritorious."[99]

The Statutory Declarations Act, 1835[100] provided for the substitution of a declaration in a large number of cases in which at that time an oath or an affidavit was necessary. The declaration was to be of the same effect as the oath or affidavit for which it was a substitute. The standard form of declaration, as later amended, was: "I A.B. do solemnly and sincerely declare, that... and I make this declaration conscientiously believing the same to be true, and by virtue of the Statutory Declaration Act, 1835". (In Chapter 2 of this book, page 87, there is an example of a statutory declaration made under this Act – the declaration of conscientious objection to vaccination.) With regard to false statements, the offence of perjury could not be committed as this is confined to false statements on oath (or affirmation). But the Act provided with regard to declarations that "any person who shall wilfully and corruptly make and subscribe any such declaration, knowing the same to be untrue in any material particular, shall be guilty of a misdemeanour."

The Act gave power to the Commissioners of the Treasury to substitute declarations for required oaths or affidavits in the proceedings in a number of departments of government: these included customs and excise matters, the Post Office, the War Office, the Army Pay Office, the Treasury, the Board of Trade, the

India Board, and the National Debt Office. The Commissioners were given the same power with regard to any office under their control, direction or superintendence. The Act substituted declarations for the oaths taken by churchwardens, sidesmen, and pawnbrokers; and in matters relating to the Turnpike Acts, the paving of streets, the taking out of patents, and transfers of stock at the Bank of England.

The Universities of Oxford and Cambridge and all bodies which by law or "by any valid usage" were authorised to administer or receive oaths were to substitute declarations. It was made illegal for Justices of the Peace or other persons to administer or receive voluntary oaths on extra-judicial matters. Justices and other officers authorised to administer oaths were given power to receive voluntary declarations in the form prescribed in the Act.

The Act expressly excluded from its provisions any oath or affidavit for judicial proceedings and the oath of allegiance when required for appointment to an office.

The process of substituting declarations for oaths was taken further by the provisions of the Promissory Oaths Act, 1868.[101] The Act substituted declarations for the promissory oaths required on accepting an employment or office in all cases except those in which the law specifically provided for such oaths. With regard to the oath of allegiance the Act stated that no person should be required or authorised either to take this oath or to make a declaration to the like effect unless specifically required by law to take the oath. At the present time most civilians never take the oath of allegiance.

The making of legal declarations, especially declarations in writing, has become very common in modern times. In addition to declarations made under the Statutory Declarations Act, legal declarations have been provided for in many branches of law, for example, the laws concerning income tax and social security. While many of these declarations are assertory, some declarations are promissory. An example of a promissory legal declaration is the declaration promising secrecy required from those attending at polling stations or at the counting of votes at parliamentary and local government elections.[102] In the twentieth century, while many citizens make legal declarations fairly frequently, most citizens take oaths very rarely.

Rights of Affirmation for All Religious Objectors 1854–1868

In the middle of the nineteenth century rights of affirmation were extended to all who had religious objections to swearing. This extension of rights was made in three Acts, the first being the Common Law Procedure Act, 1854.[103] In the debate on this Bill in the House of Lords the Duke of Argyll pointed out the anomaly of the existing position. "The principle of dispensation was already recognised by the law of the land; but the exemption was only granted to certain enumerated parties, on the ground that it was believed they had conscientious scruples to taking an oath: but could it be said that no other body of men could have these conscientious objections except Quakers, Separatists and Moravians? He knew of cases in Scotland where persons had been imprisoned rather than take the oath... There were many cases of persons who objected to take an oath, not because their fathers before them were Quakers or Separatists but because they had religious scruples on the point." In the same debate Lord Brougham referred to a case in Scotland where a person summoned as a witness and refusing, from conscientious scruples, to take an oath was imprisoned for thirty days.[104]

The Act of 1854 applied to any person giving evidence or making an affidavit or deposition in civil proceedings: if any such person "shall refuse or be unwilling from alleged conscientious motives to be sworn" the judge or other official concerned was empowered "upon being satisfied of the sincerity of such objection" to permit an affirmation instead of the oath. The legal effect of such an affirmation should be the same as that of the oath for which it was a substitute. The right of affirmation given in the Act was confined to religious objectors by the words included in the affirmation: "I do solemnly, sincerely and truly affirm and declare, that the taking of an oath is, according to my religious belief, unlawful".

In 1861 the Criminal Proceedings Oath Relief Act[105] extended the right of affirmation, on the same terms, to evidence, affidavits and depositions in criminal proceedings. In 1867 the Criminal Law Amendment Act[106] extended the right, on the same terms, to jurors in civil or criminal proceedings.

The three Acts just described did not include Scotland. Rights of affirmation for religious objectors in Scotland were allowed by a series of Acts between 1855 and 1868: the conditions were almost exactly the same as those in the corresponding English Acts. In 1855 an Act[107] allowed affirmations in civil proceedings; in 1863[108] the right was extended to criminal proceedings; in 1865 an Act[109] repealed the Acts of 1855 and 1863 and allowed rights of affirmation in all civil and criminal proceedings; in 1868 an Act[110] extended rights of affirmation to jurors.

There was no further extension of rights of affirmation for religious objectors in either part of Great Britain until the Oaths Act of 1888. Until 1888 religious objectors, except Separatists and present or former Quakers or Moravians, had no legal right to affirm instead of taking the oath of allegiance and certain other promissory oaths required for holding a number of civil and military offices.

The Position of Atheists and Agnostics in the Nineteenth Century

The legal concessions so far described in this chapter have concerned religious believers, whether adherents of non-Christian religions allowed to swear according to the forms of their own religions or religious objectors to oaths allowed to affirm. For the first group the oath had a religious, though not a Christian, sanction; for the second group, while an affirmation with no religious reference was allowed, yet those who affirmed were believers whose standards of conduct were related to their religious beliefs. But in the middle of the nineteenth century a quite different group of opponents to oaths became important: these were the considerable number of people who seriously and openly stated that they had no religious beliefs. How should these unbelievers – atheists or agnostics – be regarded by the law in relation to the taking of oaths or the making of alternative affirmations?

Many people in the nineteenth century thought that the position of atheists in relation to oaths, or alternatives to oaths, was and should be quite distinct from that of unorthodox Christians. They would have assented to the intolerant view towards atheists held by even that apostle of toleration, the philosopher John Locke. Locke wrote during the Restoration period: "Those are not at all to be tolerated who deny the being of God. Promises, covenants, and oaths, which are the bonds of human society, can have no hold upon an atheist. The taking away of God, though but even in thought, dissolves all".[111] The same kind of view was expressed by Lord Robert Montagu in 1861 in a debate in the House of Commons on an unsuccessful Affirmations Bill. "It was said that honour and honesty would prevent men from making false statements. What's honour? what is honesty without belief in God?... Honour and honesty, apart from religion, were nothing but pride and self-interest. If a man did not believe in a God he could refuse to tell a lie only because he was too proud to do so; and he could be honest only because he thought honesty the best policy... A consistent Atheist must be a bad citizen and capable of every Machiavellian scheme and falsehood. "[112] In the same debate another MP, J. Walter, stated: "How could a man be said to act from conscientious motives – that was to have a conscience – who did not believe in the distinction between right and wrong? And how could a man be said to believe in the distinction between right and wrong who did not believe in the moral government of the world? and what was the use of his believing in a moral Governor of the world unless he believed that such Governor would reward or punish men in a future state?"[113]

In John Stuart Mill's book "On Liberty", published in 1859, he referred to the then current "legal doctrine, that no person can be allowed to give evidence in a court of justice, who does not profess belief in a God (any god is sufficient) and in a future state". He cited the cases of two persons who on two separate occasions in 1857 "were rejected as jurymen, and one of them grossly insulted by the judge and by one of the counsel, because they honestly declared that they had no religious belief; and a third, a foreigner, for the same reason was denied justice against a thief."[114] At that time a court could question a person about to take the oath as to whether he believed in God and whether he believed in a future state of rewards and punishments: if his answer to either of these questions was in the negative he could be refused permission to take the oath.

In the history of the struggle for rights of affirmation for unbelievers the leading figure was Charles Bradlaugh. Bradlaugh's struggle with the law, which culminated in the passage of the Oaths Bill which he introduced in Parliament in 1888, started with his refusal in 1861 to answer in court questions concerning his religious opinions. Bradlaugh was the defendant in a civil case at Wigan County Court in April 1861. The counsel for the plaintiff asked whether he believed "in the religious obligations of an oath": Bradlaugh objected to answering any questions before he was sworn. He asked for leave to affirm, which the Judge refused, but he was willing to take the oath. The Judge asked him: "Do you believe in the existence of a supreme God?" He replied: "I object that the answer, if in the negative, would subject me to criminal prosecution." (He was probably referring to the Blasphemy Laws, which were quite frequently enforced at that time). The Judge then asked: "Do you believe in a state of future rewards and punishments?" Bradlaugh objected to the question. The Judge then said: "Then I shall not permit you to give evidence at all; and I think you escape very well in not being sent to gaol", and summed up the case as an "undefended case".[115]

In this case it was the unbeliever's own interests which suffered from the exclusion of his evidence but the treatment of unbelievers as incompetent witnesses might easily prejudice the interests of others. A striking case of this position was cited in the House of Commons in 1869 by a lawyer, George Denman. He stated that, in a case of murder in which he had acted for the prosecution, the best witness to the identity of the murderer was not allowed to take the oath. "When questioned as to his religious belief, he at once admitted that he did not believe in future reward and punishment, and his evidence, though he was to all appearances a respectable man, was in consequence, excluded."[116]

In his book "On Liberty", John Stuart Mill made a scathing attack on the legal assumption on which these exclusions were based: The assumption "is that the oath is worthless of a person who does not believe in a future state; a proposition which betokens much ignorance of history in those who assent to it... and would be maintained by no one who had the smallest conception how many of the persons in great repute with the world, both for virtues and attainments, are well known, at least to their intimates, to be unbelievers. The rule, besides, is suicidal and cuts away its own foundation. Under pretence that atheists must be liars, it admits the testimony of all atheists who are willing to lie, and rejects only those who brave the obloquy of publicly confessing a detested creed rather than affirm a falsehood. A rule thus self-convicted of absurdity so far as regards its professed purpose, can be kept in force only as a badge of hatred, a relic of persecution; a persecution, too, having the peculiarity that the qualification for undergoing it is the being clearly proved not to deserve it."[117]

The extension of the rights of affirmation in the act of 1854 (already described) was of no assistance to unbelievers because the allowed affirmation included a declaration that the taking of an oath was unlawful according to the religious belief of the affirmer. In 1861 an Affirmations Bill proposed to give wider rights of affirmation. The words to be included in the affirmation professed in the Bill were: "I do solemnly, sincerely and truly affirm and declare that an oath would not, in my judgment, oblige me more closely to speak what is true than my deliberate undertaking to do so."[118] But this Bill did not become law.

In 1869 a Bill was introduced in the House of Commons by George Denman, who stated that its purpose was to admit the evidence of two classes of witnesses, one class being witnesses considered incompetent "through some defect in the religious belief of such witness".[119] "He held that the law ought, in all cases, to leave Judge and juries to decide whether a man was to be believed, and that it should not be incumbent on the Judge to make a man stand down, and in some cases commit him to prison, if he could not, or would not, from any cause whatever, consent, before giving his evidence, to imprecate Divine vengeance upon himself in case of his evidence being untrue."[120]

Denman pointed out that "A person might not be a confirmed Atheist and yet might have a doubt as to punishment hereafter"[121] and that "the law enabled an unscrupulous person to avoid being examined by pretending to be an Atheist."[122] "He did not wish to abolish oaths. Those who wished to take them might take them;... his object was to prevent a miscarriage of justice from the arbitrary rule of excluding this evidence."[123] In contrast to the debates on the Affirmations Bill in 1861, this proposal passed the House of Commons with no expressed opposition. In the House of Lords the Bill was supported by the Lord Chancellor, Lord Hatherly, "because he had long been of opinion that it was undesirable to draw a distinction between the duty of telling the truth at all times, and the duty of telling it in a court of law. He was convinced that all that was necessary in giving evidence in a court of justice was that, instead of taking an oath, a witness should know that he had a solemn duty to perform, for any breach of which he would be liable to a legal penalty."[124] Lord Cairns objected to the wording of a clause of the Bill as allowing affirmation to a witness who simply disliked taking an oath;[125] as a result of this objection, which was supported by another Peer, the clause was reworded. The Bill was passed by the House of Lords and became the Evidence Further Amendment Act, 1869.[126]

The Act stated, in Section 4: "If any person called to give evidence in any court of justice, whether in a civil or criminal proceeding, shall object to take an oath, or shall be objected to as incompetent to take an oath, such person shall, if the presiding judge is satisfied that the taking of an oath would have no binding effect on his conscience, make the following promise and declaration: 'I solemnly promise and declare that the evidence given by me to the court shall be the truth, the whole truth and nothing but the truth'." Penalties for perjury should apply as if an oath had been taken.

The Evidence Amendment Act, 1870,[127] explained that in the 1869 Act the words "court of justice" and "presiding judge" should be deemed to include any person having by law authority to administer an oath for the taking of evidence.

There was no further extension of rights of affirmation for unbelievers before the Oaths Act of 1888. Unbelievers remained in a less favourable legal position than religious objectors in three ways: the Acts of 1869 and 1870 did not apply to Scotland and there was no corresponding Scottish legislation; the Acts did not include affidavits; and there was no extension of rights of affirmation to jurors.

In its attempt to find suitable words to delimit the class of persons who might be allowed to affirm, Parliament had decided on a description which was resented by many unbelievers. "Too much discretion was left to the Judge, who was supposed to satisfy himself... that the oath would have 'no binding effect' upon the conscience of a heretical witness. A promise is binding upon the conscience of an honest man in whatever form it may be made, and it put Freethinkers in an entirely false position to be obliged to assent to the statement that some particular form was not binding upon them. Conscientious witnesses who wished to affirm hardly knew what to answer when the Judge put the question to them, and he would not always be satisfied with the mere statement that the oath gave no additionally binding effect to the promise."[128] This description was written by Bradlaugh's daughter and its authorship

35

is appropriate, for Bradlaugh suffered through being considered a person on whose conscience the taking of an oath would have no binding effect during his long struggle for the right to take the parliamentary oath of allegiance. This dramatic struggle was the penultimate stage of the fight which led to full rights of affirmation for atheists and agnostics.

"The Bradlaugh Case" 1880–1886

When Charles Bradlaugh was elected to Parliament at the General Election in April 1880 as one of the two MPs for Northampton, he was already a well known publicist: his published views included advocacy of atheism, republicanism, land-law reform and birth control.

When the House of Commons assembled Bradlaugh claimed the right to affirm instead of taking the oath of allegiance. When invited by the Speaker to make a statement to the House with regard to his claim he said: "I have to submit that the Parliamentary Oaths Act, 1866,[129] gives the right to affirm to every person for the time being permitted by law to make affirmation. I am such a person, and under the Evidence Amendment Act, 1869,[130] and the Evidence Amendment Act, 1870,[131] I have repeatedly, for nine years past, affirmed in the highest courts of jurisdiction in this realm, I am ready to make the declaration or affirmation of allegiance." The Speaker, Sir Henry Brand, said that he had grave doubts as to the claim and desired the judgment of the House. A Select Committee of seventeen members was appointed. By a majority of one the committee decided that persons entitled under the Acts of 1869 and 1870 "to make a solemn declaration instead of an oath in courts of justice, cannot be admitted to make an affirmation or declaration instead of an oath in the House of Commons."[132]

Having been denied the right to affirm, Bradlaugh decided to take the oath. At that time the oath had ceased to contain any specifically Christian wording. Under the Promissory Oaths Act, 1868,[133] the form of the oath of allegiance was: "I do swear that I will be faithful and bear true allegiance to Her Majesty Queen Victoria, her heirs and successors, according to law. So help me God." (This, with the substitution of the name of the reigning sovereign, has remained the form since that date.) Bradlaugh immediately published in the press a statement of the reasons for his decision. The following is part of this statement: "I believed that I had the legal right to make affirmation of allegiance in lieu of taking the oath... While I considered that I had the legal right, it was then clearly my moral duty to make the affirmation. The oath, although to me including words of idle and meaningless character, was and is regarded by a large number of my fellow countrymen as an appeal to Deity to take cognizance of their swearing. It would have been an act of hypocrisy to voluntarily take this form if any other had been open to me, or to take it without protest, as though it meant in my mouth any such appeal. I am sorry for the earnest believers who see words sacred to them used as a meaningless addendum to a promise, but I cannot permit their less sincere co-religionists to use an idle form, in order to prevent me from doing my duty to those who have chosen me to speak for them in Parliament. I shall, taking the oath, regard myself as bound not by the letter of its words, but by the spirit which the affirmation would have conveyed had I been permitted to use it."[134] This statement antagonised many MPs.[135]

When Bradlaugh presented himself to take the oath his action was challenged by a member, and the Speaker allowed the intervention. The matter was referred to a Select Committee of twenty-three members. The Committee reported that Bradlaugh, by stating that he had repeatedly affirmed in courts of law, had brought it to the notice of the House that he was a person about whom the judges were satisfied that an oath was "not binding on his conscience"; that, under the circumstances, an oath taken by him would not be an oath "within the true meaning of the statutes"; and that the House could and ought to prevent him from going through the form. The Committee suggested that he be allowed to affirm with a view to his right to do so being tested in the courts.[136] A motion that he be allowed to affirm was defeated by 275 to 230 votes.[137] Bradlaugh then again presented himself to take the oath and was refused leave to do so. He was then allowed to make a speech from the Bar of the House. After this he was ordered to withdraw, first by the Speaker and then by a motion passed by the House. He refused to withdraw, was arrested by the Sergeant-at-Arms, and was held in custody in the Clock Tower for a day.

But the Prime Minister, W.E. Gladstone, wished Bradlaugh's rights to be legally determined. A few days later Gladstone moved as a standing order that members-elect, who claimed that they had the legal right to affirm, should be allowed to do so "subject to any liability by statute", and Gladstone's motion was carried by 303 to 249 votes.[138] Bradlaugh then affirmed, took his seat and voted in a division. A writ was immediately served on him (not at the instance of the Government) to recover the sum of £500, the penalty which the Parliamentary Oaths Act of 1866[139] provided for voting without having taken the oath.[140]

For nine months, 2nd July 1880 to 31st March 1881, Bradlaugh performed his work as an MP while awaiting the decision of the courts. In March 1881 the case of Clarke v. Bradlaugh[141] was heard in the Court of the Queen's Bench. The judgment was against Bradlaugh and the Court of Appeal in the same month upheld the judgment. He was held to have voted illegally because he was not a person legally permitted to affirm in lieu of the parliamentary oath. In the opinion of the judges the Evidence Acts of 1869[142] and 1870[143] were intended only to remove restrictions on the admissibility of witnesses, and the Parliamentary Oaths Act, 1866,[144] permitted affirmation only to persons already entitled to affirm "not on particular occasions but on all occasions when they would otherwise have to take an oath." Bradlaugh's seat was then declared to be vacant.[145]

In this first year of Bradlaugh's struggle most of the points at issue had emerged so that, for the purposes of this chapter, the history of his struggle during the next four and a half years can be summarised. Bradlaugh was re-elected for Northampton at a by-election in April 1881 and again at by-elections in March 1882 and February 1884 and at the General Election in November 1885. After each re-election except the last, and on a number of other occasions, he attempted to take the oath and was either refused leave to do so or excluded from the House of Commons on a majority vote of members of the House; on most of these occasions a substantial minority of some 150 to 250 members supported him. On two occasions Bradlaugh administered the oath to himself: on the first occasion this action led to his expulsion and to a writ for a new election; on the second occasion it led to his exclusion, to a new election, and to a lawsuit by the Government against him for voting without having first properly taken the oath. In June 1884 in this lawsuit[146] judgment was given against Bradlaugh; the jury decided that at the time of taking the oath he was without belief in a Supreme Being, was a person on whose conscience the oath, as an oath, had no binding force, did not take the oath according to full parliamentary practice, and did not take and subscribe the oath as an oath. In January 1885 the Court of Appeal upheld this judgment.[147]

Thus at the time of his re-election to Parliament in November 1885 it had been decided by the courts that Bradlaugh had both made an invalid affirmation of allegiance and sworn an invalid oath of allegiance. In January 1886, when the House of Commons assembled after the General Election, Sir Arthur Wellesley Peel, who had succeeded Sir Henry Brand as Speaker in 1884, decided to act on his independent authority in the matter of the oath. He stated: "We are assembled in a new Parliament, I know nothing of the Resolutions of the past... It is the right, the legal, statutable obligation, of Members when returned to this House, to come to this Table, and take the Oath prescribed by Statute... The honourable Member takes that Oath under whatever risks may attach to him in a Court of Law. But it is not for me, and I respectfully say it is not for the House, to enter into any inquisition as to what may be the opinions of a Member when he comes to the Table to take the Oath."[148] After nearly six years of struggle Bradlaugh had not won the right to affirm but he had won the right to take the oath as a known atheist.

"The Bradlaugh Case" provoked vigorous and often bitter controversy not only in the House of Commons but among the public. To some extent the direct issue was obscured by considerations of party politics and by dislike of Bradlaugh's real or imagined opinions on matters other than atheism. The direct issue was technically the validity of an atheist's oath or affirmation but with this was connected the question whether it was desirable to allow a declared atheist to be a member of the House of Commons.

In May 1880 Lord Randolph Churchill argued that "if the House admitted that Members of the House might declare, with all the authority which a Parliamentary position gave, with right, law, and justice on their side, that the words 'So help me God' were merely a ridiculous and superstitious invocation, utterly devoid of any moral force, then the whole connection between the proceedings of Parliament and a Divine sanction was in danger; and the idea, he might almost say the faith, which had for centuries animated the House of Commons that its proceedings were under the supervision and would be guided by the wisdom of a beneficent Providence, lost all its force."[149]

But Bradlaugh had many sympathisers in the country, not only among members and supporters of the National Secular Society but among Christians. The majority of the electors of Northampton continued to support him. In the House of Commons an Affirmations Bill introduced by the Government in 1883 failed to pass its Second Reading by only three votes.[150] John Bright, who throughout his long membership of the House had been allowed to affirm as a Quaker, gave consistent support to Bradlaugh's rights. In a speech in the House in May 1880 Bright asked what would result if the House set up the principle of a credal test – would it next question any member thought to be an unbeliever, though not a professed one? "I make a promise. My word is as good, and taken to be as good, as your Oath. And that is declared by an irrevocable Act of Parliament. And if Mr. Bradlaugh take this Oath, as he proposed to take it, I have no doubt that, though the last words of the Oath have no binding effect upon him, yet his sense of honour and his conscience would make that declaration as binding on him as my Affirmation is on me, and as your Oath is on you."[151]

The Oaths Acts, 1888–1978

The Bill which became the Oaths Act of 1888 was introduced by Charles Bradlaugh; it was intended firstly, to provide rights of affirmation on all occasions and, secondly, to provide these rights for all who objected to taking oaths. With regard to the first object Bradlaugh was completely successful (despite some expressed opposition to allowing atheists to serve as jurors) and those to whom the right of affirmation was given were allowed by the Act to claim it "in all places and for all purposes where an oath is or shall be required by law." Thus the Act ended all the complications and uncertainties of the period when rights of affirmation for some groups of objectors applied only to certain occasions of swearing, and the Act adopted the principle of rights of affirmation on all occasions, the principle embodied in the legislation fifty years earlier regarding Quakers, Moravians and Separatists.

With regard to the second object – to provide for all who objected to taking oaths – Bradlaugh's original proposal was considerably modified during the passage of the Bill. The original wording of the Bill read: "Every person objecting to being sworn shall be permitted to make his solemn affirmation."[152] To this wording a considerable number of MPs objected because, in their view, it would enable people, who thought that their obligation to speak the truth on oath was greater than it would be on affirmation, to choose to affirm because they were prepared to lie or to speak carelessly. W.A. Macdonald stated: "There were many people who would be slow to speak falsely, if they thought they would have to take God to witness that they were speaking the truth; whereas they would think it a much less heinous offence to speak untruly if they were allowed to make a mere affirmation." He hoped it would be made clear that "it was only persons who had conscientious objection to taking the oath who would be allowed to affirm."[153] A solicitor, Sydney Gedge, stated that "when the name of the Almighty is invoked a deeper sense of seriousness and responsibility is felt. A man who has no wish to be untruthful will yet state things to which he would not swear. My long experience as a solicitor leads me to believe that if the sanction of the oath were done away with in Courts of Justice many more untrue statements, and certainly a great many more inaccurate statements, would be made by witnesses than are made under the existing system."[154] In the debates, stress was laid on the desirability that the law should be such as would lead to as much truth-speaking as possible in courts by using whatever method was most binding on a man's conscience. As a result of the objection taken to the original wording the clause was altered so as to confirm rights of affirmation to those who had conscientious objections to swearing. The Bill passed its Second Reading in the House of Commons by 250 to 150 votes. It was then amended in committee and passed its Third Reading by 147 to 60 votes. The Bill was passed in the House of Lords without amendment.

The Oaths Act, 1888[155] remained in force until 31st July 1978, the only amendment to it being the Oaths Act, 1961.[156] This Act, which covered any person "to whom it is not reasonably practicable to administer an oath in the manner appropriate to his religious belief", was described earlier in this chapter. The Act included Scotland, and since 1888 the law with regard to rights of affirmation has been uniform throughout Great Britain.

The Oaths Act, 1888, stated in Section 1: "Every person upon objecting to being sworn, and stating, as the ground of such objection, either that he has no religious belief, or that the taking of an oath is contrary to his belief, shall be permitted to make his solemn affirmation instead of taking an oath, in all places and for all purposes where an oath is or shall be required by law, which affirmation shall be of the same force and effect as if he had taken the oath." The offence of perjury related to an affirmation in the same way as to an oath.

Section 2 of the Act stated: "Every such affirmation shall be as follows: 'I, A.B., do solemnly, sincerely and truly declare and affirm', and then proceed with the words of the oath prescribed by law, omitting any words of imprecation or calling to witness." Section 4 of the Act prescribed the form of an affirmation in writing.

It will be noted that under the Act the right to affirm had to be claimed: no one could be compelled to affirm. But if an atheist chose to take an oath, rather than claim the right to affirm, his oath could no longer be held to be invalid. Section 3 of the Act stated: "Where an oath has been duly administered and taken, the fact that the person to whom the same was administered had, at the time of taking such oath, no religious belief, shall not for any purpose affect the validity of such oath."

Thus in 1888, nearly two hundred years after the granting of the first rights of affirmation, the law allowed full rights of affirmation to both unbelievers and religious objectors to oaths. The law retained swearing as the normal procedure and, though there are no figures available, there is little doubt that this normal procedure was and still is followed by the large majority of those concerned.

The final development occurred with the passing of the Oaths Act, 1978. This Act repealed the whole of the 1838, 1888, 1909 and 1961 Acts.

The 1978 Act again prescribes the normal form of oath and manner in which it is to be administered. Previously permitted variations from such form or manner and the provisions relating to court martials are continued. Moreover, if a person takes an oath other than in the prescribed form, "he is bound by it if it has been administered in such form and with such ceremonies as he may have declared to be binding".

The law on affirmations, effective from 1st August 1977 under the Administration of Justice Act, 1977 and from 1st August 1978, under the Oaths Act, 1978 now states simply that: "Any person who objects to being sworn shall be permitted to make his solemn affirmation instead of taking an oath." Thus, there is no longer any requirement for the person to state the reason for his or her objection, but, interestingly, the requirement that the person must object to taking an oath still survives. It is not a simple alternative. Furthermore, where it is not reasonably practicable, without inconvenience or delay, to administer an oath in the manner appropriate to a person's belief, he or she is permitted to make a solemn affirmation or, indeed may be required to do so. (In R v Pritam Singh, no copy of the Sikhs' holy book was available to the court.)

The whole of the present law regarding the rights of affirmation is contained in the Oaths Act, 1978; the Quakers and Moravians Acts 1833[157] and 1838[158] (see page 26); and the Acts of 1955[159] and 1957[160] which concern proceedings at court martial (see page 9).

In Part II of this book there will be some discussion and evaluation of the legal position with regard to oaths and affirmations.

References

1   Will. & Mar. c. 18
2   51 & 52 Vic. c. 46
3   Westermarck, Edward *The Origin and Development of the Moral Ideas* Vol. 11 p. 118
4   Ibid. Vol. I p. 59
5   Ibid. Vol. 11 pp. 118–119
6   Ibid. Vol. 11 p. 122
7   Bentham, Jeremy *Swear Not at All*. Works. 1962 Edition Vol. V. p. 191
8   *New English Dictionary*. Oxford. 1905 Edition.
9   51 & 52 Vic. c. 46. Sect. 2
10   Eliz. 1. c. 1. Sect. 19
11   9 Edw. 7.c. 39. Sect. 2 (1)
12   11 & 12 Eliz. 2. c. 37
13   48 & 49 Vic. c. 69
14   23 Geo. 5. c. 12
15   51 & 52 Vic. c. 46. Sect. 5
16   Omychurd v. Barker. 1745 (1 Atk. 21)
17   Law Times. 1961. Vol. 231. p. 286
18   1 & 2 Vic. c. 105
19   9 Edw. 7. c. 39. Sect. 2
20   R. v. Pritam Singh. All England Law Reports. 1958. Vol.l p.p. 199 – 202
21   Army Act, 1955. 3 & 4 Eliz. 2. c. 18. Sect. 102
     Air Force Act, 1955. 3 & 4 Eliz. 2. c. 19. Sect. 102
22   Naval Discipline Act, 1957. 5 & 6 Eliz. 2. c. 53. Sect. 60 (4)
23   9 & 10 Eliz. 2. c. 21
24   51 & 52 Vic. c. 46

25   Roth, Cecil *A History of the Jews in England* p. 179
26   9 Edw. 7. c. 39. Sect. 2 (1)
27   6 Geo. 3. c. 53
28   21 & 22 Vic. c. 48
29   8 & 9 Vic. c. 52
30   Jews Relief Act, 1858. 21 & 22 Vic. c. 49
31   28 & 29 Vic. c. 19
32   In Roth op. cit. pp. 257 onwards, there is a detailed history of this struggle
33   Hansard. 1853. Vol. 125. Col. 1222
34   *The New English Bible. New Testament.* 1961
35   Taylor, Jeremy *Works.* 1854 Edition. Vol. II p. 426
36   Ibid. Vol. 11 p. 445
37   Ibid. Vol. 11 p. 424–425
38   See Knox, Ronald *Enthusiasm* and Jones, Rufus M. *Studies in Mystical Religion*
39   See Rideman, Peter, of the Hutterian Brothers *Account of our Religious Doctrine and Faith.* 1540
40   Penn, William; Richardson, Richard and Others. *A Treatise of Oaths.* 1713 Edition, pp. 186 – 187
41   Ibid. pp. 6–7
42   Ibid. p. 7
43   Ibid. p. 9
44   Ibid. p. 10
45   Ibid. p. 11
46   Ibid. p. 12
47   Ibid. p. 13
48   Ibid. pp. 13–15
49   Ibid. pp. 15–16, 17–18, 20
50   Ibid. p. 24
51   Friends, Society of *Christian Faith and Practice in the Experience of the Society of Friends.* 1960. Par. 570 and Par. 571
52   Underwood, A.C. *A History of the English Baptists* p. 114 See other parts of this book for Baptist views on oaths
53   Fox, George *Journal.* Everyman Edition p. 112
54   Braithwaite, William C. *The Second Period of Quakerism* pp. 9 – 13
55   13 & 14 Car. 2. c. 1
56   16 Car. 2. c. 4
57   Braithwaite op. cit. p. 23
58   7 Ja. 1. c. 6
59   3 Ja. 1. c. 4
60   Braithwaite op. cit. pp. 14–15
61   Ibid. pp. 34 and 37
62   Ibid. p. 223
63   Ibid. p. 222
64   Ibid. p. 83–84
65   35 Eliz. 1. c. 1. 1593
66   Braithwaite op. cit. p. 108

67 Psalm 2. verse 12.
68 Foxe, John *Actes and Monuments (The Book of Martyrs)* 1563
69 Fox op. cit; pp. 231–233
70 1 Will. & Mar. c. 18
71 13 Car. 2. St. 2c. 1
72 25 Car. 2. c. 2
73 9 Geo. 4 c. 17
74 1 Will. & Mar. c. 1
75 30 Car. 2. St. 2. c. 1
76 Braithwaite op. cit. p. 181
77 7 & 8 Will. 3. c. 27. Sect. 19
78 7 & 8 Will 3. c. 34
79 Braithwaite op. cit. p. 413
80 13 & 14 Will. 3. c. 4
81 1 Geo. 1. St. 2. c. 6.
82 Braithwaite op. cit. p. 185
83 Ibid. p.201
84 8 Geo. 1. c. 6.
85 22 Geo. 2. c. 4. Sects 36 and 37
86 Bost, Ami *History of the Moravians.* Appendix
87 Holmes, John *History of the United Brethren.* Vol.I p. 323
88 House of Commons Journal. Vol. 25. pp. 727– 728
89 22 Geo. 2. c. 30
90 15 Geo. 3. c. 39
91 9 Geo. 4. 32
92 3 & 4.Will. 4c. 48
93 1 & 2 Vic. c. 77
94 Hansard Vol. 18. Col. 1012
95 3 & 4 Will. 4. c. 82
96 Statute Law Revision Act, 1890. 53 & 54 Vic. c. 33
97 Hansard Vol. 26. Cols. 415–416
98 Hansard Vol. 18. Cols. 1016–1017
99 Bentham, Jeremy *Theory of Legislation.* 1802. 1914 Edition pp. 291 – 293
100 5 & 6 Will. 4. c. 62
101 31 & 32 Vic. c. 72
102 Representation of the People Act, 1949, 12 & 13 Geo. 6. c. 68 2nd Schedule. Clause 32.
103 17 & 18 Vic. c. 125. Sect. 20
104 Hansard Vol. 131. Cols. 1265 – 1266
105 24 & 25 Vic. c. 66
106 30 & 31 Vic. c. 35. Sect. 8
107 Affirmations (Scotland) Act, 1855. 18 & 19 Vic. c. 25
108 Oath Relief in Criminal Proceedings (Scotland) Act, 1863, 26 & 27 Vic. c. 85
109 Affirmations (Scotland) Act, 1865. 28 & 29 Vic. c. 9
110 Jurors' Affirmation (Scotland) Act, 1868. 31 & 32 Vic c. 39

111 Locke, John *First Letter Concerning Toleration*. Works. 1824 Edition. Vol. V. p. 47

112 Hansard Vol. 163. Col. 959

113 Hansard Vol. 163. Col. 964

114 Mill, John Stuart *On Liberty*. Everyman Edition. p. 90

115 Bonner, Hypatia Bradlaugh and Robertson, John M. *Charles Bradlaugh*. Vol. l pp 168– 169

116 Hansard Vol. 195. Col. 1804

117 Mill op. cit. p. 91

118 Hansard Vol. 163. Col. 962

119 Hansard Vol. 194. Col. 406

120 Hansard Vol. 195. Col. 1802

121 Hansard Vol. 195. Col. 1804

122 Hansard Vol. 195. Col. 1803

123 Hansard Vol. 195. Cols. 1804–1805

124 Hansard Vol. 198. Col. 678

125 Hansard Vol. 198. Col. 987

126 32 & 33. Vic. c. 68

127 33 & 34. Vic. c. 49

128 Bonner & Robertson op. cit. Vol. l. p. 289

129 29 & 30. Vic. c. 19

130 32 & 33. Vic. c. 68

131 33 & 34. Vic. c. 49

132 Bradlaugh, Charles *Speeches* p. 1

133 31 & 32. Vic. c. 72

134 Bonner & Robertson op. cit. Vol. II pp. 221 – 222

135 Arnstein, Walter L. *"The Bradlaugh Case"* p. 41. See this book for details of the case.

136 Bonner & Robertson op. cit. Vol. Il p. 233

137 Ibid. Vol. II p. 238

138 Ibid. Vol. Il p. 240–245

139 29 & 30 Vic. c. 19. Sect. 5

140 Bonner & Robertson op. cit. Vol II pp. 246 and 248

141 Clarke v. Bradlaugh (1881) 7 Q.B.D. 38

142 32 & 33 Vic. c. 68

143 33 & 34 Vic. c. 49

144 29 & 30 Vic. c. 19

145 Bonner & Robertson op. cit. Vol. II pp. 260–262

146 Attorney General v. Bradlaugh (1885) 14 Q.B.D. 667

147 Bonner & Robertson op. cit. Vol. II pp. 351–358

148 Hansard Vol. 302. Col. 23

149 Hansard Vol. 252. Col. 335

150 Bonner & Robertson op. cit. Vol. Il p. 340

151 Hansard Vol. 252. Cols. 211, 213–214

152 Hansard Vol. 323. Col. 1222

153 Hansard Vol. 323. Cols. 1222–1223

154 Hansard Vol. 323. Col. 1209

155 51 & 52 Vic. c. 46

156 9 & 10 Eliz. 2. c. 21
157 3 & 4 Will. 4. c. 48
158 1 & 2 Vic. c. 77
159 3 & 4 Eliz. 2. c. 18
     3 & 4 Eliz. 2. c. 19
160 5 & 6 Eliz. 2. c. 53

Chronological Table of Acts Relating to Oaths or Affirmations

Date

1559	Oath of Allegiance & Supremacy	1 Eliz. 1. c. 1.
1593	Abjuring the Realm	35 Eliz. 1. c. 1.
1605	Oath of Allegiance & Supremacy	3 Ja. 1. c. 4
1609	Oath of Allegiance & Supremacy	7 Ja. 1. c. b.
1662	Act against Quakers	13 & 14 Car..2. c. 1
1678	Declaration against Transubstantiation	30 Car. 2. St. 2. c. 1
1689	Oaths of Allegiance & Supremacy	1 Will. & Mar. c. 1.
1689	Toleration Act	1 Will. & Mar. c. 18
1696	Quakers' Affirmations at Elections	7 & 8 Will. 3. c. 27
1696	Quakers' Affirmations	7 & 8 Will. 3. c. 34
1702	Quakers' Affirmations	13 & 14 Will. 3. c. 4
1715	Quakers' Affirmations	1 Geo. 1. St. 2. c. b
1722	Quakers' Affirmations	8 Geo. 1. c. b.
1749	Moravians' Affirmations	22 Geo. 2. c. 30.
1749	Quakers' Affirmations	22 Geo. 2. c. 46
1765	Oath of Abjuration	6 Geo. 3. c. 53
1775	Oaths and Affirmations	15 Geo. 3. c. 39
1828	Quakers' & Moravians' Affirmations	9 Geo. 4. c. 32
1833	Quakers & Moravians Act	3 & 4 Will. 4. c. 48
1833	Separatists' Affirmations	3 & 4 Will. 4. c. 82
1835	Statutory Declarations Act	5 & 6 Will. 4. c. 62
1838	Quakers & Moravians Act	1 & 2 Vic. c. 77.
1838	Oaths Act	1 & 2 Vic. c. 105
1845	Jewish Municipal Declarations	8 & 9 Vic. c. 52
1854	Common Law Procedure Act	17 & 18 Vic. c. 125.
1855	Affirmations (Scotland) Act	18 & 19 Vic. c. 25
1858	Oath of Allegiance	21 & 22 Vic. c. 48
1858	Jews Relief Act	21 & 22 Vic. c. 49
1861	Criminal Proceedings Oath Relief Act	24 & 25 Vic. c. 66
1863	Oaths Relief in Criminal Proceedings (Scotland) Act	26 & 27 Vic. c. 85
1865	Affirmations (Scotland) Act	28 & 29 Vic. c. 9.
1866	Parliamentary Oaths Act	29 & 30 Vic. c. 19.
1867	Criminal Law Amendment Act	30 & 31 Vic. c. 35
1868	Jurors' Affirmation (Scotland) Act	31 & 32 Vic. c. 39
1868	Promissory Oaths Act	31 & 32 Vic. c. 72

1869	Evidence Further Amendment Act	32 & 33 Vic. c. 68
1870	Evidence Amendment Act	33 & 34 Vic. c. 49
1885	Criminal Law Amendment Act	48 & 49 Vic. c. 69
1888	Oaths Act	51 & 52 Vic. c. 46
1909	Oaths Act	9 Edw. 7. c. 39.
1933	Children & Young Persons Act	23 Geo. 5.c. 12
1955	Army Act (Section 102)	3 & 4 Eliz. 2. c. 18
1955	Air Force Act (Section 102)	3 & 4 Eliz. 2. c. 19
1957	Naval Discipline Act (Section 60)	5 & 6 Eliz. 2. c. 53
1961	Oaths Act	9 & 10 Eliz. 2. c. 21
1963	Children and Young Persons Act	11 & 12 Eliz. 2. c. 37
1978	Oaths Act	Eliz. 2. c. 19

CHAPTER 2

Compulsory Vaccination Against Smallpox

Introduction

The history of conscientious objection to compulsory vaccination shows sharp contrasts in several respects with the history of objection to oaths.

The first contrast is in the type of compulsion. Oaths were an institution of social life from time immemorial and were connected with many kinds of activities; compulsory vaccination was one of the early measures of modern public health legislation and enforced a specific remedy against the specific evil of smallpox.

The second contrast is that the obligation to take an oath was an obligation affecting the individual's own conduct whereas the Vaccination Acts compelled parents to take certain actions with regard to their children. Thus, in addition to problems of the comparative rights of the individual and society, compulsory vaccination raised problems of the comparative rights of children and parents.

The third contrast is that, while objection to oaths was always connected with religious belief, or unbelief, there was in most cases no direct connection between religious opinions and objection to vaccination. The controversy about vaccination was, in most cases, concerned with different decisions as to the assessment of complicated evidence and with the right choice between two courses both of which involved risks. The fourth contrast is that, while objectors to oaths were always a small minority, objectors to vaccination became, in England and Wales, a large minority, and in the years 1935 to 1938, a small majority. Opposition to vaccination was a popular movement in a considerable number of places and the compulsory provisions of the law were resisted not only by individuals but by a number of the local authorities responsible for enforcement. But, despite these contrasts, there is some similarity in the history of the problems raised by conscientious objection to oaths and to vaccination and in the solutions adopted to meet these problems. In both cases conscientious law-breaking led eventually to provision for legal conscientious objection and in both cases the legal right of objection, originally restricted, later became available substantially to all who claimed it.

Compulsory vaccination in Scotland was controlled by a series of Vaccination Acts completely separate from those covering England and Wales. For this reason the following account covers England and Wales only and at the end of the chapter there is a short account of the history of compulsory vaccination in Scotland.

The Antecedents to Compulsion

When compulsory vaccination was first introduced in 1853, the country had experienced smallpox as a serious and widespread disease for at least two centuries. Before the compulsory registration of deaths, from 1837 onwards, the statistical information was very incomplete. In a report to the Board of Health in 1857, its Medical Officer estimated that in the periods 1660–1679 and 1728–1759 the annual smallpox death rate per 100,000 population exceeded 400 and that in the period 1771–1780 it exceeded 500.[1] In London in the eighteenth century the figures recorded in the Bills of Mortality showed twenty-nine epidemics each responsible for at least 10% of the total deaths from all causes in the year of outbreak.[2]

There was a rapid decrease in the number of deaths from smallpox in the early part of the nineteenth century. In the seven years 1848–1854 the average annual number of deaths in England and Wales was 5,229 and the average annual death rate per 100,000 population was 31 for males and 27 for females.[3] Most of these deaths were in early childhood; it was estimated in 1853 that of those dying from smallpox 11% were aged under four months, 25% under one year, and 75–80% under five years.[4] This fact was an important reason why the original legal compulsion was applied not to the population in general but to babies.

Early in the eighteenth century the practice of variolation was introduced into this country. "Variolation was simply the inoculation of healthy individuals with the contents of the skin lesions of a natural case in the vesicular stage in the hope that by this means a mild attack of smallpox, which would protect the subjects against infection by natural means, would develop."[5] In 1746 a hospital for smallpox and inoculation was established by voluntary subscription in London and 1,000 persons were inoculated during its first ten years. The practice of inoculation was continued by the successor of this hospital up to 1822. Inoculation was made illegal in 1840,[6] about forty years after the first experiments with vaccination.

In 1798 Edward Jenner inaugurated the practice of vaccination by inoculating several persons with cowpox having observed that those who had suffered from naturally acquired cowpox seemed to be immune from smallpox. In 1800 the first vaccination station was started and in 1803 several others were started. In 1802 the government, after investigations by a Parliamentary Committee, awarded a grant of £10,000 to Jenner and in 1807 the Royal College of Physicians reported strongly in favour of vaccination. In 1809 the National Vaccine Board was established which administered vaccination stations with vaccinators paid from public funds and also supplied lymph to other vaccinators. The supply of lymph was maintained by the method of "arm to arm" vaccination in which lymph was taken from the arms of vaccinated persons to be used to vaccinate others; this continued to be the main method up to 1899.

In 1840, during a severe smallpox epidemic, "An Act to extend the Practice of Vaccination"[7] was passed, making it the duty of local authorities to provide facilities for vaccination. At that time the only types of local authority which existed in every area were the Boards of Guardians administering the relief of the poor in the Poor Law Unions. In the years following the Poor Law Amendment Act of 1834[8] the parishes in England and Wales were systematically grouped into Poor Law Unions, each with its Board of Guardians elected by the ratepayers, and there were 626 Unions in 1841. These Boards had been made the responsible authorities for the registration of births, marriages and deaths in 1836.[9] They were now made the authorities for the administration of the Vaccination Acts. They remained the vaccination authorities until their abolition in 1930 although in the intervening period many other public health functions came to be performed by other types of local authority.

The Vaccination Act, 1840,[10] directed Boards of Guardians to contract with their Medical Officers or with any legally qualified medical practitioners for the vaccination of all residents. The arrangements were to be made under regulations made by the Poor Law Commissioners and the remuneration of the vaccinators was to depend on the number of successful primary vaccinations. An amending Act of 1841[11] provided that the expenses of vaccination should be paid from rates and other funds for poor relief and that persons using the facilities for public vaccination should not, by doing so, be subject to any of the disabilities or disqualifications attached to the receipt of poor relief.

In 1853 the Epidemiological Society, founded in 1850, reported on its investigation into the existing position with regard to vaccination. On the basis of available figures, which included only those vaccinated under the provisions of the Vaccination Acts, they reported the number of vaccinations of children aged under one year in the year 1851–1852 as about 194,000. This figure was about 32% of the number of births in that year. They found great differences in the proportions of infants vaccinated in different areas and that, in general, vaccination was more neglected in rural districts than among town populations.[12]

The Vaccination Act, 1853

The Bill which became the Vaccination Act, 1853, was introduced as a Private Member's Bill in the House of Lords by Lord Lyttleton. He stated that, "It was unnecessary... to speak of the certainty of vaccination as a preventive of the small-pox, that being a point on which the whole medical profession had arrived at complete unanimity."[13] He supported this statement by quoting figures supplied by the Epidemiological Society with regard to the history of smallpox mortality in this country, and with regard to the comparison of mortality in England and Wales with mortality in various countries which had made vaccination directly or indirectly compulsory. He considered that, with compulsion, the country would continue to have all the good results of the existing system and an increase of them. To the objection that compulsion would be an undue interference with the liberty of the subject he replied: "It might very well be argued that parents had no right, even looking to their own children alone, to allow them to take the disease; but the proper object of the Bill was to prevent persons spreading the infection to others – which he considered in reality a criminal act."[14] Lord Shaftesbury, in supporting the Bill, emphasised the serious effects on future health of many non-fatal cases of smallpox. He considered that the voluntary system had been tried for a long time and had failed. With regard to the reasons for failure he stated: "This omission to have their children vaccinated did not arise to so great an extent as was sometimes supposed from prejudice – though, no doubt, that did prevail in a great many instances – but was chiefly due to indifference or neglect, because directly the small-pox broke out in a district they crowded by hundreds and thousands to have their children vaccinated."[15] In the House of Commons Viscount Palmerston urged in support of the Bill that "The object was prevention by means of timely foresight and precaution and the class of society for whom that foresight and precaution were required was the poorest, and that which was the least likely to have recourse to such measures voluntarily."[16]

There was no vote taken at any stage in the passing of the Bill and no speaker in either House questioned the desirability of vaccination. But three speakers in the House of Commons opposed the introduction of compulsion. One of these speakers, Sir George Strickland, stated: "The mother must be compelled to vaccinate; but in a rich man's house that was impossible. The House was going to force everyone to give up prejudices against vaccination. If they acted more on the old English principle, and left people to the voluntary and to their own good sense, the object would be more rapidly and successfully attained."[17] Compulsion was also opposed by some members of the medical profession. Ten medical practitioners in Hull, in a memorial sent to Lord Lyttleton, stated that, "the attempt to make vaccination compulsory will probably have a tendency to make a beneficial and salutary boon odious and unpopular, simply because it is compulsory and not voluntary."[18] The British Medical Journal, in a leading article, stated: "till an efficient system of voluntary vaccination be attractively placed within the reach of all, it would be monstrous to inflict upon the community compulsory submission to poor-law vaccination, a system which, from its unpopularity and meanness, can exercise only a very limited protective power."[19]

The compulsory provisions of the Vaccination Act, 1853,[20] applied to all children born after the first day of August 1853. The obligation was imposed on the parent of the child, or in exceptional cases, on the person having "the care, nurture or custody" of the child.

Under Section 2 the father or mother was obliged to have the child vaccinated within three months of birth; in the exceptional cases where some other person was responsible this period was increased to four months. Unless the child had already been vaccinated by a duly qualified medical practitioner, and such vaccination duly certified, he was to be taken to be vaccinated by the vaccinator appointed by the Board of Guardians for his area of residence (Section 2) and on the eighth day following the date of vaccination he was to be taken to the same vaccinator for inspection (Section 3). Thus the public vaccination service continued to be free of charge and organised in the same way as before, but no parent was compelled to use it if he preferred to pay for vaccination by a private doctor. The vaccinator had to give a certificate of successful vaccination to the parent and to send a duplicate to the Registrar of Births of the sub-district (Section 4). The vaccinator could also give two alternative certificates. He could give a certificate of postponement for two months, renewable for the same period, if he was of the opinion that the child was "not in a fit and proper state to be successfully vaccinated" (Section 5).

If he was of the opinion that a child vaccinated by him was "insusceptible of the vaccine disease" he could give a certificate to this effect (Section 7). The parent who possessed either of these certificates was held to be complying with the law. The Registrar of Births was instructed to serve a notice requiring vaccination on the parent of any child not already vaccinated; this was to be done with regard to any child born in his sub-district, within seven days of the registration of the birth. (Section 9). An offence was committed by the parent or other person responsible if, after receipt of such a notice, he failed to have the child vaccinated within the prescribed period and taken for subsequent inspection. The penalty for this offence was a fine not exceeding twenty shillings (Section 9) to be recoverable before any two Justices of the Peace for the area concerned (Section 12).

The Period 1853–1867

During the period before the next important change in legislation, in 1867, there was no consistent decrease from year to year in mortality from smallpox. In the twelve years 1855 to 1866 the number of deaths varied between 1,290 in 1861 and 7,624 in 1864.

But a comparison of the average for 1855–1866 with the average for 1848– 1854 shows a decrease in annual mortality from 5,229 to 3,934 and a decrease of about a third in the mortality rate per 100,000 population, which had fallen to 19.5.[21] With regard to the age distribution of mortality, deaths of children under five decreased from 62% of total deaths from smallpox in the decade 1851–1860 to 54% in the next decade,[22] and from 103 to 65 per 100,000 children under five.

There seems little doubt that in the period between 1853 and 1867 there was a large increase in the proportion of infants vaccinated compared with the period before 1853. The figures of infants vaccinated by the public vaccination service (which are the only figures available) shows a rise in the proportion of successful vaccinations to births from 32% in 1851–52 to an average of 70% in the eight years 1859 – 60 to 1866 – 67. In these eight years, however, there was no consistent trend in the figures, the maximum being 89.7% in 1862–63 and the minimum 61.9% in 1865–66.[23]

It had become clear by 1866 that there were some important defects in the existing law in relation to its desired object of securing universal successful infant vaccination; some of these defects were in the system of vaccination, some were in the machinery for enforcing compulsion. Critics of the system argued that there were in fact large numbers of inefficient vaccinations and that the public system did not either ensure that vaccinators had adequate qualifications or give them sufficient financial incentive to efficiency. They also argued that there was insufficient control by the central government of the vaccination activities of Boards of Guardians and that some Boards were very lax in the performance of their duties.

With regard to the enforcement of compulsion, critics noted three main defects in the law. First, in a prosecution of a parent for failure to have his child vaccinated, the prosecution had to prove the delivery to him of the prescribed form of notice. Second, there was, in many areas, no officer responsible for prosecuting offenders. An Act of 1861[24] had given Boards of Guardians permission to appoint persons to institute and conduct prosecutions but such an appointment was not obligatory and, while provision was made for the cost of the proceedings, no power was given to pay any remuneration to the person appointed. Third, it had been decided by the Court of Queen's Bench that when a parent had once been fined for neglecting to have a child vaccinated, no further proceedings could be taken against him with regard to the vaccination of that child. In the opinion of one critic,[25] this meant that "the Act, instead of being compulsory, permits the option of submitting to vaccination, or escaping it on payment of twenty shillings". These three hindrances to the enforcement of compulsion were removed in the Acts of 1867 and 1871.

The Vaccination Acts, 1867 and 1871

A Bill to consolidate and amend the laws relative to vaccination was introduced by the Government in 1867. The debates in the House of Commons on this Bill showed, in contrast to the debates in 1853, that some speakers objected to vaccination itself, not merely to compulsion. For example, W.H. Barrow stated: "It was the opinion of many medical men now that vaccination had produced disease to a dangerous extent... His objection was founded upon statements made by a number of parents, some of them medical men, whose children had died or suffered great injuries to their constitution from vaccination."[26] This reason for objection to vaccination later influenced many resisters to compulsion, and resisters were also influenced by two other arguments which were voiced in this debate – first, that "there were many cases of persons being attacked by smallpox after having been vaccinated"[27] and second, that diseases other than smallpox, particularly syphilis, might be transmitted in the process of arm-to-arm vaccination.[28] (The speaker who made this last point was not opposed to vaccination but was urging the importance of ensuring that both the child vaccinated and the child from whom vaccine was taken were in a healthy state.)

In addition to the argument that a voluntary system would be more effective in promoting vaccination, there were various other arguments used by speakers opposing compulsion. Two speakers thought it undesirable to use compulsion on a matter on which medical men were not all agreed. Sir J.C. Jervoise asked: "If even with a revelation people could not agree upon theological matters, how could it be expected that they should agree to a rigorous enactment on a subject like this on which doctors notoriously differed?"[29] Colonel Bartelot stated that out of 750,000 parents "there were 250,000 who could not read or write; yet they were liable to a fine of 20s. if they did not follow the forms supplied under the Act."[30] N. Kendall said that he opposed the Bill "because he thought sufficient regard had not been paid to the feelings of the lower classes"[31] and Thomas Chambers opposed it "because he was persuaded that even if it were passed an agitation would be commenced which would not cease until the Act was repealed".[32] J.W. Henley, while not opposing compulsion in itself, stated that no attempt was made under the Bill "to conciliate the prejudices or consult the convenience of the people who were compelled to vaccinate their children. The Bill was one of pure coercion..." and he criticised a number of the provisions, including the obligation to attend at vaccination stations and the obligation to supply vaccine to other children if required.[33]

At the Second Reading of the Bill in the House of Commons, W.H. Barrow moved the adjournment and was defeated by 98–7 votes; there was no other vote taken in the full House and there was no vote on any of the amendments proposed in Committee. The British Medical Association's Committee on Parliamentary Bills regretted that many clauses of the Bill were "hurried through Committee about 2 a.m. after an exhausting debate on the Reform Bill notwithstanding the notice-paper was crowded with amendments".[34] In the House of Lords the Bill was referred to a Select Committee which made only a few verbal alterations.[35]

The Vaccination Act, 1867,[36] was a Consolidating Act and all previous Vaccination Acts were repealed. The Act came into force at the beginning of 1868. It was enacted that each Board of Guardians was to divide its area into "vaccination districts" (Section 2) and contract with a medical practitioner to act as "public vaccinator" for the district (Section 3). No person was to be appointed as a public vaccinator or act as a deputy for a public vaccinator unless he possessed qualifications prescribed by the Privy Council (Section 4) and the Privy Council might authorise payments to public vaccinators from central funds at a rate not exceeding one shilling for each child successfully vaccinated; these payments were in addition to those received from the Guardians (Section 5).

The Privy Council was authorised to make regulations regarding the re-vaccination of applicants by the Public Vaccinator (Section 8). Such regulations were made, providing, under different conditions at different periods, for free re-vaccination for those who desired it;

re-vaccination was never made compulsory with regard to anyone already successfully vaccinated.

Several important changes were made in the provisions regarding compulsion and its enforcement. The obligation of the parent to have his child vaccinated within three months of its birth remained unchanged. In the case of some other person having custody of the child it was enacted that such person should have the child vaccinated within three months of receiving its custody (Section 16). In the case of any parent using the public vaccination service the obligation remained to take the child for subsequent inspection and two further obligations were added; that the vaccinator should be allowed, if he saw fit, to take lymph from the child for the performance of other vaccinations, and that, if the vaccination of the child was unsuccessful, the parent should, if directed by the vaccinator, have the child again vaccinated and inspected (Section 17). The penalty for neglect of vaccination or inspection remained a maximum fine of twenty shillings and costs could also be charged unless the parent rendered "a reasonable excuse for his neglect" (Section 29).

The Act authorised Boards of Guardians to "Pay any officer appointed by them to prosecute persons charged with offences under this Act, or otherwise to enforce its provisions" (Section 28). This provision was greatly strengthened by Section 5 of the amending Act of 1871[37] which compelled all Boards of Guardians to appoint such officers, to be known as "Vaccination Officers". This same Section, as interpreted by a short explanatory Act in 1874,[38] gave the same power to the Local Government Board to make regulations regarding the enforcement of the Vaccination Acts by Guardians and Vaccination Officers as it had with regard to Guardians and their officers in matters relating to the relief of the poor. Under this power the local Government Board, in a general order made in 1874, directed that (with a modification with regard to repeated prosecutions), "The Guardians shall, in all cases in which the provisions of the Vaccination Acts for enforcing vaccination have been neglected, cause proceedings to be taken against the persons in default, and for this purpose shall give directions, authorising the Vaccination Officer to institute and conduct such proceedings." The order also provided that the Vaccination Officer should take such proceedings as were necessary in any case in which the Local Government Board directed him to do so.[39]

The Act of 1867 removed the necessity for the proof, in a prosecution for neglect of vaccination, that the defendant had received notice of the requirements of the law (Section 34) though the Act continued the existing provision that such notice should be given to the parent by the Registrar of Births (Section 15).

To meet the objection that a penalty for neglect of vaccination could, under the Act of 1853 and under Section 29 of the Act of 1867, be inflicted only once, the latter Act contained a further provision for coercing the recalcitrant. Section 31 provided that, if the officer responsible for enforcing the Act gave information in writing to a Justice of the Peace that he had reason to believe that any child in his area under the age of fourteen had not been successfully vaccinated, that he had given notice to the parent to have the child vaccinated, and that this notice had been disregarded, then the Justice might summon the parent to appear before him with the child. "Upon the appearance, if the Justice shall find, after such examination as he shall deem necessary, that the child has not been vaccinated, nor has already had the smallpox, he may, if he see fit, make an order under his hand and seal directing such child to be vaccinated within a certain time; and if at the expiration of such time the child shall not have been so vaccinated, or shall not be shown to be then unfit to be vaccinated, the person upon whom such an order shall have been made shall be proceeded against summarily, and unless he can show some reasonable ground for his omission to carry the order into effect, shall be liable to a penalty not exceeding twenty shillings. "

The importance of this provision was that a recalcitrant parent could now have persistent action taken against him. There was no legal limit to the number of occasions on which he could be summoned to appear before the Justice, nor, if on each occasion the Justice thought fit to make the order to vaccinate, to the number of occasions on which he could be prosecuted, until he either complied with the law or the child passed the age of fourteen.

Thus the legislation of 1867 and 1871 provided an efficient system for enforcing compulsory vaccination and this object was attained with considerable success during the succeeding years. In each of the fourteen years 1872 to 1885 the number of primary vaccinations was more than 84% of the number of births and the average over the whole period was 85.4%. When allowance is made for the large number of babies dying under the age of three months

– 6.7% of births in 1881–85[40] – the figures show that probably well over 90% of surviving babies had been vaccinated. As the total number of vaccinations is not known prior to 1872 (the figures not including vaccinations by private doctors) it can be stated only that this percentage is probably higher than in the period 1853 to 1867; it is certainly higher than in any period since 1885.

But the period when compulsory vaccination began to be efficiently enforced coincided with the period when there began to be widespread opposition to vaccination, and the very efficiency of enforcement had the consequence that the most determined opponents of vaccination, if they were parents, became lawbreakers, prosecuted, sometimes repeatedly, in magistrates' courts. From 1867 to 1898 Parliament, the Government, Boards of Guardians, Vaccination Officers, and Justices of the Peace had to face the problem of how to deal with a considerable number of cases of illegal conscientious objection.

The Reasons for Opposition to Vaccination

At the time of the debates on the Vaccination Bill of 1867 there were not only individual opponents of vaccination throughout the country but there was also some organised opposition. A lecturer to the British Medical Association in 1866 quoted the opinion of a Government investigator that "though objection to vaccination existed in isolated instances in several places, and although in one or two places there was strong local prejudice" yet on the whole less than one per cent of omission to vaccinate was due to anything but indifference and idleness or to real want of opportunity.[41] In the same year an article in The Lancet expressed astonishment that there were still some individuals who doubted the efficacy of vaccination and even denounced it as injurious. The article continued: "It is true that the majority of those persons are amongst the most ignorant, and therefore most prejudiced of mankind, but now and then persons with some pretensions to be regarded as authorities join the ranks of the malcontents... The Compulsory Vaccination Act has called into existence an 'Anti-Compulsory Vaccination League'"[42] This League sent a deputation to the Government in 1867 and asked that there should be a commission of enquiry into the hygienic value of vaccination and the policy of payment from public funds and suggested that, pending such enquiry, compulsory vaccination should be suspended.[43] In the debates in the House of Commons on the Vaccination Bill, 1867, W.H. Barrow stated that "He had received communications from a great number of persons, not only in England but on the Continent, thanking him for the protests he had felt it his duty to make against the system of vaccination"[44] and a supporter of the Bill referred to "those well-meaning but ill-informed men by whom the walls of the city had been placarded" on the subject of communication of disease by vaccination.[45]

Those parents who objected to the vaccination of their children did not necessarily become defendants in court: whether or not they did so depended mainly on two circumstances – the efficiency with which the compulsory provisions of the law were enforced and the attitude of the parent. For example, one strong opponent of vaccination obviously favoured eventual obedience to the law combined with a comminatory protest, for he published in 1866 the following form of protest to be sent to the convicting justice and to the Home Secretary. "Know all men by these presents, that I... having been forced against my will to vaccinate my child, which operation I consider as the sure promoter of disease, if not death, by poisoning the blood, do solemnly protest against such tyranny, and hereby invoke the judgment of the Almighty on those who may have been the means of passing such infamous, arbitrary and unnatural laws."[46]

There is no means of knowing how many objecting parents obeyed the law or their reasons for doing so. They might be deterred by the legal penalties involved; they might fear the publicity of a prosecution or consider it a disgrace; they might consider that their duty to obey the law overrode their duty to act on their opinions about vaccination; or there might be other reasons for their compliance. There is good reason to believe that in the last two decades of the nineteenth century the number of parents willing to be prosecuted was much smaller than the total number who objected to vaccination and that many complying objectors used their influence as electors to induce their Boards of Guardians not to enforce the law.

The following are examples of prosecutions in the first two years after the Act of 1867 came into force. In Sheffield one of the first persons summoned was a herbalist who was himself a member of the Board of Guardians.[47] At least two of the parents prosecuted in

1869 were themselves doctors.[48] A Leeds chemist had his fine and costs paid by the local branch of the Anti-Compulsory Vaccination League.[49] A Yorkshire tanner chose to go to prison for seven days as the alternative to a fine of 20s. and costs.[50]

In the Minority Report of the Royal Commission on Vaccination it was stated that in 1853 there were few or no signs of opposition to vaccination amongst the population and a general acquiescence in the assumption that the abatement in the virulence of smallpox from the commencement of the nineteenth century had been due almost entirely to vaccination. But, stated the Report, in the 1870s "resistance to the law began to spread widely and the main point on which recalcitrants insisted was that experience proved the impotence of vaccination to prevent epidemics".[51] The starting point of large-scale resistance to vaccination was the smallpox epidemic of 1870 to 1872.

This epidemic, reputed to have come from France, started in the East End of London in October 1870. After a period of more than twenty years, in which the highest mortality in a single year was 7,264, the figures rose to 23,062 in 1871 and 19,022 in 1872. The last epidemic of comparable severity had been in 1837 to 1840 with a total mortality of over 40,000; in that epidemic most of the deaths were of children under five. In 1871 – 72, in contrast, only 32% of deaths were in this age group. The proportion of the population over the age of five attacked by smallpox during this epidemic was greater than at any time since the early eighteenth century.[52] There are no available figures of the total number of cases as smallpox was not yet compulsorily notifiable; on the basis of the fatality rate of cases admitted to the smallpox hospitals of the Metropolitan Asylums Board – 18% to 19% – total deaths in England and Wales would represent some 221,000 to 234,000 cases of smallpox. An epidemic on this scale, after nearly twenty years in which a considerable proportion of infants had been vaccinated, inevitably led many people to question the claim of the enthusiasts for infant vaccination that it would lead to the decrease of smallpox.

Another claim of the supporters of vaccination was questioned on the evidence of this epidemic: the claim that vaccination safeguarded the individual who was vaccinated from contracting smallpox. Many people who had been vaccinated suffered from smallpox during the epidemic. Even children, whose vaccination in infancy was fairly recent, were not safe: by July 1871, 6,854 vaccinated persons had been admitted to smallpox hospitals under the Metropolitan Asylums Board.[53] The smallpox hospitals admitted, in 1870–72, 195 cases of vaccinated children under five and 786 cases of vaccinated children between five and ten. Vaccination did not seem even to protect these children from death for, in these hospitals during this period, there were 38 deaths of vaccinated children under five and 60 deaths of vaccinated children between five and ten.[54]

The shock produced by the epidemic was all the greater because of the absolute faith in vaccination which had been shown by many of its supporters. In contrast to continental countries, where the value of revaccination had been realised, in England the Vaccination Acts from 1840 onwards "were founded on the entirely false Jennerian concept that infant vaccination provided lifelong immunity and revaccination was really unnecessary".[55] Voluntary revaccination by Public Vaccinators had been allowed in the 1867 Act but only at a fee of two-thirds the fee for primary vaccinations, and in 1871 an official statement said that revaccination could be performed "so far as this is not inconsistent with the more imperative claims for primary vaccination".[56] Some authorities realised the importance of revaccination. A leading article in *The British Medical Journal*[57] stated "Every one admits that vaccination does not confer absolute and permanent immunity. In as much as it is not permanent, repeated vaccinations are desirable..." But the official statement of 1871 opined that by well performed and successful vaccination in infancy "most people are completely ensured for their whole lifetime against an attack of smallpox and in a proportionately few cases, where the protection is less complete, smallpox, if it be caught, will in consequence of vaccination generally be so mild a disease as not to threaten death or disfigurement." The grim facts of the epidemic conflicted with inflated claims such as this, and the sceptics did not find convincing the defence that many "vaccinated" persons had in fact been unsuccessfully or inefficiently vaccinated. It was very natural that experience of the epidemic, in comparison with the official claims in support of infant vaccination, should lead many people to hold the opposite extreme view – that infant vaccination was useless as a protection.

This effect of the epidemic was well exemplified in the evidence given before the Royal Commission on Vaccination by a Congregational Minister who had been prosecuted. "I was in the very midst of the epidemic... I visited during that time scores of my friends who lay at the point of death; stood by and saw them die... I did not observe one case from all my enquiries where they were unvaccinated; they had all been vaccinated (I inquired in every case that I possibly could) yet they died." To the question: "Were you an opponent of vaccination at that time?" he replied: "I was not strictly an opponent, I was considering the question at the time..."[58]

Another witness before the Commission stated that in the epidemic in 1871 he and one sister were revaccinated; six weeks later he contracted smallpox and a week after this she contracted it. The seven other persons in the house were not revaccinated and did not contract smallpox. "That set me to think about it, and I have had ample reason since to confirm me in the opinion that I had formed that vaccination was no preventative." He acted on his opinion and was fined four times.[59]

Thus the conviction that infant vaccination was useless was one important reason why some parents resisted the law. The other important reason for resistance was the belief that vaccination was injurious to the child. Of course an individual might object for both these reasons and sometimes for other reasons in addition. For example, a Bridgwater coachbuilder, prosecuted in 1871, said that vaccination did not prevent smallpox, that it was a dangerous operation, and that compulsory vaccination was an infringement of the liberty of the subject.[60] A Select Committee of the House of Commons in 1871 occupied eight sittings "in hearing the evidence of persons who assert that vaccination is useless and injurious."[61]

Nearly twenty years later, among some thirty objectors who had been prosecuted who gave evidence before the Royal Commission on Vaccination, belief in the harmful effects of vaccination on the child was the reason given by several for their resistance to the law. For example, a Surrey carpenter who had been imprisoned stated: "I gave the magistrates the reason that I saw so many children suffering around me, and the number of parents who tell me they have got no rest for weeks together after the vaccination of their children owing to the children's suffering..."[62] A foreman tailor from Keighley, twice imprisoned, said that he was set against vaccination by seeing the case of a child vaccinated at the age of twelve months who could never walk afterwards.[63]

A photographer from Andover, prosecuted sixty times, stated: "I remember a very shocking death that occurred from vaccination in Andover in my early days... The child died something like six weeks after it was vaccinated thoroughly rotten; it was previously a healthy child, born of healthy parents... I have known many other cases, but that was the most distressing case; it suffered horribly, and died simply rotten."[64] Evidence was given that a father had been fined twice though he had shown the magistrate a copy of the death certificate of another of his children certifying vaccination as a primary cause of death.[65] A doctor, on behalf of the royal Commission, investigated more than six hundred cases reported to the Commission as being cases of death or more or less serious injury resulting from vaccination.[66]

In 1894 The British Medical Journal stated: "We do not believe that vaccination properly performed on a healthy child ever causes death."[67] In contrast, it is now recognised that in a very small proportion of cases vaccination, however carefully performed, is followed by the serious complication of generalised vaccinia or of post-vaccinial encephalomyelitis, and that in some of these cases the complication leads to death. In the present state of medical knowledge this risk cannot be avoided; it is not only admitted by the Government Department concerned but special reports are made on as many of these cases as possible. Presumably these complications accounted for some of the cases of deaths and serious illness which so impressed the objectors to vaccination in the late nineteenth century. But there were also risks which do not exist now in this country. Vaccinators did not take present precautions to avoid sepsis: lancets were not sterilised between patients but merely washed in warm water.[68] General standards of cleanliness were much lower than they are now. The congregation of infants at vaccination stations probably led to a spread of infection between them at a time when the importance of isolation was not realised. In 1871 the Lancet reported a case in which a father was imprisoned in lieu of a fine for not taking his child to be inspected after vaccination, his reason being that in his house there was a child Iying dead from smallpox. The Lancet headed this report "How to Make Vaccination Unpopular" and gave its view that the law should forbid the use of vaccination stations by anyone living in an infected house.[69]

Another cause of possible risk was the system of arm-to-arm vaccination which was the common method of vaccination up to 1899; in that year the public vaccination service universally adopted the method of vaccination with glycerinated calf Iymph which had been first used in this country in 1881.[70] The Royal Commission on Vaccination strongly recommended this change because the use of calf Iymph would completely avoid the risk of the transmission of syphilis in arm-to-arm vaccination. The Commission considered this risk to be very small but realised that it had been feared by many people and that it was natural that parents should regard with abhorrence the taking of any such risks.[71]

In the later years of the nineteenth century the general mortality rate of infants was very high. The average annual percentage of children born who died under the age of one year was 14.2% in the 1880s and 15.3% in the 1890s;[72] in 1895 and 1896 more than a quarter of total deaths were infant deaths. A doctor, writing to The British Medical Journal in 1898, cited figures such as these and commented: "So that just in the year when illnesses and the number of deaths are at the maximum vaccination compulsorily takes place; can it be wondered that people who have not had a scientific education, hearing of illness after illness, death after death, pretty soon after vaccination ascribe to it half the diseases that occur?... Many diseases – 'bad arms', inflammation of the arm, abscesses, eczema, impetigo – and most diseases and most deaths that occur soon after vaccination are put down by many people with great conviction to be the direct or indirect result of vaccination."[73] It is clear that a parent's feeling and decision on the matter of his child's vaccination would be influenced by the deaths and serious illnesses which he believed to be the result of vaccination, whether or not his belief was actually justified in particular cases.

Thus, in most cases, the decision of objectors seems to have been based not on general principles but on an assessment of the facts differing from that made by official opinion and, resulting from this, a contrary decision as to the comparative rightness of exposing their children to the risks of vaccination as against exposing them to the risks of being left unvaccinated. There was no difference of ultimate aim in the vaccination controversy: both parties regarded smallpox as a serious evil, both parties acted in the way that they thought would best safeguard the health of children. As the matter involved parental responsibility and parental affection, many people, on both sides of the controversy, felt very strongly, held their opinions with great tenacity, and acted from deep conviction.

The decision of objectors was, however, sometimes based, wholly or partly, on a general principle. For example, a witness before the Royal Commission, who had been fined thirty-four times, gave as one of his reasons "feeling that my children as given me from the hands of God were perfect and needed nothing done to them beyond, I objected on that ground."[74] An objector in 1900 stated: "I consider vaccination a direct violation of the laws of natural theology; not only that, it is a diabolical practice of inoculating animal diseases into the human system."[75] The general principle of objection to the cruelty to animals involved influenced some opponents of vaccination in the period after vaccination from calf lymph became the normal method. The general principle of the right of parents to make the important decisions with regard to their children's welfare would not in itself make those who held that principle opponents of vaccination. But this principle influenced some believers in vaccination to oppose compulsion and stiffened the resistance of objectors to vaccination. For example, a witness before the Royal Commission, who had been fined thirteen times, stated: "Another reason is that I am the guardian of my child, and I think it is the duty of the law to protect me – that I have the right to decide what is best for my child."[76] The religious sect known as the Peculiar People included vaccination with other forms of medical care as being forbidden to them by their religion (see Chapter 9). But in most cases of objection to vaccination there was no direct connection with religious beliefs.

However, the religious attitude towards the authority of conscience, especially among Nonconformists, probably strengthened the resistance of some objectors. For example, the leaders of the strong resistance movement in Leicester "were, almost to a man, God-fearing dissenters."[77]

Consideration by Parliament of Repeated Prosecutions, 1870–1871

The earliest problem of illegal conscientious objection to be considered seriously by Parliament was the problem of repeated prosecutions of the same individual. Before 1867 only one conviction for refusal of vaccination was possible in relation to any one child. Under the Act of 1867 only one conviction was possible, under Section 29, for the original refusal of a parent to have his child vaccinated within three months of birth, but in addition, under

Section 31, an indefinite number of orders could be made by a Justice for the vaccination of an unvaccinated child, and on each occasion when a parent refused to obey such an order he could be prosecuted and convicted. Under the Act of 1867 there was no legal limit to the number of times a recalcitrant parent could be convicted on account of the same child until the child attained the age of fourteen.

In 1870 J. Candlish, MP for Sunderland, introduced a Bill to limit the number and amount of penalties which could be imposed on a parent on account of the same child. The Bill was not taken further than the Second Reading Debate in which the Home Secretary, H.A. Bruce, stated his intention to appoint a Select Committee.

In February 1871 a Select Committee of the House of Commons was appointed to enquire into the operation of the Act of 1867 and to report whether the Act should be amended; the Committee consisted of fifteen members.[78]

The Committee approved of the general enforcement of compulsory vaccination and recommended that the appointment of Vaccination Officers by Boards of Guardians should be obligatory; this recommendation was implemented in the amending Vaccination Act, 1871.[79] But the Committee drew a distinction between the parents who left their children unvaccinated because of neglect, carelessness or procrastination and "those parents, very few in proportion to the whole population, who assert that vaccination will do harm". With regard to this last class of parents the Committee opined that "it becomes necessary to weigh the claims of the parent to control, as he thinks fit, the medical treatment of an infant child, as against the duty of the State to protect the health of the community, and to save the child itself from a dreadful disease."[80]

With regard to repeated prosecutions Candlish, not himself an objector, stated that he knew of fifty cases in which a parent had been prosecuted several times. One example was a Derbyshire newsagent who had been convicted thirteen times, ten of the convictions being in a period of twelve months, had suffered several distraints on his goods, and, having no goods left, was now in prison. The Committee expressed "great doubt whether the object of the law is gained by thus continuing a long contest with the convictions of the parent."[81] Their statement continued:

"The public opinion of the neighbourhood may sympathise with a person thus prosecuted, and may in consequence be excited against the law; and, after all, though the parent be fined or imprisoned, the child may remain unvaccinated." The Committee recommended that "whenever, in any case two penalties, or one full penalty, have been imposed upon a parent, the magistrate should not impose any further penalty in respect of the same child."[82] In the Bill which became the Vaccination Act, 1871, a clause was included in the terms of this recommendation.[83] This clause was approved in the House of Commons by 57 to 12 votes but in the Committee Stage in the House of Lords it was defeated by 8 to 7 votes.[84] As the Government considered the passing of the Bill to be urgent they did not contest the decision of the House of Lords on this clause and the legal possibility of an unlimited number of prosecutions on account of the same child remained for the next twenty-seven years.

Resistance to Compulsion 1871–1898

After the Act of 1871 and a short explanatory Act of 1874 there was no further legislation concerning vaccination until 1898. After the epidemic of 1870–72 the average annual number of deaths from smallpox was considerably lower than in the mid-nineteenth century and decreased each decade; as compared with about 4,370 in the 1850s and about 3,440 in the 1860s the average annual deaths in England and Wales were 2,045 in 1873 – 79, 1,291 in the 1880s, and 399 in the 1890s. From 1873 to the end of the century the maximum annual figure was 4,278; deaths exceeded 1,000 in only eleven of the twenty-seven years, and in each of four years from 1889 onwards the number of deaths was under 50.

During the period after 1870 a number of measures other than vaccination became important as means to the prevention and control of smallpox. There was a great extension of infectious diseases hospitals in London under the Metropolitan Asylums Board, established under an Act of 1867:[85] in the period 1870–1885 nearly 60,000 smallpox patients were admitted to the Board's hospitals. Under the Public Health Act of 1875[86] local sanitary authorities were enabled to provide hospitals and many authorities established hospitals for infectious diseases, though only about a third of them had done so by 1895.

Various Acts gave powers for the removal of smallpox patients to hospital and for the cleansing and disinfecting of premises and their contents. From 1875 onwards many of the larger provincial cities, by private Acts, provided for the compulsory notification of smallpox. In 1889[87] a general Act was passed which allowed the local authorities which adopted it to compel the notification of smallpox and some other infectious diseases, and an Act of 1899[88] made such notification compulsory in all areas.

In the early twentieth century legislation allowed certain other compulsory measures of isolation and certain measures of sanitary control of persons entering the country. Some critics of compulsory vaccination urged that these other methods of controlling smallpox, along with improvements of housing and sanitation, were more useful than vaccination and that the expenditure and effort devoted to infant vaccination diverted attention and resources from them.

For example, the Minority Report of the Royal Commission considered the universal enforcement of vaccination "inexpedient because it concentrates attention on a safeguard proved to be insufficient in itself, and leads to the neglect of sanitation and isolation, which our evidence shows to be more effective."[89] In 1901 Bernard Shaw, as a member of St. Pancras Borough Council, objected to general infant vaccination as a diversion of energy from the improvement of housing conditions.[90]

The figures for total vaccination of infants, first available in 1872, showed that in the years 1872 to 1885 the percentage of infants vaccinated to total births never fell below 84%. But from 1885 to 1897, the last year when the figure was unaffected by legal exemptions, the percentage declined each year. In the period 1886 to 1891 the average figure was 80.25%: in 1891 the figure was 75.8%. In the period 1892 to 1897 the average figure was 68.9%: in 1897 the figure was 62.4%. This decline in the percentage of infants vaccinated was due to the opposition to vaccination which had both direct and indirect results. The direct result was the refusal of many objectors, even after prosecution, to allow their children to be vaccinated. The indirect result was that many Boards of Guardians ceased to use their full powers to enforce the law or, in more extreme cases, ceased entirely to enforce the compulsory provisions of the Vaccination Acts. The magnitude of the effect on the number of vaccinations which could be produced by strong local opposition combined with non-enforcement of the law is shown in the case of Leicester. Here an Anti-Vaccination League was founded in 1869 and at a National Anti-Vaccination Conference, amid a crowd of 100,000 people, "A copy of the Vaccination Act was ceremonially burned amid scenes of wild enthusiasm."[91] The percentage of infants vaccinated in Leicester fell from 86.1% in 1874 to 1.3% in 1897.[92]

According to a return presented to the House of Commons in 1890, there had been, in a period of about ten years from July 1879 onwards, 11,408 cases of fines inflicted in England and Wales for breaches of the vaccination laws.[93] In Gloucester there had been 250 prosecutions in three and a half years before the Guardians resolved to discontinue them in 1887.[94] In Oldham there had been 1,622 prosecutions in seven years prior to 1886 when they were discontinued.[95] In cases where both father and mother were available it was usually the father who was prosecuted. The number of cases of imprisonment in England and Wales in the ten years from 1879 onwards was 115.[96] Imprisonment could not be inflicted as an initial penalty: it was imposed only in default of the payment of fines or costs. Under the Summary Jurisdiction Act, 1879,[97] the length of imprisonment in lieu of fine and costs was a maximum of seven days for an amount not exceeding 10s, fourteen days for an amount not exceeding £1, and one month for an amount not exceeding £5. The maximum fine for refusal of vaccination was 20s., so that even when costs were also charged, as was often the case, the offender would not be liable to imprisonment for more than one month. In fact offenders imprisoned seem usually to have been in prison for seven days or fourteen days. In at least one case a woman was imprisoned.[98]

Imprisonment with hard labour was illegal for refusal of vaccination, though it was sometimes mistakenly imposed. In general, objectors in prison in lieu of payment of a fine were treated in the same way as other offenders serving terms of imprisonment without hard labour. This fact was bitterly resented by some of those sympathising with the objectors and there were a number of questions on the matter in the House of Commons. In 1893 a Bill was introduced with a clause providing that an objector imprisoned for non-payment of a fine should be treated in the same way as persons imprisoned for debt;[99] this was already the position of objectors who had not been fined and were in prison only for non-payment of costs.[100] This Bill did not become law but the conditions of imprisonment of objectors were later changed by the Act of 1898.[101]

The small number of cases of imprisonment, in comparison with the number of cases fined, may seem surprising in view of the fact that a fine of 20s, which would now be regarded as a small penalty, at that time meant a payment exceeding the weekly wage of some objectors. There seem to have been several circumstances which limited the number of imprisonments. Firstly, it was very common for the fine inflicted to be smaller than the maximum allowed. Sometimes the fine was as low as 1s. Secondly, the fine was sometimes paid for the objector by sympathisers and this would be particularly likely in areas with a strong anti-vaccination movement. Thirdly, it was fairly common for distraint to be made on the goods of the objector if he was unable or unwilling to pay the fine.

Very soon after the passing of the Act of 1867 some Boards of Guardians were showing extreme reluctance to enforce it. The Northampton Guardians in 1870 carried a motion "that the Act be not enforced", one Guardian stating that he "thought that fathers and mothers were the best judges of what they ought to do".[102] However, soon afterwards they reversed this decision after receiving a letter from the Medical Department of the Privy Council informing them that they would not be allowed to jeopardise the lives of Her Majesty's subjects with impunity.[103] In 1875 the ultimate sanction was used against the Keighley Guardians: the Court of the Queen's Bench issued a writ of *mandamus* commanding them to enforce the law. The Royal Commission described and commented on the result of this action as follows: "In default of obedience they were committed to prison. After a short incarceration they were let out on bail. When subsequently brought before the Court to answer for their contempt, they were released on entering into their own recognizances to come up for judgment when called upon. By the terms of the recognizance they were bound while guardians to do nothing in disobedience to the Vaccination Acts or to cause their operation to be in any way disturbed. The proceedings proved, however, quite ineffectual so far as vaccination was concerned. The same course was pursued afterwards as before... Experience shows that when the guardians represent a local community opposed to vaccination this method of putting pressure upon them is inoperative to promote it."[104]

There were in 1870 Boards of Guardians for 667 Poor Law Unions in England and Wales. The members of each Board were the local Justices of the Peace and, in addition, members elected by all ratepaying occupiers and all owners of land or buildings, without distinction of sex.[105] Those entitled to vote had a number of votes (varying from one to twelve) in proportion to the rateable value owned or occupied. After 1872[106] voting was by ballot. After 1875[107] women could be elected as Guardians. The Local Government Act, 1894,[108] abolished cumulative voting and ex-officio Guardians and also provided that, in those areas of Poor Law Unions falling within Rural Districts, the persons elected as Rural District Councillors should also act as the Guardians appointed for those areas. By 1891 the number of Boards had decreased to 648. From 1871[109] the Government Department responsible for the control of the vaccination activities of local authorities was the Local Government Board. In 1919[110] the Ministry of Health became the responsible Department and remained so until the ending of compulsory vaccination.

In a considerable number of areas a large minority, if not a majority, of the population were against vaccination. At Derby, in 1871, an objector on his release from prison was received by bands of music and "several thousand people with a large red flag carried in front."[111] At Gloucester, in 1885, a canvass held by the local anti-vaccination society showed that, out of over 4,000 replies, 75% did not believe in vaccination and another 17%, though believing in vaccination, thought that it should not be compulsory.[112] A strong local opposition to vaccination meant not only that there were large numbers of defaulting parents to be prosecuted, if the law was enforced, but also large numbers of electors who considered the candidates' attitude to enforcement of the law important in deciding their choice at Guardians' elections. "In some districts guardians have been elected from time to time solely because they have pledged themselves not to prosecute those who fail to have their children vaccinated", stated the Royal Commission.[113] The evidence before the Commission of a member of the Halifax Board of Guardians is an example of how Guardians resented their predicament. The Board's reason for discontinuing prosecutions was "that we found it utterly impossible in the face of public opinion to carry out the Act... we feel that the guardians ought not to have the odium of carrying out the Act thrust upon them; we feel that our duties are sufficiently burdensome already." The majority on the Board against compulsory vaccination included some who "believe in the merits of vaccination itself but they refuse to compel others."[114]

Thus the Guardians in areas with strong local opposition to vaccination had to decide between, on the one hand, their legal duties under the Vaccination Acts and the constant pressure of the Local Government Board to make them fulfil these and, on the other hand, the difficulties and odium of enforcing the law, their duties as elected representatives, and often also their personal opinions. Board after Board ceased to prosecute offenders against the compulsory provisions of the Acts. An enquiry by the Royal Commission at the end of 1891 found that at that date nearly a fifth of the Boards (122 out of 648) were not enforcing the law.[115] The appointment of the Royal Commission in 1889 had itself added to the number of non-enforcing Boards, as it was considered by some Boards that, while the whole question of vaccination and its enforcement was under consideration, this was a reason for not enforcing the law. 46 out of the 122 non-enforcing Boards in 1891 had acted for this reason and some other Boards followed their example between 1891 and the Final Report of the Commission in 1896.[116] Even the Local Government Board found it difficult to bring pressure on recalcitrant Boards while the whole subject was under consideration by the Commission.[117]

The Royal Commission on Vaccination, 1889–1896

The Royal Commission on Vaccination was appointed in May 1889 to enquire and report on the following matters:

(1) The effect of vaccination in reducing the prevalence of, and mortality from, smallpox.

(2) What means, other than vaccination, can be used for diminishing the prevalence of smallpox; and how far such means could be relied on in place of vaccination.

(3) The objections made to vaccination on the grounds of injurious effects alleged to result therefrom; and the nature and extent of any injurious effects which do, in fact, so result.

(4) Whether any, and, if so, what means should be adopted for preventing or lessening the ill effects, if any, resulting from vaccination; and whether, and, if so, by what means, vaccination with animal vaccine should be further facilitated as a part of public vaccination.

(5) Whether any alterations should be made in the arrangement and proceedings for securing the performance of vaccination, and, in particular, in the provisions of the Vaccination Acts with respect to prosecutions for non-compliance with the law.

The Chairman of the Commission was Baron Herschell. Fifteen other persons served as members, of whom six were members of the medical profession and six were members of the House of Commons. Three members died before the Commission presented its final report. The Commission published seven reports, the first in 1889 and the final report in 1896. Most of these reports consisted of the evidence, both oral and documentary, supplied to the Commission; the Commission's recommendations were contained in the Fifth Report in 1892[118] and the Final Report in 1896.[119] The Commission considered a large amount of evidence, including the evidence of many anti-vaccinationists. Some anti-vaccination witnesses were advised, and some had their expenses of the journey to London paid, by the London Society for the Abolition of Compulsory Vaccination, founded in 1880, the predecessor of the National Anti-Vaccination League, founded in 1896.[120]

The following account does not cover all the conclusions of the Royal Commission but is concerned only with those referring to the principle of compulsion, the methods of enforcement, and the means to diminish opposition to vaccination. The majority of the Commission favoured the retention of compulsory vaccination. They opined that "it is better for the child and better for the community that it should be vaccinated than that it should remain unvaccinated. A parent can have no inherent right... to prevent or neglect its vaccination". Their reason for advocating compulsion was that "If no penalty were attached to the failure to vaccinate, it is, we think, certain that a large number of children would remain unvaccinated from mere neglect on the part of their parents or indisposition to incur the trouble involved, and not because they thought it better in the interests of their children".[121] There were two dissenting recommendations on the matter, each signed by two members of the Commission. In one of these recommendations it was opined that, if public vaccination were offered at the home of the child, together with medical treatment for any untoward results of vaccination, much objection to vaccination would cease. "The right of the parent on grounds of conscience to refuse vaccination for his child being conceded, and the offer of vaccination under improved conditions being made at the home of the child, it would in our opinion be best to leave the parent to accept or reject this offer". The retention of compulsion in any form would cause irritation and hostility in the future, as it had done in the past.[122] In the other dissenting recommendation the authors stated: "On the whole, we are of opinion that a resolute and universal enforcement of vaccination is neither possible, nor expedient, nor just... It is unjust, because to meet a danger often remote by a defence at best uncertain, it overrides parental responsibility and disregards parental feelings."[123]

The Commission unanimously recommended that there should be a legal limit to the number of repeated prosecutions. After the failure of the Government to secure such a legal limit in the Vaccination Bill of 1871, a direction was included in a General Order in 1874 that, in any case in which there had been one prosecution under Section 31 of the Act of 1867, the Vaccination Officer could take no further proceedings under that Section with regard to the same child until he had brought the circumstances of the case to the notice of the Guardians and received their special directions on the case.[124] Thus the decision whether to prosecute repeatedly a defaulting parent rested not with the Vaccination Officer but with the Guardians. The Local Government Board's general policy was against an unlimited repetition of prosecutions, but the Board had no legal power to interfere with the Guardians' exercise of their discretion in the matter.

In addition to those Boards of Guardians which discontinued all prosecutions there were other Boards which limited the number of prosecutions on account of the same child. But there had been numerous cases in which a parent had been repeatedly prosecuted. For example, in Oldham between 1879 and 1886, seventeen parents had been fined four times or more, including ten who had been fined seven times or more. The following are examples of extreme cases cited before the Royal Commission: a parent prosecuted sixty times in respect of nine children, with a total of £40–12–6 in fines and costs, and distraint on two occasions;[125] a parent prosecuted seventy-nine times on account of two children, with a total of £75 in fines and costs;[126] a parent imprisoned three times with a total imprisonment of seven weeks.[127]

The Commission recommended unanimously in their Fifth Report in 1892 and in their Final Report in 1896 that constantly repeated penalties in respect of the same child should no longer be possible. They considered that, while in some cases the possibility of repeated prosecutions secured compliance with the law, yet the general result of repeated prosecutions of those who honestly objected to vaccination was to cause irritation and to foster anti-vaccination propaganda, so that fewer children were vaccinated than if there had been a limit to the number of repeated prosecutions. "The penalty was not designed to punish a parent who may be considered misguided in his views and unwise in his action, but to secure the vaccination of the people. If a law less severe or administered with less stringency would better secure this end, that seems to us conclusive in its favour."[128]

Another unanimous recommendation of the Commission, made in their Fifth Report and repeated in their Final Report, was that persons imprisoned under the Vaccination Acts "should no longer be subjected to the same treatment as criminals". In the opinion of the Commission, to treat as criminals those offenders who regard vaccination as "likely to be injurious to the health of their children and are well-conducted and in other respects law-abiding citizens" was not "calculated to secure obedience to the law or to add to the number of the vaccinated."[129]

The most important recommendation made by the Commission with regard to objectors to vaccination was the recommendation to allow some kind of legal exemption for conscientious objectors. This idea had been put forward at least as early as 1871, when the chief legal adviser to the Poor Law Board proposed to the Select Committee of the House of Commons that, when prosecuted, an offender should escape the penalty if he took an oath in the court that he had a conscientious objection to his child being vaccinated.[130] The Select Committee rejected the suggestion "that the parents' declaration of belief that vaccination is injurious might be pleaded against any penalty" as it believed that "if the law were thus changed it would become a dead letter".[131]

Under the Act of 1867, Section 29 referred to "a reasonable excuse for his neglect" as excepting a parent from committing an offence and Section 31, referred to "some reasonable ground" for a parent's omission to obey the order of a Justice of the Peace as excusing from liability to a penalty. Various defendants in court pleaded that their conscientious objections to the vaccination of their children should be held to be reasonable excuses, and to come under these legal exceptions. Such pleas were nearly always unsuccessful. Occasionally the magistrates considered that the parent had a "reasonable excuse" if another child of his had suffered severely as a result of vaccination.[132]

In 1885 a public meeting at Gloucester passed a resolution expressing an earnest hope that "the magistrates will in the future either accept a conscientious objection as a reasonable excuse or show their regard for it by inflicting a mere nominal fine."[133] The amount of the fine was, of course, a matter for the discretion of the Magistrates and they could perfectly legally regard the fact that an offence was committed for conscientious reasons as being relevant to their decision as to the amount of fine to be imposed. The Magistrate also had discretion as to whether to make an order for vaccination under Section 31 of the Act of 1867.

Two members of the Royal Commission, who dissented from the proposals of the other members of the Commission with regard to legal conscientious objection, made the same proposal as that rejected by the Select Committee in 1871. "We think that in all cases in which a parent or guardian refuses to allow vaccination the person so refusing should be summoned before a magistrate, as at present, and that the only change made should be to permit the magistrate to accept a sworn deposition of conscientious objection and to abstain from the infliction of a fine."[134]

The majority of the Commission, on the other hand, recommended some method to protect from prosecution those who were "honestly opposed" to vaccination. "When we speak of an honest opposition to the practice we intend to confine ourselves to cases in which the objection is to the operation itself, and to exclude cases in which the objection arises merely from an indisposition to take the trouble involved." They had reached the conclusion, after much study of the subject, that it would conduce to increased vaccination if, while general compulsion remained, "a scheme could be devised which would preclude the attempt (so often a vain one) to compel those who are honestly opposed to the practice to submit their children to vaccination".[135] They gave two examples of alternative possible schemes. First, "if a parent attended before the local authority and satisfied them that he entertained such an objection, no proceedings should be taken against him." Second, a statutory declaration to that effect before any one now authorised to take such declaration, or some other specified official or officials, might be made a bar to proceedings. They added: "We do not think it would be any real gain to parents who had no conviction that the vaccination of their children was calculated to do mischief to take either of these steps rather than submit them to the operation."[136] However, they gave their view that in the first instance the change in the law should be temporary, say for five years, while its effects should be carefully watched.[137]

The Vaccination Act, 1898

The Vaccination Bill, 1898, was introduced in the House of Commons in March by H. Chaplin, the President of the Local Government Board. It received the Royal Assent in August and came into force immediately with regard to provision for legal conscientious objection and at the beginning of 1899 with regard to the other change in the law. The Act[138] was to remain law for five years only; it was subsequently renewed annually between 1904 and 1921 by Expiring Laws Continuance Acts and made permanent by the Expiring Laws Act, 1922.[139] The Act was not a Consolidating Act: it amended the Vaccination Act, 1867.[140] Apart from provisions relating to objectors to vaccination, the main changes in the law were as follows. The period during which it was compulsory for a child to be vaccinated was changed from three months to six months after its birth (Section 1 (1)). This change was recommended by the Royal Commission and made the law on this matter in England and Wales identical with the law in Scotland. It became illegal to compel the vaccination of a child born in a hospital or institution at any time earlier than six months after its birth (Section 1 (5)). The Public Vaccinator was to postpone the vaccination of a child "if, in his opinion, the condition of the house in which it resides is such, or there is or has been such a recent prevalence of infectious disease in the district, that it cannot safely be vaccinated" (Section 1 (4)).

Under normal circumstances the parent using the public vaccination service was no longer required to take the child to a vaccination station. Instead, on the parents' request, the Public Vaccinator was obliged to visit the child's home in order to vaccinate it (Section 1(2)), and, if a child was still unvaccinated four months after its birth, the Public Vaccinator was obliged, after giving at least twenty-four hours' notice, to visit the child's home and to offer to vaccinate it (Section 1(3)). In the public vaccination service arm-to-arm vaccination was replaced by vaccination with "glycerinated calf Iymph or such other Iymph as may be issued by the Local Government Board" (Section 1(3)), and the Public Vaccinator no longer had the right to take Iymph from a vaccinated child.

The original Bill included a clause designed to limit to two the number of prosecutions on account of the same child. The President of the Local Government Board, in supporting this proposal, stated: "Repeated penalties have often been enforced without securing the vaccination of the child, on the one hand, and, on the other, they have a tendency to bring the vaccination law into bad odour, and to rouse opposition to it which could not otherwise exist."[141] A further clause was added during the passage of the Bill so that the matter was covered by two Sections of the Act. Section 3 provided that: "An order under Section 31 of the Vaccination Act of 1867, directing that a child be vaccinated, shall not be made on any person who had previously been convicted of non-compliance with a similar order relating to the same child." Section 4 provided that: "No proceedings under Section 31 of the Vaccination Act of 1867 shall be taken against any parent or person who has been convicted under Section 29 of the said Act on account of the same child, until it has reached the age of four years." The joint effects of these two Sections were that a parent could be punished only twice on account of the same child – once under Section 29 and once under Section 31 of the Act of 1867 – and that, if there were two prosecutions, there would normally be an interval of three years or more between them.

In the Committee Stage of the Bill, a clause was added which became Section 5 of the Act. This section provided that "Persons committed to prison on account of non-compliance with any order or non-payment of fines or costs under the Vaccination Acts shall be treated in the same way as first-class misdemeanants."

The inclusion in the Act of provision for legal conscientious objection was achieved only after a considerable struggle in Parliament. The original Bill contained no such provision. In his speech introducing the Bill, the President of the Local Government Board rejected the suggestion that an objector might be exempted after making a statutory declaration, stating: "The effect of this, it seems to me, would be to make the law a dead letter wherever people wish and choose to do so."[142] In the debate on the Second Reading, Sir Walter Foster, a doctor, stated that he believed that more children would be vaccinated if the law provided for the honest objector as "Every man who is imprisoned for a breach of the Vaccination Law makes hundreds of converts – or perverts if you like to term it so – to his view of the Vaccination Law."[143] At the Committee Stage he moved an amendment to allow a statutory declaration of conscientious objection: this amendment was defeated by 26 to 24 votes.[144] Later in the Committee Stage another doctor, Sir William Priestley, carried by 20 to 11 votes an amendment that would allow a parent, faced by a second prosecution on account of the same child, to gain legal exemption if he satisfied the court that he conscientiously believed that vaccination would be prejudicial to the health of the child.[145] At the Report Stage, Sir Walter Foster again proposed his amendment: there was a long debate and he received considerable support from members of the Government party. A.J. Balfour, for the Government, offered to insert a clause in the Bill embodying the same principle and a clause was later moved by the Government and adopted, on a division, by a comparatively small majority.[146] This clause became Section 2 of the Act.

Section 2 provided that "No parent or other person shall be liable to any penalty under Section 29 or Section 31 of the Vaccination Act of 1867, if within four months from the birth of the child he satisfies two justices, or a stipendiary or metropolitan police magistrate, in petty sessions, that he conscientiously believes that vaccination would be prejudicial to the health of the child, and within seven days thereafter delivers to the vaccination officer for the district a certificate by such justices or magistrate of such conscientious objection." In the case of children born before the passing of the Act the four months was to be reckoned from the date of the passing of the Act.

When the Bill reached the Committee Stage in the House of Lords, Lord Faversham moved to strike out this clause providing for conscientious objection and his motion was carried by 40 to 38 votes in spite of a defence of the clause by the Prime Minister, Lord Salisbury, and by Lord Lister. At the renewed debate in the House of Commons, the Government refused to make concessions and the motion to disagree with the Lords was carried by 129 to 34 votes. The Bill, with the clause included, finally passed the Third Reading in the House of Lords by 55 to 45 votes.[147] Thus, forty-five years after the introduction of compulsory vaccination the legal right of conscientious objection to it was conceded. The conscientious law-breakers and the many other anti-vaccinationists had not succeeded in abolishing compulsion, but 'they had gained the right for the objecting parent to preserve his children from vaccination without breaking the law.

The Period 1898–1907

After seven years in which annual deaths from smallpox had never exceeded 550 the figure rose in 1902 to 2,464. In the smallpox epidemic in London in 1901 – 02 there were 9,496 notified cases and 1,543 deaths.[148] In the whole of England and Wales in 1902-03 there were 21,306 notified cases and 3,224 deaths.[149] In 1904 there were 507 and in 1905 there were 116 deaths. This was the last large epidemic of virulent smallpox in Great Britain.

The proportion of successful vaccinations of infants to total births, which was 61% in 1898, rose every year to 75.4% in 1903. From 1905 to 1907 it decreased from 75.8% to 70.9%. It seems likely that this increase in the proportion of infants vaccinated was caused to a considerable extent by the various changes in the law made by the Act of 1898. In the public vaccination service the performance of vaccination in the child's home made the operation easier and more convenient for the mother and the visit of the Public Vaccinator to the home gave him an opportunity to persuade the parent. The discontinuation of arm-to-arm vaccination removed some of the fears of harmful results of vaccination. The introduction of legal conscientious objection made Boards of Guardians and Vaccination Officers willing to administer the law more stringently, made the Government more willing to coerce recalcitrant authorities, and made public opinion more willing to support the general enforcement of the Vaccination Acts.

For some years after 1898 a few Boards of Guardians continued to resist the compulsory provisions of the Acts. For example, the Leicester Guardians, who stated that there were 70,000 unvaccinated children in their area,[150] refused to fill a vacancy for a Vaccination Officer. After being served with a writ of mandamus they eventually agreed to make the appointment but appointed an anti-vaccinationist. The Court of the Queen's Bench would not discharge the writ for this appointment and a few months later they appointed an officer willing to enforce the law.[151] However, in 1902 they were again in legal difficulty through resolving that their Vaccination Officer should not prosecute without their instructions. In an appeal the Divisional Court ruled: "That it is the duty of the Vaccination Officer to take proceedings when he thinks proper, and if the guardians interfere with him he is not bound to obey them."[152]

This ruling was in line with an important judgment made by the Court of the Queen's Bench in 1897: "that a Vaccination Officer has authority of his own motion to institute proceedings without a special authority from the Guardians."[153] This judgment made the enforcement activities of a resolute Vaccination Officer independent of the views of his employing Board of Guardians and strengthened the hands of the Local Government Board in coercing recalcitrant Guardians.

In a General Order issued in 1898 the Local Government Board further strengthened its position by directing that no appointment of a Vaccination Officer could be made without its approval and that Guardians must require the due performance of the various duties imposed upon the officer by the Vaccination Acts, and, in case of any continued neglect by the officer, must report the matter to the Board.[154] A number of MPs strongly disagreed with the removal of the control of prosecutions from the elected Guardians and in the years 1900 to 1906 several unsuccessful Bills were introduced to restore the authority to the Guardians.

In the period 1898 to 1905 there was a considerable campaign with the object of making re-vaccination legally obligatory. An unsuccessful amendment on the matter was moved at the Committee Stage of the Vaccination Bill of 1898.[155] In 1903 the recently founded Imperial Vaccination League sent a deputation to the President of the Local Government Board and this deputation urged general re-vaccination at the age of ten or twelve.[156] In 1904 a Re-vaccination Bill was introduced in the House of Commons but withdrawn.[157] In the same year a Bill was passed in the House of Lords which provided for the re-vaccination of all children, except those legally exempted for conscientious objection, within twelve months of attaining the age of twelve. Lord Lansdowne stated that the Government considered re-vaccination desirable and had encouraged and facilitated it, but they had not thought it desirable to legislate on the matter.[158] Pressure of business prevented the consideration of the Bill in the House of Commons.[159] In 1905 a Government spokesman in the House of Lords said that the Government relied on the opinion of the Royal Commission that compulsory re-vaccination was impracticable.[160]

The provisions of the Act of 1898 allowing legal conscientious objection were immediately used by large numbers of parents. Between the 12th August 1898, when these provisions came into force, and the end of the year 203,413 certificates of exemption were received by Vaccination Officers relating to 230,147 children.[161] A large number of these certificates were for children born before the passing of the Act. During the nine years 1899 to 1907 the total number of exemptions was just under 400,000. The average annual number of exemptions as a proportion of births was 4.8% during this period and the percentage in single years varied between 3.6% in 1899 and 1902 and 8.4% in 1907.[162] Thus, before this system of exemptions was replaced by another system at the beginning of 1908, parents had obtained certificates for more than 630,000 children. Some objectors to vaccination refused to apply for exemption but their numbers were very small in comparison with the numbers of those who took advantage of the change in the law.

Yet though a large number of objecting parents were enabled to obey their consciences without breaking the law, some parents who claimed exemption failed to obtain it. The way in which this system of exemptions worked in practice, and the problems which arose will be discussed in detail in Chapter 11. The following account will therefore describe only briefly the main points which led to criticism of the system.

Under Section 2 of the Act of 1898 the parent applying for exemption had to satisfy the magistrates in petty sessions that he conscientiously believed that vaccination would be prejudicial to the health of the child. The magistrates decided whether to grant a certificate of exemption or to refuse to grant it. The law imposed upon magistrates the duty of making a quite new type of judgment and initially no guidance was given to them as to how their powers should be exercised. Later some guidance was given to magistrates. The Lord Chief Justice in 1904 and the Home Secretary in 1906 made statements with regard to the principles on which magistrates should base their judgments. (These statements are quoted in Chapter 11.) But the decision remained with the magistrates and there was no right of appeal against their decision.

Nearly all critics of the system deplored the lack of uniform principles of treatment of applicants by different magistrates. Some magistrates granted certificates with little or no examination of the applicants; others refused certificates even after a long cross-examination. Magistrates, like other citizens, often held strong views on the highly controversial subject of vaccination, and some magistrates based their decision on their own views of vaccination, not on those of the applicants. "Some magistrates appeared to think that they ought to be satisfied that vaccination would be harmful to the child", stated the Lord Chief Justice in 1904, and "He desired to point out that this was not the question which Magistrates had to decide."[163]

There was no information available as to the number of applications refused but the Home Secretary stated in 1906 that he received frequent complaints of the refusal of certificates.[164] If the objector who was refused a certificate acted on his opinions he became a law-breaker and there were a number of cases cited in the House of Commons of prosecutions of objectors who had been refused legal exemption. Thus this system of exemptions was not successful in eliminating the conscientious law-breaker.

The Vaccination Act, 1907

In 1906 there was a debate in the House of Commons on the motion of Arnold Lufton that "vaccination ought no longer to be obligatory on those who regard it as useless or dangerous." During this debate, in addition to the criticisms of the existing exemption system already noted, there was mention of the burden on a poor applicant in the loss of wages and other expenses which his attendance at petty sessions might entail. It was stated that there was sometimes discrimination against poor applicants, and that the poor workman was often at a disadvantage because he was nervous and unable to express his objections as well as the wealthier objector. Sir William Collins, a member of the Royal Commission, said that the Commission had unanimously desired that the honest objector to vaccination should not be subject to any penalty, but that, owing to the way in which magistrates had interpreted their duties with regard to exemptions, compulsion in a modified form was still being carried out. The President of the Local Government Board, John Burns, joined in criticising the existing system and stated that he proposed to institute an enquiry as to the direction which new legislation should take.[165]

The Vaccination Bill, 1907, proposed to replace the existing system of exemptions by the provision that an objector could secure legal exemption merely by making a specified statutory declaration; the Bill contained no other provisions.

The Bill was introduced on behalf of the Government by the President of the Local Government Board, John Burns. In the debate on the Second Reading he stated, with regard to the existing system, "Owing to the presence of the word 'satisfies' we have a state of things which... is not respectful to the law, is a nuisance, and should be abated as soon as possible."[166] Some magistrates, he said, had exceeded their powers and done things not contemplated by those who formed the Act of 1898. By requiring the applicant to satisfy the Bench of the reality of his conscientious conviction-an impossible task-the administration of the Act was injured and a new set of martyrs made to uphold the banner of anti-vaccination. Under the proposed provisions the statutory declaration could be made before any one of 10,000–12,000 Commissioners for Oaths or 17,000–18,000 Justices of the Peace.[167]

In opposing the Bill Sir Henry Craile objected to the substitution of a secret signature of a declaration for a public statement in court "with the aid that publicity gives to distinguish between ignorance, carelessness, or prejudice and a conscientious belief."[168]

Another opponent of the Bill, Sir John Batty Tuke, said that "The really honest conscientious objector was not numerically dangerous. But unluckily even the honest conscientious objector dragged in his train a large number of persons who had no settled convictions on the subject, such as ignorant or careless parents or guardians." He predicted that the result of such persons merely making a declaration without giving reasons for belief would be to reduce the proportion of infant vaccinations to 50% or even lower.[169]

The Bill passed its Second Reading by 122 to 14 votes. In the Committee Stage an amendment was carried against the Government to give either parent the right to make the statutory declaration.[170] But in the House of Lords this amendment was rejected and the wording restored to its original form[171] and this decision was accepted by the House of Commons.[172] The result was that in the Act the right was given to the "parent", interpreted as the father, or the mother if the father was not available.

The Bill continued the wording of the Act of 1898 in the description of the ground for exemption-that the objector "conscientiously believes that vaccination would be prejudicial to the health of the child." In the Committee Stage in the House of Commons Sir William Collins moved an amendment to omit this statement of belief and to let the declaration take the form of a simple objection.

The President of the Local Government Board opposed the amendment, saying that "if the floodgates of medical controversy were opened they might have to sit even longer than the Royal Commission" and urging that the prospects of the Bill should not be jeopardised. The amendment was withdrawn.[173]

The Vaccination Act, 1907,[174] came into force at the beginning of 1908. In Section 2 the provisions of that Section were substituted for Section 2 of the Act of 1898. Section 2 (1) provided that "No parent or other person shall be liable to any penalty, under Section 29 or Section 31 of the Vaccination Act of 1867, if within four months from the birth of the child he makes a statutory declaration that he conscientiously believes that vaccination would be prejudicial to the health of the child, and within seven days thereafter delivers or sends by post the declaration to the vaccination officer of the district." Section 2 (3) provided that "A statutory declaration made for the purposes of this section shall be made in the form set out in the schedule to this Act, or in a form to the like effect."

In the Schedule to the Act the Form of Declaration was as follows: "I (name and address) being the parent (or person having the custody) of a child named (name and date of birth) do hereby solemnly and sincerely declare that I conscientiously believe that vaccination would be prejudicial to the health of the child, and I make this solemn declaration conscientiously believing the same to be true, and by virtue of the Statutory Declarations Act, 1835."[175] This was followed by the date and signature of the person making the declaration and then "Declared before me" (place and time) and the signature of the Commissioner for Oaths, Justice of the Peace or other officer authorised to receive a statutory declaration.

The Period 1908–1948

After the epidemic in the first few years of the twentieth century smallpox ceased to be a major problem of public health. Between 1906 and 1948 the number of deaths in England and Wales never exceeded 100 in any year and only in one year exceeded 50. In the forty-three years 1906 to 1948 average annual deaths numbered 12.

There is now a recognised distinction between the virulent type of smallpox with which this account has so far been concerned, now termed "variola major", and a usually mild type of smallpox, now termed "variola minor" . In a book published in 1962 an authority on smallpox, C.W. Dixon, writes: "Smallpox is an acute virus infection and... the virus appears to exist in only two distinct variants-that giving rise to variola major and that giving rise to variola minor... When a number of cases occur and the epidemiological pattern is clear, variola major and variola minor appear to be two distinct variants which have never been known to change from one into the other."[176]

In the ten years 1911 to 1920, notified cases of variola major were nearly 300 in two years, between 100 and 200 in four years, and under 100 in the other four years. In the years 1921 to 1948 the number of notified cases never exceeded 100 in any year and in twelve of these years there were no cases.[177]

The first recognised outbreak of variola minor in this country occurred in 1919. From this year until 1934 cases occurred every year. Between 1923 and 1932 there were each year more than 2,000 notified cases in England and Wales, and between 1926 and 1930 there were more than 10,000 notified cases each year. Over the whole period there were more than 81,000 notified cases. The case mortality was under 0.5% and the total number of deaths during the period was about 200. There were no cases of variola minor in the years 1936 to 1948.[178]

The number of successful infant vaccinations as a proportion of births was 75.8% in 1905, the highest figure reached since 1891.

From 1905 the figure fell every year, except for two years during the First World War, to its first minimum of 38.3% in 1921. From 1922 to 1930, except for one year, the figure was above 40%, with a maximum of 47.8% in 1923. This increase was largely due to the epidemic of variola minor during those years. From 40.1% in 1930 the figure fell to 34.0% in 1937 and 1938 and then to 31.5% in 1940. There was then an increase and the average figure for 1942 to 1946 was 40.4%. The last year in which more than half the children born were successfully vaccinated was 1912; on the eve of the Second World War the proportion was only just over a third; in the year of the legislation abolishing compulsion the proportion was rather over two-fifths.

The figures of the proportion of infants born for whom their parents received exemption on conscientious grounds varied up to 1938 roughly inversely to the figures of the proportion vaccinated. The introduction of the system of exemption by statutory declaration at the beginning of 1908 resulted in an immediate doubling of the proportion exempted – 17.0% in 1908 compared with 8.4% in 1907. The figure then rose every year to 36.5% in 1914. In 1921 the proportion reached its first maximum of 45.0%; in that year considerably more infants were exempted than were vaccinated. The figure then fell to about 37% in 1923 and 1924 during the early years of the epidemic of variola minor. The Ministry of Health Report for 1923–24 stated: "In consequence of local epidemics of smallpox in many parts of the country there was a considerable increase in the amount of vaccination performed, and many of those who sought the protection of vaccination for themselves and their families, when smallpox threatened, were persons who had previously made declarations of conscientious objection to vaccination."[179]

From 40.7% in 1927 the proportion of exemptions increased every year to its maximum of 51.0% in 1937. During each of the four years 1935 to 1938 slightly more than 50% of children born were exempted. The proportion then decreased every year to 38.8% in 1943, the last year for which the figure was published. The actual number of exemptions each year averaged about 259,000 in the ten years 1908 to 1917 and about 295,000 in the ten years 1928 to 1937.

A return for 1918 showed how greatly the amount of anti-vaccination opinion varied between different parts of the country. In that year the proportion of exemptions was 38% in England and

30% in Wales and Monmouthshire. In England the proportion was over 50% in ten geographical counties, with a maximum of 22% in London. In Wales and Monmouthshire the proportions ranged from just over 50% in Monmouthshire to 8% in Anglesey.[180]

In the amending Vaccination Order issued by the Local Government Board in 1907 it was laid down that the Registrar of Births should include the form of declaration of conscientious objection with the notice of requirement of vaccination given to every person when registering a birth.[181] In 1923, because of the epidemic of variola minor, the Ministry of Health rescinded this requirement and instead ordered that arrangements should be made for the parent to obtain the form of declaration on request.[182] However in 1924 a new order restored the previous position.[183] Also in 1923 the Ministry of Health sent a circular to Boards of Guardians, urging that exemption from penalties should be secured only in conformity with the law and the Home Secretary circularised Clerks of Justices, calling attention to certain cases in which irregularities had occurred in connection with declarations of conscientious objection and urging the strict observance of the requirement of the law.[184]

The only legislative measure concerned with vaccination in the years between 1907 and 1946 was the Local Government Act, 1929,[185] which came into force on the 1st April 1930. This Act abolished the Poor Law Unions and their governing Boards of Guardians. All the functions relating to vaccination which were formerly performed by the Boards of Guardians were transferred, in the County of London, to the councils of the City of London and the Metropolitan Boroughs (Section 18) and, in the rest of England and Wales, to the County Councils and County Borough Councils (Section 2).

The Ending of Compulsion

In 1932 the Minister of Health communicated with the associations of the new vaccination authorities – the County Councils Association, the Association of Municipal Corporations, and the Metropolitan Boroughs Standing Joint Committee – asking for any proposals they desired to make for facilitating the general acceptance of vaccination and preventing the spread of smallpox. From the replies received it appeared that "the majority of Authorities concerned favour the replacement of the compulsory provisions of the Vaccination Acts by provision for the free vaccination, with Government Iymph and under the control of the Local Authorities, of persons presenting themselves or of children presented by their parents for vaccination or re-vaccination."[186]

In 1946 the Chief Medical Officer of the Ministry of Health stated in his report: "Long freedom from serious outbreaks of smallpox has fostered the public indifference to vaccination... For some time before 1939 the enforcement of the Vaccination Acts against those parents or guardians who did not comply with the law has been falling into abeyance, and in the war years it has been abandoned. Compulsion is now a dead letter, many representations to this effect have been made by local authorities, to resuscitate it seems impracticable, and the question of its removal from the statutes has been under consideration."[187]

In March 1946 the Minister of Health was asked in the House of Commons whether "in view of the greater success which has been achieved in diphtheria immunisation, he will consider making vaccination non-compulsory and instituting a widespread publicity campaign to encourage it."[188] At that time diphtheria immunisation was the only example, other than vaccination, of preventive inoculation of children on a large scale. Some local authorities had started immunisation schemes in the 1930s and in 1940 a national scheme was started, with the provision of free prophylactics by the Ministry of Health. Every local authority was urged to provide a scheme of free immunisation for children and by 1946 every authority had done so.[189] There was a strong propaganda campaign. In the period 1940 to 1946 about 3,000,000 children under five and about 3,600,000 children between five and fifteen were immunised[190] and it was estimated that, at the end of 1946, of the total number of children under fifteen 62.2% had been immunised. This result was achieved without any kind of legal compulsion.[191]

A clause abolishing compulsory vaccination was included in the provisions relating to vaccination and immunisation in the National Health Service Bill, 1946. Compulsion was ended without any debate or vote on the matter at any stage in the passing of the Bill. At the Committee Stage the Minister of Health, Aneurin Bevan, was asked his reasons for proposing the end of compulsion. In his reply he said: "... the reason compulsory vaccination has been dropped is chiefly because large numbers of people were contracting out and it was undesirable to continue to make it compulsory. At the same time... very strong propaganda is carried on by the Ministry of Health urging people to have their children immunised against diphtheria and quite remarkable results are being achieved."[192]

The National Health Service Act, 1946,[193] came into force on the 5th July 1948. Section 26 (5) of the Act stated: "The Vaccination Acts, 1867 to 1907, shall cease to have effect." Thus, when the Act came into force, compulsory vaccination ended, ninety-five years after it was first established and fifty years after conscientious objection to it became legal.

Vaccination became one of the duties of the Local Health Authorities-County Councils and County Borough Councils - established under Part III of the Act. Section 26 (1) stated: "Every local health authority shall make arrangements with medical practitioners for the vaccination of persons in the area of the authority against smallpox..." Section 26 (3) provided that, in making arrangements for vaccination, the local health authority should give every medical practitioner providing general medical services in the area under Part IV of the Act an opportunity to provide the service. Section 26 (4) gave the Minister of Health power to supply vaccines free of charge to local health authorities and to medical practitioners providing vaccination services under this section of the Act.

As a result of these legal changes the office of Public Vaccinator ceased to exist and there was no longer any general obligation to perform vaccination in the child's home. The schemes of local health authorities were "designed, in general, to afford facilities for group vaccination... at sessions held at child welfare centres, school clinics etc. or for individual inoculation by the family doctor."[194] All vaccination, including re-vaccination, under these schemes was free of charge. Official policy continued to recommend the vaccination of all infants.

In the first eighteen months after the ending of compulsion the number of infant vaccinations was only 27% of the number of births and in 1950 the figure was only 23.8%. But in the subsequent nine years the figure rose every year till it reached 45% in 1959, a proportion higher than that in any year since 1927.

In February 1962, during an outbreak of smallpox, Dr. Donald Johnson, in the House of Commons, moved the introduction of a Bill for the compulsory vaccination of infants, with a conscience clause similar to that in the Act of 1907. The opposing speaker,

Dr. J. Dickson Mabon, stated that the Bill if passed "would be a retrogressive measure resented by the medical profession" and that "Experience of immunisation against polio and diphtheria showed that intelligence and good sense weighed more than compulsion in a campaign with the public". The motion to introduce the Bill was defeated by 186 to 77 votes.[195]

Compulsory Vaccination in Scotland

The following account gives a short history of compulsory vaccination in Scotland, noting the main differences between the Scottish law and the law in England and Wales.

Compulsory vaccination in Scotland was established ten years later than in England and Wales by the Vaccination (Scotland) Act, 1863,[196] which affected all children born after the beginning of 1864. In 1863 the number of deaths from smallpox in Scotland was 1,646 and the annual average number for the eight years 1855 to 1862 was 883.[197]

Section 8 of the Act placed the obligation to have the child vaccinated primarily on the father-in his absence the obligation was placed on the mother, and in the absence of both parents it was placed on the person having the "care, nurture, or custody of the child." (This contrasted with the English Act of 1853[198] which placed the obligation on the father or mother and the Act of 1867[199] which placed it on the "parent".)

The same Section provided that the child must be vaccinated within six months of its birth. (This period was in contrast to the period of three months specified in the English Act of 1853: in the Act of 1898[200] the specified period in England and Wales was increased to six months.)

Under the same Section it was the responsibility of the parent to transmit a certificate of successful vaccination, signed by a medical practitioner, to the Registrar of Births for the District. The medical practitioner concerned could, alternatively, give a certificate of postponement for two months, renewable for the same period (Section 9), or after three successive vaccinations he could give a certificate of insusceptibility (Section 10).

If the Registrar had not received a certificate within the prescribed period he was to send a notice to the parent and, if the parent had not produced a certificate within ten days, he was to pay 1s. for the notice and a penalty not exceeding 20s. (Section 17). Section 18 provided for continued action against a defaulting parent in a somewhat similar way to that provided for in Section 31 of the English Act of 1867.

The Inspector of the Poor of the Parish was, every six months, to report defaulters to the Parochial Board who "shall issue an order to the Vaccinator appointed by them to vaccinate the persons named in such list" and give written notice of such order to the parents concerned. Unless a certificate had already been produced, refusal to allow a child to be vaccinated under such an order was an offence and "for every such offence" the parent was liable to a penalty not exceeding 20s. Thus, as in England and Wales under the Act of 1867, repeated punishments on account of the same child were possible and in Scotland there was no later change in the law limiting the number of such punishments. A contrast with the English law was that the Act, in both Section 17 and Section 18, specified imprisonment for not more than ten days as the alternative to the payment of the penalty.

The Vaccination Authorities were the Parochial Boards set up under the Poor Law Amendment (Scotland) Act, 1845.[201] The Parochial Board of every Parish or combination of Parishes was to appoint one or more medical practitioners as vaccinators for the area (Section 1) but the board of Supervision (the Government Department concerned) might modify this provision and appoint travelling vaccinators "in insular, highland and other districts... where, from the difficulty of travelling and other causes this might seem advisable" (Section 12). Vaccinators appointed under the Act were to be paid a fee for each successful vaccination (Sections 2 and 12) and the Parochial Board was to defray the expenses of vaccination from the funds for the relief of the poor (Section 6).

Parochial Boards, vaccinators and other officers were to conform to the regulations of the Board of Supervision (Section 5) and, where a Parochial Board failed to perform any of its duties, it should be lawful for the Board of Supervision to perform these duties (Section 27).

Under the Local Government (Scotland) Act, 1894,[202] Parochial Boards were succeeded by Parish Councils, which became the vaccination authorities. Under the Public Health (Scotland) Act, 1897,[203] Parishes ceased to be the only local authorities concerned with vaccination, as Burghs, Districts and Counties were allowed to "defray the cost of vaccinating or re-vaccinating such persons as to them may seem expedient". The Local Government (Scotland) Act, 1929,[204] abolished Parish Councils and under this Act vaccination functions were to be exercised only by County Councils and the Councils of Large Burghs, (Burghs with a population of 20,000 and upwards).

There were some important differences in practice between the Scottish and English vaccination systems. The great majority of vaccinations in Scotland were carried out by private medical practitioners[205] and the duties of the vaccinators appointed by the Parochial Boards were confined to vaccinating defaulters and the children of persons in receipt of poor relief.[206] (In contrast, in England and Wales 47% of vaccinations in 1898, 72% in 1908, and 66% in 1918 were performed by the Public Vaccinators).[207] In Scotland vaccination stations were exceptional and most vaccinations were performed in the child's home.[208] (In England and Wales in the public vaccination service vaccinations were normally performed at stations until this was changed in the Act of 1898).

In the years immediately succeeding the Act of 1863 the proportions of total births vaccinated were very high: for example, in 1865 the proportion was 88% of all births and 96% of all those who did not die during the first six months after birth.[209] There was much less resistance to vaccination in Scotland than in England and Wales and this seems to be the main reason why provision for legal conscientious objection was not introduced into the Scottish law of compulsory vaccination until nine years after its introduction in England and Wales, even though the Royal Commission on Vaccination had recommended that any such provision, if made, should apply to the whole of the United Kingdom[210] and the subject of prosecutions of Scottish objectors had been raised in the House of Commons on several occasions in the early twentieth century.

In 1907 a Bill to make such provision was introduced in the House of Lords. In a speech opposing the Bill, Lord Balfour said that there was no demand of any sort for the Bill in Scotland. There had been nothing in Scotland analogous to the circumstances in England when the Act of 1898 was passed. Not a single local authority in Scotland had refused to perform its duty. "The agitation, such as it was, was concentrated in one or two places, and over nearly the whole of Scotland he had never seen the slightest sign of discontent..." On the other hand, Lord Tweedmouth said that considerable representations in favour of the Bill had been made to the Scottish Office, and he thought that "if a man who lived in England and Wales went north across the Tweed he should carry with him the same rights that he had in England".[211] The Bill was passed in the House of Lords and subsequently in the House of Commons.

The Vaccination (Scotland) Act, 1907,[212] came into force on the 28th August 1907. Its provisions were substantially the same as those of the English Act of 1907,[213] allowing exemption from penalties if the parent or person responsible for the child made the required statutory declaration: in Scotland this could be done within six months of its birth (as contrasted with four months under the English Act or, for a child already born, within six months of the passing of the Act.) Thus the law in Scotland changed directly from making no provision for legal conscientious objection to making provision for exemption by statutory declaration and Scotland never experienced the system of exemption conditional on satisfying a judicial body, which existed in England and Wales from 1898 to 1907.

The National Health Service (Scotland) Act, 1947,[214] abolished compulsory vaccination from the 5th July 1948, when the Act came into force. Section 26 (5) stated: "The Vaccination (Scotland) Acts 1863 to 1907... shall cease to have effect". Local Health Authorities-the councils of Counties and Large Burghs-were obliged to make arrangements for voluntary vaccination and the provisions regarding vaccination were substantially similar to those of the English National Health Service Act.[215]

References

BMJ = British Medical Journal
R.C. Vaccination = Royal Commission on Vaccination

1   BMJ 1889 Il p. 1057
2   Paul, Hugh *The Control of Communicable Diseases* pp. 164–165
3   General Board of Health. Papers Relating to the Sanitary State of the People of England. 1858
4   Report of Epidemiological Society. BMJ 1853 p. 593
5   Hutchinson, J.R. in Ministry of Health Report 1945–46 p. 119
6   Vaccination Act, 1840, 3 & 4 Vic. c. 29
7   Ibid.

8   4 & 5 Will. 4. c. 76
9   6 & 7 Will. 4. c. 86
10 3 & 4 Vic. c. 29
11 4 & 5 Vic. c. 32
12 BMJ 1853 p. 593
13 Hansard Vol. 125 p. 1002
14 Hansard Vol. 125 p. 1009
15 Hansard Vol. 125 p. 1010
16 Hansard Vol. 129 pp. 471–2
17 Hansard Vol. 129 p. 474
18 BMJ 1853 p. 472
19 BMJ 1853 p. 313
20 16 & 17 Vic. c. 100
21 Paul op. cit. p. 165
22 Creighton, Charles *A History of Epidemics in Britain* Vol. II p. 625
23 Poor Law Board Return. Quoted BMJ 1870 II p. 15
24 Vaccination Acts Amendment Act, 1861, 24 & 25 Vic. c. 59
25 A.B. Steele. Quoted BMJ 1866 II p. 249
26 Hansard Vol. 187 p. 1870
27 Sir J.C. Jervoise. Hansard Vol. 187 p. 1871
28 J.W. Henley. Hansard Vol. 187 p. 1879
29 Hansard Vol. 187 p. 1871
30 Hansard Vol. 187 p. 1873
31 Hansard Vol. 188 p. 649
32 Hansard Vol. 188 p. 649
33 Hansard Vol. 187 p. 1880
34 BMJ 1867 II p. 70
35 BMJ 1867 II p. 90
36 30 & 31 Vic. c. 84
37 34 & 35 Vic. c. 98
38 37 & 38 Vic. c. 75
39 Local Government Board Order, 31.10.1874. Articles 16 & 17
40 Ministry of Health Report 1948 – 49 p. 224
41 BMJ 1866 II p. 250
42 *Lancet* 1866 I p. 548
43 BMJ 1867 I p. 273
44 Hansard Vol. 187 p. 1870
45 R. Lowe. Hansard Vol. 187 p. 1883
46 BMJ 1866 II p. 702
47 BMJ 1868 II p. 112
48 BMJ 1869 I p. 522 and II p. 13
49 BMJ 1869 I p. 336
50 BMJ 1869 II p. 617
51 Final Report of R.C. Vaccination, 1896 c. 8270 p. 218
52 Creighton op. cit. Vol II pp. 624, 625 & 626
53 *Lancet* 1871 II p. 94
54 Report of Metropolitan Asylums Board. Quoted in pamphlet by L.
    Loat "The Truth about Vaccination and Immunisation" p. 23

55 Dixon, C.W. *Smallpox* p. 286
56 Ibid. p. 293
57 BMJ 1870 I p. 608
58 Third Report of R.C. Vaccination, 1890 c. 6192. pp. 2–3
59 Second Report of R.C. Vaccination, 1890. c. 6066. p. 211
60 BMJ 1871 II p. 359
61 *Lancet* 1871 I p. 766
62 Second Report of R.C. Vaccination p. 206
63 Ibid. p. 218
64 Ibid. pp. 190–191
65 Ibid. p. 206
66 R.C. Vaccination. Appendix IX
67 BMJ 1897 II p. 1468
68 Dixon op. cit. p. 289
69 *Lancet* 1871 I p. 833
70 Ministry of Health Report 1945–46 p. 119
71 BMJ 1896 II p. 456
72 Ministry of Health Report 1948 – 49 p. 224
73 BMJ 1896 II p. 449
74 Second Report of R.C. Vaccination p. 187
75 BMJ 1900 II p. 1620
76 Second Report of R.C. Vaccination p. 204
77 Nethercot, Gerald, Article in *The Listener* 1.2.1962
78 BMJ 1871 I p. 184
79 34 & 35 Vic. c. 98
80 *Lancet* 1871 I p. 766
81 *Lancet* 1871 I pp. 320–321
82 *Lancet* 1871 I p. 766
83 BMJ 1871 I p. 671
84 BMJ 1871 II pp. 251 and 252
85 Metropolitan Poor Law Act, 1867. 30 & 31 Vic. c. 6
86 Public Health Act 1875 c. 55
87 Infectious Diseases (Notification) Act, 1889
88 Do. Act of 1899
89 Final Report of R.C. Vaccination. Par. 296
90 BMJ 1901 II p. 1099
91 Nethercot op. cit
92 Pamphlet of National Anti–Vaccination League
93 Final Report of R.C. Vaccination p. 135
94 Sixth Report of R.C. Vaccination c. 7993 p. 10
95 Ibid. p. 15
96 Final Report of R.C. Vaccination p. 135
97 Summary Jurisdiction Act. 1879 c. 49
98 Second Report of R.C. Vaccination p. 204
99 BMJ 1893 I p. 1130
100 BMJ 1891 I p. 1102
101 Vaccination Act 1898 61 & 62 Vic. c. 49 Sec. 5
102 BMJ 1870 I p. 65

103　BMJ 1870 I p. 115
104　Final Report of R.C. Vaccination p. 133
105　Poor Law Amendment Act, 1834
106　Ballot Act, 1872
107　1875 Act enabling women to be guardians
108　Local Government Act, 1894 c. 73
109　Local Government Board Act, 1871. 34 & 35 Vic. c. 70
110　Ministry of Health Act, 1919
111　BMJ 1871 I p. 406
112　Sixth Report of R.C. Vaccination p. 9
113　Final Report of R.C. Vaccination p. 133
114　Third Report of R.C. Vaccination pp. 3–4
115　Final Report of R.C. Vaccination p. 134
116　BMJ 1895 I pp. 115 and 624
117　BMJ 1895 I p. 450
118　Fifth Report of R.C. Vaccination, 1892 c. 6666
119　Final Report of R.C. Vaccination, 1896 c. 8270
120　Pamphlet: A Thumb-Nail Sketch of the Work of the National Anti-Vaccination League. pp. 1,5,6
121　Final Report of R.C. Vaccination. Par. 523
122　Ibid.
123　Ibid. Par. 296
124　Local Government Board Order 31.10.1874. Article 16.
125　Second Report of R.C. Vaccination pp. 190 – 191
126　Ibid. p. 205
127　Ibid. pp. 218–219
128　Final Report of R.C. Vaccination Par. 522
129　BMJ 1892 I p. 1032
130　*Lancet* 1871 I p. 590
131　*Lancet* 1871 I p. 766
132　Second Report of R.C. Vaccination p. 202
133　Report of R.C. Vaccination. p. 9
134　Final Report of R.C. Vaccination, Minority Recommendation of Sir Guyer Hunter and Jonathan Hutchinson
135　Ibid. Par. 524
136　Ibid. Par. 525
137　Ibid. Par. 526
138　61 & 62 Vic. c. 49
139　12 & 13 Geo. 5. c. 50
140　30 & 31 Vic. c. 84
141　Hansard Vol. 54 p. 1678
142　Hansard Vol. 54 p. 1678
143　Hansard Vol. 56 p. 430–431
144　BMJ 1898 I p. 1665
145　BMJ 1898 II p. 111
146　BMJ 1898 II p. 257
147　BMJ 1898 II p. 429
148　Dixon op. cit. p. 203

149 Taylor, Stephen *Battle for Health* p. 52
150 BMJ 1899 I p. 1344
151 BMJ 1899 II pp. 256,872,1492,1751,1820
152 Moore v. Keyte 1902. BMJ 1902 I p. 668
153 Bramble v. Lowe 1897
154 Local Government Board Order 18.10.1898. Articles 11 and 28
155 BMJ 1898 II p. 189
156 BMJ 1903 I pp. 165 – 168
157 BMJ 1904 I pp. 628 and 1156
158 BMJ 1904 I pp. 1507– 1508
159 BMJ 1904 II p. 200
160 BMJ 1905 I p. 615
161 Parliamentary Return No. 89 H.C. Session 1899
162 Ministry of Health Report 1919 – 20. Part I p. 148
163 Address to Grand Jury at Warwickshire Assizes. BMJ 1906 I p. 1322
164 Home Office Circular 18.5.1906
165 BMJ 1906 I pp. 1003– 1004
166 Hansard Vol. 174 p. 1278
167 BMJ 1907 I p. 1327
168 Hansard Vol. 174 p. 1278
169 Hansard Vol. 174 p. 1271
170 BMJ 1907 I p. 1452
171 BMJ 1907 II p. 409
172 BMJ 1907 II p. 546
173 BMJ 1907 I p. 1510
174 Edw 7. c. 31
175 5 & 6 Will. 4. c. 62
176 Dixon op. cit. p. 1
177 Ibid. p. 211
178 Ibid p. 211–212
179 Ministry of Health Report 1923 – 24 p. 12
180 Ministry of Health Report 1919–20 Part I. p. 149
181 BMJ 1907 II p. 921
182 Ministry of Health Report 1923 – 24 p. 13
183 Ministry of Health Report 1924 – 25 p. 13
184 Ministry of Health Report 1923 – 24 p. 12
185 19 Geo. 5. c. 17
186 Ministry of Health Report 1932 – 33 p. 57
187 Report of Chief Medical Officer to Ministry of Health 1939 – 45 p. 24
188 Hansard Vol. 420 p. 250
189 Report of Chief Medical Officer to Ministry of Health 1939–45 p. 28–29
190 Ministry of Health Report 1946 – 47 p. 23
191 Ministry of Health Report 1948 – 49 p. 36
192 Hansard Vol. 420 Col. 401–2
193 9 & 10 Geo. 6. c. 81
194 Ministry of Health Report 1948 – 49 p. 258
195 *The Guardian* 15.2.1962
196 26 & 27 Vic. c. 108

197 Creighton op. cit. Vol II p. 622
198 16 & 17 Vic. c. 100
199 30 & 31 Vic. c. 84
200 61 & 62 Vic. c. 49
201 8 & 9 Vic. c. 83
202 57 & 58 Vic. c. 58 Sects. 8 and 21
203 60 & 61 Vic. c. 38 Sect. 77
204 19 & 20 Geo. 5. c. 25 Sects. 1 and 2
205 Debate on Vaccination (Scotland) Bill, 1907. BMJ 1907 II p. 362
206 Statement by Lord Advocate. BMJ 1903 I p. 752
207 Ministry of Health Report 1919 – 20 Part I pp. 148 and 152
208 *Lancet* 1871 I p. 628 and BMJ 1907 II p. 362
209 Returns of Registrar General for Scotland BMJ 1867 I p. 546
210 Final Report of R.C. Vaccination Par. 526
211 BMJ 1907 II p. 362
212 7 Edw. 7. c. 49
213 7 Edw. 7. c. 31
214 10 & 11 Geo. 6. c. 27
215 9 & 10 Geo. 6. c. 81

Chronological Table of Acts Relating to Vaccination

Date

1840	Vaccination Act	3 & 4 Vic. c. 29
1841	Vaccination Act	4 & 5 Vic. c. 32
1853	Vaccination Act	16 & 17 Vic. c. 100
1861	Vaccination Acts Amendment Act	24 & 25 Vic. c. 59
1863	Vaccination (Scotland) Act	26 & 27 Vic. c. 108
1867	Vaccination Act	30 & 31 Vic. c. 84
1871	Vaccination Act	34 & 35 Vic. c. 98
1874	Vaccination Act	37 & 38 Vic. c. 75
1894	Local Government (Scotland) Act (Sections 8 & 21)	57 & 58 Vic. c. 58
1897	Public Health (Scotland) Act (Section 77)	60 & 61 Vic. c. 38
1898	Vaccination Act	61 & 62 Vic c. 49
1907	Vaccination Act	7 Edw. 7. c. 31
1907	Vaccination (Scotland) Act	7 Edw. 7. c. 49
1929	Local Government Act (Sections 2 & 18)	19 Geo. 5. c. 17
1929	Local Government (Scotland) Act (Sections 1 & 2)	19 & 20 Geo. 5. c. 25
1946	National Health Service Act (Section 26)	9 & 10 Geo. 6. c. 81
1947	National Health Service (Scotland) Act (Section 26)	10 & 11 Geo. 6. c. 27

CHAPTER 3

Compulsions for Military Purposes Before the Twentieth Century

Introduction

To most British citizens during the First World War military conscription appeared to be a new and strange institution for, unlike her continental neighbours, Britain in 1914 had no compulsory service in her navy, army, or reserve Forces and no legally compulsory military training of any kind. But this belief in the newness of conscription was only partially justified. It was true that the kind of military conscription imposed in 1916 was a completely new phenomenon in Britain: never before had the law conscripted all men of military age for full-time service in the Forces or in other work of vital national importance. But the principle of compulsion was not new: for many centuries, under the prerogative of the Crown or under legislation, some men had been compelled to serve in the navy, army or militia when occasion required. These old compulsions had been largely forgotten because for about eighty years they had not been applied in practice, and during that period Britain's wars had been fought by the voluntarily enlisted members of her regular Forces supplemented, in some cases, by voluntary reserve Forces and by volunteers for service in a particular war.

This chapter is concerned with the old forms of compulsion, and with conscientious objection to them, from the seventeenth century onwards. The chapter will first give an outline of the history of compulsions relating to the navy; the army; and the militia and other reserve Forces. The chapter will then describe the history of conscientious objectors to these compulsions and the legal concessions made to them.

The whole of this chapter covers England and Wales only.

The History of Compulsions (1) The Navy

The legal assumption of the right of the Crown to conscript seamen for service in the navy goes back to the time when the King had few ships of his own and in time of war commandeered for his service both ships and sailors. This legal right to conscript seamen was used as required throughout the seventeenth, eighteenth and early nineteenth centuries. The right then fell into disuse though it was not abrogated by statute.

The seafaring classes formed a permanent reserve from which the peace-time navy could draw its large increases in time of war. In theory only seamen or watermen were liable for impressment into the navy, but in practice a press-gang would sometimes go beyond its legal limits. The following passage describes the effects of the methods of the press-gang on sailors in the navy at the time of the naval mutinies of 1797. "Many of them had been kidnapped, torn forcibly, sometimes with knocking on the head, not only from seamen's taverns or wharf-side brothels, but from their wives and families amid riots and tumults of would-be rescuers. Worse still, perhaps, they had been seized as they entered home waters after a voyage abroad of two or three years. . .; pounced on when in sight of their homes – often without the pay due to them - and shipped on to warships for an indefinite period, without prospect of release until the end of the war, whenever that might be. . ."[1]

The naval historian Professor Michael Lewis writes that impressment "was good in law and sanctioned by age-old tradition. The Government of the day... was undoubtedly empowered to impress seafaring men, and the seamen of Britain invariably accepted the fact in principle. What they did object to were the conditions which obtained in practice..."[2] He estimates that in the last five years of the eighteenth century about half of the average ship's company were recruited by the press-gang.[3] A considerable further number were recruited by other forms of compulsion or duress applied, for example, to debtors, convicted prisoners, and rogues and vagabonds.

Compulsory impressment was discontinued in the course of the twenty-five years after the peace of 1815. The right to impress was never formally renounced, though an Act of 1835[4] provided that, with certain exceptions, no person should be detained in the naval service against his will for more than five years. In the same year a register of seamen was established and in 1853 an Act[5] established voluntary long-term service for ten years. Improved conditions of service attracted more volunteers. The naval rating became a specialised man, distinct from the merchant seaman, and the men who had completed their time formed a reserve.

The History of Compulsions (2) The Army

Compulsory impressment for army service was imposed in several periods during the seventeenth century, as is shown by the following examples. In 1625 twelve thousand soldiers were impressed and landed in Holland in order to march on the Palatinate. G.M. Trevelyan points out that the Petition of Right in 1628 did not ask for impressment to be forbidden: "For all knew that, so long as no standing army was allowed, the press-gang must be used in emergencies to fill the ranks of the hasty levies by which England then waged war."[6] He also notes that, in the ill-managed foreign expeditions of that period, public opinion would not "suffer any but rogues and weaklings, whom their neighbourhood could well spare, to be carried off."[7] In the Second Bishops' War of 1640 a regular army was raised by the press-gang; this enforced enlistment was greatly resented and whole companies deserted. An Act of 1640[8] authorised Justices of the Peace to impress men for the war in Ireland. In the early stages of the Civil War impressment was important to both sides: more than half of the infantry were pressed men. This was also the situation in the first year of Parliament's New Model Army, but after 1645 impressment into this army became rare and it ceased after 1651, when ten thousand men were impressed to serve in Ireland. Under Charles II there was no legal protection against impressment and, for example, in 1678 there were ten thousand pressed British soldiers in the French service in Flanders.

After the Revolution of 1688 the position became very different. The impressment of soldiers by the direct orders and under the sole authority of the Crown ceased. Officers who were authorised to raise regiments, or the men under them, sometimes pressed recruits, and there are recorded cases of successful appeals to the Crown or the House of Commons against such compulsory enlistment.[9] Compulsory enlistment under statutory authority, for the army as distinct from reserve Forces, was not after 1688 applied to the general population, even during the French Wars of 1793 to 1815.

There were, however, three classes of men on whom compulsion or duress was applied – debtors, convicted prisoners, and men without a regular means of livelihood. During the wars with France under William III and Anne an Act of 1696[10] and two subsequent Acts were passed; in these Acts relief to insolvent debtors of military age was made conditional on their enlistment in the army or navy or their provision of substitutes, and the same principle can be traced up to an Act of 1760.[11]

With regard to convicted prisoners the Mutiny Act of 1702[12] provided that persons "convicted or attained of capital felonies and offences" could be pardoned on condition of enlistment in the army or navy. This principle continued to be applied for more than a hundred years, and during the Peninsular War of 1808 to 1814 several regiments were recruited in this way.

Men without a regular means of livelihood were made liable to be impressed during four periods of war in the eighteenth century. The first period was during the War of the Spanish Succession, when five similar Acts were passed between 1703 and 1711. The Act of 1703[13] ordered Justices of the Peace to "raise and levy such able-bodied men as had not any lawful calling or employment or visible means for their maintenance and livelihood" to serve as soldiers. After certain formalities the man was to be "deemed a listed soldier". Similar principles were applied in two Acts passed in 1743[14] and 1744[15] during the War of the Austrian Succession. During the Seven Years' War two Acts in 1756[16] and 1757[17] made the same classes liable to be impressed if between the age of seventeen and forty-five, not under a certain height, and not "known Papists". During the War of American Independence two Acts of 1778[15] and 1779[19] authorised the impressment of the same classes of men, except that Papists were no longer disqualified and that the second Act covered men between the ages of sixteen and fifty. In all these periods the impressment was either for a stated number of years or until the end of the war.

The History of Compulsions (3) The Militia and Other Reserve Forces

The term "militia" first came into use during the seventeenth century but the principle goes back as far as the Saxon "fyrd". Legislation dates from the Statute of Winchester in 1285,[20] which obliged every freeman between the ages of 15 and 60 to provide in his house weapons to keep the peace, and protected him from being forced to serve outside his county "save upon the coming of strange enemies into the realm". Throughout its history the militia had three main purposes – to train the ordinary citizen in the use of arms; to defend the country against rebellion and foreign invasion; and, until the establishment of modern police forces from 1829 onwards, to act in emergencies to assist in keeping the peace. The militia was a local force organised in each county; and it could not without special statutory authority be used for service abroad, and it very rarely was so used.

After the Civil Wars Parliament re-established the county militia in two Acts of 1649 and 1650 and in 1655 Cromwell appointed new militia commissioners for the counties with the duty of raising a force. Those who refused to train were to be fined £20 and the obstinate imprisoned.

Parliament after the Restoration was very averse to the maintenance of a standing army but it trusted a militia under the control of the county aristocracy and gentry and composed of men, who, not being professional soldiers, were likely to form a separate power not amenable to parliamentary control. The Militia Acts of 1661[21] – 1662[22] and 1663[23] provided the system on which the militia was organised until its reorganisation in 1757. In each county the militia was under the command of a Lieutenant appointed by the Crown and the Lieutenant appointed all officers. Property owners were required to furnish men, horses and arms in proportion to the value of their property and persons of small means were required to contribute to a parish rate for the purpose. In theory the militia were called under arms for a few weeks in every year but in practice the levy was erratic.

During the Seven Years' War, in a series of Acts between 1757[24] and 1762,[25] the militia system was reorganised. The Acts authorised the establishment of a militia of about 32,000 men, infantry soldiers between the ages of 18 and 45, to be raised from each county in specified proportions. Militiamen were to serve for three years and train for twenty-eight days each year. The main method of recruiting men was by ballot, which was introduced for the first time with parliamentary sanction. Every man chosen by ballot was compelled either to serve himself or to pay a forfeit of £10, to be applied in providing a substitute. Bounties were given to balloted men serving personally and they could also be given to volunteers. The Crown, after informing Parliament, could "embody" the militia – that is, call it out for service – in case of rebellion, invasion, or imminent danger of invasion. When embodied, the militia could be put under officers of the regular army to serve in any part of the kingdom. In the course of the next sixty years the militia were embodied for periods during the Seven Years' War, the War of American Independence, and the French Wars of 1793 to 1815. The Militia Acts were consolidated in an Act of 1786[26] and this was the Act in force when Britain entered into War with Revolutionary France early in 1793. The next consolidating Act was the Militia Act, 1802,[27] which remained the Principal Act for fifty years.

During the period between 1793 and 1815 there were passed at least thirty Acts dealing with the militia or allied matters and no attempt will be made here to describe all their provisions. The exigencies of war demanded different numbers of active and reserve soldiers at different periods but at no period were all or nearly all men of military age recruited for full-time service. After the expulsion of British troops from the Netherlands in 1794 they were not again engaged in Europe before the peace of Amiens in 1802, though they were serving in the West Indies. When Britain resumed war with France in 1803 there was soon a great demand for reserve Forces to meet Napoleon's threat of invasion. In 1808 the Peninsular War started and British troops were in Europe from then until the end of the wars in 1815. In the ten years 1804 to 1813 the effective strength of the rank and file of British Forces in January of each year varied between about 134,000 and 203,000 in the army and between 71,000 and 90,000 in the militia.[28] In 1812 there were also 214,000 men in the local militia.[29] There were also large numbers of men enrolled in another reserve Force – the Volunteer Corps: the number in 1803 – 1804 was estimated as about 380,000[30] and in 1812 as about 69,000.[31] Recruits to this Corps were mainly from a higher social class than the militiamen; members of the Corps were exempted from liability for militia service so that, though their recruitment was voluntary, it was affected to some extent by the compulsions applied with regard to the militia. There was no compulsory recruitment for the regular army, as distinct from reserve Forces (with the exception of the duress applied to certain debtors and prisoners, described earlier in this chapter). This meant that there was usually no compulsion for service outside the British Isles (with a possible exception c. 1813). Of the total of about 250,000 men recruited for the army between 1803 and the end of September 1813, recruits from the militia numbered 93,000[32] – 37% of the total – but these men transferred to the army as volunteers.

From 1757 onwards the kinds of compulsion employed with regard to the militia varied under different Acts and also as between localities. The constant element of compulsion was that exercised on county and parish authorities. It was the responsibility of these authorities to recruit the number of men allotted to them as their quotas under any particular Act and in several Acts provision was made that the authority should pay a specified fine for each recruit deficiency. The parish could fulfil its obligation by enlisting volunteers, or by the compulsory method of the ballot, or by a combination of these methods. Voluntary enlistment was usually secured by payment of a bounty and maximum rates for such bounties were laid down in the various Acts. When the method of the ballot was employed the man balloted had three options – to serve personally, to provide a substitute, or to pay a specified fine. The price of substitutes varied with the comparative scarcity of men willing to serve and the fine, which was £10 in the Militia Acts, 1757 to 1802, was raised to £20 in the Militia Act, 1807.[33] If the fine was not paid it could be levied by distress on the balloted man's property.

Thus it was only the man with little or no property who was compelled to serve personally in the militia; if he could produce money or property either to pay for a substitute or to pay the required fine he could, if he preferred to do so, pay for his exemption from personal service. In the early nineteenth century most balloted men preferred to pay for exemption; for example, out of about 26,000 men raised in about twelve months under the Militia Act of 1807, 88% were substitutes.[34] In the words of G.G. Coulton: "The old militia pressed with almost deliberate unfairness upon the poor man... A minority served because they had drawn an unlucky number in the ballot, and were too poor to buy substitutes. The substitutes were, in a sense, volunteers, but under a system which no man respected."[35] The period of service in the militia varied at different times but never exceeded five years. Under the Militia Act of 1802 the age limit for militia service was from eighteen to forty-five and the annual period of training was twenty-one days. Certain groups were exempted from compulsion, including the clergy and "any poor man who has more than one child born in wedlock".

During the period of war between 1793 and 1815 several Acts were passed which gave compulsory powers for raising reserve Forces outside the ordinary militia system. The Cavalry Act of 1796[37] provided for a cavalry force to be raised as an augmentation of the militia.

The Act imposed a liability on all owners of horses, kept for the purpose of riding or of drawing a carriage, to provide one horse and horseman for every ten horses kept. Owners of less than ten horses had their horses included in groups of ten, and a ballot decided on which owner the liability should rest. An amending Act[38] of the same year allowed compulsion to be suspended in any district where there were sufficient volunteers. The Army Reserve Act of 1803[39] provided for the use of the militia ballot machinery to provide an army of reserve to serve at home as second battalions to certain established regiments; this Act continued in force until 1806. The Annual Training Act of 1806[40] envisaged a scheme to train for twenty-four days 200,000 men each year, but this scheme was never implemented. The Local Militia Acts of 1808[41] and 1812[42] authorised the raising by ballot of men aged eighteen to thirty for a local militia, in areas where there were below a certain number in the militia and Volunteer Corps and where sufficient volunteers could not be obtained. Under these Acts a balloted man could not provide a substitute but he could procure exemption for two years by the payment of a fine of £10, £20, or £30 according to his means. Members of the local militia served for four years and could be trained for up to twenty-eight days annually. Under the Local Militia Act of 1816[43] the machinery of the ballot was suspended and after this date the local militia fell into disuse.

In the period between 1815 and 1852 the numbers in the militia became comparatively small. Britain during this period was not engaged in any major wars. From 1829[44] onwards police forces of the modern type began to be created and by 1867 there were

24,000 members of police forces in England and Wales; the militia were thus progressively less needed for police functions. The Militia Act, 1829,[45] suspended the ballot, but the ballot was put in force by an Order in Council at the end of 1830 and continued in force till early 1832. This was the last time that the ballot was employed. The suspension of the ballot was continued annually first under this Act and then under the Militia Ballot Act, 1860[46] and the Militia (Ballot Suspension) Act 1865,[47] and finally by including a provision in the annual Expiring Laws Continuance Acts. The Act of 1860 amended the ballot machinery. There were consolidating Militia Acts in 1852[48] and 1882.[49] Under the Territorial and Reserve Forces Act, 1907,[50] the militia disappeared.

Finally by the Territorial Army and Militia Act, 1921,[51] all the enactments still in force with regard to the militia were repealed. Thus, though the power to recruit men by ballot was part of the law until 1921, in practice compulsory recruitment ceased in 1832 and the militia, for the rest of its history, was recruited entirely from volunteers.

The History of Conscientious Objection

Conscientious objection to military service was not a new phenomenon in the seventeenth century. In the first two hundred years of Christianity many Christians held that military service was incompatible with their faith. In later periods most Christians did not adopt this position. The general view of Christians in England in the seventeenth century is expressed in the Thirty-Seventh Article of Religion of the Church of England, promulgated in the middle of the sixteenth century. Part of this Article reads: "It is lawful for Christian men, at the commandment of the magistrate, to wear weapons and serve in the wars." But there had been some dissentients from this view in England since the fourteenth century. For example, a Lollard petition to the Parliament of 1395 declared that "all wars were against the principles of the New Testament, and were but murdering and plundering the poor to win glory for kings".[52] In 1530 an Ecclesiastical Commission found a sect holding, among "divers heretical opinions", that "Christian men among themselves have nought to do with the sword", and an early English Anabaptist was charged, among other heresies, with asserting: "I am bound to love the Turk from the bottom of

110

my heart."[53] A sect known as "The Family of Love", which had members in England for about a hundred years from the middle of the sixteenth century, rejected war, and so did the Muggletonians, a sect originating in England in 1652. The first English Baptists had considerable contact with the Dutch Mennonites, who refused military service, and during the seventeenth century some English Baptists objected to military service, though many Baptists served as soldiers during the Civil Wars.[54]

The Quaker Peace Testimony

The Society of Friends, commonly known as Quakers, originated in 1652. In 1651 George Fox, the founder of the Society, while in prison at Derby, was offered a captaincy in the militia. He refused the offer and recorded: "I told them I knew from whence all wars did arise, even from the lust, according to James his doctrine,[55] and that I lived in the virtue of that life and power that took away the occasion of all wars."[56] Several of the leaders among the early Quakers had been soldiers and eighty-five soldiers or former soldiers are known to have become Quakers before 1660.[57] But it did not prove possible for a Quaker to remain a soldier and very soon objection to participation in fighting became one of the fundamental Quaker "testimonies". In 1661, just after the Fifth Monarchy Rising, in a declaration to Charles II, the "harmless and innocent people of God called Quakers" stated: "All bloody principles and practices we (as to our own particular) do utterly deny, with all outward wars, and strife, and fightings with outward weapons, for any end, or under any pretence whatsoever; and this is our testimony to the whole world... And we do certainly know, and so testify to the world, that the Spirit of Christ which leads us into all Truth, will never move us to fight and war against any man with outward weapons, neither for the Kingdom of Christ, nor for the kingdoms of this world. . . So we, whom the Lord hath called into the obedience of his Truth, have denied wars and fightings, and cannot again any more learn it:..."[58] It was on this basis that individual Quakers became conscientious objectors to military service; the following are four seventeenth-century examples.

George Girdler in 1667, refusing service in the Kent Militia, declared that he was "refusing, not in contempt of the King or any of his officers, but in obedience to the Lord, who had showed him mercy, and had called him from carnal weapons to love enemies according to Christ's doctrine, and not to take up arms against them."[59]

Philip Ford in 1679 appeared before the Lieutenancy at the Guildhall for not bearing arms in the Trained Bands of the City of London. The Chairman said to him: "You say you can pay tribute to Caesar. This is a tribute to appear with your arms at the King's command." Ford replied: "Christ Jesus the Prince of Peace who paid tribute to Caesar gives the word of command to his followers to love their enemies, do good to those that hate them and despitefully use them and persecute them. And your command to your followers is to kill your enemies. So that I choose rather to obey the captain of my salvation than you, whatever he may suffer you to inflict upon me for so doing."[60]

Thomas Lurting, a sailor who had served under Admiral Blake at Santa Cruz in 1657, decided that he could not fight, while actually engaged in a battle outside Barcelona. "Lurting's ship opened fire on a castle, and Lurting occupied himself with one corner of the place, the guns of which had found the range of the vessel. He was on the forecastle watching the effect of his shot when it suddenly flashed through him, 'What, if now thou killest a man?' Putting on his clothes, for he had been half stripped, he walked on the deck as if he had not seen a gun fired, and when asked if he was wounded, said, 'No, but under some scruple of conscience on the account of fighting'. [61]

Thomas Chalkley was pressed for the navy in 1694 at the age of nineteen. After a night in the hold of the ship he was asked whether he would serve the King. He recorded: "I answered that I was willing to serve him in my business and according to my conscience; but as for war or fighting, Christ had forbid it in His excellent Sermon on the Mount; and for that reason I could not bear arms, nor be instrumental to kill or destroy men."[62]

The Legal Position of Quakers

In the later seventeenth century and early eighteenth century a considerable number of Quakers were impressed for the navy. A seaman ran a constant risk of impressment and, for example, Thomas Lurting was impressed several times after the date of the incident just described. The pressed Quaker, disobeying orders, was sometimes subjected to continued physical ill-treatment in an attempt to break his resistance. For example, Richard Seller, a fisherman, pressed at Scarborough, maintained his principles despite much ill-treatment and an unenforced sentence of hanging. In 1678 and 1679 the Society of Friends tried to relieve "the often sufferings of Friends by being impressed into the King's ships of war" by appointing a member to endeavour to secure their discharge at the expense of the Society, and his efforts met with considerable success. Again in 1706 and 1707 the Society acted in obtaining the discharge of impressed members. In the same two years it also obtained the discharge of some members impressed for the army under the legislation conscripting men without a regular means of livelihood.

The compulsions relating to the militia did not usually involve compulsory personal service with no alternatives for the individual. If Quakers had objected only to their own personal service as militiamen, few Quakers with sufficient means to pay for a substitute or to pay the alternative financial contributions required would have been involved in law-breaking. But Quakers interpreted their testimony against war as including objection to making payments as an alternative to personal service. For example, the annual meeting of the Society in 1760 stated: "We are sorrowfully affected to find that some Friends in a few counties have failed in the maintenance of our Christian testimony against wars and fighting, by joining with others to hire substitutes, and by the payment of money to exempt themselves from personal service in the militia: a practice inconsistent with our testimony to the reign of the Prince of Peace."[63]

Quakers also objected to providing specific property, for example horses or carriages, to paying fines, and to paying rates for the purposes of the militia or for other specifically military purposes. For example, the annual meeting of the Society, referring to the Militia Act, 1762, stated: "It is our sense and judgment, that we cannot, consistent with our well known principles, actively pay the rate or assessment which, by virtue of the militia act, may be imposed on such counties as shall not raise the militia; because such money is required expressly for, and in lieu of, such militia: nor rates or assessments made for advancing the hire, or enlisting-money of volunteers, nor the money to be raised and given to militia men."[65]

The normal method of enforcing the payment of fines or rates was by distraint on the property of the Quakers concerned. "They could relieve their consciences where taxes were imposed for general purposes and war-budgets were lumped in with other Government expenditures, but whenever a tax was collected solely for military purposes the Friends resisted it as they did tithes and suffered 'distraints for war'."[66] Quakers felt that they could not conscientiously "actively" make payments for military purposes; in contrast, legal distraint forcibly took their goods without involving their consent.

The earliest known instances of distraints were in 1659 and instances occurred at intervals for the next two hundred years. The amount of distraints varied in different periods and also in different localities. In the later seventeenth century: "In Kent and Sussex, where the fear of foreign invasion was ever present, and in London, whose train-bands... were formed as an efficient force, the hand of the law fell most heavily on Friends. The minute-books of Kent Quarterly Meetings show only fourteen years in the period 1660 to 1702 in which there is no record of fine or imprisonment for this cause." Kent Friends were brought before the courts for such matters as "refusing to send out three parts of an arms" or "not sending in half a man to a muster with a month's pay." The distraints for fines were often much in excess of the sum required, for example, "a silver cup worth 50s. for a fine of 20s." and "one more worth £7 for a fine of 30s." A few Kent Friends were imprisoned during the earlier years of the period; in 1661 one was in prison for nineteen weeks.[67]

In the period between 1715 and 1757 there was comparatively little militia activity in most parts of the country, except in 1745 when the militia was embodied on account of the Jacobite Rebellion. During the consideration of the Bill which became the Militia Act of 1757 the Chairman of the House of Commons Committee assured a Quaker deputation "that it could not be possible to obtain a total exemption from some expense, but that nothing of this kind was intended to be inflicted as any punishment for not complying, but as a reasonable compensation to the country."[68] This Act[69] included the first legislative concession made to Quakers concerning their obligations with regard to the military forces. It provided that, if a Quaker was chosen by the militia ballot and refused to serve or to provide a substitute, the militia authorities should, if they thought proper, hire a substitute and meet the expense by distraining on the goods of the Quaker. This provision was continued in subsequent militia legislation.

In the Militia Act, 1762,[70] a limitation of the costs of distraint was made in the case of Quakers who refused to pay a rate which might be levied by a parish to give bounties to volunteers; subsequent legislation included a similar provision.

Under three pieces of legislation passed during the war period 1793 to 1815 a Quaker could be allowed to pay a fine smaller than the normal amount.

Under the Cavalry Act, 1796,[71] a person liable to provide a horse and horseman paid a penalty of £20 for failing to provide a horse and £15 for failing to provide a horseman. An amending Act[72] in the same year provided that a Quaker could apply to be struck off any list of persons liable and instead fined £1 for each horse kept for the purpose of riding or drawing a carriage. Under the abortive Annual Training Act, 1806,[73] the authorities might levy on a Quaker such proportion of the normal fine of £10 as they thought proper according to his means, not being less than £1 or more than £7. Under the Local Militia Acts, 1808[74] and 1812,[75] in which the normal fine imposed was £10, £20 or £30 according to means, the authorities might levy on a Quaker such a proportion of the normal fine as they thought proper "according to the situation in life and property of such person", and there is record of cases in which this discretionary power was used.

"From 1761 until 1815... distraints for the militia and other local rates levied for war purposes are constantly recorded and reach a formidable total."[76] After 1815 the burden of distraints was much smaller; by the middle of the nineteenth century distraints had almost disappeared. In 1873 the Society of Friends discontinued the practice, which had prevailed for more than two hundred years, of collecting from all areas in the country the records of distraints on account of Quaker "testimonies"; in the seventeen years up to 1873 there was recorded only one case of distraint for "military demands" in each of five years and none in the other years.

But during the period of war between 1793 and 1815 distraints in some years totalled considerable amounts. For example, the returns made for the year 1797–98 showed the total value of goods taken by distraint as at least £1,947 and the returns for the year 1803–04 showed a total of £2,840.[77] The military purposes for which distraints were made included, in one or both of these years, the militia, the cavalry, the army, the "army of reserve", and the navy. There were also distraints for refusal to carry soldiers' baggage. This was a legal obligation imposed in some legislation; for example, under Section 95 of the Militia Act of 1802[78] power was given to constables, on a justice's warrant, to order persons having carriages to provide them temporarily for certain purposes. That Quakers objected to obeying this compulsion is shown by the evidence of distraints and by the decision of their annual meeting in 1810: "It is the judgment of this meeting that it is inconsistent with our known testimony against war, for Friends to be in any manner aiding and assisting in the conveyance of soldiers, their baggage, arms, ammunition, or other military stores ."[79]

How did distraints affect the individuals concerned? The following examples are taken from the records of distraints for military purposes on Quakers in Lancashire and Essex for the year 1803–04.[80]

In Lancashire 11 individuals suffered distraints to a total amount of £235; the distraints were all on account of the provision of militia substitutes and the amounts of the original demands varied between £9-10s and £22-4s.

In Essex 32 individuals, including 3 women, suffered distraints to a total amount of about £330; the amounts of the original demands varied between 1s.8d. and £25. The following are some examples of the reason for the demand, the amount of the demand and charges, and the kind of goods taken:

(1) Militia substitute; £12-12s. plus 8s. charges; wearing apparel.
(2) Militia substitutes; £12; barley and wheat.
(3) Fine for refusal to convey baggage; £5 plus 10s. charges; flour.
(4) "Military purposes"; 3s. plus 9s. charges; silver spoon and two candlesticks.
(5) "Military purposes"; 14s. plus 10s. charges; two gallons of gin, saucepan and knife.
(6) Militia rate; 2s. plus £1-0s.6d. charges; cheese.

After the passing of the Militia Act of 1779 it became important to Quakers that the legal position should be made clear with regard to obligations for personal service. This Act[81] provided that a man chosen by the militia ballot who did not enrol for service, provide a substitute, or pay the required fine, and who had insufficient distrainable property to meet the fine, should be compulsorily enrolled in the militia. In 1782 a Quaker without property was chosen by ballot and refused to serve and the militia officer pressed for his compulsory enrolment. An opinion deprecating this course was obtained from the Attorney-General, who stated: "It would be harsh measure if the legislature made any law pressing upon tender consciences,..."[82] The Militia Act of 1786[83] settled the question by confining the provision as to compulsory enrolment to "any person chosen by ballot (not being a Quaker)" and this was continued in subsequent legislation. Exemption from personal military service was specifically given in an Act in 1803[84] which provided that "no person being one of the people called Quakers shall be liable to military service under this Act" and there were similar provisions in the abortive Annual Training Act, 1806,[85] and in the Local Militia Acts, 1808[86] and 1812.[87] This complete legal protection from compulsory enlistment contrasts sharply with the position during the First World War, when Quaker objectors who had failed to obtain from tribunals exemption from military service, or who had refused to comply with their conditions of exemption, were compulsorily enlisted in the army.

The Militia Act of 1786 substituted imprisonment for compulsory enrolment as the ultimate legal sanction in the case of a propertyless balloted Quaker. It enacted[88] that, if a Quaker had insufficient distrainable property to meet the cost of providing a substitute and it appeared "that such Quaker is of sufficient ability to pay the sum of ten pounds", then it should be lawful for the Deputy Lieutenants "to commit such Quaker to the common gaol, there to remain without bail or mainprize for the space of three months" or until he paid the sum of money paid to the substitute. This provision was continued in the Militia Act of 1802.[89] In the Local Militia Act of 1808[90] it was enacted that, when a balloted Quaker had no distrainable property to pay the fine levied, "then it shall be lawful for any deputy-lieutenant or justice of the peace, if he shall think fit, to commit such Quaker... to prison, there to remain for any time not exceeding one month, unless such sum shall be sooner paid and satisfied." The Local Militia Act of 1812[91] repeated this provision, adding the limitations that it must appear on enquiry that the Quaker "is of sufficient ability to pay such fine of £10" and that no Quaker committed to prison "shall be confined among felons." It seems that under the Acts of 1786 and 1812 men unable to pay £10 were not liable to imprisonment, and it is clear that under the Local Militia Acts the authorities were given discretion as to whether to commit to prison.

In 1788 there was a case of imprisonment under the Militia Act, 1786. In the period of war from 1793 onwards there were two or three cases of imprisonment almost every year and from 1808 the numbers were greater. Under the Militia Acts the period of imprisonment was three months; under the Local Militia Acts the period was not exceeding one month, and that a shorter sentence was often imposed is shown in an enquiry made by the Society of Friends for the year 1809 –10.[92] This enquiry found that in that year twenty-four men, members of, or associated with the Society, had been imprisoned under the Local Militia Act, 1808. Of the twenty-one men for whom the period of sentence was recorded, five were imprisoned for twenty-eight days and sixteen for fourteen days. In twenty cases the authorities used their powers of discretion to exempt from imprisonment. After 1815 there were very few cases of imprisonment and the suspension of the militia ballot after 1832 meant that after that date there was no occasion for imprisonment of a balloted Quaker. The consolidating Militia Act, 1852,[93] repealed the provision of the Act of 1802[94] which allowed the imprisonment of balloted Quakers so that, even had the ballot been again imposed, there would have been no cases of imprisonment after that date.

Two types of concession, other than those already described, were made to Quakers in the Militia Act, 1802, and both were continued in subsequent legislation. It was enacted[95] that if any Quaker holding the office of constable, overseer, headborough, or tythingman should refuse or neglect to perform duties concerned with the militia, the Justices of the Peace were allowed, and in some cases required, to appoint a person to perform these duties. If such a person was appointed the Quaker became discharged from such duties and free from any penalty for not performing them. The other concession was in relation to the duty newly imposed upon householders in 1802 to supply lists of all men aged 18 to

45 residing in their homes. It was enacted[96] that if a householder produced evidence that he was a Quaker the list should instead be made by a constable or other officer.

The Moravian Brethren

Legal concessions to conscientious objectors to military service in the eighteenth and early nineteenth centuries were confined to members of two religious bodies – the Quakers and the Moravian Brethren. The general history of the Moravian Brethren was described briefly in Chapter 1 of this book (page 25). Many of the Bohemian Brethren in the fifteenth and sixteenth centuries held the view that a Christian could not, with a good conscience, bear arms, and this view was also held by their spiritual descendants, the Moravian Brethren, in the eighteenth century. Objection to military service was not in the eighteenth century a tenet held collectively by the Moravian Brethren but a considerable number of their members were objectors. In 1739 a group of Moravians who had settled in Georgia migrated to Pennsylvania because their refusal to take up arms had displeased other settlers.[97] In England in 1744 some of the Moravian ministers in Yorkshire "were imprisoned in order to compel them to military service."[98]

In their petition to Parliament in 1749 the deputies representing the Moravian Brethren included a request: "That their bearing arms as militia, or otherwise, in America, may be dispensed with; and that they may, with regard thereto, but put on such a footing as is suitable to their conscience; being willing to make such compensation, in lieu thereof, as shall be thought reasonable."[99] It will be noted that, in contrast to the Quakers, the Moravians seem to have had no objection to making payments in lieu of personal military service.

The Act of 1749,[100] which was passed in reply to this petition, provided that any Moravian residing in the British colonies in America who should be summoned to bear arms or do military service should, on application, be discharged from such personal service, provided that he paid such sum of money as should be assessed on him in lieu of such service.

In 1803 the first legal provision was made for Moravians with regard to military service in England. In that year an Act[101] exempted all members of the Moravian Brethren from personal military service and they were also exempted under the abortive Annual Training Act, 1806,[102] and under the Local Militia Acts, 1808[103] and 1812.[104] The Act of 1803 extended to Moravians a number of other legal concessions already made to Quakers. The Acts of 1806, 1808, and 1812 included Moravians with Quakers with regard to most of the concessions granted and the other special provisions enacted.

A Methodist Objector

There was in the eighteenth century at least one case of an individual, not either a Quaker or a Moravian, who resisted military service because he was what would now be termed a "Christian pacifist". The Acts Of V43[105] and 1744,[106] which allowed the impressment into the army of men without a regular means of livelihood, were used to impress several of the early Methodist preachers, as was recorded with indignation by John Wesley in his Journal.[107] Among those impressed was John Nelson, a stonemason and itinerant preacher. He recorded in his Journal that in 1744 he was impressed by the order of "several of the inhabitants of the town, who did not like so much preaching."[108] He refused to take money as a soldier and stated before a court-martial: "I shall not fight; for I cannot bow my knee before the Lord to pray for a man and get up and kill him when I have done; for I know God both hears me speak and sees me act, and I should expect the lot of the hypocrite if my actions contradict my prayers."[109] After about two months his friends provided a substitute and persuaded the authorities to release him from the army.

References

1   Mainwaring, G.E. and Dobree, Bonamy *The Floating Republic*, Penguin Edition p. 23
2   Lewis, Michael *The Navy of Britain* p. 322
3   Ibid. pp. 312 and 317
4   5 & 6 Will. 4. c. 24
5   16 & 17 Vic. c. 69
6   Trevelyan, George Macaulay *England under the Stuarts*, Pelican Edition p.137
7   Ibid. p. 140
8   16 Car. 1. c. 28
9   Clode, Charles M. *The Military Forces of the Crown* Vol. 11 pp. 8 and 585

10   7 & 8 Will. 3. c. 12
11   1 Geo. 3. c. 17
12   1 Anne Stat. 2. c. 20
13   2 & 3 Anne c. 13
14   17 Geo. 2. c. 15
15   18 Geo. 2. c. 10
16   29 Geo. 2. c. 4
17   30 Geo. 2. c. 8
18   18 Geo. 3. c. 53
19   19 Geo. 3. c. 10
20   13 Edw. 1. c. 6
21   13 Car. 2. c. 6
22   13 & 14 Car.2.c.3
23   15 Car. 2. c. 3
24   30 Geo. 2. c. 25
25   2 Geo. 3. c. 20
26   26 Geo. 3. c. 107
27   42 Geo. 3. c. 90
28   Clode op. cit. Vol. 11 p. 436
29   Ibid. Vol. I pp. 328–331
30   Ibid. Vol. I p. 115
31   Ibid. Vol. I pp. 328–331
32   Ibid. Vol. I p. 558
33   47 Geo. 3. (Sess. 2) c. 71
34   Clode op. cit. Vol. I pp. 291–293
35   Coulton, G . G . *The Case for Compulsory Military Service* pp . 355–357
36   42 Geo. 3. c. 90
37   37 Geo. 3. c. 6
38   37 Geo. 3. c. 23
39   43 Geo. 3. c. 82
40   46 Geo. 3. c. 90
41   48 Geo. 3. c. 3
42   52 Geo. 3. c. 38
43   56 Geo. 3. c. 3
44   Metropolitan Police Act, 1829
45   10 Geo. 4. c. 10
46   23 & 24 Vic. c. 120
47   28 & 29 Vic. c. 46
48   15 & 16 Vic. c. 50
49   45 & 46 Vic. c. 49
50   7 Edw. 7. c. 9
51   11 & 12 Geo. 5. c. 37
52   Hirst, Margaret E. *The Quakers in Peace and War. An Account of their Peace Principles and Practice* p. 27
53   Ibid. p. 29
54   Underwood, A.C. *A History of the English Baptists* pp. 54 & 64
55   James Ch. 4 vv 1 and 2 A.V.
56   Fox, George *Journal*, Cambridge Edition, 1911. Vol. I p. 68

57 Hirst op. cit. pp. 527–529
58 Printed Document. 1661. In Library of the Society of Friends.
59 Minutes of Kent Quarterly Meeting. Quoted in Hirst op. cit. p. 76
60 Hooke, Ellis Record of Sufferings 1679. Quoted in "Fellowship" 1.5.1960
61 Braithwaite, William C. The Beginnings of Quakerism p.521. Based on tract published in 1710.
62 Chalkley, Thomas Journal p.7. Quoted in Hirst op. cit. p. 178
63 Friends, Society of Extracts Relating to Christian Doctrine, Practice and Discipline 1861
64 2 Geo. 3. c. 20
65 Friends, Society of Extracts from Minutes and Advices of Yearly Meeting 1783
66 Jones, Rufus M. *The Later Periods of Quakerism* Vol. I p. 157
67 Hirst op. cit. pp. 75–76
68 Ibid. p. 197
69 30 Geo. 2. c. 25. Sect. 26
70 2 Geo. 3. c. 20. Sect. 88
71 37 Geo. 3. c. 6
72 37 Geo. 3. c. 23. Sect. 26
73 46 Geo. 3. c. 90. Sect. 20
74 48 Geo. 3. c. 111. Sect. 23
75 52 Geo. 3. c. 38. Sect. 50
76 Hirst op. cit. p. 199
77 Minutes of Yearly Meetings 1798 and 1804. Manuscript in Library of the Society of Friends.
78 42 Geo. 3. c. 90
79 Minutes of Yearly Meeting 1810. Manuscript in Library of the Society of Friends.
80 Records of Distraints for Lancashire and Essex Quarterly Meetings. Manuscript in Library of the Society of Friends.
81 19 Geo. 3. c. 72. Sect. 22
82 Hirst op. cit. p. 207
83 26 Geo. 3. c. 107. Sect. 26
84 43 Geo. 3. c. 96. Sect. 12
85 46 Geo. 3. c. 90. Sect. 20
86 48 Geo. 3. c. 111. Sect. 23
87 52 Geo. 3. c. 38. Sect. 50
88 26 Geo. 3. c. 107. Sect. 35
89 42 Geo. 3. c. 90. Sect. 50
90 48 Geo. 3. c. 111. Sect. 23
91 52 Geo. 3. c. 38. Sect. 50
92 Abstract of the Returns made to an Inquiry respecting Cases of Imprisonment, or of Exemption from Imprisonment under the Local Militia Acts. Manuscript in Library of the Society of Friends.
93 15 & 16 Vic. c. 50. Sect. 33
94 42 Geo. 3. c. 90. Sect. 50
95 42 Geo. 3. c. 90. Sect. 27
96 42 Geo. 3. c. 90. Sect. 33

97 Bost, Ami *History of the Moravians* p. 305
    Holmes, John *History of the United Brethren* Vol. I p. 369
98 Holmes op. cit. Vol. I p. 223
99 House of Commons Journal. Vol. 25 pp. 727–728
100 22 Geo. 2. c. 30
101 43 Geo. 3. c. 120. Sect. 2
102 46 Geo. 3. c. 90. Sect. 20
103 48 Geo. 3. c. 111. Sect. 23
104 52 Geo. 3. c. 38. Sect. 50
105 17 Geo. 2. c. 15
106 18 Geo. 2. c. 10
107 Wesley, John *Journal*. Everyman Edition. Vol. I pp. 212, 467-468, 470, 503–504, 507, 517
108 Nelson, John *Journal* p. 113
109 Ibid. p. 129

Chronological Table of Acts Concerning Military Compulsions

Date		
1285	Statute of Winchester	13 Edw. 1. c. 6
1640	Impressment for Army	16 Car. 1. c. 28
1662	Militia Act	13 & 14 Car. 2. c. 3
1696	Enlistment of Debtors	7 & 8 Will. 3. c. 12
1702	Enlistment of Convicted Prisoners	1 Anne Stat. 2. c. 20
1703	Impressment for Army	2 & 3 Anne c. 13
1743	Impressment for Army	17 Geo. 2. c. 15
1744	Impressment for Army	18 Geo. 2. c. 10
1749	Exemption of Moravians	22 Geo. 2. c. 30
1756	Impressment for Army	29 Geo. 2. c. 4
1757	Impressment for Army	30 Geo. 2. c. 8
1757	Militia Act	30 Geo. 2. c. 25
1760	Enlistment of Debtors	1 Geo. 3. c. 17
1762	Militia Act	2 Geo. 3. c. 20
1778	Impressment for Army	18 Geo. 3. c. 53
1779	Impressment for Army	19 Geo. 3. c. 10
1779	Militia Act	19 Geo. 3. c. 72
1786	Militia Act	26 Geo. 3. c. 107
1796	Cavalry Act	37 Geo. 3. c. 6
1796	Cavalry Act	37 Geo. 3. c. 23
1802	Militia Act	42 Geo. 3. c. 90
1803	Army Reserve Act	43 Geo. 3. c. 82
1803	Defence of the Realm Act	43 Geo. 3. c. 96
1803	Defence of the Realm Act	43 Geo. 3. c. 120
1806	Annual Training Act	46 Geo. 3. c. 90
1807	Militia Act	47 Geo. 3. (Sess.2) c. 71

1808	Local Militia Act	48 Geo. 3. c. 111
1812	Local Militia Act	52 Geo. 3. c. 38
1816	Local Militia Act	56 Geo. 3. c. 3
1829	Militia Act	10 Geo. 4. c. 10
1835	Service in Navy	5 & 6 Will. 4. c. 24
1852	Militia Act	15 & 16 Vic. c. 50
1853	Service in the Navy Act	c. 69
1860	Militia Ballot Act	23 & 24 Vic. c. 120
1865	Militia (Ballot Suspension) Act	28 & 29 Vic. c. 46
1882	Militia Act	45 & 46 Vic. c. 49
1907	Territorial and Reserve Forces Act	7 Edw. 7. c. 11
1921	Territorial Army and Militia Act	11 & 12 Geo. 5. c. 37

CHAPTER 4

Compulsory Military Service During the First World War

Introduction

There was an interval of about eighty years between the abandonment of the use of compulsory powers in the recruitment of the militia and the navy in the 1830s and the imposition of conscription for military service in 1916. Both the purposes and the methods of the new conscription were very different from those of the old. In contrast with the old compulsions for the navy, the new conscription applied no special compulsions to seamen and there was nothing corresponding to the brutal and arbitrary methods of the press gang. In contrast with the old compulsions for the militia, the new conscription imposed an obligation for full-time service in either the Armed Forces or work of national importance on nearly all men of military age and the enforced military service was not confined, as in the militia, to service within the British. Isles. The main reason for the imposition of conscription, eighteen months after the outbreak of the First World War, was the urgent need for increased manpower in the forces fighting abroad; any confinement of area of service and any system of ballot would have defeated the objects of the measure.

As the new conscription was universal there was no longer any possibility of providing substitutes for service, as was common in the militia; nearly every fit man of military age was legally required to perform full-time personal service. As a corollary of this, the law could not provide for the conscientious objector, as it did with regard to militiary service, by accepting a money payment in place of personal service and, if necessary, collecting it by distraint on his property. Thus, with regard to the conscientious objectors of the First World War, the problem which faced the legislators and administrators was not only whether, and on what grounds, exemption from military service should be given but also what conditions, if any, should be imposed on those exempted. The solution adopted was to impose a condition of some form of alternative personal service in the case of nearly all those to whom exemption was given. The condition and problems of "alternative service" thus appeared for the first time in the history of conscientious objection to compulsory military service.

During the nineteenth and early twentieth centuries there had been great changes in public opinion with regard to the morality of warfare. The belief that a Christian should not participate in war ceased to be confined (or almost confined) to Quakers and Moravians. A number of religious sects founded during the nineteenth century – the Plymouth Brethren, the Christadelphians, the Seventh Day Adventists, the International Bible Students' Association – held views which involved opposition to military service by all or a large number of their members. The Peace Society, founded in 1816, included both Anglicans and Nonconformists and held that "war is inconsistent with the spirit of Christianity and the true interests of mankind".[1] Many Christians came to question the justifiability of war and among the conscientious objectors of the First World War there were objectors not only from the sects already mentioned but from the Catholic Church, the Church of England, the Presbyterian Churches, and all the main Nonconformist denominations. Another important source of objection to military service was the growing Labour movement with its emphasis on the importance of the ordinary man and on the international solidarity of the workers. Thus, when conscription was imposed it was found that there was a great variety of views among those who applied for exemption as conscientious objectors.

The Conscription Controversy in the Early Twentieth Century

During the early twentieth century there was a revival of interest in the principles and problems of compulsory military service. In 1902 the National Service League was founded as a non-party organisation to further the ideals of compulsory service. In 1904 a Royal Commission on the Militia and Volunteer Forces, under the presidency of the Duke of Norfolk, made a majority report in favour of compulsion. It rejected the militia ballot as old fashioned and unequal in its effects and recommended a period of full-time military training for all able-bodied men, followed by one or two short periods of retraining. Such training would adopt "the principles which have been adopted, after the disastrous failure of older methods, by every great State of the European continent... We are convinced that only by the adoption of these principles can an army for home defence, adequate in strength and military efficiency to defeat an invader, be raised and maintained in the United Kingdom..."[2] These proposals were rejected by the Government of A.J. Balfour.

Bills which proposed to enact some kind of compulsory military training, though not in the form proposed by the Norfolk Commission, were introduced in the House of Commons in 1908 and 1913 and in the House of Lords in 1909 and March 1914; all were either defeated or withdrawn. In the debate on the Bill in 1913 the problem of the conscientious objector was raised. A Quaker M.P., Arnold Rowntree, argued that in the long run compulsory military training would destroy religious freedom for many people and said that thousands outside the Society of Friends would object to such training. Keir Hardie, the founder of the Independent Labour Party, stated that "the Socialist Party of the world is not merely opposed to war; it is opposed to militarism and especially to military compulsion, and therefore we oppose the Bill... because of its principle of compelling citizens to become soldiers, however much their principles may be opposed to their doing so."[3]

Early in 1913 Lord Roberts opened a national campaign in favour of conscription and in the same year the Voluntary Service Committee was formed, which opened a campaign to maintain the voluntary principle in the Armed Forces. This Committee included in its case against compulsion the argument that the objection to military service on ethical and religious grounds was widespread and was an objection which even those who did not agree with it could not easily condemn.

Thus there was considerable debate on the principles and problems of compulsion in the decade prior to the outbreak of the First World War but no measure of compulsion was enacted. In his book "Conscription Conflict" on which the foregoing short account is based, Denis Hayes concludes: "Peace-time conscription did not come because the people would not have it."[4]

Compulsory Military Training in Australia and New Zealand

However, in another part of the Commonwealth – Australia and New Zealand – compulsory military training was introduced in 1911. The relevance of this fact to the history of conscription in Great Britain is that in 1916 both the British Government introducing conscription and some of those opposing it knew of what had happened in the administration of the schemes in Australasia.

The Australian scheme covered boys and men aged fourteen to twenty-five, the New Zealand scheme those aged twelve to twenty-one; both were schemes of part-time military training. The Australian Act gave power to the Defence Department to exempt conscientious objectors "upon such conditions as may be prescribed"; this was interpreted to mean that certain religious objectors could fulfil their legal obligation by training only in ambulance and other non-combatant duties. In both countries there was considerable opposition to compulsory training, some parents were punished for refusing to register their children, and some youths who refused to comply with the law were imprisoned in military institutions. The solitary confinement of a boy of sixteen in Australia and of some boys in New Zealand aroused considerable public protest.[5]

The Coming of Conscription

At the outbreak of war in August 1914, of the five Great Powers involved – Britain, France, Russia, Germany, and the Austro-Hungarian Empire – Britain was the only country without conscription. Germany had five million and France nearly four million men of military age who had received training in the Forces.[6] In contrast Britain, though possessing a strong navy, had a comparatively small professional army and, for home defence, a voluntary Territorial Force. Almost immediately a force of nearly 100,000 men was sent to resist the German invasion of Northern France. Casualties were very high but by the end of 1914 there had been a large increase in the strength of the armed Forces as a million volunteers had enlisted.[7] "While the country was volunteering to such an extent that the Government was hard pressed to provide

128

the required accommodation, clothing and weapons, the clamour of the conscriptionists was largely stilled."[8]

In a debate in the House of Lords in January 1915 the Lord Chancellor, Lord Haldane, who, as Secretary of State for War, had opposed peace-time conscription, stated: "It has been laid down that any subject at a time of emergency may be asked to give himself and his property for the defence of the nation... We hope to solve our problem by this magnificent response which is being made, and which gives us, after all, men who are to a certain extent picked, who come because of their enthusiasm, and men who are better than the dead level which compulsory service gives you. . . But at a time of national necessity any other consideration must yield to national interest and we should bar nothing in the way of principle if it should become necessary."[9]

The first Coalition Government, formed under H.H. Asquith in May 1915, introduced a Bill for setting up a National Register to enable the Government to calculate the supply of man-power available for military service and war industry. This Bill received the Royal Assent in July and became the National Registration Act, 1915.[10] The Act made provision for a compulsory register of all males and females between the ages of fifteen and sixty-five except those in the Armed Forces. The ordinary date of registration was 15th August 1915; an amending Act in February 1918[11] covered those attaining the age of fifteen or discharged from the Forces after the original date of registration. The particulars required from the persons registered included marital status, number and type of dependants, occupation and employer, and whether the person was skilled in and able to perform work other than that in which he was engaged. Certificates of registration were issued and these were required to be produced on demand to any authorised person. The register was completed within a few weeks of the passing of the Act and showed that there were about five million men of military age in Great Britain not serving in the Forces. Excluding those who were medically unfit or indispensable to war industry it was estimated that about one and three quarter million men were available for military service.[12]

In October 1915 Lord Derby was appointed as Director of Recruiting and under the "Derby Scheme" a personal canvass was made of every man between the ages of eighteen and forty-one. Each man was invited to "attest", that is to pledge himself to join the Forces when called up. Attested men would be placed in two classes, single and married, each being divided into age-groups.

Men would be called up by class and age-group as and when required. No married men could be called up until after all the single men had been dealt with. An assurance was given that if single men did not attest in sufficient numbers the married men would not be held to their attestation pledge. The tribunals, which later functioned under conscription, were first set up under this scheme. Their function was to consider the applications of attested men or their employers for postponement of their calling up on the ground of either personal hardship or the national importance of their civilian work. In the early months of the war many men had joined the Forces from occupations of great importance to the war effort; one of the functions of the tribunals was to help to prevent the enlistment, whether voluntary or compulsory, of men whose civilian work was considered of more value to the war effort than their services in the Forces.

In December 1915 Lord Derby reported that out of about 2,200,000 civilian single men of military age only 1,150,000 had enlisted or attested under the scheme – a million single men had not responded. This fact, combined with the previous assurance to the married men who attested, was one of the causes of the enactment of conscription for single men a month later.

There had been a growing opinion in favour of conscription as the war progressed. Initial hopes of a short war had vanished. The casualties of trench warfare were frequently very heavy, for example, 60,000 British casualties in the Battle of Loos in Autumn 1915.[13] The high recruitment figures of the early months of the war had not been maintained: a Cabinet Committee reported in September 1915 that over the last six months about 80,000 men a month had been recruited. It was obvious that the country's full resources of manpower were not yet mobilised for a war which it was now realised would be a long and costly struggle. Lloyd George, who became Prime Minister at the end of 1916, stated in his "War Memoirs": "Looking back after the event, no one can now doubt that the adoption of conscription was vitally necessary for carrying the War through to victory."[14] Conscription was advocated also on grounds of fairness, by British people who emphasised the inequalities of sacrifice as between the men on active service and the available men who did not enlist and by the leaders of France which, with its available men conscripted, had contributed far more in effort and sacrifice to the war on the Western Front.

The first measure of conscription, covering unmarried men and widowers without dependants, was introduced on 4th January 1916 and received the Royal Assent on 27th January, as the Military Service Acts 1916.[15] It received the support of a large majority of the House of Commons. The Home Secretary, Sir John Simon, resigned in protest and the First Reading of the Bill was opposed by 105 M.P.s. Those voting in this minority included nearly all the Irish M.P.s; in the vote on the Second Reading of the Bill the Irish members abstained on the ground that the Bill did not extend to Ireland, and the minority voting against the Bill was reduced to 39 as against a vote of 431 in support of it. In the House of Lords the temporary nature of conscription was stressed by the Lord Chancellor, Lord Haldane, who stated: "The Bill does not profess to be and is not an attempt to establish upon a permanent basis the liabilities of the citi7ens of this country to military service... This Bill is a war measure, temporary and limited in its application, and it is intended for one purpose and for one purpose only – namely to provide us with a number of men who are indispensable if we are to maintain our existing military functions, if we are to meet the obligations to which we are already committed, and if we are to carry the war to a successful issue."[16]

The General Provisions of the Military Service Acts

Six Military Service Acts were passed in the three years 1916 to 1918: of these the first two were the most important.

The Military Service Act, 1916,[17] applied to all men (with certain exceptions which included ministers of religion) who were British subjects ordinarily resident in Great Britain, aged over eighteen and under forty-one, and either unmarried or widowers with no children dependent on them. Such men would be "deemed as from the appointed date to have been duly enlisted in His Majesty's forces for general service with the colours or in the reserve for the period of the war, and to have been forthwith transferred to that reserve."[18] The appointed date was 2nd March and proclamations made under the authority of the Act called up various groups of reservists at different dates and a reservist not reporting for service when called up could be punished and could be taken to his unit under armed escort. A man "deemed" to be in the reserve came under the Army Act 1881[19] and the Reserve Forces Acts 1882[20] to 1907.

Certificates of exemption could be granted on four grounds: (a) the importance in the national interest of the man's civilian work; (b) serious hardship on account of "exceptional financial or business obligations or domestic position"; (c) ill-health or infirmity; (d) conscientious objection.[21] Any exemption could be absolute, conditional or temporary. A certificate of exemption could be reviewed or renewed at any time on the application either of the holder or of a person authorised by the Army Council, and it could be withdrawn or varied by the reviewing authority. It was laid down in the Act that no exemption could be conditional on employment "under any specified employer or in any specified place or establishment"[22] though a later Act[23] removed this prohibition in the case of conscientious objectors.

Two types of authority were at this time authorised to grant exemptions. Any Government Department, after consultation with the Army Council, might give certificates to men or classes or bodies of men employed by the Department or certified by the Department to be engaged in work of national importance within its sphere of interest. Other exemptions were the responsibility of tribunals, to which application was made by, or in respect of, the man for whom the exemption was desired. The constitution of the tribunals was specified in the Second Schedule of the Act and Clause 5 of this Schedule gave the power to make by orders in council, regulations and instructions with respect to the constitution, functions and procedure of tribunals.

The other five Military Service Acts passed during the War extended or amended the provisions of the Military Service Act, 1916.

The Military Service Act (Session 2), 1916,[24] became law on 25th May. In the House of Commons the Second Reading of the Bill had been passed by 328 to 36 votes. The most important provision of the Act was the extension of conscription to married men of military age; thus the promise of preferential treatment for married men was honoured, but only to the extent that the married men had an additional four months of freedom from compulsion. The Act also provided that youths should be compulsorily recruited when they attained the age of eighteen, though as far as possible youths under nineteen should not be sent abroad. Officers and men of the Territorial Force could be transferred to other branches of the army without their consent and time-expired men ceased to be excepted. Returned prisoners of war and repatriated men who had given a pledge not to take up arms were excepted from conscription.

The Military Service (Review of Exceptions) Act, 1917,[25] which became law on 5th April, dealt mainly with men previously rejected on medical grounds. The military authorities were authorised to call up for re-examination, on the expiration of six months after his discharge or rejection, any man discharged for disablement or ill health, any man rejected for medical reasons, and any Territorial classified as not fit for foreign service. Men disabled by enemy action in war and certified agricultural workers were excepted from these provisions.

The Military Service (Conventions with Allied States) Act, 1917,[26] became law on 10th July. The Act authorised the ratification by Order in Council of conventions with any allied Government imposing a mutual liability to military service on British subjects in that country and on subjects of that country in the United Kingdom. Men affected must first be given the opportunity to return home if they applied to do so.

The Military Service Act, 1918,[27] became law on 6th February. The Act empowered the Director General of National Service to order the withdrawal of certificates of exemption from any men or classes or groups of men exempted wholly or partly on occupational grounds. Men from whom certificates were withdrawn would be unable to obtain any further exemption on grounds of occupation.

The Military Service (No. 2) Act, 1918,[28] which became law on 18th April, was passed in response to the need for further recruits arising from the serious military situation – there had been over 300,000 recent British casualties, and this situation on the Western Front[29] led also to the sending abroad of youths under nineteen. The Act raised the upper age-limit for compulsory recruitment to fifty-one and gave power for the age limit to be raised to fifty-six, generally or for certain classes, if desired by both Houses of Parliament. Proclamations could be made cancelling any exemptions which had been given on grounds other than ill health or conscientious objection and such proclamations were made cancelling, with certain exceptions, the exemptions of men born in the years 1895 to 1900 inclusive. The Act also made the law regarding exceptions and exemptions stricter in various other ways. Thus there was a constant trend in the five Military Service Acts to include more men in compulsory military service, and to except or exempt fewer men from service in the Forces.

The Law of Conscientious Objection

The debates in Parliament on the various stages of the first Military Service Bill are of great interest both in their general discussions of the principles involved in allowing legal conscientious objection and in the insight shown by several speakers into the problems involved and the difficulties likely to arise in the administration of the law.

A few speakers expressed the view that no exemption of any kind should be given but no amendment to this effect was introduced. Several speakers opined that to allow exemption for conscientious reasons was illogical. For example, William Joynson-Hicks (later Lord Brentford) stated: "I am not at all sure that in war time the State has not a right to call upon every man to take his share in the defence of the country. The conscientious objector seeks to exercise his right of private judgment against the needs of the State... Whatever may be his conscientious objections, the needs of the State are above and beyond a man's conscientious objections, feelings and desires. Is it reasonable that these conscientious objectors should have all the advantages of the State, all the advantages of the protection of their lives, their homes, their wives, and their children and everything that is dear to them, their church, their chapel, their religion, everything protected by our naval and military forces, and that they are not to serve in either of these forces? But for that Navy what would be the position of the conscientious objector in England who claimed the right not to fight?"[30] Bonar Law stated: "I have no hesitation whatever in expressing the view that the State has the right, the absolute right, to demand service of any one of its citizens if it thinks it is his duty to do so. I think that is the essence of the State". But the speaker continued that the question was "not has the State the right to take a particular course, but is it wise to take a particular course". He then referred to the exemption of Quakers under the Militia Act and to concessions to conscientious objectors in Australia[31] and both these precedents were also quoted by the Prime Minister, H.H. Asquith, when introducing the Bill.[32] The Home Secretary, Herbert Samuel, asked what was the alternative to the proposed exemption of conscientious objectors: should these objectors be punished by the courts? "Is it really contemplated that now, when for the first time you are making military service compulsory in this country, it should be accompanied by the arrest and imprisonment of a certain number of men who unquestionably, by common consent, are men of the highest character, and, in other matters, good citizens?" He was sure M.P.s "would not wish to contemplate that there should be anything in the nature of religious persecution."[33]

In addition to the decision on whether to make provision of any kind for legal conscientious objection, Parliament had to make three main decisions on the matter: (1) what the law was to mean by a "conscientious objection"; (2) what conditions (if any) should be imposed on legally recognised objectors; (3) how the decision should be made in the case of the individual, as to whether he should be legally recognised as an objector and under what conditions.

(1)   The Military Service Act, in Section 2: Subsection 1 (d), stated that application for exemption might be made "on the ground of a conscientious objection to the undertaking of a combatant service. " This was the wording used in the Bill when introduced and it remained unaltered, but there were four amendments which proposed alterations.

William Joynson-Hicks moved to substitute the words "on the ground that the applicant was on 15th August 1915, the date of National Registration, a member of the Society of Friends or of any other recognised religious body one of whose fundamental tenets is an objection to all war." He stated: "My Amendment is designed to meet the case of the man who has a real religious conscientious objection and to exclude the man who shelters himself behind what he calls a conscientious objection, and who is at heart a slacker and a shirker."[34] Bonar Law replied that the Government could not accept the amendment and said: "If there is any right whatever or exemptions on account of conscience it does not apply to any particular denomination, and it is a question of a man's own heart and conscience."[35]

Major Newman proposed that the clause in the Bill should be worded "conscientious objection to the taking of human life". He wished to remove any expression that would afford a means of avoiding military service.[36]

Edmund Harvey, a Quaker M.P., moved an amendment that the clause should read "conscientious objection to the undertaking of military service or combatant service". He wished to make it clear that there were a great number of conscientious objectors who objected to any form of military service.[37] Earlier in the debate he had stated: "There are men who are prepared to go into the Royal Army Medical Corps, or other branches of the Army, who would be glad to do that, but who cannot but feel that it is contrary to their deepest religious and conscientious instincts that they should take part in taking life. Although that class exists, and I am very glad that their position should be met, they are really a minority of the conscientious objectors."[38] This amendment was supported by the votes of 53 M.P.s.

In the House of Lords an amendment was moved by Lord Courtney of Penrith that the clause should read "conscientious objection to undertake any service or engage in any action in support of the war or to the undertaking of combatant service." This amendment was moved just after Lord Courtney had stated that a conscientious objection might arise in several ways. There were those who objected to war altogether, but there were others equally important who, while not objecting to war altogether, thought that the nation was not justified in regard to the present war. Lord Courtney gave instances of respected historical figures who objected to particular wars in which Britain was engaged. He asked the House to consider the difficulties involved in attempting to make men fight against their will, or even to make them assist in upholding a war which they profoundly refuted and in which they would not, under any penalty, take part.[39] In rejecting the amendment the Marquis of Lansdowne said that, while he respected the conviction of men who objected to a great deal more than the shedding of blood, yet the proposed words averted much too far – they would make it possible for a man to reject an employment, however pacific, if the result of his acceptance was to liberate another man for the army.[40]

In the light of the knowledge of what happened in the administration of the provisions of the Military Service Act, it is clear that this clause of the Act was unfortunately worded. A considerable number of tribunals took the view that, as the applicant had to establish an objection "to the undertaking of combatant service," they had no power to exempt him from anything but combatant service; they therefore gave decisions which made all successful applicants liable for non-combatant military service. This view was erroneous, but some tribunals persisted in it even after the Government Department concerned had communicated with them pointing out that another Subsection of the Act clearly allowed them to give other kinds of exemption to conscientious objectors.

(2) The kinds of exemption possible were covered in Section 2: Subsection 3 of the Act and the wording was as follows: "Any certificate of exemption may be absolute, conditional or temporary, as the authority by whom it was granted thinks best suited to the case, and also in the case of an application on conscientious grounds may take the form of an exemption from combatant service only, or may be conditional on the applicant being engaged in some work which in the opinion of the tribunal dealing with the case is of national importance." The last sentence was added by a Government amendment during the passage of the Bill. Several M.P.s had instanced cases in which pacifists in considerable numbers were already engaged, in a civilian capacity, in ambulance or relief work to meet needs arising from the war.

In the House of Lords Viscount Peele moved an amendment limiting the exemption which could be given to a conscientious objector to exemption from combatant duties only. He said that he did not see why conscientious objectors should be exempted from some duties connected with the war.[41] The Marquis of Lansdowne objected to the amendment and said that, in the Government's view "it is much better that the tribunals should be in a position to give what I may call, without disrespect, the out-and-out conscientious objector an absolute dispensation."[42]

(3) The third decision to be made by Parliament was what should be the test of conscientious objection in the case of the individual man who came under the provisions of conscription. The Act gave every man affected the right to apply to a local tribunal and the decision as to whether to exempt him, and under what conditions, if any, was to be made by the local tribunal, with an appeal against the decision to an appeal tribunal. The tribunals, which were already functioning under the "Derby Scheme", were to be continued, with some changes, to judge applications for exemptions under conscription.

The functions of the tribunals covered decisions as to exemption not only on the ground of conscientious objection but on the other possible grounds of exemption – the national importance of the man's civilian work, serious hardship, and ill-health or infirmity. Edmund Harvey moved an amendment that, in the case of an application on conscientious grounds, there should be an appeal to a specially constituted tribunal. He said it would readily be appreciated that tribunals suited for other purposes were not suited to deal with the applications of conscientious objectors.[43] Walter Long, the President of the Local Government Board, replied that the existing tribunals would be strengthened, and maintained that the tribunals should be so constituted that the cases of conscientious objectors should be fairly and fully considered.[44]

Several members expressed the view that to test an individual's conscientious objection by any kind of tribunal would prove unsatisfactory. Both Philip Snowden[45] and Charles Trevelyan referred to the experiences of objectors to compulsory vaccination in the period when such objectors had to satisfy magistrates in court in order to secure exemptions. Charles Trevelyan stated: "Sitting as a justice of the peace, I have sometimes had my colleagues trying to prevent a man who had a conscientious objection to having his children vaccinated from getting the certificate. I have known a man with such a prejudice against granting the certificate that it was with great difficulty that his colleagues made him obey the law as a justice. It is quite possible that you may have an unreasonable tribunal."[46] He also questioned in principle the judging of a man's conscience by a tribunal: "There is a military service or local tribunal which, if it thinks just in the circumstances, may grant a certificate. How can conscientious objection be just in the circumstances of one man and be unjust in the circumstances of another man? Who is to tell except the man himself? The only judge of a man's conscience is the man himself. To put it under a local tribunal is to deny the individual conscience."[47]

R.L. Outhwaite moved an amendment that a man should be entitled to apply for exemption "on the ground that he has made a declaration on oath before two justices that he entertains a conscientious objection to the undertaking of military service".[48] Philip Snowden supported the motion, saying he had not heard from the Government "how they expect the tribunal is going to discover whether an applicant has a conscientious objection or not".

In New Zealand (under the law enacting compulsory military training) "there have been so many conscientious objectors whose appeals have been refused by the Court that a special prison had to be provided for them".

In the case of compulsory vaccination the House of Commons in 1907 "accepted a logical conclusion, and said that if the applicant makes a declaration that he has a conscientious objection, then the justice shall be compelled to accept that."[49]

In opposing these views, Herbert Samuel, the Home Secretary, had said earlier that it was suggested that "what you ought to do is simply to accept the word of the individual that he does object on conscientious grounds to taking part in this war. I am afraid, if you agree to that, there would be a very considerable number of unconscientious conscientious objectors and it might be regarded as a mere matter of form, by men of a certain class, to say, 'We do not want to serve, and all we have to do is to call ourselves conscientious objectors, and there will be no further trouble, but we shall be exempt'. The Government have considered that proposal, and feel sure that it would not be accepted by the House generally, or by the country, as a satisfactory solution of the problem."[50] The Amendment was defeated by 287 to 37 votes.

Tribunals and their Decisions

Thus the Military Service Act, 1916, made exemption on grounds of conscientious objection subject to the decision of tribunals. The Act itself and regulations made under it governed the constitution, powers, and principles of procedure of tribunals. There were in 1916 over 2,000 local tribunals in Great Britain; the area covered by the tribunal usually corresponded to the area of the local authority and the tribunal members were appointed by the Borough or District Council concerned. These local tribunals heard and judged all applications for exemption from residents in their areas. Both the applicant and the "military representative" had the right of appeal to an appeal tribunal. There were 83 appeal tribunals in Great Britain; their members were appointed by the Crown. If an appeal tribunal granted leave to do so an appeal could be made from it to the Central Tribunal, whose members were appointed by the Crown. The Minister responsible was the President of the Local Government Board with regard to England and Wales and the Secretary for Scotland with regard to that country.

The practical effects of the provision made by Parliament for legal conscientious objection depended largely on the way in which tribunals exercised their powers. In Chapter 11. this subject will be discussed at some length and a more detailed account of the tribunal system will be given. The following account is concerned only with a general summary of the decisions of tribunals.

With regard to an application on conscientious grounds the tribunal could make one of four decisions – no exemption; exemption from combatant service only; exemption conditional on the applicant engaging in work of national importance; and absolute exemption, that is exemption with no conditions. It could also make an exemption temporary. In the absence of official figures it is not possible to give an accurate account of the relative numbers of the decisions of these four kinds made by tribunals (in contrast to the account which can be given of the decisions of tribunals in the Second World War).

There are no statistics with regard to applicants on conscientious grounds who were refused any exemption and afterwards complied with the law, entering the Services when called up. But there are careful estimates for other groups made by John W. Graham, a contemporary author much involved in work for conscientious objectors, in his book, Conscription and Conscience.[51] The following summary is based on his figures.

There were about 3,300 men in the Non-Combatant Corps of the army. These were men who were exempted from combatant service only and who accepted that decision. The figure does not include many men who were "deemed" to be members of the Non-Combatant Corps by the decision of the tribunal but who refused such service because it offended their consciences.

There were about 6,250 men who were exempted on condition that they performed various forms of civilian work of national importance and who complied with this condition by performing such work. In most cases these exemptions were given by tribunals but, for example, the Government exempted, without requiring individual applications to tribunals, several hundred members of the Friends' Ambulance Unit who were already serving abroad when conscription was introduced.

Thus, according to these estimates, about 9,550 conscientious objectors were given types of exemption which they were willing to accept and were able to obey their consciences without breaking the law. There were also a few cases of absolute exemption, not included in these figures.

In contrast, 6,261 men were arrested and taken under arrest into the army. Some of these had ignored the tribunals but a large majority had applied to tribunals for exemption on conscientious grounds and had been either given no exemption or given types of exemption which they could not conscientiously accept.

These results of the decisions of tribunals could be judged in two very different ways. It could be argued on the one hand, that they were evidence of remarkable toleration. Britain was in the midst of a war in which casualties were very high, in which there was an urgent need for more men in the Forces, in which millions of men were fighting under appalling conditions and millions of their relatives and friends were living in constant anxiety for their safety, and in which the achievement of victory was still uncertain. Yet the ordinary citizens who were members

141

of tribunals were willing to allow over nine thousand men to contract out of what was generally regarded as their obvious duty in a national emergency solely because of their personal views and feelings.

It could be argued, on the other hand, that it was a disgrace that over six thousand men, most of them generally law-abiding citizens engaged in useful work and some of them highly respected, should be treated as criminals, subject in some cases to brutal treatment in the army and in many cases to long periods of imprisonment. According to this view British people, in the struggle against Prussian militarism, were adopting the same militaristic attitude, disregarding the British tradition of religious and civil liberty, and persecuting fellow-Christians for following Christian standards.

The Grounds of Objection

At this point in the story more must be said about the views of objectors and it is very difficult to give a fair and adequate description of these. The essence of conscientious objection is that it is the result of the decision of an individual as to what it is right or wrong for him to do in a particular situation. As no individuals have identical original constitutions, and, as no individuals have identical experiences of life, the feelings, values and motives involved probably differed somewhat between every objector. When the grounds of objection were formulated in words some of these differences disappeared but, even when formulated in words, there were many different grounds of objection and individuals who had a number of reasons for their objections might place varying emphasis on the comparative importance of these reasons. All that will be attempted here is to give an account of some of the grounds of objection which led or helped to lead considerable numbers of individuals to become objectors, and to give some varied examples of the statements made by individuals at tribunals or before civilian or military courts.

It is impossible to make any statistical estimate of the numbers of objectors holding different kinds of views.

A large number, probably the majority of objectors, based their objections on their interpretations of their Christian faith. There were some objectors from all, or nearly all, the Christian denominations in Great Britain and also some objectors of Jewish faith.

In the case of many denominations the objector disagreed with the great majority of his fellow-members who supported the War. But there were some denominations which held collective views adverse to military service and in which a large number of members were objectors: this was true of the Society of Friends (Quakers), the Christadelphians, the Brethren ("Plymouth Brethren"), the Seventh-Day Adventists, and the International Bible Students' Association (later known as Jehovah's Witnesses), and it may have been true of some other small bodies.

With the exception of the Quakers, the members of the denominations just mentioned believed in the imminent Second Coming of Christ. This belief led them to separate themselves as far as possible, from the affairs of "the world".

These special views with regard to their duty as believers awaiting the Second Coming were combined with views on the duty of a Christian to refuse to take human life which they shared with many other Christian objectors.

Christian objectors all held that the teaching of Christ forbade them, as Christians, to perform combatant service in the War. Some objectors found their authority in the actual words of Christ as reported in the Bible, often supported by the "Thou shalt not kill" of the Ten Commandments (Exodus 20 v. 13). Other objectors based their objection on what they understood to be the general spirit of the life and teaching of Christ. All held that their duty as Christians was their highest obligation, overruling any contrary duty demanded by public opinion or required by the law. The following are examples of Christian grounds of objection from statements made by individual objectors:

In the teaching of Christ there is no room for suspicion, jealousy and hate, only the conquering love that casts out fear. It is fear that bids the nations arm and fight against each other; until, therefore, we accept in all its literal meaning the negative commandment, 'Thou shalt not kill', and the positive commandment, 'Love one another, even as I have loved you', until then we shall not only have war, but shall fail in all duty before God and Man.[52]

I believe in one God and Father of the whole human race, and that every man, however degraded and rebellious, is infinitely precious in His sight. If His nature is a love so powerful that it embraces even enemies; if He

143

numbers the very hairs of man's head, and forgets not even the sparrows and the grass of the field, then surely the destruction of human life, still more of brotherly relationships, which war causes, is a flat contradiction of His will.[53]

I stand here reverently to witness for the heroic Christianity of Jesus Christ; for the belief that the only way to overcome evil is to conquer it by indomitable Love and unwavering service. By this I mean a love that never admits defeat, that goes on loving and serving regardless of risk, regardless of possible consequences – in literal interpretation of our Master's orders: 'Love your enemies, do good to them that hate you, and pray for them that despitefully use you and persecute you'.[54]

I understand and honour those, my comrades, who have enlisted in the army to fight, as they believe for the right. The greatest sacrifice I have ever made is to withhold from sharing with them their sublime self-surrender. But I too am enlisted, not merely for three years or the duration of the war, under a Captain who also calls for adventure and sacrifice in His name: whose commands to me are unmistakable, not only to act towards enemies in a very different spirit, and to overcome them redemptively with very different weapons from those which are being used on the battlefields today; but also to proclaim His commands and to win recruits to His cause.[55]

It is only as nations believe in and apply the principle of Christianity that they can be saved from the tyranny of fear and suspicion, and from the evil of war. I long that my country may lead the world out of this bondage into the Truth that shall make it free, and I am convinced that it is only by the steadfastness of individuals that this can ever come about.[56]

A sea of death and darkness is flooding Europe today. God holds in readiness an ocean of love and light to purge away that hateful flood. 'Thou shalt not fear man, thou shalt not hate man, thou shalt love thy fellow-man as thyself, even if that fellow-man be the hated and despised Samaritan or the brutal Roman oppressor.' So rang out once Christ's call to love, so it rings out again today.[57]

During the war two organisations were formed of pacifists and other war-resisters. The Fellowship of Reconciliation was formed in December 1914 and was an undenominational association of Christian pacifists. One of its objects, in the wording accepted in 1916, was "To bind together in a spiritual fellowship, all those who hold that, as Christians, they are committed to the endeavour after a way of life in which Love as revealed in the life and death of Jesus Christ must be supreme and that they are therefore unable to take part in war, and are called to a common quest after a more Christian order of society, in accordance with the mind of Christ."[58]

The other organisation, the Non-Conscription Fellowship, was formed in November 1914 and dissolved in November 1919. Its membership was open to all men likely to be liable for military service who would refuse to bear arms from conscientious motives and its members included men who held a great variety of political and religious opinions. In a statement made soon after the end of the war, Clifford Allen, one of its most active officers, gave the following account of the views of those members who did not base their conscientious objections on Christian grounds. Some of these members "advanced what was known as a moral objection. By this they meant that they entertained fundamental beliefs either about the value of human personality or about the relationship of human beings to each other. Each precluded them from engaging in war. Conscience related man to man. Some of them were followers of Tolstoy, but the greater number were socialists who believed in the brotherhood of man as genuinely as Christians believed in the fatherhood of God. Others, who have sometimes been called political objectors, resisted conscription not so much because they were convinced that all war was morally wrong, or because they believed in any supernatural religious creed; they resisted conscription because it seemed to them a fatal infringement of human liberty; because they feared that industrial freedom would be menaced by military compulsion; because they believed that the foreign policy of this country made Britain worthy of at least some measure of blame for the war; or because they believed that the war had been engineered on both sides by groups of men representing a capitalist system of society, against which system they protested."[59]

The following are examples of non-Christian or not specifically Christian grounds of objection from statements made by individual objectors.

I am a Socialist, and so hold in all sincerity that the life and personality of every man is sacred, and that there is something of divinity in every human being, irrespective of the nation to which he belongs. I cannot betray my belief in the brotherhood of man. To me, war is murder, and will only become impossible when an increasing number of those who share this conviction remain true to this belief, and refuse to take part in warfare, whatever be the pretext for which it is waged. [60]

While men continue to recognise national boundaries, and to fight for merely national ideals instead of strivingfor thegood of collective humanity, no such thing as Brotherhood is possible... Freedom and militarism are irreconcilable – hopelessly and eternally irreconcilable. Military service demands the renunciation of personal liberty and responsibility. It substitutes machines for men; regiments for individuals. [61]

Were I prepared to take sides in this fratricidal struggle I should not know whichtouphold,for,asfaraslcandetermine,allthebelligerentsareegually responsiblefor the war, having been led into it blindfold by a criminal system of secret diplomacy. As I am a believer in universal brotherhood I cannot support my country merely because it is my country. Nationality is a mere accident of birth. [62]

I hold that all war is immoral... In this war in particular, I am so convinced of the shameful betrayal of the common people of the world by their statesmen and rulers, in the preparation for, and the prosecution of this war, that I believe it to be my duty to the workers, to the International Brotherhood, and to my country to stand firmly against this war. [63]

For any nation to accuse another of committing atrocities or violating treaty obligations appears to be as consummate a piece of hypocrisy as that of a thief accusing robbers of dishonesty. Every nation has done things equivalent to these within the last thirty years. War is the greatest forcing ground for atrocities and falseness ever established by man. . . I love my country too much to countenance such a crime. I must be loyal to God and humanity and in being loyal to them I shall be serving in the highest way I know the real interests of our people and our country. [64]

The next two statements appeal to the objector's personal experience of the War. One objector, looking back at his experience in relief work in a devastated area in France, wrote:

If I had not lived in Sommeilles and known how the people who had suffered during a week of the German occupation felt about the suffering and bleeding to death of their own people, I should never have become a conscientious objector. Before I lived at Sommeilles I believed that war was wicked and avoidable, but there were several times when I

146

nearly enlisted. At Sommeilles I learnt that none of the issues mattered so much as stopping the appalling suffering.[65]

An officer who refused to continue his service stated at his court-martial in April 1918:

I am resigning my commission because I now believe that 'national responsibility' is an insufficient excuse for committing acts in the name of the nation, which no sane person would be guilty of as an individual. I believe that if I now continue to act as a soldier I should be guilty of the greatest crime it is possible for a human being to commit:. . . the unspeakable crime of resolving to destroy the lives of unknown persons whose individual characters – whether supremely good or evil – you have no means of knowing, but who, nevertheless, you must endeavour to kill for the solitary crime of being obedient to the laws of their own nation. The designed and intentional killing of any person against whose personal character you can make no charge is, I consider, murder of the worst possible kind.[66]

The Fate of the Law-Breakers

It was stated earlier in this chapter that 6,261 objectors were arrested. (This figure and the other figures with regard to arrested objectors are based on detailed records kept by the Conscientious Objectors' Information Bureau.) These men were arrested because they did not obey their call-up notices and, with the exception of a few cases where mistakes were made, they were called up because they were not legally exempt from military service and were therefore "deemed" to be soldiers in the reserve. There were four reasons why objectors could be in this position. Some objectors had ignored the tribunals, making no application for exemption. A considerable number of objectors had applied to the tribunals but had been refused any kind of exemption; they were therefore deemed to be soldiers. Another large group of objectors had been exempted only from combatant duties; they were therefore deemed to be soldiers to be employed only in non-combatant duties and those who refused to enlist for such service were arrested. The fourth group were objectors who had been exempted on condition that they engaged in various forms of civilian work considered to be of national importance. If an objector so exempted refused to comply with the conditions imposed on him by his tribunal he came under the following provision of the Military Service Act, 1916 (Section 3 (3)),[67] "Where a certificate of exemption ceases to be in force owing to... the failure to comply with the conditions on which the certificate was granted... the man to whom the certificate was granted shall" after a certain period, which was altered in an amending Act "be deemed to have been enlisted and transferred to the reserve in the same manner as if no such certificate had been granted".

The "appointed day" when the Act came into force was 2 March 1916 and a proclamation required men born in 1886 to 1896 inclusive to enlist at various dates up to the middle of the month. By the end of March at least ten objectors[68] had been arrested and by the end of April over a hundred.[69] The usual procedure was for the man to be arrested by the police and then taken before a magistrate where proof was given of his liability and refusal to serve and where he could make a statement. He was then formally fined £2 (very often never paid) and handed over to the military escort who took him to the unit to which he had been called up or to an army distribution centre.

Objectors who had received from the tribunals exemption from combatant service were nearly always called up to units of the Non-Combatant Corps; other objectors could be enlisted in units in any branch of the army. On arrival at his unit the objector, if determined to continue his resistance, soon committed some act of technical disobedience, such as refusing to salute or to wear khaki. He was now legally a soldier subject to the provisions of army law.

During the passage of the Military Service Bill some M.P.s had expressed the fear that an objector might become liable to the death penalty under the Army Act, but Government spokesmen had argued that this was very unlikely. These fears were aroused again when it was learned (by a letter thrown from a train) that seventeen objectors under detention in a unit of the Non-Combatant Corps had been sent out to France on 7th May 1916. Further groups of objectors were sent to France in May and early June. Various ministers were approached and the Prime Minister, H.H. Asquith, wrote to the Commander-in-Chief forbidding any executions without the knowledge of the Cabinet.[70] On June 22nd, in reply to a statement in the House of Commons that it was rumoured that death sentences had been imposed, the Under Secretary for War, H.J. Tennant, said that he had no information,[71] but on June 29th he stated "it was

148

the case that courts martial held in France had sentenced certain men professing conscientious objections to death for offences punishable by death under the Army Act. In all these thirty-four cases the sentence had been commuted to penal servitude by the Commander-in-Chief in France."[72]

In fact, four objectors had been sentenced on June 15th and thirty on June 19th.[73] In all cases the sentences were commuted to ten years' penal servitude (and none of those sentenced actually remained in prison after April 1919).[74] It seems clear that the passing of these death sentences was not an action instigated by the Government. The taking of objectors to France, the threats made to them of a possible death penalty for disobedience to military order there, and the pronouncement of the sentences were all part of the attempt of some army authorities to break the resistance of objectors in the army and to deter others from following their example. The objectors concerned did not cease their resistance because of the threat of the death penalty; one of those later sentenced to death wrote to his mother from France (in a letter smuggled out): "We have been warned today that we are now within the war zone, and the military authorities have absolute power, and disobedience may be followed by very severe penalties, and very possibly the death penalty... Do not be downhearted if the worst comes to the worst; many have died cheerfully before for a worse cause."[75] Though objectors were sent to France after June 1916 there were no more death sentences.

This imposition of death sentences was the most extreme result of deeming objectors to be soldiers. The army used its ordinary methods of inducing defaulters to be obedient soldiers and was confronted with persistent resistance of a kind which it had rarely previously experienced. The objectors were not mutineers but they were often persistent defiers of authority. Sentences of military detention brought no solution of the problem for "as drill was a part of detention, the conscientious objectors were perpetually committing further acts of disobedience behind prison walls, bringing liability for further punishment."[76] There were a considerable number of cases, particularly in the first few months, in which great physical brutality was used in attempts to compel obedience from the objector and a number of these cases led to questions in Parliament.[77] Much of this brutality was illegal and this was stated clearly in a letter from the War Office to army officers in

September 1916. Parts of this letter read: "I am commanded by the Army Council to inform you that it appears from reports which have been received by this Department that in certain instances attempts have been made by Commanding Officers to compel conscientious objectors to perform their military duties by ignoring acts of grave insubordination and ensuring compliance by physical means. I am, therefore, to request that you will be good enough to take steps to ensure that such a procedure, if it is taking place, immediately ceases. It should be clearly pointed out to all concerned... that any special treatment in the way of coercion other than by the methods of punishment laid down in the Army Act and King's Regulations is strictly prohibited, and that very serious notice will be taken of any irregularities in this respect which may come to light."[75] Illegal brutality had largely stopped before the date of this letter and was rare after it. But there were certain brutal punishments which were legal for soldiers on active service, the most notorious being Field Punishment No. 1 commonly known as "crucifixion" - this consisted in attachment by handcuffs, straps or ropes to a fixed object (often in a very painful position) for two hours on three days out of four for a maximum of twenty-eight days.[79] A number of objectors in army units abroad suffered from this and similar punishments. One objector commented: "I feel that we have no special cause to complain that we C.O.s were treated in this way – we were exceptional cases, and militarism was making a special effort to break us in. The shamefulness of the system lies in the fact that the ordinary soldier is liable to such punishment for the merest trivial offence."[80] The punishment of "crucifixion" was abolished in 1923 [81]

Under the Army Act the power of a Commanding Officer was limited to ordering what were considered minor punishments; serious punishments could be inflicted only as the result of the decision of a court-martial and an objector had the right to ask for trial by such a court. An important decision with regard to court-martial sentences was made in Army Order X issued on 27th May 1916. This stated: "Where an offence against discipline has been committed, and the accused soldier represents that the offence was the result of conscientious objection to military service, imprisonment and not detention should be awarded." Such a sentenced soldier was to be committed to the nearest civil prison.[82] This order was not a command, as courts martial had independent judicial powers, but it led ultimately to the award of sentences of imprisonment to nearly all objectors in the army who showed that they intended to continue their resistance.

At the time of the issue of Army Order X, 689 objectors had been arrested; at the end of June the figure was 1,451; at the end of July 1,715 objectors had been arrested and 866 had been sentenced by courts martial.[83] It was clear that these figures would go on increasing, for the process of application and often appeal to tribunals and the subsequent interval before call-up delayed the dates of arrest, and the second Military Service Act,[84] conscripting married men, which had become law on 25th May, led to large additional numbers of objectors. It was clear also that decisions of tribunals had resulted in the arrest of many objectors who would have been willing to perform civilian alternative service. At the end of June the Government decided to offer an alternative to imprisonment in what became known as the "Home Office Scheme."

In a statement in the House of Commons on June 28th the Prime Minister, H.H. Asquith, explained that the cases of soldiers coming under Army Order X would first be sifted to show that there was prima facie evidence of conscientious objection to military service. For this purpose court-martial and tribunal records would be consulted and, if these did not provide sufficient evidence, further investigations would be made, including enquiry by categorical questions to the objector concerned. In all cases when a prima facie case of conscientious objection was established the Army Council would depend on the advice of the Central Appeal Tribunal. The men whom this Tribunal held to be genuine conscientious objectors would be released on undertaking to perform work of national importance under civilian control. They would be transferred to Section W of the Army Reserve and would cease to be subject to military discipline so long as they continued to carry out satisfactorily the duties imposed upon them. The kinds and conditions of their work would be determined by a committee appointed by the Home Secretary. Objectors who refused information required from them, or who were rejected by the Central Tribunal, would remain in custody.[85]

By means of the Home Office Scheme a large number of arrested objectors were saved from any long period of imprisonment or detention. During the whole of the war period 3,750 objectors

151

were released to work under this scheme. Up to the end of July 1917 only 158 men had been considered by the Central Tribunal to be not genuine conscientious objectors. A considerable number of objectors refused to work under the scheme and at least 26 men returned from the scheme to prison either voluntarily or for some breach of the rules.[86] An account of the kinds of work and conditions which prevailed under the Home Office Scheme will be given later in this chapter.

Between the end of July 1916 and the beginning of 1917 the number of objectors who had been arrested had doubled, rising to a least 3,250;[87] in March 1918 the number was about 5,300[88] and in January 1919 over 6,100.[89] Not all those who were arrested received prison sentences, for example some were rejected or discharged from the army on medical grounds. About 350[90] objectors accepted combatant or non-combatant service. Those who accepted combatant service had been successfully coerced into abandoning their principles. This was probably true also of some of those accepting non-combatant service, but probably some found non-combatant service acceptable and had disobeyed the law because they had received no exemption and had been enlisted in combatant units. According to the Report of the Prison Commissioners, 3,733 objectors in the year 1917–18 were received into prison after court-martial sentences,[91] some individuals being received more than once. In March 1918 there were over 1,100[92] objectors in prison – nearly a fifth of the total male prisoners in local prisons. A month before the Armistice there were over 1,300 objectors in prison and 200 ex-prisoners in custody in the army awaiting another court-martial.[93]

A sentence of imprisonment did not release from the army: at the end of his sentence an objector was returned to his army unit where, if he again disobeyed orders, he spent a few days in the guardroom and then received a further sentence of imprisonment from a court-martial. The experience of Arthur Creech Jones, related in the House of Commons in 1939, was typical of the experience of objectors arrested in 1916 and not released under the Home Office Scheme. "I went before a court martial and... I was sentenced to a period of six months imprisonment with hard labour. I served my period... and was then taken back to my regiment, given a military order, court-martialled afresh and sentenced to one year's hard labour. That sentence I also served, I was again taken back to my regiment, given another military order, refused to obey, was court-martialled again, and had to go for two years' hard labour.

I served the two years' hard labour and went back to my regiment four months after the war was over. I still refused to obey military orders and was sentenced to another period of two years' hard labour... It was recognised all through this course that I was a perfectly genuine person. Nevertheless I had been caught up in the military machine and the 'cat and mouse' arrangements began to operate."[94]

During the whole period up to the end of July 1919 a total of 5,739 objectors were sentenced by court martial. 1,548 objectors were sentenced more than once and of these 893 were sentenced more than twice. The total number of court-martial sentences was 8,608.[95] There are no complete figures regarding the length of imprisonment of individuals, but the number of 1,548 objectors sentenced more than once probably corresponds roughly to the number in prison for more than a short period. At least 843 objectors were in prison for twenty months or more; [96] some were in prison for nearly three years. The majority of long-term prisoners were "absolutists", who were not willing to accept any conditions for exemption from military service, but there were objectors not deemed genuine by the Central Tribunal, some objectors returned from service under the Home Office Scheme, and probably some objectors who would have accepted some forms of alternative service though not service under the Home Office Scheme.

Most objectors in prison for long periods were serving sentences of imprisonment with "hard labour". This was considered by the law to be the most severe form of imprisonment and a two years' sentence, which, with full remission, lasted for twenty months, was the maximum sentence of imprisonment for any offence, longer terms of imprisonment being under the easier conditions of "penal servitude".[97] But, as the result of a succession of sentences, hundreds of objectors served, with brief intervals in guardrooms, total periods of imprisonment with hard labour exceeding twenty months. Considerable concern was expressed about the conditions of long-term imprisonment of objectors not only by those who agreed with the objectors, but by others, for example, in the churches and in labour organisations. The Government acted in two ways to mitigate the situation. First, it made certain concessions with regard to conditions of imprisonment. From May 1917 it was arranged that an objector returning for a second or subsequent term of imprisonment within a month of discharge from prison should not have to spend the first month of the sentence in solitary confinement, as was normally required in a sentence of imprisonment with hard labour. In December 1917 it was announced in Parliament[98] that objectors who had served sentences of twelve months' (with remission ten months') imprisonment, with hard labour should receive certain improvements of conditions under a prison rule originally made for Suffragette prisoners. These concessions included more periods of exercise, more frequent visits and permission to wear their own clothes.

It was also conceded that these objectors might converse during exercise periods, whereas previously prison rules had forbidden conversation at any time and the ingenious devices often used to communicate had led to punishment if discovered.

In the same announcement in Parliament a second kind of mitigation was described. The Home Office would, from time to time, report to the War Office names of objectors reported by the prison medical officers to be in a poor state of health and therefore recommended for release. Under this arrangement 50 objectors were released between December 1917 and April 1918,[99] and 8 had been released prior to the announcement. Over the whole period up to July 1919, 342 objectors were released from prison on medical grounds.[100]

The Armistice on 11th November 1918, did not lead to any immediate change in the position regarding imprisonment and over 300 objectors received court-martial sentences in the period of eight months after the Armistice.[101] In answer to the growing demand for the release of objectors the main Government argument was that such release would give them preference in obtaining employment in comparison with men in the Forces not yet demobilised. But at the beginning of April 1919 the Government announced in Parliament that all objectors and other prisoners sentenced under the Army Act would be released when they had served sentences amounting to two years (with remission twenty months). They would also be discharged from the army.[102] Under this arrangement a total of 843 objectors were released.[103] In June the War Office started a general commuting of the sentences of objectors[104] and at the end of July the Government announced in Parliament that all objectors had been released.[105] The number of objectors released under these arrangements in June and July was 221.[106] By early August all objectors who had been arrested had been both released and discharged from the army. One objector released in April records that he received a few weeks later "a form from the War Office recording that I had been discharged from the Army and stating that my behaviour had been so bad that if I ever attempted to join the Army again I would be subject to a sentence of two years' imprisonment with hard labour. The War Office certainly has no sense of humour".[107]

Nearly all the men who were sentenced by court-martial to imprisonment or detention, and who represented that their offence was the result of conscientious objection to military service, including those released to work under the Home Office Scheme, were disfranchised for a period by the Representation of the People Act, 1918,[105] which became law on 6th February 1918. Section 9 (2) of this Act disqualified the objector "during the continuance of the present war and a period of five years thereafter from being registered or voting as a parliamentary or local Government elector". This Section also disfranchised objectors who had received exemption from all military service, but an objector could avoid disfranchisement if he obtained from the Central Tribunal "before the expiration of one year after the termination of the war" a certificate that he had been engaged in ambulance or other recognised work abroad, or that he had satisfactorily complied with his condition of exemption, or that, having received absolute exemption, he had been engaged in work of national importance. Objectors who performed non-combatant service in the army were not disfranchised.

The clause disfranchising conscientious objectors was added to the original Bill by an amendment moved by Sir George Younger, a member of the Central Tribunal. In its original form the amendment disqualified all objectors except those who performed non-combatant service in the army; considerable opposition to this amendment was expressed in the House of Commons and over 170 M.P.s voted against it.[109]

Among the opponents of the amendment was Lord Hugh Cecil, who opposed it on Christian grounds. The following is part of his speech: "... it is the very essence of the conscientious objector's position that he says the State has, up to a certain point, undoubtedly authority over him, but that in this respect he is bound to obey a higher law than the law of the State – a religious law or a moral law which prohibits him from obeying the law of the State...

To those who in all sincerity think it is wicked to fight in war – for them it is wicked to fight in war – it ceases to be a mere delusion, and it becomes truly operative upon the conscience... What, then, can we say in this case? We can only say their conscience is mistaken. I say it... I am sure they are thoroughly and utterly mistaken, but are you going to disqualify people and punish them for being mistaken in their opinions? If you do you are surely back again to the old familiar ground of religious persecution. . . I am most anxious that this country should maintain the proposition that there is a higher law, that we view with admiration any appeal to that higher law, and that we will not listen to the doctrine that the State's interest is to be supreme, but on the contrary that we will make our authority conform to the higher standard and keep the State within its proper function, and within its proper scope... It is in the belief in that higher region of allegiance, which imposes upon us something more than the State can ask from us, and which gives us something that the State can never give, that we should vindicate the great cause that we have in hand. We are fighting, we sometimes say, for civilisation. I would rather say that we are fighting that civilisation may remain a Christian civilisation, and certainly, according to a Christian civilisation, it is wrong to force the conscience of the sincere... I hope, therefore, that this Amendment will be rejected. I hope it, first of all, because it is a retrospective law, and so contrary to all sound principles of legislation. I hope it still more because it appears to enforce the law of the State as superior to the moral law..."[110]

Forms of Alternative Service

The conscientious objectors who served in various ways as an alternative to combatant service in the forces were in three main groups – those performing non-combatant duties in the army; those doing various forms of civilian work according to the conditions of their exemptions; those who had been arrested and were released to work under the Home Office Scheme.

According to John W. Graham's estimates there were about 3,400 conscientious objectors performing non-combatant duties in the army – 3,300 in the Non-Combatant Corps and 100 in the Royal Army Medical Corps.[111] The Non-Combatant Corps was formed soon after the introduction of conscription. In the words of an official description, it "was formed with a view to the employment of soldiers who have a conscientious objection to the taking of life. They are therefore required to perform any and all duties other than those of a combatant nature, namely the bearing of arms and instruction in the use thereof."[112] Members of the Corps were engaged, both at home and abroad, in a variety of jobs; these included stretcher-bearing, work in hospitals, quarrying, loading and unloading goods, and sanitary work.

The official definition of duties "of a combatant nature" was confined to "the bearing of arms and instruction in the use thereof." This was explained on several occasions by spokesmen for the War Office when questions were asked in the House of Commons about objectors punished for refusing to handle munitions. For example, in December 1917 the Under Secretary of State for War, refusing to interfere with the arrest of nine men in France for this reason, stated "men in the Non-Combatant Corps can be called upon to carry out any duties other than those of a combatant nature".[113] A considerable number of cases occurred in which men in the Corps were punished for refusing duties which offended their consciences. For example, at Abancourt, in December 1917, seventeen men were sentenced to eighty days or more Field Punishment No. 1 "for refusing to handle military supplies."[114] Men in the Corps could be sent for employment with other corps provided that it was in a "non-combatant capacity."[115]

Some conscientious objectors in the Royal Army Medical Corps disobeyed military orders when they were transferred to combatant units at various times after mid-1917. A number of these men had voluntarily enlisted before the introduction of conscription and had therefore no legal exemption from combatant service. To meet this situation, according to a statement by the Under Secretary for War in the House of Commons in July 1917, "Instructions have been issued under which any men drafted from the Royal Army Medical Corps who claim to be conscientious objectors to combatant service will have their claims investigated" by the War Office "and if they are substantiated the men will be transferred either to the Non-Combatant Corps or back to the Royal Army Medical Corps."[116] However, these instructions were not always observed – in the summer of 1918 about fifty men in Egypt were sent by court-martial to military prisons for refusing on conscientious grounds to accept transfer to combatant units.[117]

According to the estimate made by John W. Graham there were about 6,250 conscientious objectors who were exempted on condition that they performed various forms of civilian work of national importance and who complied with this condition by performing such work. This estimate is the total of estimates of 1,200 working under the Friends' Ambulance Unit, 200 working under the Friends' War Victims Relief Committee, and 900 doing a variety of kinds of work according to the decisions of tribunals.[115]

The Friends' Ambulance Unit, whose membership was not confined to Quakers, was formed soon after the outbreak of war "to render voluntary non-military service in relief of the suffering and distress resulting from war". In October 1914 it started work in the dressing-sheds at Dunkirk. Its work in France and Flanders included the staffing of hospitals, hospital ships, ambulance trains, ambulance convoys, and recreation huts, and relief work among Belgian refugees; at the time of the Armistice there were 640 members (including nurses) engaged in this work. The Unit also had, at various times, up to about 400 members working in four hospitals in Britain.

A large majority, but not all, of the members of the Unit were pacifists. Under conscription those members working abroad were given a collective exemption by the War Office.

The General Service Section of the Friends' Ambulance Unit was formed early in 1916 as the result of the decisions of tribunals to give conditional exemption to a number of conscientious objectors, members of, or closely associated with, the Society of Friends, who were willing to work for the Unit and who, for various reasons, could not be absorbed into ambulance work. This Section of the Unit was responsible for 442 men at the time of the Armistice. The majority were working in agriculture but there were some employed in educational and welfare work and in various other types of work. Some members, in addition to other conscientious objectors, worked under two other Quaker organisations – the Friends' War Victims Relief Committee and the Friends' Emergency Committee for the Assistance of Germans, Austrians and Hungarians in Distress.[119]

"The difficulties about work of national importance became so great that the Government set up a Committee to advise Tribunals about it, and to endeavour to bring the work and the workers together."[120]

The Committee on Work of National Importance was set up by the Board of Trade in March 1916. Its membership included a pacifist M.P. – Edmund Harvey – and its first chairman was H.W. Pelham, so that it was commonly known as the "Pelham Committee".

Over the whole of the war period it was responsible for the work of 3,964 conditionally exempted objectors, including 1,400 Christadelphians. The Committee did not supersede the authority of tribunals; it advised a tribunal when the tribunal chose to consult it about a case and the advice was not mandatory. The Committee made out a list of recognised occupations which it recommended to tribunals as being of national importance. Its preliminary list was as follows: Agriculture – farm labour, market gardening and fruit growing, seed raising, agricultural machinery making and repairs, agricultural education and organisation. Forestry – cutting, hauling and preparing timber. Food Supply – flour milling, sugar refining, margarine production. Shipping – mercantile marine, shipbuilding and repairing. Transport – railways and canals, docks and wharves, cartage connected with these. Mining, Education, Public Utility Services – sanitary services, local authorities, fire brigades, civil hospitals, work-houses, infirmaries, asylums.[121] John W. Graham comments that men under the Pelham Committee "were many of them employed under tolerable circumstances, and doing, if not their proper work, at least something useful under conditions of practical freedom."[122] This comment, in its phrase "if not their proper work", refers to one problem concerning conditions of alternative service which was important both during the First World War and later. This problem was whether the authorities, in dealing with objectors exempted on condition that they did some form of civilian work, should be primarily concerned with getting the most socially valuable service possible from the objector or whether they should be primarily concerned with equalising his position in certain respects with the position of men conscripted into the forces. In some cases the pursuit of either of these aims might lead to the same result but in many cases it did not. Objectors with special skills might sometimes be most usefully employed by being left in their existing jobs or by being allowed to take other jobs in their own occupation. But this need involve no sacrifice on their part and it was often felt that it would put them in an unfair and too easy position. During the First World War conditions were often imposed obliging an objector to make some obvious sacrifice such as changing his job or his occupation, changing his place of residence or working at a distance from his home, or working for lower remuneration or for the same pay as men in the Forces.

The "Home Office Scheme", as was explained earlier in this chapter, was devised for men who had not received exemption from military service, had been forcibly enlisted in the army, and had there disobeyed orders for conscientious reasons. Over the whole of the war period 3,750 objectors were released to work under this scheme.

The scheme was organised by a committee appointed by the Home Office under the chairmanship of William Brace, M.P: its official name was "The Committee for the Employment of Conscientious Objectors." The men were employed in groups in a number of settlements or work centres in various parts of Great Britain. In March 1917, for example, there were over 2050 men distributed in at least twenty-five centres; their work included agriculture, land reclamation, timber cutting, quarrying, road making, work in waterworks, building, and work in a variety of industries.123 Soon after this date timber cutting ceased to be included in the scheme, as many men had objected to cutting timber for the supply of the army and the War Office had assumed control of all timber supplies.124 At the large settlement in the evacuated convict prison on Dartmoor, in May 1917, "The 850 'C.O.s' are engaged for 9½ hours daily under the supervision of prison warders on the garden and 200-acre farm at Princetown; on work in connection with waterworks; on land reclamation; on the upkeep of the prison; on indoor industries; and on communal service."125

In December 1917 the Committee arranged that men employed by it might, at the Committee's discretion, after twelve months' good conduct and industry, qualify for individual employment in work of national importance.

There were two main criticisms of the Scheme by objectors and their supporters. One criticism was that the men under the Scheme were bound by many rules, often employed and organised under semi-penal conditions, and liable to be returned to prison or the army for trivial infringements of regulations. The other criticism was that they were often employed in work of low utility and with inefficient equipment and methods of work. A communication sent to the War Cabinet in September 1917 on behalf of a large number of the men in the Scheme stated: "Practically all who accepted the

Scheme did so in the belief that work of real social value would be provided thereunder... By far the main portion of the work provided under the Scheme has been economically wasteful, penal in character and such as could only be devised for punishment rather than utility. For instance, at Dartmoor, the work allotted to the conscientious objectors is exactly the same as that given out to the convicts..."[126] In addition to a number of men who were sent back to prison or the army for breach of regulations, a number returned there voluntarily because of dissatisfaction with the conditions of the Scheme.

Objectors' Views on Alternative Service

It will be clear from even this brief description of forms of alternative service that objectors performed service of many different kinds. The views of objectors on the rightness or wrongness of alternative service cannot be divided neatly between views that alternative service was right and views that it was wrong. The caution given in the description of the grounds of objection must be repeated here: the decision on what, if any, alternative service he could rightly perform was the objector's individual decision, and no general statements can cover all the reasons for the decisions of individual objectors. Some objectors were able to do work for which they felt a keen interest and concern; others accepted work which did not satisfy these conditions but which did not offend their consciences. The desire to serve their fellows at a time of great suffering and stress was the predominant motive of some objectors; in contrast, some objectors felt that to refuse to co-operate in the prosecution of the war and the machinery of conscription was the most valuable action that they could take. Some objectors were much influenced by the wish to share the risks and hardships of the men at the front; others felt that any available work in or near the front line was too directly assisting in the prosecution of the war to be possible for them.

Many objectors whose objection was confined to the actual taking of life were able to work conscientiously in the Non-Combatant Corps. Among these objectors were many Plymouth Brethren; in this denomination, while there was general objection to combatant service, members were divided on the matter of non-combatant service. In contrast, the Christadelphians objected to all military service. One of the circularised decisions of the

Central Tribunal stated "The Tribunal was satisfied that the basis of faith common to Christadelphians forbade them to take service under military authority".[127] A large majority of Quaker objectors refused all military service. The Seventh-Day Adventists had a general objection to combatant service; they had no objection to non-combatant service as such but their position was complicated by their refusal to work on Saturday, which they regarded as the divinely appointed Sabbath. For example, fourteen of their members who had accepted service in the Non-Combatant Corps, on condition that their Sabbatarian scruples were respected, were excused work on Saturdays for eighteen months, and were then ordered to work on their Sabbath and severely punished for their refusal to do so.[123]

It was quite common for tribunal members to show understanding of an objection to actual killing but to fail to understand an objection to all military service. Some of the reasons for objection to non-combatant service were given in two letters sent to the Government in March 1916 on behalf of the No-Conscription Fellowship and the Friends' Service Committee. The first letter quoted a statement of the Under Secretary for War "It will shortly be possible, I hope, to employ conscientious objectors in setting free any men fit for combatant service who may at present be employed on non-combatant duties."[129] This statement, said the letter, "bears out the contention that by undertaking non-combatant service a conscientious objector would thereby be assisting in the prosecution of war and directly releasing others to do that which he feels it is not right for him to perform himself. As to R.A.M.C. duties as an alternative, our members, with a few exceptions, can only regard the work of such a Corps as part of the military machine, its primary function being to maintain the efficiency of the fighting forces, and re-equip the wounded for further fighting."[130] The second letter, written after the establishment of the Non-Combatant Corps, stated: "The Government should understand that the men for whom we speak, can, under no circumstances, become part of this corps, which we observe will be under the control of the War Office and in every sense part of the military machine."[131]

Many objectors who were unwilling to perform any kind of military service found that they could conscientiously perform various forms of civilian alternative service. Some objectors were willing to do any form of civilian work allowed to them. (They would, presumably, have refused to work in the manufacture of munitions but, to the best of my knowledge, such work was never ordered as a condition of exemption.) In contrast, some objectors were willing to do some forms of civilian work but not others and there were various considerations which might affect this discrimination. It was very difficult, if not impossible, to draw a clear line between work which assisted in the prosecution of the war and work which did not so assist, and different individuals drew the line in different places. For example, in relation to the work of the Friends' Ambulance Unit, while many members were willing to assist in any of its activities, some felt that they could do ambulance work only for badly wounded men who would not be returned to active service and some felt that they could not do any ambulance work which was part of the medical services of the army. Another difficulty was that, as the exemptions of men of military age in work of national importance were constantly being revised, the employment of an objector might easily lead to the call-up of a man previously exempted. In the words of one objector: "He could not work on the land in order to release men for the army or engage in an industry in order to make it easier for the Government to secure men for military purposes."[132] Some objectors had a strong sense of vocation and were unwilling to perform forms of alternative service which did not satisfy this. Some objectors felt that they could not conscientiously accept any type of employment which had conditions specifically forbidding activities in peace propaganda: for example, such activities were forbidden by the regulations of the Home Office Scheme.

The objectors known as "absolutists" were so called because they were not willing to accept anything short of the "absolute" exemption which tribunals were empowered to give under the Military Service Act. A few absolutists were given this exemption but a much larger number were arrested and in prison for relatively long periods, as they refused to accept release under the conditions of the Home Office Scheme. The considerations already mentioned in relation to discrimination between forms of civilian employment influenced some objectors who adopted the absolutist position. Some other important elements in absolutist views were conviction of the evil nature of conscription and the desire to oppose it uncompromisingly and thus to help to end it; the view that individual conscience should not be subject to a bargain with the authorities; and indignation at the way in which so many objectors had been denied by tribunals the rights granted to them by Parliament. The following are five examples of absolutist views from the statements of individual objectors.

I am not prepared to undertake any form of national service as a condition of exemption from the provisions of the Military Service Act. To do so would be a bargain with a thing I believe to be utterly wrong. To consent to do one thing in order to be excused from doing another is to acquiesce in the second thing and become a party to it. I cannot acquiesce in or become a party to war. [133]

I regard conscription as a fearful evil to England – putting the whole manhood of the Nation and therefore, in effect, all opinion as well as institutions, whether religious or secular, under the control of the military. For this reason I feel bound never to acquiesce in its establishment, nor to compromise with it in any way that may facilitate its establishment. 234

I am eager and willing to help my country at all times, and I consider that, as a schoolmaster, I was already rendering my best service. To change that for some less useful occupation, or to submit to any form of military conscription would be, for me, to barter my conscience, to betray those who have suffered and died for this cause in times past, and to assist in the fastening of conscription upon this unhappy country. [135]

Whether calculated or not, the tendency of alternative service has been to split up the spiritual forces opposing militarism as a whole, and to weaken them in individuals... Alternative service almost inevitably means the sending of someone else to do what one will not do one's self. Even if there is no conscientious objection on the part of the person displaced, there is something revolting to one's sense of what is just and honourable. [136]

I more and more see that (in most cases) it is not the actual work involved in alternativism but the willingness to work in part of the war-organised machine that Absolutists are Up against. By going to prison we are protesting to the utmost against this thing which we regard as evil. [137]

The Ending of Conscription

The Military Service Act, 1916, and the Acts amending it conscripted those concerned "for the period of the war."[138] In order to define the meaning of this phrase an Act was passed ten days after the

Armistice – the Termination of the Present War (Definition) Act, 1918.[139] This Act empowered the Crown, by Order in Council without parliamentary sanction, to declare both a date for the official termination of the war with any State and a date for the official termination of the war as a whole. Under this Act the war with Germany was officially terminated on 10th January 1920 and the war as a whole was officially terminated on 31st August 1921, and six months after the latter date the Military Service Acts automatically lapsed without the necessity of legislation to repeal them.[140]

After the Armistice the continuance of conscription became an actively debated issue. In the campaign preceding the General Election of 14th December 1918 the Labour Party's Manifesto demanded "the complete abolition of conscription" and the Prime Minister, Lloyd George, stated at a meeting: "The Military Service Act was passed in order to meet a great emergency. When the emergency is passed, when the need is passed, the Act will lapse and there is no intention to renew it".[141]

However, the Government was not willing to abolish conscription immediately and in March it introduced the Bill which became the Naval, Military and Air Force Service Act, 1919.[142] The Government desired the power to retain men already serving; it did not wish to continue compulsory enlistment and stated that "no conscript has been called up since 11th November."[143] The Act, which became law on 16th April, empowered the responsible authorities in the three Services to retain any men who "cannot consistently with the public interest be released" for any period not extending beyond 30th April 1920. At the end of the period of retention the man must be "discharged with all convenient speed" and in no case later than three months after 30th April 1920. Demobilisation was in fact spread over a considerable period but on 20th May 1920 the Secretary for War, Winston Churchill, stated in the House of Commons that orders had been issued for all conscripts to be released.[144]

In the period after the Armistice different groups of conscientious objectors were differently affected. Objectors performing non-combatant duties in the Army came under the general scheme of demobilisation; in September 1919 there were still between 1500 and 2000 men in the Non-Combatant Corps.[145] Immediately after the Armistice, all the work of tribunals regarding applications and appeals was suspended, with provision for resumption in case of any resumption of compulsory enlistment.[146] A Government spokesman stated in February 1919 that work under the Pelham Committee had by then ceased.[147] By the end of April all the men employed under the Home Office Scheme had been released.[148] By August, as had already been described, all other objectors who had been arrested had been both released from prison and discharged from the army.

References

1   Hirst, Margaret E. *The Quakers in Peace and War* p. 244
2   Hayes, Denis *Conscription Conflict* p. 31
3   Ibid. p. 132
4   Ibid. p. 146
5   Hirst, op. cit. pp. 489–492
6   Hart, Liddell, *A History of the First World War* pp.52–56
7   Trevelyan, G.M. *A Short History of England* p. 544
8   Hayes, op. cit. p.148
9   Debate 18.1.1915 quoted in Hayes, op.cit. p. 152
10   5 & 6 Geo.5.c.60
11   National Registration (Amendment) Act, 1918. 7 & 8 Geo. 5. c. 60
12   Hayes, op. cit. p. 157
13   Hart, op. cit.
14   Hayes, op. cit. p. 194
15   Hayes, op. cit. pp. 202, 203, 205 5 & 6 Geo. 5. c. 104
16   Hayes, op. cit. p. 205
17   5 & 6 Geo.5.c.104
18   Sec. 1, Subsec. 1
19   44 & 45 Vic. c. 58
20   45 & 46 Vic. c. 48
21   Sec. 2 Subsec. 1
22   Sec. 2 Subsec. 3
23   6 & 7 Geo. 5. c. 15
24   6 & 7 Geo.5.c. 15
25   7 Geo. 5. c. 12
26   7 & 8 Geo. 5. c. 26
27   7 & 8 Geo. 5. c. 66
28   8 Geo. 5. c. 5
29   Hart, op. cit .
30   Hansard 19.1.16 Plt Series 1 p. 9
31   Ibid. pp. 10–11
32   Hansard 5.1.16   Plt Series 1 p. 1
33   Hansard 19.1.16 Plt Series 1 p. 19
34   Ibid. pp. 9 & 10

35   Ibid. p. 10
36   Hansard 19.1.16 Plt Series 3 p. 1
37   Ibid.
38   Hansard 19.1.16 Plt Series 2 pp. 1–2
39   Hansard 25.1.16 Plt Series 3 pp. 29, 30 ,31
40   Ibid. p. 32
41   Ibid.
42   Ibid.
43   Hansard 19.1.16 Series 3 p. 26
44   Ibid.
45   Ibid. Series 2 p. 23
46   Hansard 18.1.16 Series 1 p. 7
47   Hansard 19.1.16 Series 2 p. 18
48   Ibid. p. 22
49   Ibid. p. 23
50   Ibid. p. 19
51   Graham John W. *Conscription and Conscience*, 1922 pp. 344–352
52   Soc. of Friends Service Committee "The Absolutists' Objection to Conscription" pp. 22–23, in Graham op. cit. p. 91
53   Ibid. p. 23
54   Ibid. p. 25
55   Catchpool, T. Corder *On Two Fronts*, p. 109
56   Quoted in "Tribunal" 11.1.1917
57   Quoted in "Tribunal" 19.4.1917
58   Fellowship of Reconciliation Newssheet 25.7.1916
59   No-Conscription Fellowship "Troublesome People" p. 6
60   Tribunal 14.3.1916
61   Ibid . 8.3.1917
62   Ibid. 20.12.1917
63   Ibid.
64   Ibid. 4.10.1917
65   *We Did Not Fight* p. 140
66   Tribunal 2.5.1918
67   5&6Geo.5.c.104
68   Tribunal 6.4.1916
69   Ibid. 4.5.1916
70   Graham op. cit. p. 113
71   C.O. Hansard 15.5.–13.7.1916 p. 39–40
72   C.O. Hansard p. 40
73   Hirst, op. cit. p. 512
74   Names of men sentenced in Graham op. cit. pp. 115–116
75   No-Conscription Fellowship "Troublesome People" p. 29
76   Graham op. cit. p. 111
77   Examples in Graham op. cit. Chapter 4
78   Quoted in Graham op. cit. pp. 149–150
79   Army Act 1881 Sect. 44 Quoted in "Tribunal" 8.6.1916
80   *Troublesome People* pp. 27–28
81   Hirst, op. cit. p. 512

82 Tribunal 1.6.1916
83 Tribunal 1.6.1916, 6.7.1916 & 3.8.1916
84 6 & 7 Geo. 5. c. 15
85 Summary of Statement in Graham op. cit. pp. 222 - 223
86 From Graham op. cit. pp. 350–351
87 Tribunal 3.1.1917
88 Tribunal 21.3.1918
89 Tribunal 23.1.1919
90 Graham op. cit. p. 350
91 Report of Prison Commission 1917–18 in Tribunal 3.4.1919
92 Tribunal 7.3.1918
93 Tribunal 10.10.1918
94 Hansard 16.5.39. Vol. 347 No. 103 Col. 1697
95 Graham op. cit. p. 348
96 Graham op. cit. p. 350
97 For description of prison conditions at the time see Graham op. cit.,
    ch. 8 and S. Hobhouse & Fenner Brockway (edited) *English Prisons
    Today* 1922
98 Tribunal 13.12.1917
99 Tribunal 18.4.1918
100 Graham op. cit. p. 350
101 Tribunal 10.7.1919
102 Hansard 3.4.19 C.O. Hansard 90 p. 2040
103 Graham op. cit. p. 350
104 Tribunal 12.6.19
105 Tribunal 7.8.19
106 Graham op. cit. p. 350
107 Fenner Brockway *Inside the Left*, p. 119
108 7 & 8 Geo.5.c.64
109 Hansard 20.11.1917 & 21.11.17 C.O.'s Hansard Vol. 2 No. 48
110 Speech in House of Commons C.O.'s Hansard Vol. 2 No. 48 pp. 575,
    579, 580
111 Graham op. cit. p. 349
112 Tribunal 26.4.17 Official letters to men under Home Office Schemes
113 Hansard 10.12.17 C.O. Hansard 51 p. 616
114 Hansard 16.4.18 C.O. Hansard 66 p. 769
115 Hansard 9.4.18 C.O. Hansard 65 p. 757
116 Hansard 18.7.17 C.O. Hansard 38 p. 462
117 Graham op. cit. pp. 153–154, Tribunal 22.5.19
118 Graham p. 349
119 For the work of these three organisations see:
    Hirst op. cit. pp.494–503 & 511
    Meaburn Tatham & James E. Miles *The Friends' Ambulance Unit
    1914–1919*
    A. Ruth Fry *A Quaker Adventure* Friends War Victims Relief Committee
    Anna B. Thomas (compiled) St Stephen's House Friends Emergency
    Committee
120 Graham op. cit. pp. 98–99

121 Ibid. p. 101 (list quoted)
122 Ibid. p. 242
123 Tribunal 5.4.17 (official account quoted)
124 Ibid. 19.4.17
125 Ibid. 10.5.17
126 Ibid. 13.9.17
127 Case No. 2 (R77) Quoted in Denis Hayes "Challenge of Conscience" p.373
128 Graham op. cit. pp. 152–153 Tribunal 4.4.18
129 Hansard 29.2.16
130 Tribunal 8.3.16
131 Ibid. 15.3.16
132 Ibid. 14.12.16 Court martial statement
133 Ibid. 13.7.16
134 "The Absolutist's Objection to Conscription" Letter from Guardroom, May 1917, p. 12
135 T.A.O.C. p. 16 Court martial statement April 1917
136 Catchpool op. cit. p. pp. 154 & 155
137 *The Absolutist's Objection to Conscription* pp. 15–16
138 5 & 6 Geo. 5. c. 104 Sect. 1 (1)
139 8 & 9 Geo.5.c.59
140 Hayes op. cit. p. 330
141 Hayes op. cit. pp. 318–319
142 9 & 10 Geo. 5. c. 15
143 Hansard 6.3.19 C.O. Hansard 87a p. 2008
144 Ibid. 20.5.19
145 Tribunal 2.10.19
146 Report of the Local Govt. Board 1918–1919 pp. 128–129
147 Hansard 19.2.19 C.O. Hansard No. 86 p. 1087
148 Tribunal 1.5.19

Chronological Table of Acts Relating to Compulsory Military Service during the First World War

Date		
1881	Army Act	44 & 45 Vic. c. 58
1882	Reserve Forces Act	45 & 46 Vic. c. 48
1915	National Registration Act	5 & 6 Geo. 5. c. 60
1916	Military Service Act	5 & 6 Geo. 5. c. 104
1916	Military Service (Session 2) Act	6 & 7 Geo. 5. c. 15
1917	Military Service (Review of Exceptions Act)	7 & 8 Geo. 5. c. 12
1917	Military Service (Conventions with Allied States) Act	7 & 8 Geo. 5. c. 26
1918	National Registration (Amendment Act)	7 & 8 Geo. 5. c. 60
1918	Representation of the People Act (Section 9)	7 & 8 Geo. 5. c. 64
1918	Military Service Act	7 & 8 Geo. 5. c. 66
1918	Military Service (No. 2) Act	8 & 9 Geo. 5. c. 5
1918	Termination of the Present War (Definition) Act	8 & 9 Geo. 5. c. 59
1919	Naval, Military and Air Force Service Act	9 & 10 Geo. 5. c. 15

CHAPTER 5

Compulsory Military Service During the Second World War

Contrasts with the Position in the First World War

There were several important contrasts between the Second World War and the First World War with regard to both military conscription and conscientious objection to it.

(1) In the Second World War the process of conscription was well planned and systematic. The possibility of war had been foreseen for several years. Compulsory military training was enacted three months before the War and compulsory military service was enacted on the day of the outbreak of war.

(2) During the Second War the range of legal compulsion was much wider than during the First War. For the first time in our history women were conscripted for military service. Legal compulsion was applied not only with regard to military service but with regard to the civilian work of large numbers of men and women and with regard to part-time assistance in Civil Defence and fire-watching. (These non-military compulsions will be discussed in Chapter 7.)

(3) After the First War compulsory enlistment ceased at the Armistice and the last conscripts were discharged eighteen months after that date. After the Second War compulsory enlistment of men continued for fifteen years and the last conscripts were not discharged until May 1963 – eighteen years after V E Day.

(4) The number of men conscientious objectors in the Second War was at least three times the number in the First War – 48,000 or more as compared with about 16,000.

(5) In the National Service (Armed Forces) Act of 1939 the wording of the provision exempting conscientious objectors avoided the ambiguity of the corresponding wording in the Military Service Act of 1916.

(6) The tribunals under the National Service Act were concerned only with decisions as to the exemption of conscientious objectors; they had no functions with regard to the other kinds of exemption dealt with by the tribunals of the First War. These tribunals had members appointed by a central government department; the chairmen of local tribunals were county-court judges (or their Scottish equivalent) and there was no army representative present at tribunal sessions to present the case against exemption. For all these reasons the tribunals, in general, treated those applying for exemption as conscientious objectors more judicially and more efficiently than did their predecessors during the First War.

(7) By 1939 the public were more familiar with the views of conscientious objectors than the public of the First War and there was much less antagonism to objectors. Both Parliament and the administrators of the law were concerned to fit objectors into useful work which they could conscientiously perform and to minimise the occasions for law-breaking. A much larger proportion of objectors was exempted without being involved in any breach of the law.

(8) In the Second War, though there were between three and four thousand convictions of conscientious objectors for offences against the law of compulsory military service, only a few of these objectors were in prison for periods longer than a year.

The Coming of Conscription

The introduction of conscription in May 1939 came after at least three years of fear of the possibility of a major war and of increase of armaments in preparation for that contingency. R.B. McCallum wrote that the settlement made at the end of the First World War "provided a system for the preservation of peace, which held out some prospect of success and for which it could be claimed that it was much better than no system at all. This system broke down by the beginning of 1936. Its end can be defined by two precise and clearly marked events, the occupation of Addis Ababa by Italian troops and the occupation of the Rhineland by German troops."[1] The first of these events was a successful act of military aggression despite economic sanctions applied by members of the League of Nations; the second was a breach of the provisions of the Treaty of Versailles. The world disarmament conference of 1932–1934 had failed.

Adolf Hitler, who became German Chancellor in January 1933, had taken Germany out of the League of Nations later in that year and had imposed military conscription in March 1935 (another breach of the Treaty of Versailles).

The imposition of conscription in Germany followed closely the publication in Britain on 4th March 1935 of a "Statement Relating to Defence". A.J.P. Taylor described this Statement as "a landmark in British policy. It announced that the British government had ceased to rely on collective security and were now going to rely on the older security of armed force... Hitler used the British White Paper as his excuse for restoring conscription in Germany on 16th March. The National government, on their side, accepted this as a justification for their new line of policy."[2] The same historian wrote that 1936 "saw the beginning of British rearmament, though few people appreciated this at the time. Real events happened in the back rooms. In November 1935 the armament plans were recast in order to prepare for a great war, not merely to fill a few gaps. Effective rearmament began soon afterwards."[3]

Between 1935 and Spring 1939 the expenditure on the armed forces was more than quadrupled, the largest increase being for the Air Force.[4] In mid-1939 the total number of men in the Armed Forces was 480,000.[5] After the Munich Crisis of September 1938 the serious development of Civil Defence services started and in January 1939 a Voluntary National Service Campaign was inaugurated. This Campaign asked for recruits both for the Armed Forces (and their reserves and Auxiliary Services) and for Civil Defence and certain other civilian services. Up to the end of

August 1939 nearly one and a half million men and women had enrolled, about 75% of them for whole-time or part-time Civil Defence.[6]

In February 1939 a target was set for the expansion of the army to thirty-two divisions – six regular and twenty-six territorial. The army chiefs' opinion was that "once the army really began to grow, they could not rely on voluntary recruits. They therefore wanted some measure of compulsion to provide a reservoir of half-trained men for the army of the future."[7] On 31st March the British Government guaranteed military assistance in case of a threat to Polish independence and made an alliance with the Polish Government. On 26th April the Prime Minister, Neville Chamberlain, announced in the House of Commons that compulsory military training would be introduced. He stated: "We cannot but be impressed with the view, shared by other democratic countries and especially by our friends in Europe, that despite the immense efforts this country has already made by way of re-armament, nothing would so impress the world with the determination of this country to offer a firm resistance to any attempt at general domination as its acceptance of the principle of compulsory military service, which is the universal rule on the Continent."[8]

The following day the Prime Minister moved a resolution: "That this House approves the proposal of His Majesty's Government to introduce as soon as possible a system of compulsory military training as announced on 26th April; regards such a system as necessary for the safety of the country and the fulfilment of the undertakings recently given to certain countries in Europe."[9] The Leader of the Opposition, C.R. Attlee, moved for the Labour Party an amending resolution which "regrets that His Majesty's Government, in breach of their pledges, should abandon the voluntary principle which has not failed to provide the man-power needed for defence, and is of opinion that the measure proposed is ill-conceived, and, so far from adding materially to the effective defence of the country, will promote division and discourage the national effort."[10] The Government resolution was carried by 376 to 145 votes:[11] those voting against the resolution included, in addition to members of the Labour Party, members of the small Liberal Party and some other Opposition M.P.s. On 8th May the Second Reading of the Military Training Bill was carried by 387 to 145 votes.[12]

The General Legal Provisions Concerning Compulsory Military Service

The Military Training Act, 1939,[13] which became law on 26th May, provided, with certain exceptions, that all male British subjects ordinarily resident in Great Britain, while between the ages of twenty and twenty-one years, should be registered for military training. Men so registered were liable, after medical examination, to be called up at any time within a year of their registration, but provision was made for postponement of liability for training. They were to be enlisted for four years as militiamen under the Territorial and Reserve Forces Act, 1907,[14] and their service was to commence with six months' continuous military training, which could not take place elsewhere than within the United Kingdom or the Channel Islands. Equivalent training could be given in the Navy or Air Force. Under this Act 240,000 men were registered on 3rd June and the first conscripts were called up on 1st July. The Act was to remain in force for three years: it expired on 26th May 1942. But on the outbreak of war its provisions were superseded by Section 12 of the National Service (Armed Forces) Act, 1939, and those registered or liable to be registered under the Military Training Act came instead under the provisions of the National Service Act.

The Bill which became the National Service (Armed Forces) Act, 1939,[15] passed through all its stages in two days, 2nd and 3rd September, and received the Royal Assent on 3rd September – the day on which Britain declared war on Germany. Only 7 MPs voted against the motion to introduce the Bill. Including the two tellers, these nine MPs comprised the four members belonging to the Independent Labour Party and in addition four Labour members and one Independent, three of these being Quakers.

The Act covered male British subjects resident in Great Britain or subsequently entering the country; it provided for the making of Royal Proclamations imposing liability for service with the Armed Forces on men in any age group between the limits of eighteen and forty-one. The Act contained provisions making the Ministry of Labour and National Service responsible for administering compulsory registrations of those liable for military service, compulsory medical examinations of those registered, and the service of "enlistment notices" on those who had been medically examined. This procedure meant that the military authorities had no control over the man liable for service until the date of enlistment specified in the enlistment notice: after that date he was deemed to be enlisted in the Force specified in the notice "until the end of the present emergency." Men liable for service were allowed, usually at the time of registration, to express a preference for naval or air force service, but there was no guarantee that the preferred service would be available.

Men in certain classes were exempted from liability for service under the Act: these classes included men already members of the Armed Forces; men who were severely mentally ill or mentally deficient; men registered as blind; and any man who was "a man in holy orders or a regular minister of any religious denomination". All other men were subject to compulsory registration but many who registered were not called up for military service because they were in one of the following classes. (1) Men who were classified in Grades III or IV at their medical examinations – about 16% of those examined over the whole period 1939–46 – were not normally called up for service.[16] (2) A large number of men were not called up because of the importance of their civilian work to the war effort or to necessary civilian services. A Schedule of Reserved Occupations had been in preparation since 1937 and it came into force at the outbreak of war. Men above the age specified for each occupation in the Schedule were, in general, ineligible for acceptance into the Armed forces either as volunteers or under the National Service Acts. The Schedule was constantly revised in the light of the changing man-power requirements of the Armed Forces and industry. This system of block reservations was supplemented by provision for individual deferment of calling up, and after the end of 1941 individual deferment gradually replaced block reservation.[17] (3) The legal provisions for conscientious objection (in the next Section of this chapter) exempted many objectors from liability to be called up and a considerable number of other objectors never became liable because they refused to take their medical examination. (4) The Act allowed an individual to have his liability for service postponed on account of exceptional hardship and during the war period about 214,000 men were allowed postponement for this reason.[18]

The National Service (Armed Forces) Act, 1940,[19] made it clear that the exemption from liability of those already members of the Armed Forces did not apply to members of the Local Defence

Volunteers (later the Home Guard) whose services were part-time. The National Service Act, 1942,[20] passed in December of that year, reduced to seventeen years and eight months the age at which men could be compulsorily registered but the lowest age at which they could be called up remained at eighteen.

During the period of the war a total of thirty-nine registrations were held under the National Service Acts 1939 and 1942. Men between the ages of twenty and twenty-three were registered in 1939, men between twenty-three and thirty-five were registered in 1940, and by the middle of 1941 registration had covered all men between twenty and forty-one. After that date, first men aged nineteen and then men aged eighteen were registered and from the middle of 1943 all registrations were of men aged between seventeen years eight months and eighteen.[21] Official figures show that, including those registered under the Military Training Act, 1939, a total of 8,355,500 men were registered during the war period.[22] The total number of men posted to the Armed Forces under the Military Training Act and the National Service Acts was 2,985,000 up to the end of June 1945.[23] (The total number of men in the Armed Forces in mid-1945 was 4,653,000,[24] not including those in the Home Guard.)

To meet the urgent need for more men in the Civil Defence Forces two kinds of provision were made in the National Service Act, 1941,[25] passed in April. The Act conferred a right on men liable for military service to express a preference for Civil Defence. The Act also provided that any man liable for military service could be compulsorily enlisted in one of the Civil Defence Forces – the Police War Reserve, the National Fire Service, or the Civil Defence Reserve. About 30,000 men were posted to the Civil Defence Forces under these provisions, mainly between April 1941 and July 1943.[26]

Later in the War somewhat similar methods were used to meet the urgent need for men in mining. From September 1942 certain men were allowed to opt for underground work in coal or other mines as an alternative to military service and about 22,300 men made this choice. From December 1943 to the end of May 1945 certain young men liable for military service work were compulsorily allocated to underground work in coal mines – they were commonly known as "Bevin boys" (after Ernest Bevin, Minister of Labour and National Service). The allocation was made by ballot and about 21,800 men were allocated in this way.[27]

The National Service (Foreign Countries) Act, 1942,[28] enabled conscription to be applied to British subjects in foreign countries: the Act was applied only in Egypt. The Allied Powers (War Service) Act, 1942,[29] provided for the making of Orders in Council imposing on men of military age of any allied country a liability to be enlisted in the British Armed Forces if they did not enlist in their own national forces. Orders in Council were made applying these provisions to the nationals of nine allied countries.[30]

The National Service (No. 2) Act, 1941,[31] passed in December, provided that by Royal Proclamation men between the ages of forty-one and fifty-one could be made liable for military service. A proclamation was made in March 1942 making men liable between the ages of forty-one and forty-six, "but, in fact, only doctors and dentists in the age groups 41 to 45 were considered for service in the Armed Forces and these were offered commissions in their professional capacity."[32] Men between forty-one and fifty-one were registered not under the National Service Acts but under the Registration for Employment Order of March 1941.[33] This Order was made under the Defence Regulations and was one of the measures of control of civilian employment: (it will be described in Chapter 7). Under this Order nine registrations were held between April 1941 and September 1942 and a total of 1,933,000 men were registered.[34] Thus, in practice, most men over forty-one were not compulsorily called up for full-time military service. But many men above this age were compulsorily enrolled for part-time service in the Home Guard.

The Home Guard (at that time entitled the Local Defence Volunteers) was formed in May 1940 to meet the threat of invasion. Service in the Home Guard was part-time, not exceeding forty-eight hours in every four weeks, and was unpaid. Legal provisions relating to the Home Guard were made under the Defence Regulations. For the first twenty months of its existence the Home Guard included only volunteers – over a million men enrolled soon after its formation. But the National Service (No. 2) Act, 1941,[35] provided for the making of Defence Regulations compelling part-time service in the Forces, and in January 1942 power was given to the Minister of Labour and National Service or any National Service Officer to direct any male British subject in Great Britain to enrol in the Home Guard.[36] In practice compulsion was applied only to men between the ages of eighteen and fifty-one. Men in the classes exempted in the National Service Act, 1939, and legally recognised conscientious objectors were exempted from liability for enrolment, and there was provision for consideration of medical fitness and for appeal against enrolment on grounds of exceptional hardship. Between January 1942 and September 1944, when compulsory enrolment was suspended, about 946,200 directions to enrol were issued. The Home Guard was disbanded at the beginning of 1946.[37]

The National Service (No. 2) Act, 1941,[38] made women subject to compulsory military service for the first time in British history. (Some M.P.s opposed this extension of conscription.) The legal provisions with regard to exempted classes, postponement on grounds of hardship, and conscientious objection applied to women in the same way as they applied to men. But in the case of women two additional classes were exempted from compulsory military service: no married woman (unless legally separated from her husband) and no woman with a child of her own under the age of fourteen living with her was liable for compulsory recruitment. A Royal Proclamation under the Act immediately (December 1941) made women liable between the ages of twenty and thirty-one and in January 1943 the lower age limit was changed to nineteen. In practice the age range was much smaller: "Only women born in the years 1918 to 1923 inclusive (broadly those aged 19 to 24 inclusive at the date of call-up) were, in fact, called up."[39]

There were no registrations of women under this Act; women between the ages of twenty and thirty-one had already been compulsorily registered for civilian employment under the Registration for Employment Order of March 1941[40] and those aged nineteen were registered in 1942 under the same Order. Those women who were made liable for military service were, in practice, compelled either to enter one of the Women's Auxiliary Services – the Women's Royal Naval Service, the Auxiliary Territorial Service, or the Women's Auxiliary Air Force – or to enter certain specified forms of civilian employment. In the first period of conscription for women they could opt for work in Civil Defence: later this option was withdrawn. Throughout the whole period of conscription women could opt for certain priority civilian employments including munitions work, work in agriculture, and domestic work in hospitals. A considerable number of women were already engaged in work considered to be of vital national importance (including not only certain industrial work but also teaching and nursing) and such women were not asked to change their employment: some others had their obligations deferred. As a result of all these circumstances only about 126,000 women were posted under the Act to the Women's Auxiliary Services (compared with the 461,000 total membership of these Services in mid-1943). The compulsory enlistment of women in these Services was suspended in January 1944 and ended in May 1945 with the end of the war with Germany.[41] The liability of women for compulsory military service was formally ended under the National Service Act, 1947.[42]

The Law of Conscientious Objection

In the debate on the Second Reading of the Military Training Bill the Prime Minister, Neville Chamberlain, who had been a member of the Birmingham Tribunal in the First World War, made it clear that the Government accepted the principle of legal exemption for conscientious objectors and wished to avoid the kind of attempt to coerce them which occurred so frequently in the First War. He stated: "We all recognise that there are people who have perfectly genuine and very deep-seated scruples on the subject of military service, and even if we do not agree with those scruples at any rate we can respect them if they are honestly held. But there is a great variation in the way in which people are affected by scruples of this kind. There is the most extreme case, where a man feels it his duty to do nothing even to aid or comfort those who are engaged in military operations, although it may well be that those military operations have been forced upon us by the aggression of some other country. Probably that is the smallest of all classes of conscientious objectors. But it often happens that those who hold the most extreme opinions hold them with the greatest tenacity. We learned something about this in the Great War, and I think we found that it was both a useless and an exasperating waste of time and effort to attempt to force such people to act in a manner which was contrary to their principles". After describing the proposed categories of exemption and the proposed tribunal system he stated: "We can lay down the general line on which we want the tribunals to proceed, but it is impossible to do more than that in a general way, and the particular circumstances of each individual must be investigated and judged by the local tribunal before it is possible to decide into which of the categories, if any, that individual ought to be allocated.

I want to make it clear here that in the view of the Government, where scruples are conscientiously held we desire that they should be respected and that there should be no persecution of those who hold them."[43]

The provisions relating to conscientious objection were substantially similar in the Military Training Act, 1939,[44] and the National Service (Armed Forces) Act, 1939.[45] In the National Service (Armed Forces) Act, 1939, the description of a conscientious objection was much wider than that in the Military Service Act, 1916,[46] which had described it as a "conscientious objection to the undertaking of combatant service" and which had led to frequent misunderstanding of the law by tribunals (see Chapter 4 p137). Section 5 of the 1939 Act stated: "If any person liable under this Act to be called up for services claims that he conscientiously objects – (a) to being registered in the military service register, or (b) to performing military service, or (c) to performing combatant duties, he may, on furnishing the prescribed particulars about himself, apply in the prescribed manner to be registered as a conscientious objector in a special register to be kept by the Minister". Such an application gave a right to be "provisionally registered" in the register of conscientious objectors; the application was usually made when the man registered with his age group, but it could also be made at any time up to two days after taking his medical examination. This procedure covered all men between the ages of eighteen and forty-one, as they were all registered under the National Service Acts. Men aged between forty-one and fifty-one, who registered in 1941–42 under the Registration for Employment Order, had not the opportunity at the time of their registration to apply for provisional registration as conscientious objectors. But men aged between forty-one and forty-six and who, from January 1942 onwards, were considered with regard to their possible compulsory enrolment in the Home Guard, were allowed to apply for registration. The law regarding determination of their position by tribunals applied to objectors liable for compulsory enrolment in the Home Guard in the same way as it applied to objectors liable for military service under the National Service Acts.[47]

Section 5 of the 1939 Act gave the Minister power to register provisionally as a conscientious objector any man liable for military service who refused or failed to apply for registration, if the Minister considered there were reasonable grounds for believing the man to be a conscientious objector. This provision was used by the Minister on a number of occasions to deal with the cases of objectors who refused on principle to register with their age groups and, although the Act provided penalties for refusal to register, only eight objectors are known to have been prosecuted for this offence.[48]

After provisional registration as a conscientious objector the next stage was application to a local tribunal. Such written application had to be made "within the prescribed period" (usually fourteen days) and "in the prescribed manner". The objector had to state whether he objected to being registered in the military service register or to performing military service or to performing combatant duties – he could claim objection to any one or two or to all of these. After the decision of the local tribunal an applicant, if aggrieved by the decision, had the right of appeal to the Appellate Tribunal (usually within twenty-one days). The constitution of tribunals was laid down in Part I of the Schedule to the Act. (It will be described in the next Section of this chapter.) Unlike the tribunals of the First World War, the tribunals under the National Service Act were concerned only with applications on grounds of conscientious objection.

The possible decisions of tribunals were stated in Section 5 as follows and applied to both local tribunals and the Appellate Tribunals. The tribunal, if satisfied "that the ground upon which the application was made is established, shall by order direct either – (a) that the applicant shall, without conditions, be registered in the register of conscientious objectors; or (b) that he shall be conditionally registered in that register until the end of the present emergency, the condition being that he must until that event undertake work specified by the tribunal, of a civil character and under civilian control,... or (c)... that he shall be registered as a person liable under this Act to be called up for service but to be employed only in non-combatant duties; but, if not so satisfied, shall by order direct that his name shall... be removed from the register of conscientious objectors." It was also provided that "No determination of a local tribunal or the Appellate Tribunal made for the purposes of this Act shall be called in question in any court of law". Men registered by tribunals under (a) or (b) were not liable to be called up for service and men registered under (c) were to be excluded by the authorities in the Services from employment in combatant duties.

In administering these provisions, tribunals which registered an objector under (b) often specified more than one type of work; in that case, if the objector performed any of the alternative types of work specified, he was complying with his condition of exemption.

Under this Act, men registered for non-combatant duties in the Forces, though protected, were not included in the register of conscientious objectors. But this position was altered in the National Service Act, 1941,[49] which provided that in future such men should be included in the register and that men already registered for non-combatant duties should be transferred to the register. Except for this amendment, all the provisions just described remained unaltered throughout the war period.

Official figures show that in the one registration under the Military Training Act, 1939, and the thirty-nine registrations during the war period under the National Service Acts a total of 67,047 men were provisionally registered as conscientious objectors. This figure was 0.8% of the total of 8,355,500 men registered during the same period; in other words the figure was about 1 in every 125 men registering. In the early registrations the proportions were much higher: in the pre-war registration the proportion was 1.8%; in the first three registrations of the war period – up to February 1940 – the proportions were successively 2.2%, 2.1%, and 2.0%. These were all registrations of men aged between twenty and twenty-four. In the next four registrations between March and May 1940, when men aged between twenty-four and twenty-eight were registered, the proportions were all between 1% and 2%, declining at each registration. From June 1940 the proportions were all below 1% and from April 1941 they were all below 0.5% . In the period from September 1943, when the registrations were of men aged between seventeen years eight months and eighteen, the proportions were all under 0.3%.[50] As probable influences on the decline of the proportions registering as objectors, two facts may be noted: the increasing age of those registering at every registration up to June 1941 and the serious war position starting with the German invasion of Denmark and Norway in April 1940.

The figure of 67,047 is not the complete total of men who registered provisionally as conscientious objectors. It does not include men between the ages of forty-one and fifty-one who registered provisionally, mainly on account of liability for enrolment in the Home Guard. To the best of my knowledge, there are no published figures as to the number of these registrations. Objectors in this age group who appeared before tribunals are included in the total figures of applications to tribunals but the official figures do not distinguish these men from other objectors.

The total number of original applications of men considered by local tribunals was 59,192 up to the end of June 1945[51] There were thus some 8,000 men who had been provisionally registered as objectors and who had not appeared before tribunals. Some of these men were presumably recently registered objectors awaiting a tribunal hearing at the end of June 1945 and there were some provisionally registered objectors who failed to make application to a tribunal. But most of the objectors who remained provisionally registered, without determination of their status by a tribunal, were men who were exempted or deferred because of the nature of their work. Such exemption or deferment was not affected by provisional registration as conscientious objectors and usually such objectors were not called to appear before tribunals unless or until their exemption or deferment ended (unless they appeared on account of liability for service in the Home Guard).

When women were made liable for compulsory military service in the National Service (No. 2) Act, 1941,[52] they were given under the Act exactly the same rights of conscientious objection as had been given to men. The Act also provided that no woman called up for service would be required actually to use any lethal weapon, or to take part in the actual use of any lethal weapon, unless she signified in writing her willingness to do so.

It was explained in the preceding Section of this chapter (p179) that in practice there were very important differences between compulsion for military service for men and for women and these differences affected also the comparative position of male and female conscientious objectors. Women registered originally under the Registration for Employment Order, 1941.[53] Women in the age group proclaimed "as liable for military service – originally women aged between twenty and thirty-one, later women aged between nineteen and thirty-one – were allowed to apply for registration as conscientious objectors. To the best of my knowledge, there are no official figures of the total number of women who applied to be registered as objectors.

The only published figures with regard to the numbers of women conscientious objectors relate to those women who appeared before tribunals; up to the end of December 1945 local tribunals considered 1,074 original applications from women,[54] and there were no additional women objectors after that date. But this figure is no indication of the total number of women objectors, as many such objectors never appeared before tribunals. The official report of the Ministry of Labour and National Service stated: "Women in the age groups concerned who applied to be registered as conscientious objectors were offered useful work in industry if they were not already regarded as in reserved employment. Only where such work was refused, or where they specially so requested, were their applications placed before the Tribunals."[55] Denis Hayes, in his book on conscientious objection, stated: "If a woman claimed to be a Conscientious Objector the interviewing of ficer would offer her the alternative of comparatively innocuous civil work (such as work in agriculture or horticulture or as a ward-maid in a hospital), and it was only if she declined these that her case was formally dealt with under the National Service Acts and referred to a Local Tribunal for decision."[56] With regard to those women objectors who did appear before tribunals, the official figures are as detailed and informative as the figures for men objectors.

Tribunals and their Decisions

Conscientious Objectors' Tribunals were first set up under the provisions of the Military Training Act, 1939,[57] and several local tribunals held sessions before the outbreak of war. The tribunals already set up were continued under the very similar provisions of the National Service (Armed Forces) Act, 1939.[58]

The general provisions relating to tribunals were contained in Section 5 and Part I of the Schedule of this Act and in regulations made by the Minister of Labour and National Service under Section 19. The Schedule stated: "Local tribunals shall be appointed for such districts as the Minister may determine, and shall consist of a chairman and four other members appointed by the Minister: the chairman shall be a county court judge, or, in the case of a local tribunal for a district in Scotland, a sheriff or sheriff-substitute." With regard to the Appellate Tribunal, the Schedule stated: "Each division of the Appellate Tribunal shall consist of a chairman and two other members appointed by the Minister." The chairman should be a person nominated in England by the Lord Chancellor and in Scotland by the Lord President of the Court of Session. The Schedule provided that each division of the Appellate Tribunal should have one member, and each local tribunal at least one member, "appointed by the Minister after consultation with organisations representative of workers." With regard to the membership of all tribunals the Schedule stated that "the Minister shall have regard to the necessity of selecting impartial persons."

After the extension of compulsory military service to women, provision was made for including women in the membership of tribunals. An order made in January 1942[59] increased the membership of a local tribunal to seven, two of whom should be women, at least one man and one woman to be appointed after consultation with workers' organisations. The membership of each division of the Appellate Tribunal was increased to five, two of whom should be women, at least one man and one woman to be appointed after consultation with workers' organisations. In the case of local tribunals only four members, and in the case of a division of the Appellate Tribunal only two members, in addition to the chairman, were to take part in any particular session. There should be at least one woman member officiating when any case of a woman was being heard but the absence of any women members in such a case should not invalidate the proceedings.

During the war period there were nineteen local tribunals in Great Britain – twelve in England, two in Wales, and five in Scotland; several of these tribunals did not function for the whole of the period. The tribunals covered large areas and their number contrasts with the number of over two thousand local tribunals during the First World War, when the unit was usually the area of a borough or district council. There were two divisions of the Appellate Tribunal established in 1939 – one for England and one for Scotland; later four further divisions were established, making a total of six divisions in Great Britain – four for England, one for Wales and one for Scotland. This number contrasts with the eighty-three appeal tribunals, usually for county areas, of the First World War. Under the National Service Act, 1939, there was no body corresponding to the central Appeal Tribunal of the First World War: there was only one possible stage of appeal instead of two.

The following sets of figures regarding the number of applications to, and the decisions of, tribunals are all extracted from official figures which were compiled by the Ministry of Labour and National Service (though not all were published by the Ministry).

For the period between the first meeting of a tribunal in July 1939 and the end of June 1945 the total number of original applications by men considered by local tribunals was 59,192. The decisions of the local tribunals were as follows:[60]

	Number	Per Cent
Registered unconditionally as Conscientious Objectors	2,810	4.7
Registered conditionally as Conscientious Objectors	22,059	37 3
Registered for non-combatant duties in the Forces	16,784	28.4
Total registered as Conscientious Objectors	41,653	70.4
Name removed from register of Conscientious Objectors	1 7,539	29.6

These figures include an unrecorded number of men who applied to tribunals on account of their liability for service in the Home Guard; in their cases any decision except removal from the register exempted them from Home Guard duties and any condition of exemption imposed was suspended unless or until they became liable for service under the National Service Acts.

The Ministry of Labour and National Service published the following adjusted figures relating to orders made by tribunals with regard to men who had appeared before local tribunals in the period between July 1939 and the end of June 1945.[61] (These figures cover the same 59,192 men as were covered in the previous table.) The figures show the original decisions of local tribunals adjusted for (a) the effect of appeals to the Appellate Tribunal; (b) references to tribunals on the question of compliance with conditions or registration, under the National Service Act, 1941. (The figures are not adjusted for the effect of applications to the Appellate Tribunal by men sentenced by court-martial or for refusal of medical examination; these applications will be described in a later section of this chapter.)

	Number	Per Cent
Registered unconditionally as Conscientious Objectors	3,577	6.1
Registered conditionally as Conscientious Objectors	28,720	48.5
Registered for non-combatant duties in the Forces	14,691	24.8
Total registered as Conscientious Objectors	46,988	79.4
Name removed from register of Conscientious Objectors	12,204	20.6

Both the applicant and the Minister had an unrestricted right of appeal to the Appellate Tribunal against the decision of the local tribunal but, in practice, the Minister very rarely appealed. Up to the end of June 1945, of men who had appeared before local tribunals 31% had appeared before the Appellate Tribunal; in addition, some applicants were awaiting the hearing of their appeals. The Appellate Tribunal had heard appeals from nearly 58% of men whom the local tribunal had removed from the register of conscientious objectors and from 39% of men whom the local tribunal had registered for non-combatant duties in the Forces.[62]

The Appellate Tribunal could give any of the four types of decision available to the local tribunal: it could therefore worsen the position of the applicant and did so in the case of about 280 men. But, on balance, applicants benefited greatly from the exercise of their rights of appeal.

A comparison of the adjusted figures, quoted above, with the figures for original decisions of local tribunals over the same period, quoted on p187, shows that decisions on appeal added over 5,300 to the number of men registered as conscientious objectors, and decreased by nearly 2,100 the number of men registered for non-combatant duties in the Forces.[63]

The second type of adjustment made in the adjusted figures must now be explained. The National Service Act, 1941,[64] provided in Section 5 that, if the Ministry considered that a conditionally registered objector was not complying with his conditions of registration but had "reasonable excuse" for his non-compliance, they could refer his case back to his local tribunal. If the tribunal found a breach of condition with reasonable excuse it could (a) register the objector unconditionally, or (b) vary the existing condition or substitute a new condition, or (c) leave his exemption unchanged. The objector could appeal to the Appellate Tribunal which could make any of the same decisions. This legal provision gave a useful opportunity of varying the exemption in cases where circumstances, for example ill-health or lack of suitable employment, had prevented an objector from observing the conditions of his exemption. Up to the end of June 1945 under this provision local tribunals had heard nearly 5,000 cases and the Appellate Tribunal had considered appeals in about 400 cases.[65]

A comparison of the adjusted figures quoted on p188 with the figures for original decisions of local tribunals over the same period, quoted on p187, shows that the joint effect of decisions under the procedure just described, and of the decisions of the Appellate Tribunal on ordinary appeals, was to add about 770 men to the number unconditionally registered as objectors and to add about 6,660 men to the number conditionally registered. In addition, a large number of conditionally registered objectors had their conditions varied.[66]

The adjusted figures show that nearly four-fifths of the men who appeared before tribunals had their objections given some legal recognition. In the large majority of cases the legal exemption given apparently satisfied the conscience of the objector. This was a great achievement, not only from the point of view of the objector, who was able to give, and often was very keen to give, what he considered useful service without offending his conscience, but also from the point of view of the Ministry of Labour and National Service, which preferred that a man who refused to fight should be contributing in other ways to the war effort or to the maintenance of essential community services.

It is impossible to know how many men accepted the tribunal's decision with a bad or doubtful conscience but it is likely that there were a considerable number of such men among those rejected by the tribunals (that is, removed from the register of conscientious objectors). The consciences of some such men and also of some men registered for non-combatant duties in the Forces were relieved by the right given at some period to opt for service in Civil Defence or for underground work in mines (see p177). Two groups of men did not accept the decision of the tribunal. On the one hand, a considerable number of men, at some time during the War period, renounced their status as conscientious objectors and performed combatant service in the Forces and there was legal provision for those taking this action. (The are no published figures as to the total number of such men.) On the other hand, a considerable number of men illegally refused to obey the decision of the tribunal. On this matter the statistics are incomplete, being based mainly on cases known to the Central Board for Conscientious Objectors. On this basis some 3,300 objectors, up to the end of June 1945, are known to have been sentenced for offences arising from their conscientious objection to obeying the decision of the tribunal; this figure is about 5.5% of the total number of men appearing before tribunals. Some 2,950 – 3,000 men objectors are known to have been sentenced for refusal of military service or of combatant service; this figure is about 11% of the total of about 26,900 men whom the tribunals made liable for either combatant or non-combatant duties in the Forces.[67] A much smaller number of men were sentenced for the offence of failing, without reasonable excuse, to comply with their conditions as conditionally registered objectors. The Ministry of Labour and National Service reported that up to the end of June 1945, 294 men were sentenced for this offence;[68] this figure is about 1% of the number of men conditionally registered.

The figures for women objectors will now be described briefly. The Ministry of Labour and National Service published the following figures,[69] adjusted in the same way as their adjusted figures for men, of orders made with regard to women who had appeared before local tribunals up to the end of December 1945 (there were no additional women objectors after that date). The total number of orders was 1,074.

	Number	Per Cent
Registered unconditionally as Conscientious Objectors	105	9.8
Registered conditionally as Conscientious Objectors	776	72.2
Registered for non-combatant duties in the Forces	30	2.8

Total registered as Conscientious Objectors	911	84.8
Name removed from register of Conscientious Objectors	163	15.2

A comparison of these figures with the figures for original decisions of local tribunals over the same period shows that 115 women were added to the number registered as conscientious objectors by decisions of the Appellate Tribunal.[70]

The few women who were registered for non-combatant duties in the Forces were not, in fact, called up for service as there was not a non-combatant section in any of the Women's Auxiliary Services. These women were instead directed to some civil employment under the powers given by the Defence Regulations. It has already been explained that a large number of women objectors never appeared before tribunals (see p179). Those who did have tribunal hearings were not necessarily an average sample of women objectors. Denis Hayes, who had considerable knowledge of the facts, wrote: "Those whose cases were submitted to the Tribunals were usually the unconditionalists or those who hoped to get either a condition of particular work or a choice of work that the Ministry of Labour officials were unwilling to give."[71] Official figures show that, up to the end of 1946, 88 women conditionally registered as objectors were sentenced for failing, without reasonable excuse, to comply with their conditions of exemption.[72] All women objectors conditionally registered had been released from their conditions by the end of 1947.[73] In Chapter 11 there will be a further discussion of the tribunal system over the whole period 1939–1960.

The Views of Objectors

During the period between the two World Wars, questions of peace and war and problems of international relations were very widely discussed among the British public. Experience of the First World War led, among many people, to a great reaction against war, desire for limitation of armaments, and to faith in the possibility of the newly founded League of Nations. Among strong supporters of the League – in the League of Nations Union, the Labour Party and elsewhere – the fundamental divergence of view between pacifists and other peace-lovers caused little difficulty in the 1920s. But the Japanese invasion of Manchuria in 1931 and the Italian invasion of Abyssinia in 1935 raised in an acute form the question of approval or disapproval of the use by the League of military sanctions against an aggressor State. In the "Peace Ballot" of 1934 – 35, in which the questions answered related to support of the League and allied matters, about 11l/2 million people expressed their opinions. On the question of the use of economic sanctions by the League 10 million voted in favour and only 635,000 against. But on the question of the use of military sanctions 2,350,000 voted against their use (though, of course, the majority of these voters were not pacifists) compared with 6,780,000 who voted in favour of their use.[74]

The question of approval or disapproval of the use of military force also arose in an acute form with regard to the Spanish Civil War of 1936–1939 and with regard to possible military resistance to aggressive acts of the German Nazi Government, and in both these cases many pacifists found themselves divided from others with whose general political views they were in sympathy. Thus in the inter-war period, and particularly in its later years, the rightness or wrongness of pacifism had been much considered and debated not only in general but in relation to particular situations.

At the outbreak of the First World War there existed in Britain no specifically pacifist organisations other than those religious denominations whose tenets included objection to military service. The Fellowship of Reconciliation, an undenominational association of Christian pacifists, was founded in December 1914.

The No-Conscription Fellowship, founded in November 1914 with a membership open to all conscientious objectors, was dissolved in 1919. In 1921 the War Resisters International was founded; it was an international pacifist body with affiliated sections in many countries and isolated members in others. In Britain the No More War Movement was founded in 1921 and became the British section of the War Resisters International; (it later merged with the Peace Pledge Union). The statement signed by all members included the words: "I am determined not to support or take part in any war, international or civil." In October 1934 the Rev. Dick Sheppard appealed in the press for men willing to renounce war to communicate with him. As a result of the response to this appeal the Peace Pledge Union was founded in 1935, and since 1936 its membership was open to women also. The pledge made by each member was "I renounce war and I will never support or sanction another" and there was no other requirement with regard to religious or political opinions. By 1939 there had also been formed a number of pacifist groups within religious denominations (sometimes including also members outside the denomination). These groups had been formed among Catholics, Anglicans, Presbyterians, Methodists, Baptists, Congregationalists, Unitarians, and members of the Churches of Christ. In 1939, after the introduction of conscription, the Central Board for Conscientious Objectors was formed to advise and assist conscientious objectors of all types of opinion (including non-pacifists). It had no individual membership and did not engage in pacifist or anti-war propaganda. All the British pacifist groups just described and also the Society of Friends and some other bodies were "constituent bodies" of the Board.

Any generalisations about the views of conscientious objectors in the Second World War must be made with as many reservations as were made with regard to the objectors of the First World War. (See Chapter 4, p142). A former member of the South Western Tribunal, Professor G.C. Field, wrote in 1944 that the "great divergence between the positions taken up by different conscientious objectors is the first thing that experience on a Conscientious Objectors' Tribunal teaches one. On the Tribunal of which I was a member we listed adherents of fifty-one different religious bodies. And, though these did not all differ sharply from one another in the grounds of their Pacifism, a considerable number did. In addition, there were those, comparatively few in number, whose objections were based on ethical or humanitarian grounds independently of any religious beliefs. And there were a few whom we classified as political objectors, and a few, also, who could only be described as objectors on aesthetic grounds. All these agreed on the one practical conclusion of refusing to participate in actual fighting. But the further conclusions that they drew often differed as widely as the premises from which they drew them."[75]

Official tribunal statistics give no information about the grounds of objection of applicants. But the South Western Tribunal (covering Gloucestershire, Somerset, Wiltshire, Devon and Cornwall) listed the religious affiliations of men appearing before the Tribunal, and the kinds of objection of those without religious affiliations, for the two years 12th March 1940 to 20th March 1942. The number of men appearing before the Tribunal in these two years totalled 3,353[76] (over two-thirds of the number for the whole period of the War). More than 90% of applicants were listed as having religious affiliations but, as a good many Anglican applicants had only nominal affiliations with their church, the figure for active affiliation was probably about 80%.

Nearly 900 applicants – over a quarter of all applicants – were members of Second Adventist bodies: 439 Brethren ("Plymouth Brethren"), 166 Christadelphians, 155 Jehovah's Witnesses, and the remainder from five or more other bodies. The common feature of belief of members of these bodies was belief in the imminent Second Coming of Christ and in their duty to gather the faithful out of the world to await this Second Coming. This attitude involved separation, in greater or lesser degree, from the affairs of the world; for example, neither the Brethren nor the Christadelphians exercised the vote or sued in the courts for debts. Jehovah's Witnesses do not vote and would not sue each other for debt. However, they are not enjoined not to use the ordinary legal processes and therefore might sue non-Witnesses in some circumstances.

While all Christadelphians objected to all military service, combatant or non-combatant, some objectors from the Brethren were willing to perform non-combatant duties in the Forces. The Jehovah's Witnesses (the International Bible Students' Association) refused all military service, believing that their covenant with Jehovah involved an attitude of neutrality in all warfare between the nations of the world. While their principles did not necessarily involve objection to civilian work as an alternative to military service, yet many Witnesses did have this objection because they felt called to undertake religious work full-time or for a considerable part of their time and were not prepared to abandon it on the orders of a tribunal. Objectors from these three bodies refused to describe themselves as "pacifists" but, in my view, for all practical purposes they should be included in this description, their objection being to military service under the State, not to military service in a particular war.

The largest denominational group of applicants to the South Western Tribunal were the 662 Methodists – nearly a fifth of the total number of applicants. This proportionate importance was not typical of the whole country, owing to the strength of Methodism in South West England. The other denominational groups (not already mentioned) with more than 100 applicants were 531 Anglicans (practising or nominal), 302 Quakers, 187 Baptists, and 143 Congregationalists. In these denominations, except the Quakers, pacifism was not a tenet of the denomination as a whole.

Several examples of statements from "Christian pacifist" objectors in the First World War were given in Chapter 4. The following example is part of a tribunal statement in the Second World War.

I believe in the Fatherhood of God and the Brotherhood of Man. I hold that all men are brethren and I cannot take part in war against my brethren in God. I would add that God is a God of love and that he has revealed to mankind in His Son, Jesus Christ, our Lord, His way and His method of overcoming evil. This method is the method of love, best exemplified by our Saviour on His Cross. I am convinced that the Cross is the central point in the Christian faith, and that it shows forth the triumph of Love over the power of evil. Since I am accepting Christ as my Master I must adopt His methods, and I am convinced that the coming of the day when Christ shall reign supreme in the world can only be achieved by the method of that sacrificing and redemptive Love which our Lord Himself showed forth in His Life, His Death and His Resurrection.[77]

Among the smaller religious groups of applicants to the South Western Tribunal were 64 Catholics and 30 adherents of non-Christian religions – 18 Jews and 12 Buddhists and Hindus. Most Catholic objectors used different arguments from those used by other Christian objectors: they related their views to the doctrine of the Catholic Church as to the conditions which a war must fulfil in order to be a "just" war, a war in which it would be right for a Catholic to take part. These objectors considered that under modern conditions of warfare war did not fulfil the conditions of "just" war – it involved moral and physical evils so great as to exceed any possible legitimate gain to either side.

The South Western Tribunal listed 61 applicants as being members of communities, living and working together. These included members of the Society of Brothers (Hutterian) who had two "Bruderhofs" in the region. This society was founded in Central Europe in the sixteenth century and adopted the Christian pacifist position from the beginning. During the 1930s a number of German members of the Society came to Britain, some of them expelled by the Nazi Government. In Britain their "Bruderhofs" attracted some British members.

It is difficult to generalise about non-religious objections: they were very diverse and the only points in common were that they were not based on the obligations of religious belief and that they led to conscientious objection to fighting in the War. But there was a broad distinction between pacifist and non-pacifist objection.

The following example of a non-religious pacifist objection is quoted from two statements made in Court.

I am uncompromisingly opposed to war because it is futile and insane and totally incapable of solving any worthwhile problem... The purpose of conscription is to harness uniformed and bewildered young men and women to the war chariot... I believe in law and order. The tank, the tommy-gun and the bomber are the very antithesis of law and order; they are outlawry and disorder in their most abandoned and hideous garb... My crime is that I have renounced war and will no longer fight against my fellow-men... My crime is that I believe in goodwill to all men, the triumph of good over evil, and the spirit of sacrifice over the lust for power. I believe that wars will cease when men refuse to fight: and I have an abundant faith in the dynamic force of the individual example.[78]

The views of non-pacifist objectors ranged from the one extreme of those socialist objectors who would not fight in any international wars but had reservations about their position in a civil war to the other extreme of a few objectors who had no objection to military service but did object to conscription for military service. An example of the latter position was an objector who was serving in the Home Guard but could not admit the right of the State to compel military service from its members.[79] Some objectors refused to fight for the British Government but would be willing to fight severally for a Welsh, Scottish, Irish or Indian Government. For example, one objector argued "that England had no right to compel youths of the Welsh nation to join the English army."[80] In Wales, where the proportion of objectors was much larger than the proportion for Great Britain as a whole, a considerable number of men based their objections, wholly or partly, on Welsh Nationalist grounds. There were a few Communist objectors (before the German invasion of Russia) and a few National Socialist objectors (The South Western Tribunal's figures showed 11 Communists and 8 National Socialists). About the latter, Professor Field remarked: "My personal belief is that the only genuine and logical conscientious objection on political grounds would be that of a convinced Fascist. For we are unmistakably and avowedly fighting to destroy something that he believes to be good. But the Tribunals have not acted on this view."[81]

The following is an example of a socialist non-pacifist objection, quoted from the answers of a member of the Independent Labour Party to questions at a tribunal session in November 1940.

It is my conviction that the use of force is justified only if on balance it will save human life and prevent human suffering. I cannot say I would oppose all wars. Some may prevent human suffering. I would not support a victory for Hitler or for British Imperialists. I think if Britain won she would impose another Versailles Treaty. I see the drift towards totalitarianism in Britain today. I believe Hitlerism in Germany can only be destroyed by the German people themselves. All that we can do is to take an international line and repudiate the policies which produced Versailles and thus encourage the German people to revolt against the Hitler regime... I do not see the only outcome of this war as being either a British victory or a German victory. I believe that the world cannot offer any hope for humanity unless another solution is reached, and that is the common feeling of the people of all countries.[82]

A number of objectors had been objectors also in the First World War. In contrast, a number of objectors had fought in the first War. The following example is part of a tribunal statement by one such objector.

I have been a convinced pacifist since 1920. Previous to this I had served in the Army for 31/2 years (1916–1919), seventeen months of which were spent on active service in France and Belgium. These experiences convinced me (a) that no matter for what causes war is wrong, and (b) that war defeats its own object which is to establish peaceful relationships between peoples, leading to a peaceful society. I was persuaded that violence opposed by violence always sows the seeds of future violence. It was this truth that led me to become a pacifist. [83]

As will be described later in this chapter there were nearly 400 men who became objectors while serving in the Forces and were sentenced by court-martial. The following example is part of a tribunal statement by one such objector.

Upon the outbreak of war, I volunteered for service in the army but was called up with my age-group a few weeks later... and posted to an ammunition company of the R.A.S.C. I was then only 20 years of age, and had devoted little time to serious thought on the wider problems of life. Certainly I had never regarded war other than as an inconvenient but vaguely glorious affair in which I was bound by tradition to take an active part. My family has a long military record. As company dispatch rider, I served with the B.E.F. in France and Belgium and was evacuated from Dunkirk. I witnessed and experienced many things which first gave me cause to think deeply for myself and to form certain views of my own regarding war and the methods by which it is waged. My inner thoughts told me I was doing wrong in serving an organisation which I had come to see clearly existed for the main purpose of attempting to settle disputes by destroying human lik. If elt deep within me that I had helped and was still helping to do something which I knew was wrong.[84]

Alternative Service

The men conscientious objectors who served in various ways as an alternative to combatant service in the Forces were in two main classes – those performing non-combatant duties in the army, and those doing various forms of civilian work according to the conditions of exemption specified by Tribunals or according to directions given by the Ministry of Labour and National Service. There was no group of objectors similar to the group who worked under the "Home Office Scheme" in the First World War.

In the first period after the outbreak of war, tribunals sometimes tried to persuade objectors to accept service in the Royal Army Medical Corps by pointing out the essentially humanitarian nature of this service. The tribunal, when registering an objector for non-combatant duties, could not specify the type of duties to be performed, but in a number of suitable cases, tribunals added a rider recommending the objector for the R.A.M.C. Up to November 1940, the authorities found it possible to post such objectors to this Corps. But at this date the War Office refused to accept any additional objectors into the Corps, except those with specialist qualifications.[85]

But only a small proportion of the objectors registered for non-combatant duties were given this recommendation for the R.A.M.C. The others might be employed in non-combatant duties in a number of corps of the army. The Central Board for Conscientious Objectors wished the position of these objectors to be more clearly defined and in May 1940 it obtained from the War Office a statement that instructions had been or would be given to Commanding Officers that the use of lethal weapons by such objectors (even in case of emergency) was not permissible.

At about the same time arrangements were made for a special slip to be attached to the documents of all objectors called up for non-combatant duties.[86]

In April 1940 a Non-Combatant Corps was formed for the specific purpose of receiving objectors who had been registered by tribunals for non-combatant duties. The officers and non-commissioned officers of this Corps were from the Auxiliary Military Pioneer Corps: all other members of the Non-Combatant Corps were objectors registered for non-combatant duties. Up to November 1946 the total number entering the Corps was 6,766 (though a considerable number did not remain in the Corps).[87]

Army Council Instructions described the types of employment of members of the Corps as follows. "The personnel of the Non-Combatant Corps will be employed, in addition to normal administrative duties, only on general duties appropriate to their category, including: (a) Construction and maintenance of hospitals, barracks, camps, railways, roads and recreative grounds (b) care of burial grounds (c) employment at baths and laundries (d) passive air defence (e) quarrying, timber-cutting, filling in of trenches (f) general duties, not involving the handling of military material of an aggressive nature."[88]

There were some occasions on which some members of the Corps resisted orders to do work which they felt they could not conscientiously perform. "On the whole, however, the authorities were fairly scrupulous in the allotment of duties to non-combatant C.O.s, though doubt as to the ultimate purpose of the work provided constantly recurring fear to many. Hedging and ditching in fruit-growing areas, limestone quarrying, work on food and petrol distribution, laying railway lines and making roads, cooking and forestry were among the multifarious duties of the Corps."[89]

A number of special types of work were performed by members of the Corps either in the Corps itself or after transfer or attachment to other units of the army. At the suggestion of some members of the Corps, 465 members were allowed to volunteer for work in bomb-disposal. A number of companies of the Corps worked in various forms of Civil Defence or in clearing war-damaged sites. About 600 objectors helped to lay smoke screens against air attack. 400 objectors performed clerical duties in camps for prisoners of war. 162 objectors became medical orderlies in the Paratroops and some scores of these went with the Parachute Field Ambulances in the invasion of France in June 1944.[90]

Probably the largest occupational group of men performing civilian alternative service was the group of those working on the land. At the end of March 1943 there were known to be 8,500[91] conditionally registered objectors engaged in land work. Some objectors were working for individual farmers, some under the Forestry Commission, some under County War Agricultural Committees, some under Christian Pacifist Forestry and Land Units, or International Voluntary Service for Peace, some as individual producers or as members of communities of various kinds.

In addition to objectors whose normal occupation was coal-mining and who were allowed to remain in it, a considerable number of objectors became miners in the latter years of the war. From 1943 onwards, tribunals sometimes gave coal-mining as a sole or alternative condition. Some objectors took advantage of the provision allowing men to opt for underground work in mines as an alternative to military service (see p177) and 547 men already in the Non-Combatant Corps volunteered for mining. Objectors who were refused exemption or registered for non-combatant duties were included in those subject to the ballot (see p177) and a few were directed to coal mining as the result of the ballot.

The Second World War required a new form of service – Civil Defence – in which many objectors assisted not only conscientiously but enthusiastically. Tribunals often exempted objectors with the sole or alternative condition of Civil Defence work. In the early years of the War, while some local authorities willingly employed objectors in their Civil Defence services, a considerable number of authorities refused to employ them. The Government strongly deprecated this attitude and in August 1941 the Ministry of Home Security sent a circular[92] to all local authorities defining its policy. This circular stated that, while in the past the question of accepting objectors had been left to the discretion of each local authority, the position had been altered by the National Service Act, 1941, and the need for man-power was pressing. Objectors should be given the opportunity of showing that their attitude to military service was not conditioned by fears for personal safety. This circular was effective in leading many authorities to change their attitude and employ objectors. In August 1942 the fire services became incorporated in the National Fire Service, under the central government, and this Service followed the Government policy of employing objectors.

The National Service Act, 1941,[93] which provided for the possible compulsory enrolment in a Civil Defence Force of any man liable for military service (see p177), included in this provision any legally recognised objector except one unconditionally exempted. A considerable number of conditionally registered objectors were interviewed with a view to transference to Civil Defence duties and about 800[94] were enrolled in the National Fire Service. In practice, enrolment was hardly ever enforced on those unwilling to serve. The provision of the Act which allowed men liable for military service to express a preference for Civil Defence was of great value to objectors to whom tribunals had refused any exemption and to objectors who had been made liable for non-combatant duties in the army; hundreds of such objectors were enrolled in the Fire Service during the period of twelve months or so after April 1941, when the Service still needed recruits.

The Friends' Ambulance Unit started work in September 1939 and continued until June 1946: during that period 1300 men and women joined it. The work of the Unit included work in the London blitz of 1940, and work in Finland, North Africa, Greece, Syria, Ethiopia, India, China, and France after D-Day. In the last stages of the war and in the immediate post-war period many members continued their work under other relief or welfare organisations.[95]

The Friends' Relief Service, which had nearly 500 full-time

men and women workers in 1942–43, had as its main work during most of the war period various services for the victims of air raids, including evacuation hostels for children and old people. From December 1944 relief work began in liberated France, and in the last months of the War and the immediate post-war period much, and eventually nearly all, the work of the Service became concerned with overseas relief.[96] Overseas relief work in a number of countries was also organised by International Voluntary Service for Peace from February 1944 onwards.[97]

Pacifist Service Units, among other activities, had members engaged in two unusual types of work. They did pioneer work in the type of case work for "problem families" which has since become widely recognised as a desirable form of social provision. They also provided "human guinea pigs" for medical research on scabies, on calcium deficiency and on the physical conditions of shipwrecked crews.[98]

Hospital work was often included in the kinds of work specified for a conditionally registered objector, and a considerable number of men objectors found individual employment in hospitals. Unless the objectors had special skill or training their work was often that of porters or orderlies and many hospitals, very short of such staff, willingly employed them.

While many objectors changed their occupations as a result of the War, a considerable number of objectors were registered on condition that they remained in their present occupations. When the objector's present work was of national importance, for example teaching, he was often allowed to continue in it. On the other hand, tribunals sometimes thought it desirable that an objector should make an obvious sacrifice by changing his occupation, even though his present work was of national importance.

While tribunals decided the conditions of exemption, they could not guarantee that objectors could obtain employment in the occupations specified. Not only some private employers but also a considerable number of local authorities refused to employ men registered as conscientious objectors. In July 1940 the Central Board for Conscientious Objectors knew of 86 local authorities which had decided to dismiss their objector employees and 33 which had decided to suspend them for the duration of the War.[99] The Minister of Labour and National Service "left it in no doubt that he thoroughly deprecated the whole business, though having no power to intervene."[100]

The Law-Breakers and the Law Concerning Them

In the Second World War, as compared with the First World War, fewer objectors were involved in any breach of the law relating to compulsory military service; the number was lower absolutely and much lower as a proportion of the total number of objectors. The main reason for this contrast was that in the Second War tribunals gave to a much larger proportion of applicants exemptions which they could conscientiously accept.

There is a second important contrast between the two periods: in the Second War few objectors were in prison for periods of more than a year, whereas in the First War at least eight hundred objectors were in prison for twenty months or more. There were two main reasons for this contrast. In the First War all law-breakers resisting military service were compulsorily enlisted in the army which meant that, if they continued to resist, they necessarily committed repeated offences and suffered repeated punishments, unless they were seconded from the army under the "Home Office Scheme." In the Second War under thirty per cent of law-breaking objectors were in the army; the large majority remained civilians, were sentenced by civilian courts, and, when released from prison, were not necessarily obliged to commit further legal offences or prosecuted if they did so. The second reason for the contrast was that the Government and Parliament were anxious to avoid the repeated penalisation of law-breaking objectors. Legislation provided a further right of application to the Appellate Tribunal for many imprisoned objectors, and even those objectors who were not successful in their applications were usually eventually left alone without further prosecution.

There were four classes of law-breaking objectors – those sentenced in the army, (with a few in the other Armed Forces) those sentenced for refusal of medical examination, those sentenced for non-compliance with their conditions of exemption, and those sentenced for offences in relation to the Home Guard. The groups will be described in this order. The only women objectors sentenced for offences in relation to compulsory military service were sentenced for non-compliance with their conditions of exemption:

the law-breaking objectors in the other groups were all men. With regard to all objectors except those in the Forces an offence involved the possible penalty of a fine. When fines were imposed a considerable number of objectors refused to pay them and were imprisoned in lieu of payment. (The maximum imprisonment in lieu of fines plus costs was[101] – not exceeding 10s.: 7 days; exceeding 10s. but not exceeding £1: 14 days; exceeding £1 but not exceeding £5: 1 month; exceeding £5 but not exceeding £20: 2 months; exceeding £20: 3 months.) Occasionally distraint was made in lieu of an unpaid fine. In May 1939, during the passage of the Military Training Bill, an amendment was moved by a private member with the aim of preventing a repetition of the "cat-and-mouse" treatment of objectors in the army during the First World War, when more than fifteen hundred objectors were sentenced by court-martial more than once and nearly nine hundred more than twice. Arthur Creech Jones M.P. gave his own experience of four court-martial sentences. (This was quoted on p152). M.P.s and the Government were sympathetic to the aim of the amendment and its gist was embodied in the Act.[102] A similar provision was made by Section 13 of the National Service (Armed Forces) Act, 1939.[103]

This provision gave the right to apply to the Appellate Tribunal to an objector who fulfilled the following conditions. (a) He had made application for registration as an objector but had nevertheless been called up for service. (b) He had been sentenced by court-martial to penal servitude or imprisonment for three months or more for an offence committed in Great Britain. (c) He claimed that the offence was committed by reason of his conscientiously objecting to performing military service or to obeying the order in respect of which the offence was committed.

The Appellate Tribunal, if it found that the offence was committed by reason of such conscientious objection, could recommend the discharge of the objector from the Armed Forces and could register him as an objector under any of the three categories available to it with regard to ordinary appeals. If the tribunal recommended the objector's discharge the Service authorities must arrange for this.

Official figures[104] show that during the war period (up to the end of June 1945) 750 applications were heard by the Appellate tribunal under this provision. Some of the objectors concerned had been called up with no legal recognition of their objection, some had been registered for non-combatant duties in the army;

the figures do not distinguish between these two categories. Of the 750 applications, 511 (68%) resulted in discharge from the army with conditional or unconditional registration as objectors and 38 (5%) resulted in registration (for the first time) for non-combatant duties, while 201 (27%) were refused. A considerable number of these applications were not first applications; an objector whose application was refused and who received a further qualifying sentence could make a further application, and a number of objectors whose first applications were refused were eventually successful. Thus the provision resulted in the discharge from the army of more than 500 men and in their legal recognition as objectors not liable in future for military service.

During the same period the Central Board for Conscientious Objectors had knowledge of a total of 931 court-martial trials of objectors. 613 individual objectors were tried by court-martial: of these men, 386 were tried once only, 154 were tried twice, 59 three times, 11 four times, 2 five times, and 1 six times.[105] These repeated court-martial trials were not all due to unsuccessful appeals. Sentence by court-martial did not necessarily give a right of application to the Appellate Tribunal: there was no right of application if the sentence was less than three months or if military detention, not imprisonment, was imposed. For example, in March 1940 the first objector to appear before a court-martial, a Christadelphian, was sentenced to sixty days' military detention and only after a second court-martial appeared before Appellate Tribunal.[106] In the following months sentences of detention were frequent and could not be commuted to imprisonment as detention was officially classed as a lesser punishment. The War Office encouraged courts-martial to impose sentences which gave the objector the right of appeal but it could not overrule the judicial independence of the court-martial; however, gradually its advice began to take effect and sentences of detention became rare. In a few cases objectors in the army suffered long total terms of imprisonment or detention. One extreme case was that of a Jehovah's Witness whose application to the Appellate Tribunal was finally successful after he had been in prison or in detention in the army for three years and three months: he had been sentenced five times by court-martial, twice to detention and three times to imprisonment, and two previous applications to the Appellate Tribunal had been unsuccessful.[107] In most cases the persistent resister was eventually successful in obtaining from the Appellate Tribunal a recommendation for discharge but there were also some cases of men eventually discharged without this recommendation. There were a few cases of brutality to objectors in the army and there were special difficulties for objectors who committed offences overseas which were not covered by the right of appeal. But the legal provision regarding application to the Appellate Tribunal saved many objectors in the army from repeated trials by court-martial and shortened many sentences of imprisonment which, in practice, were remitted soon after the objector's recommended discharge from the army.

There was another group of men in the Services who committed legal offences for conscientious reasons: these were men who had volunteered for the Services or who had been conscripted without registering as objectors and who subsequently felt unable conscientiously to continue to perform their duties. During the war period (up to the end of June 1945) the Central Board for Conscientious Objectors knew of 391 such men who had been tried by court-martial: 301 had been tried once, 51 had been tried twice, 36 had been tried three times, and 3 had been tried four times. The total number of trials was 523.[108] (These figures are *not* included in any other figures for law breaking objectors given in this chapter.)

There were some men in this group in the early days of the war and in January 1940 Dr. Alfred Salter headed a deputation of sympathetic M.P.s to the Secretary of State for War to urge that these men should be given the right of application to the Appellate Tribunal. In May 1940 Dr. Salter was informed that an administrative concession had been made by the War Office and a similar concession was later made to men in the Royal Air Force. This concession was similar to, though not identical with, the provision of Section 13 of the National Service Act, 1939 (already described). The man sentenced by court-martial to penal servitude or imprisonment for three months or more for an offence committed in Great Britain, if he claimed that the offence was committed by reason of his conscientiously objecting to performing military service or to obeying the order in respect of which the offence was committed, could make an application to the Advisory Tribunal. The Advisory Tribunal was to be a division of the Appellate Tribunal sitting in an advisory capacity. The Advisory Tribunal could advise discharge from the army or transfer to non-combatant duties and, in practice, its advice was accepted. The tribunal could not determine the man's position after discharge by registering him as a conscientious objector.[109]

This important administrative concession has been given ever since 1940 and there has been no distinction made between the man who was originally conscripted and the man who originally volunteered for service. It is known that a considerable number of men have benefited from the right of application to the Advisory Tribunal but no official figures of the number or results of applications have been published.

The largest group of law-breaking objectors was the group of those who had no legal exemption or were registered for non-combatant duties and refused to take their medical examinations, the medical examination being the necessary preliminary to the service of an enlistment notice. With regard to this matter there were two important changes in the law during the course of the War. The National Service (Armed Forces) Act, 1939,[110] provided a maximum penalty of a £5 fine for non-compliance with the requirements of a notice to submit to medical examination. The court could also order a convicted person to be arrested or detained so as to secure his attendance for examination. The first prosecutions were in May 1940 and a considerable number of those prosecuted submitted to examination, some abandoning their stand as objectors, others resisting later in the army. With regard to those who refused to be examined, the authorities made no attempts to examine by physical force, though the objector was often taken to the medical board under arrest. Some objectors were ordered to be detained indefinitely, but the legality of this was disputed and they were all released by the end of October 1940: the practice recommended by the Home Office was that the objector should not be detained after he had been taken before the medical board, unless he was serving a sentence of imprisonment in default of payment of his fine.[111] There were 517 prosecutions of objectors under these legal provisions, according to the information available to the Central Board for Conscientious Objectors.[112] Of those who refused to submit to medical examination, the majority were prosecuted again under the new legal provisions now to be described.

The National Service Act, 1941,[113] passed in April, added a new offence with much more severe penalties. The maximum punishment for refusal to comply with a notice for medical examination remained unchanged. The court could order a convicted person to submit to medical examination at a time and place to be fixed and could order him to be detained in custody for not more than seven days and taken before the medical board by a constable. Refusal to submit to medical examination under the court order was an additional offence for which the maximum penalty was 12 months' imprisonment and/or a fine of £50 if imposed by a court of summary jurisdiction, and 2 years imprisonment and/or a fine of £100 if imposed by a higher court.

The first objectors to be prosecuted under the new legal provisions were sentenced in June 1941 and on October 16th there were 372 men in prisons in England and Wales for refusal of medical examination under court order. Of these men, 68 had received sentences of up to 3 months' imprisonment, 201 sentences of over 3 months and up to 6 months, and 103 sentences of over 6 months and up to 12 months.[114] There was considerable difference of sentencing policy between different courts; some courts imposed the maximum sentence of 12 months from the beginning, in many other courts there was a tendency for the length of sentence imposed to be increased as time went on. In a few cases magistrates imposed sentences of fine instead of imprisonment; this was common in the early period at Norwich. Norwich Magistrates Court also released one objector on probation, expressing the opinion "that a conviction would not deter him from repeating the offence but would merely prevent him from doing the work he was willing to do": however, the High Court, on the appeal of the Ministry of Labour and National Service, held that the magistrates had acted illegally.[115] In a few cases objectors elected to be tried at Quarter Sessions, where sentences of over 12 months' imprisonment could be imposed and sometimes were imposed. Only one objector is known to have been sentenced to the maximum period of imprisonment of two years (which he served with the usual one-third remission).[116]

An objector who had served his sentence of imprisonment was in no better legal position than before his sentence. Was he to be served again with a notice for medical examination with further imprisonment for refusal? In supporting a change in the law in December 1941, the Minister of Labour and National Service, Ernest Bevin, said that such an objector might be "subject to a sort of cat-and-mouse procedure. We have not yet exercised that procedure, but I think the House will agree that it is objectionable. Under this Bill, we have put a man who refuses medical examination in the same position as if he had been in the Army and had been court-martialled."[117] Thus, under Section 5 of the National Service (No. 2) Act, 1941,[118] a person provisionally registered as a conscientious objector, who had been sentenced for refusal of medical examination to imprisonment for three months or more, was given the right to apply to the Appellate Tribunal if he claimed that the offence was committed by reason of his conscientiously objecting to performing military service or combatant duties. The tribunal, if satisfied of his claim, could register him as a conscientious objector in any of the three categories available to it in the case of ordinary appeals. In most cases the successful applicant, if still in prison, was released soon after his hearing.

The first cases under this provision were heard in March 1942. Between that date and the end of June 1945 a total of 1,795 applications were heard by the Appellate Tribunal. (As a few of these applications were not first applications the number of men concerned was rather fewer.) Of these applications 60.5% resulted in a variation of the objector's legal status: in 54 cases objectors were registered (for the first time) for non-combatant duties, in 1033 cases objectors were freed from any future liability for military service (and thus for medical examination) by being registered conditionally or unconditionally.[119]

From 1942 onwards the possibility of repeated prosecutions for refusal of medical examination was confined to those men whose applications to the Appellate Tribunal for exemption from military service had been unsuccessful; to those who, for various reasons, did not exercise their right to apply to the Tribunal; and to those who had not been given a "qualifying sentence". In August 1942 the Ministry of Labour and National Service announced its future policy that objectors who had been sentenced to imprisonment for three months or more would not again be prosecuted for refusal of medical examination. This policy was adhered to in most cases for the rest of the war period. But when the objector had received a sentence of a fine or imprisonment for less than three months he was usually prosecuted again.

About a thousand objectors were given conditional exemption as the result of their applications to the Appellate Tribunal; these objectors were bound by their conditions of exemption and could be prosecuted for non-compliance. In the large majority of cases where the objectors were still legally liable for military service the Ministry of Labour and National Service used its powers under the Defence Regulations (which will be described in Chapter 7) to direct them to civilian work; up to the end of 1943 about 1,200 were so directed.[120] Most of the objectors concerned had no conscientious objection to obeying such directions. But those who refused directions (about 200 up to the end of 1943)[121] were prosecuted, sometimes more than once. (The maximum penalty at a court of summary jurisdiction was a fine of £100 and/or imprisonment for 3 months.) In most cases an objector was not prosecuted more than once for refusal of a direction if the Ministry considered that he was doing some work of value to the State.

Between June 1941 and the end of June 1945 there were known to the Central Board for Conscientious Objectors a total of 2,548 prosecutions for refusal of medical examination under the National Service Act, 1941. (As some of these prosecutions were not first prosecutions the number of men concerned was rather smaller.) It is probable that in 229 cases the objectors submitted to medical examination; in some of these cases the objectors took this course in order to join the National Fire Service, which had the same medical examination. In the other 2,319 cases the objectors were sentenced (usually to imprisonment) for refusal of medical examination under court order.[122] The large majority of the sentenced objectors were willing to do civilian work according to the decision of the Tribunal or on the direction of the Ministry of Labour and National Service and eventually they were allowed to do so by the legal authorities. But they won this right only by persistent defiance of the law.

The third group of law-breaking objectors were those who had received from tribunals exemption conditional on performing civilian work of a type specified by the tribunal, and who did not comply with their conditions of exemption. It was obvious that non-compliance might be due to circumstances outside the objector's control and therefore the law gave to the tribunal the opportunity to distinguish between such non-compliance and deliberate non-compliance. The law as established in 1939 was amended in 1941.

Under Section 8 of the National Service (Armed Forces) Act, 1939,[123] it was provided that, if an objector was reported to a local tribunal as failing to observe his conditions of exemption and the tribunal was satisfied that this was the case, he should be required to apply afresh to the local tribunal, which could register him as an objector in any of the three available categories and could alter his previous conditions of exemption. If the objector failed to apply to the tribunal when required to do so, the Minister should register him as a person liable for non-combatant duties in the Forces.

Tribunals were left to decide whether the objector's non-compliance was due to circumstances beyond his control or whether it was deliberate and, if the latter, whether they wished to penalise him. Out of 321 cases of non-compliance, 262 applied to tribunals: of those who applied to tribunals, 2 were registered unconditionally, 155 were registered conditionally (with or without variation of conditions), and 105 were registered for non-combatant duties in the Forces.[124]

Thus, in a number of cases, registration for non-combatant duties was used as a penalty for non-compliance with conditions of exemption, there being no other penalty provided by law. This position was changed in the National Service Act, 1941.[125] Section 5 of this Act distinguished between cases in which there was "reasonable excuse" for non-compliance and cases in which there was not such excuse. In cases in which the Ministry of Labour and National Service considered that there was reasonable excuse it was to refer the case to the local tribunal. The position when the tribunal found a breach of condition with reasonable excuse has been described earlier in this chapter (pp.188–9). If the tribunal found a breach of condition without reasonable excuse it was to report the matter to the Ministry. In this case, and in a case of non-compliance not reported to a tribunal, the Ministry could prosecute the objector. A new legal offence was created – the offence of failing without reasonable excuse to comply with the condition of exemption. ("Reasonable excuse" could be accepted as a defence in court.) The maximum penalty for this offence was a fine of £50 and/or imprisonment for 12 months if imposed by a court of summary jurisdiction, and a fine of £100 and/or imprisonment for 2 years if imposed by a higher court.

The first prosecutions for this new legal offence were in November 1941. Between this date and the end of June 1945, according to the figures reported by the Ministry of Labour and National Service, 378 objectors – 294 men and 84 women – were sentenced for this offence.[126] The variations of sentences given to men can be illustrated from three of the cases in 1941 – one was fined £5 with costs, one was sentenced to six months' imprisonment and one to twelve months' imprisonment. The maximum sentences given to men during the war period were sentences of fifteen months' imprisonment imposed on two objectors who elected to be tried by Quarter Sessions. The first prosecutions of women were in 1943. The maximum sentences given to women were three of six months' imprisonment and one of twelve months' imprisonment; in the latter case the sentence was reduced to six months' imprisonment on the objector's appeal to Quarter Sessions.[127]

Imprisonment for non-compliance with the condition of exemption, unlike imprisonment for refusal of medical examination, gave no right of further application to the Appellate Tribunal. The reason for this contrast was that, while the Government recognised conscientious objection to military service, it consistently refused to recognise any general right of conscientious objection to civilian work. But the Ministry of Labour and National Service did not exercise its legal powers to prosecute repeatedly all objectors who continued to disregard their conditions of exemption. There were some repeated prosecutions, particularly when the first sentence had been one of a fine only, and there were some cases in which an objector, previously imprisoned, was served with a direction to employment under the Defence Regulations and sentenced for refusal of the direction. But before long "though no declaration of policy was ever made except in the usual non-committal form, a conscientious objector who had served three months or more for refusing a Tribunal condition was in actual fact left to his own devices."[128]

A number of objectors pleaded conscientious objection as a "reasonable excuse" for non-fulfilment of their conditions of exemption. In most cases this plea was unsuccessful but it was allowed in at least two cases by divisions of the Appellate Tribunal and in at least one case by a court. However, after the war period, in 1946, the Lord Chief Justice, in dismissing an appeal, ruled against this possible interpretation of the term "reasonable excuse" as a defence in a prosecution for non-fulfilment of the condition of exemption.[129]

The reasons for refusal to fulfil conditions of exemption were usually objection to co-operation in any way in the war effort or in military conscription, or a strong sense of vocation for other types of work, or a combination of these two reasons. (The majority of women prosecuted were Jehovah's Witnesses who refused to abandon their religious work.) This "absolutist" or "unconditionalist" position was maintained not only by those who refused to fulfil their conditions of exemption but also by many of those (to be described in Chapter 7) who refused to obey directions to work or other regulations of industrial conscription, and by many of those who received unconditional exemption from tribunals and who therefore were allowed to choose their work without legal restriction.

The fourth group of law-breaking objectors were those prosecuted under the Defence Regulations for offences in relation to compulsory duties in the Home Guard; there were 59 such prosecutions known to the Central Board for Conscientious Objectors.[130] It was explained earlier in this chapter that men liable for service in the Home Guard were given the same right to apply to tribunals as those liable under the National Service Acts and that all those registered by tribunals as conscientious objectors were exempted from Home Guard duties. It was therefore usually only objectors who were rejected by tribunals who were obliged to commit offences for conscientious reasons. The following are two examples of Home Guard prosecutions. In January 1943, an objector removed from the register by the tribunal was fined £5 for failing to enrol in the Home Guard when directed to do so. (The maximum penalty for this offence on summary conviction was a fine of £100 or imprisonment for three months or both.) A man who had voluntarily enrolled in the Home Guard in 1941 later changed his views and successfully applied to the tribunal for registration as a conscientious objector: he was prosecuted for being absent from Home Guard duties, sentenced to a fine of £10 or one month's imprisonment, and served the imprisonment.[131] (The maximum penalty for this offence was a fine of £10 or imprisonment for one month or both.)

References

Cmd. 7225 = Report of the Ministry of Labour and National Service for the Years 1939–1946
CBCO = Central Board for Conscientious Objectors

1 McCallum, R.B. *Public Opinion and the Last Peace* p. 8 (1944)
2 Taylor, A.J.P. *English History 1914–1945* pp. 376–377 (1965)
3 Ibid. pp. 389–390
4 Ibid. p. 411 note 2
5 Cmd. 7225 p. 35
6 Ibid. p. 8
7 Taylor op. cit. p. 433
8 Hansard Vol. 346 Col. 1343–51
9 Hansard Vol. 346 No. 90 Col. 1343
10 Hansard Vol. 346 No. 90 Col. 1352
11 Hansard Vol. 346 No. 90 Col. 1457
12 Hansard Vol. 347 No. 97 Col. 162
13 2 & 3 Geo. 6. c. 25
14 7 Edw. 7. c. 9
15 2 & 3 Geo. 6. c. 81
16 Cmd. 7225 p. 22 and 358
17 Ibid. pp. 13–21
18 Ibid. pp. 22–24
19 3 & 4 Geo. 6. c. 22
20 6 & 7 Geo. 6. c. 3
21 Cmd. 7225 p. 335
22 Hayes, Denis *Challenge of Conscience. The Story of the Conscientious Objectors of 1939–1949* p. 382
23 Cmd. 7225 p. 26
24 Ibid. p. 35
25 4 & 5 Geo. 6. c. 15
26 Cmd. 7225 p. 29
27 Ibid. pp. 25 and 143
28 5 & 6 Geo.6.c.29
29 5 & 6 Geo.6.c.30
30 Cmd. 7225 pp. 10 – 11
31 5 & 6 Geo. 6. c. 3
32 Cmd. 7225 p. 11
33 (Statutory Rules and Orders) 1941. No. 368
34 Cmd. 7225 pp. 43 and 337
35 5 & 6 Geo. 6. c. 3
36 S.R. & O. 1942. No. 91
37 Cmd. 7225 pp. 30 and 146
    CBCO Broadsheet No. 15
38 5 & 6 Geo. 6. c. 3
39 Cmd. 7225 p. 31
40 S.R. & O. 1941. No. 368

41 Cmd. 7225 pp. 30–35 and 139
42 10 & 11 Geo. 6. c. 31
43 Hansard Vol. 346 No. 95 Col. 2099
44 2 & 3 Geo. 6. c. 25
45 2 & 3 Geo. 6. c. 81
46 5 & 6 Geo. 5. c.104
47 S.R. & O. 1942. No. 91
48 Hayes op. cit. p. 8
49 4 & 5 Geo. 6. c. 15. Sect. 6
50 Hayes op. cit. p. 382
51 Cmd. 7225 p. 25
52 5 & 6 Geo. 6. c. 3
53 S.R. & O. 1941. No. 368
54 Cmd. 7225 p. 142
55 Ibid. p. 34
56 Hayes op. cit. pp. 17–18
57 2 & 3 Geo. 6. c. 25
58 2 & 3 Geo. 6. c. 81
59 S.R. & O. 1942 No. 93
60 CBCO Bulletin. August 1945
61 Cmd. 7225 p. 25
62 CBCO Bulletin. August 1945
63 Ibid.
64 4 & 5 Geo. 6. c. 15
65 CBCO Bulletin. August 1945
66 Ibid.
67 CBCO Bulletin. September 1945
68 Cmd. 7225 p. 24
69 Ibid. p. 142
70 CBCO Bulletin. March 1946
71 Hayes op. cit. p. 50
72 Cmd. 7225 p. 143
73 Ministry of Labour and National Service. Report for 1947 Cmd. 7559 p. 23
74 Livingstone, Adelaide *The Peace Ballot. The Official History* Gollancz, 1935, Supplementary Sheet
75 Field, G.C. *Pacifism and Conscientious Objection* pp. 3–4
76 These and following figures from Hayes op. cit. table p. 26
77 Hayes op. cit. pp. 27–28
78 CBCO Bulletin. May 1943
79 Hayes op. cit. p. 55
80 Ibid. p. 55
81 Field op. cit. p. 15
82 Hayes op. cit. pp. 30–31
83 Ibid. p. 28
84 CBCO Bulletin. June 1943
85 Hayes op. cit. p. 120
86 Ibid. pp. 120–122

87   Ibid. pp. 123 and 387
88   Ibid. p. 125
89   Ibid. p. 127
90   Ibid. pp. 127–130
91   CBCO Bulletin. July 1943
92   Circular No. 169/1941. Quoted Hayes op. cit. p. 184
93   4 & 5 Geo. 6. c. 15
94   Cmd. 7225 p. 25
95   Hayes op. cit. pp. 231–236
     Davies, A. Tegla *Friends Ambulance Unit*
96   Hayes op. cit. pp. 236–240
97   Ibid. pp. 230–231
98   Hayes op. cit. pp. 219–226
     Stephens, Tom (edited) *Problem Families*
     Mellanby, Kenneth *Human Guinea Pigs*
99   Hayes op. cit. p. 204
100 Ibid. p. 205
101 Summary Jurisdiction Act, 1879
102 2 & 3 Geo. 6. c. 25
103 2 & 3 Geo. 6. c. 81
104 CBCO Bulletin. August 1945
105 CBCO Bulletin. September 1945
106 Hayes op. cit. pp. 78 – 80
107 Ibid. pp. 108,110
108 CBCO Bulletin. September 1945
109 Hayes op. cit. pp. 80–82
110 2 & 3 Geo. 6. c. 81. Sects. 17 (1) and 3 (5)
111 Hayes op. cit. pp. 134– 142
112 Ibid. p. 389
113 4 & 5 Geo. 6. c. 15. Sect. 4
114 Statement in House of Commons by Home Secretary 16.10.1941
     Hansard Vol. 374 No. 107
115 Eversfield v. Story (1942) 1 K.B. 437 (1942)
     Hayes op. cit. pp. 147– 150
116 Hayes op. cit. p. 162
117 Hansard Vol. 376 No. 13 9.12.1941 Cols. 1428–35
118 5 & 6 Geo. 6. c. 3
119 CBCO Bulletin. August 1945
120 Statement of Minister of Labour and National Service
     Hayes op. cit. p. 172
121 Ibid.
122 CBCO Bulletin. September 1945
123 2 & 3 Geo. 6. c. 81
124 Hayes op. cit. pp. 249 and 384
125 4 & 5 Geo. 6. c. 15
126 Cmd. 7225 p. 143
127 Hayes op. cit. pp. 251–256
128 Ibid. p. 257

129 Ibid. pp. 251–255
130 Ibid. p. 389
131 CBCO Bulletin. January 1943

Chronological Table of Acts Relating to Compulsory Military Service during the Second World War

Date		
1907	Territorial & Reserve Forces Act	7 Edw. 7. c. 9
1939	Military Training Act	2 & 3 Geo. 6. c. 25
1939	National Service (Armed Forces) Act	2 & 3 Geo. 6. c. 81
1940	National Service (Armed Forces) Act	3 & 4 Geo. 6. c. 22
1941	National Service Act	4 & 5 Geo. 6. c. 15
1941	National Service (No. 2) Act	5 & 6 Geo. 6. c. 3
1942	National Service (Foreign Countries) Act	5 & 6 Geo. 6. c. 29
1942	Allied Powers (War Service) Act	5 & 6 Geo. 6. c. 30
1942	National Service Act	6 & 7 Geo. 6. c. 3
1947	National Service Act	10 & 11 Geo. 6. c. 31

CHAPTER 6

Compulsory Military Service
1945 – 1960

The Process of Demobilisation

The history in this chapter is continuous with the history in Chapter 5, as the compulsory registration and enlistment of young men continued without any break at the end of the War. But after the end of the war with Germany, on 8th May 1945, and still more after the end of the war with Japan on 15th August 1945, it became possible to start demobilising large numbers of men who had volunteered or been conscripted for service in the War.

Plans for demobilisation had been made well in advance. In a White Paper issued in September 1944[1] two principles were stated: that military requirements must override all other considerations, and that the arrangements must be such as would be readily understood and accepted as fair by the Armed Forces and must not be too complicated for practical application. The main scheme of demobilisation, under which more than four-fifths of both men and women were released, grouped members of the Services into release groups based on a combination of age and length of service since the beginning of the War, two months of war service being equivalent to one year of age. Thus those who were older and those who had given long service had priority and there was special priority for those aged fifty and over and for married women. Release proceeded at different rates in the different Services and sometimes as between officers and other ranks. There was a second scheme for those urgently needed in industry and this included also releases of some individual specialists and some releases for purposes of education or training; age and length of service were often considerations with regard to selections under this scheme. There were also men and women discharged for other reasons including medical or compassionate reasons.

In mid-1945 there were 4,635,000 men in the Armed Forces. In 1945 1,342,000 were discharged and in 1946 2,545,000 were discharged; at the end of 1946 the total number in the Armed Forces had fallen to 1,361,000. In 1947 592,000 were discharged and at the end of that year all who had been called up before 1944 had been released. In the next fifteen months up to the end of March 1949 a further 587,000 were discharged and at the end of March 1949 all who had been called up before 1947 had been released. The scheme of demobilisation according to age and length of service did not apply to those called up from 1947 onwards.[2]

In mid-1945 the total number in the Women's Auxiliary Services was 437,000. From these services and the Nursing Services of the Forces 172,000 were discharged in 1945 and 231,000 in 1946. At the end of 1946 the total number in the Women's Auxiliary Services had fallen to 79,000. In 1947 47,000 were discharged and at the end of that year all those who had been called up before 1944 had been released. As the compulsory enlistment of women was suspended in January 1944 and never resumed, 1947 was the last year in which conscripted women were serving and from that time the Women's Auxiliary Services included only volunteers.[3]

The demobilisation schemes applied to conscientious objectors who were registered for and performed non-combatant duties in the Forces, in exactly the same way as they applied to other members of the Forces. Conditionally registered objectors were legally liable to obey their conditions of exemption "until the end of the present emergency." After the end of the War there was a delay of seven months before the release of objectors from their conditions was authorised by the National Service (Release of Conscientious Objectors) Act, 1946,[4] which became law on 26th March. This Act applied to objectors the same principles as those applied in the demobilisation schemes. Objectors were to be classed in groups, similar to those in the Services, according to age and length of service, the service to be reckoned from the date on which the objector was conditionally registered. They were to be released from their conditions soon after the date at which both officers and men in the same group in the army had been released. (Objectors could also be released if urgently needed in

219

their ordinary occupations or for purposes of education or training.) Under these provisions a considerable number of objectors, whose corresponding groups in the army had been demobilised, including all married women, were released in April 1946 and the large majority (22,452 men and 690 women) had been released by the end of 1946. In 1947 the 54 women who remained conditionally registered were released. Between the beginning of 1947 and the end of June 1950 2,948 conditionally registered men were released; this number included all those registered before 1949. From the beginning of 1949 objectors were registered for a fixed period and the Act of 1946 did not apply to them.[5]

The General Provisions of the National Service Acts

With regard to conditions of call-up and length of compulsory service there were temporary provisions in the years prior to 1949; from 1949 onwards matters were regulated by the National Service Act, 1948,[6] and amending Acts.

After the end of the War the call-up was normally restricted to men aged under thirty.[7] From the beginning of 1947 the call-up was (with some exceptions) limited to those born in 1929 or later and men were normally called up on reaching the age of 18.[8] In 1945 and 1946 the length of service of those called up was determined by the provisions, already described, relating to discharge according to age and length of service. For those called up in 1947 and 1948 there was a fixed length of service which was gradually decreased to the term fixed under the National Service (Amendment) Act, 1948.[9] Those called up in the first half of 1947 served a maximum of two years and three months; the period was then progressively reduced until those called up at the end of 1948 served for eighteen months.[10]

The National Service Act, 1947,[11] contained provisions regulating National Service from 1949 onwards. This Act formally ended the liability of women for compulsory military service. The consolidating National Service Act, 1948[12] (with amending Acts) regulated National Service from 1949 until the end of conscription and this Act repealed the National Service Acts 1939–1947.

With regard to the duration of conscription the Act provided (in Section 61) that no man attaining the age of eighteen after 1 January 1954 should be liable to be called up under the Act, provided that a later date might be substituted by Order in Council. The later date of 1 January 1959 was substituted by the National Service Act, 1948 (Duration) Order, 1953.[13] In a White Paper issued in April 1957[14] the Government announced its intention not to call up men under the National Service Acts after the end of 1960; in fact the last registration for National Service was in January 1959 and the last call-up was in November 1960.

The National Service Act, 1948[15] imposed the obligation of a period of full-time service followed by a period of part-time service. The period of full-time service imposed by the Act was twelve months but before the Act came into force this period was increased to eighteen months by the National Service (Amendment) Act, 1948.[16] This period of eighteen months was served by men who were called up from the beginning of 1949 and who completed their service before 1 October 1950. Following the outbreak of war in Korea in June 1950, the Government took measures to increase the strength of the Armed Forces. The period of full-time service was increased to two years by the National Service Act, 1950;[17] this increased period applied to men called up from 1 October 1950 and to men who had not completed their service before that date. Two years remained the period of full-time service until the end of conscription. Even in the last years of conscription, when the Government was reducing the number of National Service men in the Forces, it decided to achieve this object by gradually increasing the age of call-up, not by decreasing the period of service. A White Paper in October 1955[18] stated: "The main purpose of national service now is to supplement the regulars and so provide sufficient active forces to meet the country's needs...A reduction in the period of national service would rob the Services – in particular the Army and the R.A.F. – of a large number of experienced national service men... at a time when as trained men they are making their most effective contribution to the Forces." As the last call-up was in November 1960, most National Service men had been discharged by the end of 1962. However, under Section 1 of the Army Reserve Act,[19] passed in February 1962, power was given to retain certain National Service men for an extra six months, the reason being the needs of the Army in West Germany. Among those whose service was lengthened under this provision were a few hundred called up in November 1960 and these last conscripts were discharged in May 1963.[20]

The National Service Act, 1948,[21] as amended by the National Service (Amendment) Act, 1948,[22] imposed the following obligations with regard to part-time service. After completion of his full-time service a man should be deemed to be a member of a Reserve Force attached to his former branch of service for a period of four years. During this period he could be required to undergo training for a maximum of sixty days during the whole period and twenty-one days in any year; the Service authorities could serve on him a training notice requiring him to attend at the time and place specified in the notice, with penalties for non-compliance. If he was accepted as a volunteer in the Territorial Army or various other Reserve Forces and engaged to serve for not less than four years he was exempted from his National Service obligations for part-time service. Under the National Service Act, 1950[23] the period of part-time service was reduced to three and a half years.

The periods of training specified in the Acts were maximum periods and there were considerable differences in the length of periods for which men were actually obliged to train, differences between the various branches of the Services and between one year and another.

In a White Paper issued in October 1955[24] the Government stated that, from the beginning of 1956, with the exception of a few men in certain special groups, reservists would not be required to train for more than a total of twenty days, including one continuous period of training, and those who had already done one period of continuous training would not be required to do further training.

The National Service Act, 1948[25] made liable for service "every male British subject ordinarily resident in Great Britain who has attained the age of eighteen years and has not attained the age of twenty-six years." With regard to two groups of men the upper age limit was raised: registered doctors and dentists were made liable if aged under thirty (by the National Service (Amendment) Act, 1948),[26] and men abroad during the last year of normal liability were made liable if aged under thirty-six (by the National Service Act, 1955).[27]

During the post-war period forty-nine registrations were held under the National Service Acts: the first was on 1 September 1945 and the last was on 10 January 1959. These registrations included men born in the twelve years between 1 October 1927 and 30 September 1939; no men born later than September 1939

222

were registered or conscripted. Up to the middle of 1956 the ages of those registering varied between the limits of 17 years 8 months and 18 years 2 months: in the registration from July 1956 to January 1958 those registering were aged between 18 and 19, and in the two last registrations the ages varied between 19 and 19½. The total number of men registered over the whole period was about 3,631,500.[28]

Published figures show that of the men born in 1929 and 1930 over three quarters joined the Forces, as conscripts or volunteers, before reaching the maximum age of liability;[29] of those born in later years the proportions were lower. Of those born in 1929 the position in October 1953[30] was that about 78% had joined the Forces, about 13% had been exempted as medically unfit, and about 8% had not been called up because they were coal miners, agricultural workers, or merchant seamen. These three occupations were numerically the most important groups in which, in the post-war period, all or many workers were in practice exempted from the call-up, but there were several smaller groups exempted for all or part of the period. In addition to those exempted, many students, apprentices, and others who were being educated or trained had their call-up deferred until the end of their education or training. During most of the post-war period the great majority of these deferred men were eventually called up but at the end of the period of conscription deferment often meant escape from the call-up – there were over 100,000 men with deferment in November 1960[31] and these men were never called up.

The total number of men in the Forces decreased greatly from 4,635,000 in mid-1945 to 1,361,000 at the end of 1946. The number then decreased every year till mid-1950 when it was about 663,000. As a result of the war in Korea, which started in June 1950, the number increased to 848,000 at the end of 1952. The number then decreased every year: it was 745,000 at the end of 1956 and 488,000 at the end of 1960 (the latter figure was about the same number as in mid-1939).[32]

Between 1 July 1945 and 17 November 1960, when the last National Service men were called up, about 2,272,000 men were posted to the Forces under the National Service Acts. Of the 1,902,300 men posted in the years 1947–1960, 72% were posted to the Army, 25% were posted to the Air Force, and 3% were posted to the Navy.[33]

The effect of conscription on recruitment to the Forces is not adequately represented by the numbers posted under the National

Service Acts. A large number of men liable for National Service joined the Forces on regular engagements, especially on three-year engagements in the Army and Air Force. For example, in the seven years 1952–1958 187,000 men volunteered for the Army (compared with 693,000 conscripted), 135,000 men volunteered for the Air Force (compared with 221,000 conscripted), and 18,000 volunteered for the Navy (compared with 27,000 conscripted).[34] Presumably many of these men would not have volunteered if they had not been thereby exempted from National Service.

The Numbers and Views of Conscientious Objectors

In the forty-nine post-war registrations under the National Service Acts the total number of men who registered provisionally as conscientious objectors was 9,102. (In addition, at least 21 men were registered provisionally by the Minister because they had refused to register and there were reasonable grounds for thinking that they were conscientious objectors.) The total number provisionally registered as objectors over the whole period was 0.25% – 1 in 400 – of the total number registered. This proportion was much smaller than the proportion of 0.8% in the total War period. But in the last two years of the War, in registrations of men aged 17 years 8 months or a little older, the proportion was only 0.23%, and the proportion was only somewhat smaller – 0.19% – in the registrations of men of the same age between September 1945 and the end of 1950. The proportion rose to 0.26% in the period 1951–1954 and to 0.35% in the period 1955–1959.[35]

Post-war conscription was not distinguished from war-time conscription by being conscription for military training only, as was the intention of the abortive Military Training Act of 1939.[36] The post-war conscripts were not only being trained for military service, they were also acting as ordinary members of the Forces; except for the length of their service, they were no more restricted in their possible obligations than were the volunteer members of the Forces. But there were two important contrasts between post-war conscription and conscription during the Second World War.

During the War conscription was for the predominant purpose of fighting originally against Germany and later also against Italy and Japan, a purpose which was probably approved by a large majority of British citizens. In contrast, post-war conscription was in order to maintain the desired strength of the Armed Forces and these Forces were used for a wide variety of special purposes. These purposes included, during the whole period, the maintenance of an army in West Germany and, for parts of the period, the maintenance of an army in Austria and the maintenance of forces, with in some cases armed action, in Greece, Palestine, the Suez Canal Zone, Korea, Malaya, Kenya, Cyprus and some other areas. To some of these activities there were more British citizens opposed than were opposed to the war against Germany, Italy and Japan, and this opposition was reflected in the views of some conscientious objectors. The peace-time conscript was being enlisted for purposes which he could not foresee, legally liable to perform any military duties ordered by the Government of the day. He might find himself employed in activities of which he approved or in activities of which he disapproved, and he had no say in the matter. This feature of peace-time conscription was in sharp contrast to the conscription for the known purposes of the Second World War.

The second important contrast was with regard to the age of the conscripts. The men conscripted in the War were a substantial proportion of all men aged between eighteen and forty-one. In contrast, the call-up from 1947 onwards affected only young men: the majority were between the ages of eighteen and twenty and the others were mainly in their early twenties. In the War the general body of citizens consented to the conscription of themselves to further policies which they had had opportunities to help to determine. In peace-time Parliament imposed conscription on young men, the majority of whom had never had the right to vote, to further policies about which these young men had never been consulted.

A large number of the objectors to peace-time conscription based their objections on what they held to be the obligations of their Christian faith. Such types of objection have been adequately exemplified in the previous three chapters of this book. The following statements of individual objectors have been selected to exemplify objections related to the special conditions and problems of the period 1945–1960.

One objector was a member of the world citizenship movement and believed that as a member of that organisation he should not take part or serve in any national army: he would not refuse to serve in a world government force.[37] Another objector holding similar views stated that force was only justified in support of war on behalf of law accepted by all States.[38]

The next examples are of objections related to contemporary methods of warfare. An objector, who said that he might have been willing to fight in the last war, "argued that the military defence strategy of this country was, ultimately, based on the use of thermonuclear weapons. It was therefore impossible to accept military service without assenting to the use of these weapons, and they raised issues which were entirely new in the history of warfare. His conscience forbade him to give that assent."[39]

Another objector, a scientist, stated:

I cannot deny my responsibility as an individual for the use of the atomic bomb and napalm, for modern scientific research into bacterial warfare and guided missiles and all the ghastly weapons which mankind is feverishly engaged upon producing in order to hasten the apocalyptic end of humanity. The basis of my belief is that war, possibly the lesser evil in the past, cannot be anything but the greatest possible evil in the future, and so my conscience forbids me to support, by means of military service, the present policy of my own country in this matter.[40]

Another objector stated:

I believe that modern warfare is morally degrading to all who participate in it... In recent years, more and more, the mass extermination and terrorisation of civilian populations has become the normal method of waging war... In the Korean War the British Government acquiesced in the use of the napalm bomb against the civilians of that country. I regard this wholesale slaughter of human beings as morally unjustifiable, and I refuse to be a party to the commission of atrocities under the guise of deknding civilisation.[41]

One objector appealed to the United Nations Convention on Genocide, which made genocide a crime under international law. He argued that, as genocide was defined as the killing of groups of people, all modern war was genocide.[42]

The next examples show objections to particular objectives of the activities of the Forces. One objector stated:

I am called up now, at eighteen, for a certain cause and I do not believe in that cause. I am told I am defending freedom. But I believe that in Kenya, Malaya and British Guiana freedom is not being defended by the British troops. I do not believe that the British way of life defends freedom. If I were a member of the British Armed Forces I would be liable to be ordered to do something which I would regard as morally wrong.[43]

An ex-officer, discharged from the army for refusal to obey orders in Kenya, stated to a tribunal:

It seemed to me that the Africans had everything in common with the ordinary people in England and were struggling for the same things that British people had themselves struggled for in the past. . . I love England so much that I do not wish to see her name dragged in the mud as a result of the things I saw taking place in Kenya.[44]

A few weeks prior to the Suez Crisis in 1956 a National Service officer in the reserve, in a letter to the national press, wrote:

I am evidently liable to be called up for a Middle East war which seems imminent... Clearly my moral duty would be to refuse to participate in a war I believed to be aggressive, or to carry out orders involving bloodshed and destruction in a cause I believe to be morally invalid... What is the legal position for the many who, like me, would object conscientiously to service in this specific war on political and moral grounds but who are technically members of the forces already and who have no religious or other objection to war as such, in a just cause?[45]

Tribunals and Their Decisions

There was no break in the tribunal system at the end of the War and the war-time tribunals continued to function. But the number of applicants was much smaller than during much of the War period – during the six years from the meeting of the first tribunal in July 1939 to the end of June 1945 local tribunals considered 59,192 new cases of men, an annual average of 9,865 cases; during the fifteen and a half years from July 1945 to the end of 1960 local tribunals considered 10,390 new cases of men, an annual average of 670 cases.[46] After the end of 1945 there were no new applications to tribunals from women conscientious objectors and the following description of the post-war tribunal system is concerned only with men objectors.

There were nineteen local tribunals in existence at some time during the War period but by the end of the War three of these had been dissolved. During 1947 the number of local tribunals was reduced from fifteen to eight and in 1948 the number was reduced to seven. From May 1948 for the rest of the period there were seven local tribunals of which one was in Scotland and one in Wales. There were six divisions of the Appellate Tribunal in existence at some time during the War period; by the end of 1947 these had been reduced to three. For the rest of the period there were three divisions – London, Manchester and Edinburgh.

Under the National Service Act, 1948[47] an alteration was made with regard to the statutory qualifications of chairmen of local tribunals: the chairman of a tribunal had henceforth to be in England and Wales either a county court judge or a barrister of at least seven years' standing, in Scotland either a sheriff or sheriff substitute or an advocate of at least five years' standing. The number of members of a local tribunal, including the chairman, remained as seven, of whom five participated in any particular session. The number of members of a division of the Appellate Tribunal, including the chairman, remained as five, of whom three participated in any particular session. But, with regard to both local tribunals and the divisions of the Appellate Tribunal, the legal obligation to include women members, introduced in January 1942 as the result of the conscription of women, was not continued in the Act. However, some women continued to serve on, or were appointed to, tribunals.

The law administered by tribunals in the post-war period remained substantially the same as the law administered by them during the War. But there were some changes in the law with regard to conditional exemption. For objectors who were registered conditionally before the end of 1948, the length of time for which the condition applied was determined on the same principles as those applying to members of the Forces. From the beginning of 1949 objectors registered conditionally were, under Section 17 of the National Service Act, 1948,[48] registered for the current period of full-time National Service, which was at first eighteen months and was increased to two years from October 1950. In addition to this period the objector was bound by his condition for a further sixty days; these sixty days were regarded as the equivalent of the

National Service man's obligation to undergo part-time training after completing his full-time service. (It is interesting to note that, unlike the law in some other European countries, e.g. France and Holland, British law did not compel objectors exempted for civilian work to engage in this work for a substantially longer period than they would have been compelled to serve in the Forces.)

Under Section 17 of the 1948 Act, the conditionally registered objector might be compelled to submit to medical examination to ascertain his fitness for the prescribed work and to undergo such training as the Minister might direct to fit him for that work. Under Section 19 of the Act an objector who, after the lapse of a month, failed to undertake or ceased to undertake work specified by the tribunal could be directed by the Minister to undertake such work. The war-time power of tribunals to specify alternative forms of work was not changed and tribunals often gave a choice between two or three alternative forms of work, for example, agriculture, forestry and hospital work.

The following sets of figures regarding the number of applications to and the decisions of tribunals are all extracted from official figures which were compiled by the Ministry of Labour and National Service (though not all were published by the Ministry).

For the period of 15½ years between July 1945 and the end of 1960 the total number of original applications considered by local tribunals was 10,390. The decisions of the local tribunals were as follows.[49]

	Number	Per Cent
Registered unconditionally as Conscientious Objectors	263	2.5
Registered conditionally as Conscientious Objectors	4,246	40.9
Registered for non-combatant duties in the Forces	2,059	19.8
Total registered as Conscientious Objectors	6,568	63.2
Name removed from register of Conscientious Objectors	3,822	36.8

The proportion of applicants refused exemption was considerably higher over the post-war period as a whole than the War period as a whole, when, out of 59,192 applicants, 29.5% were refused exemption by local tribunals. (See figures on p. 187). But during the later years of the War period, from January 1943 to June 1945, the proportion was 37.4% and this was a higher proportion than the proportion of 34.2% in the period July 1945 to December 1947. There is thus no evidence that it was the coming of peace that led to an increase in the proportion rejected by tribunals. But there was another factor which probably did influence the proportion of rejections – the age of the applicants. From the beginning of 1943 until the middle of 1956 the age of registration was between 17 years 8 months and 18 years 2 months, whereas between 1939 and June 1941 the ages of registration were between 20 and 41, and in the years 1939 to 1941 the proportion of rejections was only 28.2%.[50] As there was considerable variation in the yearly figures over the post-war period they do not supply conclusive evidence for my view that the greater proportion of rejections in that period was partly due to the youth of many of the applicants. But this conclusion seems probable, as an objector aged eighteen, especially if not brought up in a pacifist tradition, would be less likely to be able to produce the kind of evidence from others of his sincerity available to an older objector, and might also be less able to express his views in a convincing way.

Unpublished figures assembled by the Ministry of Labour and National Service[51] show that the final legal position of applicants for the 11 years 1949–1959 was as in the following table. These figures adjust the decisions of local tribunals in the same way as the figures for the Second World War for (a) decisions on appeal to the Appellate Tribunal, (b) decisions on references to tribunals on failure to comply with conditions of exemption with reasonable excuse. But the figures are also adjusted for (c) decisions on applications of original objectors after a court-martial sentence, (d) decisions on applications after a sentence for refusal of medical examination. As the adjustments in (c) and (d) were not made with regard to the figures for the Second World War, the two sets of figures are not strictly comparable. The total number of applicants for the years 1949 to 1959 was 8,106.

	Number	Per Cent
Registered unconditionally as Conscientious Objectors	250	3.1
Registered conditionally as Conscientious Objectors	4,385	54.1
Registered for non-combatant duties in the Forces	1,422	17.5
Total registered as Conscientious Objectors	6,057	74.7
Name removed from register of Conscientious Objectors	2,049	25.3

If these figures are compared with those for the Second World War (p.188) it will be seen that, even with the inclusion of adjustments (c) and (d) noted above, the proportion of applicants refused exemption was considerably higher than the 20.6% refused exemption during the War period.

If these adjusted figures are compared with the figures for decisions of local tribunals over the same period it is shown that the net result of the four kinds of alteration of the original local tribunal decisions was to add 1,034 to the total number of applicants registered as conscientious objectors, to add 59 to the number unconditionally registered, to add 1,182 to the number conditionally registered, and to decrease by 207 the number registered for non-combatant duties in the Forces. In addition a number of conditionally registered objectors had their conditions varied.

During the 11 years 1949 to 1959 the three divisions of the Appellate Tribunal considered a total of 2,713 ordinary appeals: of the men appealing 2,052 had been refused any exemption by the local tribunal, 469 had been registered for non-combatant duties in the Forces, and 192 had been conditionally registered. During the same period local tribunals made decisions on 204 cases with regard to failure to comply with conditions of exemption with reasonable excuse and the Appellate Tribunal also made decisions with regard to 7 of these cases. The Appellate Tribunal made decisions on 52 applications (not all of them first applications) from original objectors applying after sentence by court-martial and also, acting as the "Advisory Tribunal, " on a number of cases of men sentenced by court-martial who had become objectors while in the Forces.

(The figures for these latter cases are not available.) The Appellate Tribunal also made decisions on 137 applications of men applying after sentence for refusal of medical examination.[52]

During the years 1951 and 1952 tribunals dealt with several hundred cases outside the National Service Acts. These were cases of reservists called up under the provisions of the Reserve and Auxiliary Forces (Training) Act, 1951.[53] This Act authorised the recall for a period of fifteen days' training of "Z" reservists in the Army and "G" reservists in the Air Force – these were men compulsorily in the reserve as a consequence of their full-time service during the years 1939 to 1948. Under the Act over 300,000 reservists were recalled for training during the two years, 1951 and 1952, in which the Act was applied.

The Act was the first piece of twentieth-century legislation imposing compulsory military service which did not provide for legal exemption of conscientious objectors. But during the parliamentary debates on the Bill an undertaking was given by the Government that a reservist summoned for training would be allowed to apply to a local tribunal and to appeal to the Appellate Tribunal. The tribunals would act in an advisory capacity but the Service Departments would accept their advice.[54] (There was no corresponding concession for National Service reservists liable for part-time training under the National Service Act, 1948[55] and amending Acts, under provisions described earlier in this chapter).

In this advisory capacity local tribunals considered 541 cases of reservists in 1951 and 401 cases in 1952; the Appellate Tribunal considered 183 cases in 1951 and 125 cases in 1952. In 1951 either the local tribunal or the Appellate Tribunal decided that 255 reservists (47.1% of those applying) should be "regarded as conscientiously objecting to military service";[56] in 1952 the tribunals decided in this way with regard to 259 reservists (64.6% of those applying).[57] (These figures are not included in any other tribunal figures in this chapter.) In Chapter 11 there will be a further discussion of the tribunal system over the whole period 1939 to 1960.

The Law-Breakers

The call-up of reservists under the Reserve and Auxiliary Forces (Training) Act, 1951[58] resulted in prosecutions of 73 objectors who had applied unsuccessfully to the tribunals.[59] The maximum penalty for failing to obey a training notice was a £25 fine or a month's imprisonment or both; for failure to attend for medical examination the maximum penalty was a fine of £25. A number of those prosecuted were convicted of both these offences. There were some sentences of imprisonment but in many cases fines only were imposed.

Except for these law-breaking reservists and for war-time objectors breaking the law in relation to the Home Guard, the law-breakers in the post-war period were in the same legal groups as the law-breakers during the Second World War.

With regard to these three groups of law-breakers – those sentenced for refusal of medical examination, those sentenced for non-compliance with their condition of exemption and those sentenced by court-martial – the main provisions of the law remained as they were in the later years of the War period. Minor changes in the law will be mentioned in the following description.

As was the case during the War period, the largest class of law-breakers consisted of men, refused any exemption by tribunals or registered for non-combatant duties in the Forces to which they objected, who refused to take their medical examinations. (The available figures do not distinguish between law-breakers subject to these two tribunal decisions.) For the years 1947–1960 the Annual Reports of the Ministry of Labour and National Service gave figures of the number of men sentenced each year for refusal to obey a court order for medical examination. (It cannot be assumed that all the men sentenced for this offence were conscientious objectors but probably the large majority were.) Over this whole period of fourteen years the total figure was 1,274, a yearly average of 91, and in each of the eight years 1952–1959 more than 100 men were sentenced. But the total figure for the period is greater than the number of individuals affected, as there were a considerable number of second prosecutions of the same individual, sometimes occurring in a different year from that of the first prosecution. The Ministry's Reports for the years 1948–1957 gave figures of the number of men sentenced a further time during the same year, and in five years of this period 35 or more men were so sentenced.[60]

There were a number of contrasts with the position of those refusing medical examination during the War period. In the first place it seems clear that a much larger proportion of those registered

233

by the tribunals for combatant or non-combatant military service refused to take their medical examinations. On the basis of the Ministry's figures for the years 1949–1959, compared with the adjusted tribunal figures for the same years, the proportion was 32% (though this figure is too high, for reasons already given). The corresponding proportion for the War period, (based on cases known to the Central Board for Conscientious Objectors) was 8.5%, increased to 11% if court-martial sentences are also included[61] (see Chapter 5, p. 189). It seems very likely that one reason for the much larger proportion of illegal resisters to military service was the refusal by tribunals of any exemption to a considerably larger proportion of applicants.

A second contrast was the fact that in the post-war period courts tended to be more lenient in their sentences and quite often imposed fines instead of imprisonment. The following example is of penalties imposed on prosecutions for refusals of medical examination under court order during one year of the period. In 1958 the Central Board for Conscientious Objectors had knowledge of 48 cases; of these cases 33 were sentenced to imprisonment. Two objectors had sentences of 12 months' imprisonment and one objector had a sentence of 9 months' imprisonment; in these three cases the length of imprisonment was shortened on appeal to Quarter Sessions. There were 8 sentences of six months' imprisonment and the other prison sentences varied between one month's and four months' imprisonment. In 16 prosecutions fines only were imposed, varying in amount between £2 and £50.[62]

The comparative leniency of courts in the post-war period was one reason why a larger proportion of offenders than in the War period were prosecuted more than once. The Ministry of Labour and National Service had rules under which it did not prosecute a man again if he had served a sentence or sentences amounting to three months' imprisonment or more. In other cases it did not prosecute more than twice except where it considered that the previous sentences were "derisory."[63] There were in the 1950s a number of third prosecutions when fines only had been imposed in the previous sentences. Another possible reason for the larger proportion of repeated prosecutions was the fact that from June 1947 the Ministry ceased to make general use of its power, under the Defence Regulations, to give directions to civilian work, and from the end of 1949 discontinued any use of this power. (See

Chapter 7, p. 255–6). During the War the Ministry often used this power instead of prosecuting a second time objectors who refused to take their medical examinations.

Another contrast with the position in the War period was that a much smaller proportion of men sentenced applied to the Appellate Tribunal. On the basis of the official tribunal figures and of the figures for sentences already quoted, applications in the years 1949–1959 were only 11.7% of sentences during the same years; the corresponding figure for the War period was 77 4%.[64] One reason for this contrast was that the more lenient policy of many courts in the post-war period resulted in a considerable number of sentences of a fine or of imprisonment for less than three months, and neither of these sentences gave the objector the right to apply to the Appellate Tribunal. On the other hand, if the objector received a qualifying sentence he would know that the Ministry's policy meant that he would not be prosecuted again and he might not consider it worthwhile to apply to the tribunal. Another probable reason for the contrast was the fact that a considerable number of those sentenced were unwilling to accept any tribunal condition of exemption. For example, in the sample for 1958 already quoted, 26 out of the total of 48 cases were Jehovah's Witnesses who usually adopted this position. An "unconditionalist" was not very likely to be awarded unconditional exemption by the Appellate Tribunal, and an award of conditional exemption would not improve his legal position.

With regard to non-compliance with the conditions of exemption imposed by the tribunal, the law in the post-War period was the same as in the later years of the War period. For the offence of non-compliance without reasonable excuse, official figures showed 246 convictions of men and 4 convictions of women in the period from July 1945 to the end of 1960. (The convictions of women were in the first eighteen months of this period.) The Annual Reports of the Ministry of Labour and National Service showed the figure for each year from 1947 to 1960; over the whole of this period the average yearly figure was 15 but in the years 1956 to 1959 the yearly average was 28.[65] The official figures were of convictions, including convictions on second prosecutions, so that the number of individuals convicted was somewhat smaller. Over the period 1949 to 1959 convictions were 3% to 4% of the number of objectors conditionally registered during that period; this figure is considerably higher than the figure of about 1% during the War period. (See Chapter 5, p. 190). The great variation of sentences imposed is shown in the example of the thirteen sentences in 1959 known to the Central Board for Conscientious Objectors. There were six sentences of imprisonment – one of twelve months (reduced on appeal to Quarter Sessions), one of six months, two of three months, one of two months, and one of one month. There were seven sentences of fines, varying between £50 and £10. Of the twelve individuals concerned eight were Jehovah's witnesses.[66]

With regard to court-martial sentences there were two changes in the law during the period 1945 to 1960.

The Courts-Martial (Appeals) Act, 1951,[67] provided for the establishment of a Courts Martial Appeal Court to which any person convicted by a naval, army, or air-force court martial could, with the leave of the court, appeal against his conviction. As the Act did not provide for appeals against sentence, the new provision was of little value to conscientious objectors.

The second change in the law was of great value to some objectors. The war-time law had given the right to apply to the Appellate Tribunal to an objector sentenced by court-martial to imprisonment for three months or more but not to an objector sentenced to military detention. The National Service Act, 1947,[68] confirmed by Section 21 of the National Service Act 1948,[69] extended the right to an objector sentenced by court-martial to military detention for three months or more.

As was the case during the War period, conscientious objectors sentenced by court-martial were in two groups with regard to their legal position. (See Chapter 5). In the first group were men who had registered provisionally as conscientious objectors but had been rejected by tribunals or registered for non-combatant duties in the Forces to which they objected. They had taken their medical examinations and had been called up for combatant or non-combatant military service. If sentenced to imprisonment or, (from 1949 onwards), to military detention for three months or more, they had the statutory right to apply to the Appellate Tribunal. For this group of objectors there are no official published figures with regard to court-martial sentences but there are official figures with regard to applications to, and decisions of, the Appellate Tribunal.

The official figures show that between July 1945 and the end of 1959 there were 110 applications to the Appellate Tribunal after court-martial sentences. (As a number of these were not first applications, the number of individuals concerned was smaller.) Of these applications, 70 resulted in a recommendation for discharge from the Forces and 3 resulted in a recommendation for transference to non-combatant duties; the other applications were rejected.[70]

The second group of objectors sentenced by court-martial were those who had volunteered for the Forces or had been conscripted without registering provisionally as conscientious objectors, and had then become objectors while full-time members of the Forces or while in one of the Reserves. From 1951 onwards this group included men who had performed their full-time National Service and then objected to performing their legally required part-time service. Such men were not allowed to apply to a tribunal (as were the "Z" and "G" reservists described earlier in this chapter) until after receiving a court-martial sentence. This group of objectors had no statutory rights of application to the Appellate Tribunal but, by an administrative concession, they were allowed to apply to the "Advisory Tribunal" (the Appellate Tribunal functioning under another name) if they received sentences of imprisonment or (from 1949 onwards) of military detention for three months or more. For this group there are no official published figures with regard to either court-martial sentences or applications to the Advisory Tribunal.

For the years 1952 to 1955 the Central Board for Conscientious Objectors published classified figures regarding cases known to it of objectors in the Forces in both these groups.[71] The Board's annual published figures for these four years showed a total of 127 men applying to the appellate or Advisory Tribunal after a court-martial sentence. Of these, only 22 men had originally provisionally registered as conscientious objectors and were claiming their statutory right to apply to the Appellate Tribunal. The other 105 men were taking advantage of the administrative concession allowing them to apply to the Advisory Tribunal; this group included 49 National Service men who had completed their full-time service and had then refused to perform their part-time service. The numbers of individuals concerned were less than these totals as some men applied to the tribunal in more than one year. At this period, while a first unsuccessful application to the tribunal meant that the man remained in the Forces, he was usually discharged after serving a second court-martial sentence even if not successful with the tribunal.[72]

The following is an example of the results of tribunal applications. In 1955 eight men who had originally provisionally registered as conscientious objectors applied to the Appellate Tribunal: of these, six were recommended for discharge from the Forces. Seventeen men serving full-time in the Forces who had become conscientious objectors applied to the Advisory Tribunal: of these, five were recommended for discharge, four of them on their second application to the Tribunal. Thirteen men refusing part-time National Service applied to the Advisory Tribunal: of these, ten were recommended for discharge, two of them on their second application.[73]

Compulsory Retention in the Forces

The phenomenon of conscientious law-breaking on account of objection to military service did not disappear with the ending of compulsory National Service. Since November 1960 no one has been compulsorily enlisted in the Forces, and since May 1963 all full-time members of the Forces originally volunteered for enlistment. But, though enlistment has been voluntary, members of the Forces have been compulsorily retained for long periods. Thus there has remained, and still remains, the problem of the treatment of men and women who become conscientious objectors to military service at some time between their voluntary enlistment and the end of their period of engagement.

REFERENCES

Cmd. 7225 = Report of the Ministry of Labour and National Service
for the Years 1939–1946

CBCO = Central Board for Conscientious Objectors

1   Cmd. 6548
2   Cmd. 7225 pp. 35, 225–226 and 360–361
     Ministry of Labour and National Service. Reports for 1947, 1948 and
     1949
3   Cmd. 7225 pp. 35, 225–226 and 360–361
     Ministry of Labour and National Service. Report for 1947 Cmd. 7559:
     pp. 27–28
4   9 & 10 Geo. 6. c. 38
5   Cmd. 7225 p. 153
     Ministry of Labour and National Service. Reports for 1947, 1948, 1949
     and 1950
6   11 & 12 Geo. 6. c. 64
7   Cmd. 7225 p. 130
8   Ministry of Labour and National Service. Report for 1947, Cmd. 7559.
     p. 15
9   12 & 13 Geo. 6. c. 6
10   Ministry of Labour and National Service. Report for 1949, Cmd. 8017.
     p. 2
     Ibid. Report for 1950. Cmd. 8338. p. 7
11   10 & 11 Geo. 6. c. 31
12   11 & 12 Geo.6.c.64
13   S.l. 1953 No. 1771
14   Cmd. 124
15   11 & 12 Geo. 6. c. 64
16   12 & 13Geo.6.c.6
17   14 Geo. 6. c. 30
18   Cmd. 9608
19   Army Reserve Act 1962 c. 10
20   The Guardian 11.5.1963
21   11 & 12 Geo. 6. c. 64
22   12 & 13 Geo. 6. c. 6
23   14 Geo. 6. c. 30
24   Cmd. 9608
25   11 & 12 Geo. 6. c. 64 Sect. 1
26   12 & 13Geo.6.c.6
27   3 & 4 Eliz. 2. c. 11
28   Hayes, Denis *Challenge of Conscience. The Story of the Conscientious
     Objectors of 1939–1949* p. 382
     Cmd. 7225. p. 335

Ministry of Labour and National Service. Annual Reports for the Years 1947–1960

29 Ministry of Labour and National Service. Report for 1955. Cmd. 9791
    Ibid. Report for 1956. Cmd. 242
30 Ibid. Report for 1953. Cmd. 9207. p. 17
31 Ibid. Report for 1960. Cmd. 1364. p. 11
32 Cmd. 7225. pp. 35 and 225–226
    Ministry of Labour and National Service. Annual Reports for the Years 1947–1960
33 Cmd. 7225. p. 145
    Ministry of Labour and National Service. Annual Reports for the Years 1947–1960
34 Ministry of Labour and National Service. Annual Reports for the Years 1952–1958
35 Hayes op. cit. p. 382
    Ministry of Labour and National Service. Annual Reports for the Years 1948–1960
36 2 & 3 Geo. 6. c. 25
37 Statement in court. 17.1.1950. Private information.
38 Statement to Tribunal 20.1.1948. Private information.
39 Peace News 9.11.1956
40 Peace News 25.2.1955
41 Peace News 15.10.1954
42 Peace News 18.2.1955
43 Peace News 10.12.1954
44 Peace News 23.4.1954
45 The Manchester Guardian 19.9.1956
46 Hayes op. cit. p. 383
    Ministry of Labour and National Service. Annual Reports for the Years 1947–1960.
47 11 & 12 Geo. 6. c. 64. Fourth Schedule
48 11 & 12 Geo. 6. c. 64
49 Hayes op. cit. p. 383
    CBCO Bulletin. August 1945
    Ministry of Labour and National Service. Annual Reports for the Years 1947–1960
50 Hayes op. cit. p. 383
    CBCO Bulletin. August 1945
    Supplement to CBCO Bulletin. September 1945
51 Ministry of Labour and National Service: figures supplied to CBCO
52 Ibid.
53 14 & 15 Geo. 6. c. 23
54 Hansard 26.2.1951. Vol. 484 Cols. 1761–1869
55 11 & 12 Geo. 6. c. 24
56 Ministry of Labour and National Service. Report for 1951. Cmd. 8640. p. 15
57 Ibid. Report for 1952. Cmd. 8893. pp. 15–16
58 14 & 15 Geo 6. c. 23

59 CBCO Annual Report for 1952–53
60 Ministry of Labour and National Service. Annual Reports for the Years 1947–1960
61 CBCO Bulletin. August 1945 and September 1945
    Ministry of Labour and National Service. Annual Reports for the Years 1949–1959
    Ibid. Figures supplied to CBCO
62 Unpublished records of CBCO
63 Statements in House of Commons 15.5.1947 and 29.1.1952
64 CBCO Bulletins. August 1945 and September 1945
    Ministry of Labour and National Service. Annual Reports for the Years 1949–1959
    Ibid. Figures supplied to CBCO
65 Cmd. 7225 p. 143
    Ministry of Labour and National Service. Annual Reports for the Years 1947–1960
66 Unpublished records of CBCO
67 14 & 15 Geo. 6. c. 46
68 10 & 11 Geo. 6. c. 31
69 11 & 12 Geo. 6. c. 64
70 Hayes op. cit. p. 386
    CBCO Bulletin. August 1945
    Ministry of Labour and National Service: figures supplied to CBCO
71 Annual Reports of CBCO for 1952–53, 1953–54, 1954–55 and 1955–56
    The Objector. June 1953
72 Statement of Fenner Brockway in House of Commons 23.7.1953
73 Annual Report of CBCO for 1955–56

Chronological Table of Acts Relating to Compulsory Military Service 1945–1960

Date		
1946	National Service (Release of Conscientious Objectors) Act	9 & 10 Geo. 6. c. 38
1947	National Service Act	10 & 11 Geo. 6. c. 31
1948	National Service Act	11 & 12 Geo. 6. c. 64
1948	National Service (Amendment) Act	12 & 13 Geo. 6. c. 6
1950	National Service Act	14 Geo. 6. c. 30
1951	Reserve and Auxiliary Forces (Training) Act	14 & 15 Geo. 6. c. 23
1951	Courts-Martial (Appeals) Act	14 & 15 Geo. 6. c. 46
1955	National Service Act	3 & 4 Eliz. 2. c. 11
1962	Army Reserve Act	10 & 11 Eliz. 2. c. 10

CHAPTER 7

Other Twentieth Century Compulsions for Defence Purposes

Introduction

The four types of compulsion described in this chapter have the common feature that with regard to none of them was any statutory provision made for legal conscientious objection. Thus the legal position of conscientious objectors to these compulsions was very different from the position of objectors to military service. In the case of industrial conscription important administrative concessions were made which enabled some objectors to obey their consciences without breaking the law; other objectors became conscientious law-breakers. In the case of the other three types of compulsion all conscientious objection was illegal objection.

Industrial Conscription 1940–1950

The Law of Wartime Industrial Conscription

"Industrial conscription" is a convenient term to use to include the whole complex of controls of civilian labour in Great Britain established during the Second World War, in so far as these controls involved legal compulsions affecting the choice of work of the individual worker.

During the War not only was recruitment to the Armed Forces efficiently organised but from May 1940 great efforts were made to organise the available resources of civilian labour and allocate them to those industries and services most necessary for the prosecution of the War and the provision of essential community services. For this purpose it was necessary both to increase the total supply of labour available and to make many changes, varying in different periods according to the needs of the moment, in the distribution of labour between employments and often between localities.

There were two main potential sources of increased labour supply – the unemployed and people not "gainfully occupied". Between June 1939 and June 1943 (which was three months before the peak of mobilisation) the number of men (under pensionable age) and boys working in the Forces and in civilian gainful occupations increased from 13,643,000 to 14,971,000: of this increase nearly 80% was caused by the decrease in unemployment. But in the case of women the decrease in unemployment was a very minor factor in increasing labour supply compared with the increase in the number available for gainful employment. In June 1939 the number of women (under pensionable age) and girls working in gainful occupations (other than private domestic service) was 4,837,000: in June 1943 the number had increased by 57% to 7,605,000, of whom 750,000 were working part-time.[1] The recruitment, by inducement or compulsion, of two and three quarter million additional women was one of the greatest achievements of the Ministry of Labour and National Service and was of major assistance to the war effort.

In addition to the recruitment of extra labour, the war effort required large changes in the distribution of labour between various occupations and industries. Between June 1939 and June 1943 the number of members of the Armed Forces and Women's Auxiliary Services increased by over 4¼ million; the number employed in the Police, Civil Defence and the Fire Service increased by nearly 250,000; the number engaged in manufacture of equipment and supplies for the Forces increased by over 3¾ million. Over the same period the number engaged in manufacture for the home market and for export decreased by nearly 4 million; the number engaged in building and civil engineering decreased by nearly 600,000; the number engaged in the distributive trades decreased by nearly 900,000[2]

The vast changes in the employment of civilian labour necessitated by the War were not achieved by any rigid compulsory system. Prior to May 1940 very little compulsion was used except in connection with military conscription. When Ernest Bevin, at that date, became Minister of Labour and National Service in the newly formed Coalition Government, he adopted a policy of relying mainly on persuasion and the methods of voluntary collective bargaining in which he had had long experience as a trade union leader. He trusted the ordinary worker to respond to the country's needs and he addressed many meetings up and down the country explaining the nature and urgency of those needs. He was also determined that in the necessary changes of employment and locality of work the workers' wages and conditions of work should be protected and he greatly increased the provision of welfare services such as canteens and hostels. But Bevin was willing to use compulsion where he thought it necessary and he gradually increased its scope under the powers given him by the Defence Regulations until by mid-1943 there was a complicated and comprehensive system of controls in force to be used as sanctions in individual cases when neither patriotism nor economic incentive was sufficient to produce the desired results.

The only war-time legal measure of control prior to May 1940 was the Control of Employment Act[3] passed in September 1939. This Act empowered the Minister of Labour and National Service to make Orders requiring his consent to (a) the publication of advertisements for employees, (b) the engagement or re-engagement of employees. One Order was made under this Act, in April 1940. Subsequent controls of a similar kind were exercised under one of the Defence Regulations.

The Emergency Powers (Defence) Act, 1939,[4] passed ten days before the outbreak of war, gave wide powers to the Crown to make, by Order in Council, Defence Regulations for the purposes of securing the public safety, the defence of the realm, the maintenance of public order, the efficient prosecution of the war, and the maintenance of "supplies and services essential to the life of the community." But Section 1 (5) of the Act stated: "Nothing in this section shall authorise the imposition of... any form of industrial conscription."

The legal position with regard to control of employment was radically changed by the amending Emergency Powers (Defence) Act, 1940,[5] passed through Parliament in a single day on 22nd May. The historian Allan Bullock has opined: "This was the most drastic Act ever passed by a British Parliament."[6] The Act stated that the powers given in the 1939 Act should include powers to make Defence Regulations "making provision for requiring persons to place themselves, their services, and their property at the disposal of His Majesty." Under this wide authorisation the subsequent war-time control of civilian employment was exercised by means of Defence Regulations and Orders under these Regulations, without the necessity of further legislation. (Full-time military service, in contrast, continued to be regulated by the National Service Acts.)

Under the new powers given by this Act the important Defence Regulation 58A[7] was made immediately. The powers given in the first paragraph were very wide: "The Minister of Labour and National Service... or any National Service Officer may direct any person in Great Britain to perform such services in the United Kingdom... as may be specified by or described in the direction, being services which that person is, in the opinion of the Minister or Officer, capable of performing." Under the Regulation persons could be required to register prescribed particulars about themselves and in December 1941 this provision was supplemented by Defence Regulation 80B[8] which provided for compulsory directions to interview and to medical examination. In addition to giving the Minister of Labour and National Service powers to direct workers to employment, Regulation 58A also stated that the Minister "may by order make provision for regulating the engagement of workers by their employers and the duration and situation of their employment" and "may by order make provision for securing that enough workers are available in undertakings engaged in essential work."

The measures of control now to be described were exercised under the authority of Regulation 58A (which was several times amended) and Regulation 80B. These controls were in three main groups – controls to safeguard the supply of workers in "essential work"; controls of the engagement of workers; and controls concerning the registration and interviewing of workers, so that they could be allocated to officially desired employments, and concerning their compulsory direction to these employments if this was thought necessary.

It became obvious early in 1941 that greater powers were needed to secure stabilisation of labour in essential war industries and in March the Essential Work (General Provisions) Order[9] was made. In undertakings "scheduled" under this Order there were drastic restrictions on the employer's freedom to discharge and the worker's freedom to leave employment. In nearly all cases cessation of employment required the permission of a National

Service Officer, though both sides had the right of appeal to a local advisory Appeal Board. The provisions covered guaranteed wages, absenteeism, persistent lateness, and refusal to comply with lawful and reasonable orders. Eventually the Essential Work controls (including a number of separate orders for particular industries) covered 8¾ million workers in 67,500 undertakings.[10] During the War period 84% of applications to National Service Officers for permission to terminate employment were granted.[11]

The general principle of the Control of Engagement Orders was to control the engagement of workers by restricting it to engagement through an Employment Exchange or through any other agency officially approved for this purpose. There were a number of orders covering particular industries or occupations. There were also three important general Employment of Women (Control of Engagement) Orders made in January 1942,[12] covering women aged 20–30 inclusive; in April 1942,[13] covering ages 18–30 inclusive; and in February 1943,[14] covering ages 18–40 inclusive. These Orders included all women within the age groups covered with certain exceptions. The most important group excepted were women with children of their own under the age of fourteen living with them. Women in a few industries and occupations were excepted and exemption certificates could be granted to individual women or individual employers.

In addition to these general restrictions on engagement it was made an offence for an employer, without the consent of a National Service Officer, knowingly to employ a person who had been given a direction to work under another employer.[15]

There was no similar control of termination of employment (except in scheduled "essential work") but in August 1943 the Control of Employment (Notice of Termination of Employment) Order[16] provided that, with certain specified exceptions, employers must give immediate notice in writing of all cases of termination of employment of men aged 18–64 inclusive and of women aged 18–59 inclusive.

Compulsory registration for employment included both registration of persons in particular industries or occupations and general registration of men and women in certain age groups. Between July 1940 and June 1945 there were twelve registrations of "persons possessing special qualifications or skills", for example, merchant seamen, coal miners, and nurses and midwives.[17]

Under the Registration for Employment Order,[18] made in March 1941, there was a series of comprehensive registrations of men and women by age groups. All persons registering were required to give particulars of their present employment; women were required also to give particulars as to their household responsibilities and as to whether they had living with them children of their own under the age of fourteen.

The registrations of men covered only those over the age of 41, as by June 1941 men up to that age had been registered under the National Service Acts. Between April and October 1941 there were six registrations covering men aged 41 to 46 inclusive. After a nine months' gap there were three further registrations between July and September 1942 covering men up to the age of 50 years 9 months.[19] The total number of men registered was 1,933,000.[20]

There were thirty-eight registrations of women, the first being in April 1941 and the last in July 1945 and the total number registered was 11,800,000.[21] During 1941 there were eleven registrations covering women aged 20 to 31 inclusive. The sixteen registrations in 1942 included women aged 32 to 45 inclusive and also women aged 18½ to 20. There were seven further registrations of young women between 18 and 20 in the years 1943 to 1945. After a gap of nearly a year from the registration of the previous oldest age group there were between September and November 1943 four registrations of women aged between 46 and 50 years 10 months.[22] Women in this age group were regarded as available only for local work and were interviewed only in some districts.[23]

Compulsory registration provided the first information on which the Ministry of Labour and National Service could decide on further action. In some cases further action was not necessarily taken, for example, with regard to persons already in essential occupations and women with young children. If it was desired to take further action the next stage was to interview the person concerned – eight million individual interviews (mostly of women) were conducted.[24] After the making of Defence Regulation 80B in December 1941 it became an offence to refuse to obey a direction to interview or to medical examination. On the basis of the interview men and women were left in, or allocated to, priority employments (including part-time employment in the case of some women) and normally a legal direction to employment was not issued except as a last resort. "The policy and procedure to be followed in the use of directions were kept under constant review and instructions issued in relation to numerous types of cases."[25] For example, it was decided that in no circumstances should directions to employment be given to women with young children of their own living with them. A national Women's Consultative Committee, set up in March 1941, met frequently and discussed policy concerning the conscription and employment of women.[26]

The power to direct individual men and women to specified work was not used widely in the first year after the making of Defence Regulation 58A – up to July 1941 not more than 2,800 directions had been issued.[27] But, as the War developed and there came to be a general shortage of labour, the number of directions greatly increased – there were 408,000 directions issued in the year July 1942 to June 1943.[28] But the number of directions issued did not truly indicate the importance of the existence of compulsory powers. "The greater value of sanctions, as Bevin had always believed, proved to be the knowledge that they were there to be used if necessary. This supplied for most people a sufficiently powerful incentive to do voluntarily what they would otherwise be compelled to do, and a guarantee that those who tried to evade their duty would not be allowed to get away with it."[29]

A system of Local Appeal Boards was established in March 1941 to consider appeals under the Essential Work Orders and in addition workers given a direction to employment were normally allowed to appeal to these Boards. Each Appeal Board consisted of an employer's representative, a workers' representative and an independent chairman, and a woman member was included for women's appeals. Though the Board merely advised the National Service Officer, the policy of the Ministry was to accept its recommendations in nearly all cases.[30]

The Position of Conscientious Objectors

In none of the Acts, Regulations and Orders which were the framework of industrial conscription was there any mention of conscientious objection – there was no statutory provision for conscientious objectors and they had no legal rights as objectors. The law-making authorities drew a sharp distinction between conscientious objection to military service for which they had made statutory provision, and conscientious objection to civilian work, for which they refused to make any such provision.

In the administration of industrial conscription, however, some concessions were made to the objector. It was obvious, for example, that nearly all pacifists would object as strongly to making munitions as they would object to military service and that it was inconsistent to allow objection to the latter but not to the former. In a letter to the Central Board for Conscientious Objectors in February 1941 the Ministry of Labour and National Service stated: "This Department will endeavour to use its powers of direction reasonably and it is not the Minister's intention so far as can be avoided to direct persons to perform services against which they have genuine conscientious objections."[31]

In a Circular concerning Civil Defence sent in 1943 by the Ministry of Home Security to local authorities it was stated: "The Minister of Labour and National Service has pledged himself not to exercise the powers he possesses to compel persons, who profess a conscientious objection to making or handling munitions, to perform work which would involve their doing so. This pledge has been liberally interpreted to include work closely connected with, or applied to, the military side of the war effort."[32] In a letter to a woman objector from a Regional Office of the Ministry of Labour and National Service it was stated: "Those who will be required to take up other employment will, as far as possible, be able to make their own choice as to the kind of work to be undertaken. There are many types of employment such as Agriculture, Forestry, Civil Defence, Nursing etc. open to persons who have conscientious objections to undertaking war work."[33]

There is no information available as to the number of objectors who stated their objections in interviews or correspondence with Ministry officials. Though a few mistakes were made (and usually remedied) Ministry officials in general fulfilled the promise made not to direct objectors into work closely connected with the military side of the war effort. Objectors who had no objection to entering other forms of employment approved by the Ministry were not involved in any resistance to the law.

Conscientious objectors, like others given a direction to employment, were normally allowed to appeal to the advisory Local Appeal Board. Appeal Boards were not debarred from considering matters of conscience[34] and there were cases in which directions of pacifists to munitions or similar work were withdrawn after an appeal hearing. But some Boards "seemed to resent any suggestion that conscientious objection might come within their terms of reference and refused point-blank to hear any argument on the point."[35]

There are no official figures of the number of conscientious objectors prosecuted under the law of industrial conscription and the following account is based mainly on information available to the Central Board for Conscientious Objectors. The first known prosecution of a man objector was in December 1941. The man concerned was aged forty-three and had retired on conscientious grounds from a shipbuilding firm in which he had been managing director: on refusing a direction to agricultural work he was sentenced to two months' imprisonment. Three weeks later a woman aged twenty-one, a housemaid, (the first or almost the first woman objector to be prosecuted) refused a direction to domestic work in a hospital and was sentenced to a month's imprisonment on refusing to pay a fine of 40s.[36] She was probably the first woman ever to be imprisoned in this country as a conscientious objector to war (though there were some cases of women imprisoned for pacifist propaganda offences during the First World War).

The following figures (which are the best available) show the total number of prosecutions known to the Central Board for Conscientious Objectors up to the end of 1948.[37] The large majority of these prosecutions occurred during the war period, especially in 1943 and 1944 in the case of men and in 1942 and 1943 in the case of women.

The total number of prosecutions was 944–610 prosecutions of men and 334 prosecutions of women. The details were as follows:

Nature of Prosecution	Number
Men	
Directions to work and offences against the Essential Work Orders	540
Directions to interview	33
Directions to medical examination	37
Women	
Directions to work	272
Directions to interview	57
Directions to medical examination	4
Refusal to register	1

Among the prosecutions of women relating to directions to work there were 15 second prosecutions.[38] The Ministry of Labour and National Service was reluctant to prosecute women and, though there were some exceptions, it did not normally prosecute again if one sentence of imprisonment had been served. For offences under industrial conscription about 245 women were imprisoned, either as the result of a sentence of imprisonment or for refusal to pay the fine imposed.[39]

Under the Defence Regulations the maximum penalty which could be imposed on summary conviction was imprisonment for three months or a fine of £100 or both these penalties.[40] To the best of my knowledge, there was no case in which the maximum fine was imposed in addition to the maximum imprisonment, and sentences of fines in addition to imprisonment were unusual, though one man was sentenced to three months' imprisonment plus a £50 fine and one woman was sentenced to three months' imprisonment plus a £25 fine.[42] Sentences of three months' imprisonment were fairly common; at the other end of the scale fines imposed were sometimes only £2.

The scale of variation in the sentences imposed on women is shown in the following example of the first twelve known prosecutions of women objectors. In the case of seven women fines were imposed – one of £2, one of £3, three of £5, and two of £8. Five women were sentenced to imprisonment – two for fourteen days, one for one month and two for three months. In the case of one of the women sentenced to three months' imprisonment a fine of £25 was also imposed; as she refused to pay this fine an extra sentence of three months' imprisonment was imposed. Of the seven other women fined five refused to pay the fine and were imprisoned in lieu of payment.[43]

At least 200 of the prosecutions of men were cases in which the man had already served a sentence for refusal of medical examination under court order and was still legally liable for military service. As was explained in Chapter 5 (p.210), the Ministry of Labour and National Service often in such cases gave to the objector a direction to work under the Defence Regulations. If the objector refused to obey this direction he was prosecuted and in at least 160 cases[44] served his second sentence of imprisonment. In most cases the authorities then took no further action but there were about 35 cases in which there was a further prosecution because the objector was officially regarded as not being engaged in any useful work – these cases were nearly all men who were full-time workers for Jehovah's Witnesses.[45]

The views of those conscientious objectors who broke the law of industrial conscription were not a representative sample of the views of objectors as a whole. Men and women who objected only to work on munitions or other work directly concerned with military purposes were fitted into work to which they had no objection. The law-breakers were mainly men and women who objected to any co-operation in the machinery of the war effort or who, in addition to having conscientious objections to the War, felt a strong vocation for work not allowed to them by the authorities. (An individual might, of course, resist the law for both these reasons.) Among those to whom a sense of vocation was important were a considerable number of Jehovah's Witnesses, who considered that their religious work had a stronger moral claim on them than any work demanded by the legal authorities. For example, a man aged forty-five, who had been for twenty-two years a full-time minister with the Jehovah's Witnesses, was imprisoned for refusing a direction to work. He stated that he held his calling as a sacred trust from Almighty God and that his conscience therefore forbade him taking up any form of alternative service.[46]

Examples of objections to co-operation with the war effort are the following statements made by two women objectors: the first is part of a statement made in court on the occasion of a prosecution for refusal to attend for interview; the second is part of a letter to the Minister of Labour and National Service notifying refusal to register:

(1) *Prior to the outbreak of the war I was engaged upon work which I knew, in the event of war, would become increasingly essential to its prosecution, while not being direct war work. I felt, as a pacifist, that I could not honestly continue in such work, and therefore resigned on September 5th 1939, and sought work which was not connected with the war effort. I found such work and am still engaged upon it. . . Events of the past three years have only served to strengthen the certainty that the action I took in 1939 was right for me.*

Above my allegiance to the State, I place my allegiance to God and humanity. The interests of the State and of humanity are not necessarily the same, and the act of war in which the State is engaged is, in my belief, against the wellbeing of the community...

I claim that God meant me to be a free individual, not only physically, but mentally and spiritually free. He gave me my life to use as seemed best, and it is I, not the State, who must finally account for the purpose to which it is used. I cannot, therefore, give to the State the right that it claims in total war to almost total control of my life.

Finally, my objection is not merely to taking life, but to the whole process of war, and since the Registration for Employment Order was passed for the purpose of assisting the prosecution of the war, and the direction I received to attend an interview was to decide how best I could help the war effort, I could not conscientiously either register under the Order, or obey the direction to attend for an interview.[47]

(2) *I did not register because I should regard registration as giving my consent to the continued prosecution of the War by this country and to the conscription of men and women for this purpose, and I do not consent to either of these.*

I am a pacifist, that is to say I hold that the actions necessary in war cannot be justified for me for any reason whatever, though I gratefully recognise the high motives animating many of my fellow citizens who are assisting in the War. It is not right for me to assist in or consent to such actions as the bombing of German towns and the starvation of many thousands in Europe by blockade, even though the alternative may be the Nazi domination of this country. I am prepared to resist Fascism in other ways but I cannot resist it by the evil methods of war.

I am opposed to conscription because I believe that in a matter as serious as participation in war each person should take individual moral responsibility for his actions and no Government has a right to coerce him. The conscription of women for war purposes is particularly oppressive because it violates the fundamental feeling of women for the value of individual life.

If the law relating to industrial conscription had allowed me the legal right to register as a conscientious objector and to apply to a Conscientious Objectors' Tribunal for unconditional exemption, I might have taken this course. As the law stands, however, refusal to register seems to me to be the only way to make it quite clear that my services are not at the disposal of the Government for the prosecution of the War.[48]

253

Post-war Industrial Conscription

The system of controls of labour evolved during the War was not ended suddenly when hostilities ceased but was gradually modified over a period of four and a half years and was ended in March 1950. After an interval of nearly two years a modified form of control of engagement was then imposed; it lasted for more than four years, ending in April 1956. For the purposes of this chapter it is necessary to give only a summary of this history.

The Emergency Powers (Defence) Acts of 1939[49] and 1940[50] were due to expire in August 1945 but their duration was extended to February 1946 by the Emergency Powers (Defence) Act, 1945[51] After February 1946 the Defence Regulations concerning the control of labour were kept in force by being included in an Order in Council[52] under the Supplies and Services (Transitional Provisions) Act, 1945.[53] This Order continued Regulations 58A and 80B and made them applicable for certain additional purposes. Two subsequent Acts extended the purposes for which Regulations were applicable – the Supplies and Services (Extended Purposes) Act, 1947,[54] and the Supplies and Services (Defence Purposes) Act, 1951,[55] (passed during the Korean War).

In May 1945 the Essential Work Orders covered about eight and three quarter million workers. By May 1946 about five million workers had been released.[56] By the end of June 1947 there were no industries covered by the Orders.[57] The paragraphs of Regulation 58A which gave the legal power to make Essential Work Orders were revoked in 1952.[58]

After the last war-time registration of workers, in July 1945, there were no further compulsory registrations for two and a half years. Then, between January and April 1948, about 37,000 men and nearly 59,000 women were compulsorily registered under the Registration for Employment Order, 1947.[59] Registration was confined to persons in certain age-groups who were not gainfully occupied, were working as street traders, or were working in certain types of non-essential undertakings.[60] The part of Regulation 58A which gave the legal power to require persons to register was revoked in 1952.[61]

Legal directions to work began to be drastically restricted from 8th May 1945, when hostilities in Europe ceased.[62] From June 1947 the majority of directions to work were directions given to men working in coal mining or agriculture to continue working in those industries. The use of the powers of direction to interview and direction to medical examination was progressively restricted as directions to work were restricted.[63] In March 1950 it was decided to discontinue the use of any powers of direction under Regulations 58A and 80B and, in fact, no directions were given after 1949.[64] In 1953 Regulation 80B and the paragraphs of Regulation 58A authorising directions to work were revoked.[65]

In May 1945 the Control of Employment (Notice of Termination) Order[66] was cancelled.

Between May 1945 and September 1947 the number of workers controlled by Control of Engagement Orders made in May 1945,[67] December 1945,[68] and February 1947[69] was greatly reduced. But an Order made in September 1947[70] re-imposed control of engagement on a large number of workers; this Order continued in operation until March 1950 when it was revoked.[71]

Between February 1952 (during the Korean War) and April 1956 there was a modified form of control of engagement under the Notification of Vacancies Order of February 1952[72] and an amending Order of July 1952.[73] Under these Orders employers were prohibited from engaging workers aged between 18 and pensionable ages (with some exceptions) unless such persons were submitted for employment by a local office of the Ministry of Labour and National Service or by a scheduled employment agency. The effect of the Orders was to give the Ministry a wider knowledge of vacancies and contact with more persons seeking a job. But, in contrast to the position before 1950, no power of directing to work was used and there was no attempt to bring pressure on workers to accept jobs considered more important in the national interest if they preferred to accept other jobs.[74] The Orders were revoked in April 1956.[75] In July 1956 the parts of Regulation 58A not already revoked were revoked.[76]

After 1956 none of the legal controls described in this account of industrial conscription was in force.

Compulsory Part-time Civil Defence 1942–1944

Up to the end of 1941 recruitment to part-time service in Civil Defence was voluntary but on 18th December 1941 a regulation was made enabling compulsion to be applied. Under Regulation 29 BA of the Defence (General) Regulations[77] the Minister of Labour and National Service was given power to direct men and women to join the Civil Defence Services (and also the Royal Observer Corps and the Special Constabulary) for either whole-time or part-time service. The procedure was operated through the Employment Exchanges. There was a right of appeal on grounds of exceptional hardship to the Local Appeal Boards.[78] In September 1944 directions were discontinued and on 9th May 1945 an Order revoked Regulation 29 BA.[79]

Under this scheme 269,642 men and 211,962 women were given directions to part-time work in the Civil Defence Services. Of this total of 481,604, 241,994 were directed to general Civil Defence services, 78,427 were directed to First Aid Posts and Ambulances Services, and 161,183 were directed to the National Fire Service.[80]

The normal hours for part-time service were 48 hours in every four weeks. The part-time service was unpaid but subsistence in kind or a subsistence allowance could be provided.[81] The issue of compulsory orders was normally confined to men aged 18-60 and women aged 18–55 and orders were made only in some areas.[82]

Many conscientious objectors to military service had no objection to performing Civil Defence duties. But some objectors were unwilling for conscientious reasons to perform Civil Defence duties or were unwilling to perform these duties under compulsion. When the scheme was applied in Bristol in luly 1942 the Bristol Advisory Bureau for Conscientious Objectors sent to the authorities and the press a letter stating: "The meeting feels that this measure marks a further attempt to secure by coercion the compliance of the civil population in the prosecution of the war, whilst, owing to the exclusion of a conscience clause, denying to the individual the right of upholding his convictions against the claims of the State."[83]

Objectors to Civil Defence duties had no legal right of conscientious objection to these duties. A number of objectors exercised the right to appeal to the Local Appeal Board on the ground that conscientious objection was "exceptional hardship" but in no case was the appeal successful.[84] However, objectors disobeying an order were not always prosecuted and from mid-1943 the Ministry of Labour and National Service was willing to give sympathetic consideration to cases of objectors who had been unconditionally registered as conscientious objectors to military service.[85]

The total number of prosecutions known to the Central Board for Conscientious Objectors was 109. 88 men and 7 women were prosecuted. There were 101 prosecutions of men and 8 of women: it will be noted that only a few objectors were prosecuted more than once. The last prosecution was in September 1944.[86]

Under the Defence Regulations the maximum penalty which could be imposed on summary conviction was imprisonment for three months or a fine of £100 or both these penalties.[87] This maximum sentence was imposed by one court on three objectors appearing at the same session of the court: on appeal the sentence was reduced to the imprisonment only. One objector was sentenced to three months' imprisonment and a fine of £25. Eleven other objectors were sentenced to three months' imprisonment. Nine objectors had sentences of two months' imprisonment and nineteen had sentences of one month's imprisonment. Most other sentences were of fines only.[88]

Compulsory Fire-Watching 1941–1944

The dropping of incendiary bombs in the course of German air raids on Great Britain from the summer of 1940 onwards caused serious and widespread damage to property from fires; the fires also caused loss of life and injuries both directly and by illuminating targets for explosive bombs. One of the measures taken to combat incendiary bombs was the organisation of a service generally known as "fire-watching". (The official term from 1943 was "fire guard duty".) The purpose of the service was to provide people on the spot and alert during air raids, their duty being to detect the places where incendiary bombs fell and then to extinguish them or, if this was impossible, to call in the Fire Service or other assistance. At first there was no legal compulsion for this service, but early in 1941 compulsion was applied to men and in August 1942 compulsion was applied to women. Most duties were suspended from September 1944 so that in practice compulsory fire-watching existed for men for a period of between three and four years and for women for a period of about two years.

For the purposes of this chapter it is unnecessary to describe fully the detailed legal provisions concerning fire-watching, and the following account gives a general description, omitting many details. There were two sets of legal provisions, one concerning fire-watching at places of work and the other concerning fire-watching by residents in their own localities.

Under Defence Regulation 27A the Fire Prevention (Business Premises) Order[89] was issued in January 1941. This Order was applied to most vulnerable areas in the country. Under the Order the occupiers of all business premises were compelled to make adequate fire-watching arrangements; they could employ paid fire-watchers, use the services of volunteer employees, or use the legally compelled services of employees. Men aged between 18 and 60 (later raised to 63) were compelled to do fire-watching duty, when necessary, at their places of work and such duty took precedence over any similar duty in their localities of residence. This Order was replaced by another Order[90] in September 1941 and in April 1941 there was a special Order[91] made for the City of London. In August 1942 an Order[92] applied compulsion to women employees between the ages of 20 and 45.

In June 1943 Defence Regulation 27A was replaced by the Defence (Fire Guard) Regulations.[93] Under these Regulations the Fire Guard (Business and Government Premises) Order was issued in July 1943.[94] This Order continued the legal requirements already described.

The legal provisions regarding fire-watching by residents in their own localities were administered by local authorities. Under Defence Regulation 27B the Civil Defence Duties (Compulsory Enrolment) Order[95] was issued in January 1941. This Order provided for compulsory duty of men between the ages of 18 and 60 (later raised to 63). After a few months the Order was applied to the great majority of urban areas and registrations of men were held in September 1941. This Order was replaced by another Order[96] in August 1942 which also applied compulsion to women between the ages of 20 and 45. Registrations of women were held in September and October 1942. In June 1943 Defence Regulation 27B was replaced by the Defence (Fire Guard) Regulations.[97] Under these Regulations the Fire Guard (Local Authorities Services) Order[98] was issued in July 1943. This Order continued the legal requirements already described.

Compulsory fire-watching duties could not be required for more than 48 hours in each four-week period. There was no payment for compulsory duties but employers had to pay subsistence allowances and any additional travelling expenses to those fire-watching at their places of work. Duties included attendance at instruction and training, provided by either the local authorities or for employees by their employers. There were a considerable number of classes of people exempted from compulsory fire-watching duties; these classes included members of the Armed Forces, the Women's Auxiliary Service and the Home Guard, and various Civil Defence workers. A woman was exempted if she was pregnant or if she had a child aged under 14 in her care and living with her. There could be exemptions for both men and women for exceptionally long hours of work, medical unfitness, and "exceptional hardship".[99]

The legal regulations concerning fire-watching made no provision for conscientious objection. Objectors, like others affected by the regulations, had the right to apply for exemption on the ground of exceptional hardship. The local Military Service (Hardship) Committees were designated as the bodies to adjudicate on such applications. In four cases Hardship Committees regarded conscientious objection to fire-watching as exceptional hardship and gave exemption. But in the middle of 1943 a Divisional Court of the King's Bench Division, on a case before it, ruled that conscientious objection could not be considered as exceptional hardship within the Orders and that the Hardship Committee had no jurisdiction to hear the application.[100]

Conscientious objection to military service did not necessarily imply conscientious objection to obeying the legal provisions concerning fire-watching. It was only a minority, probably a small minority, of objectors who felt that they could not conscientiously co-operate with the law. These objectors did not all object to fire watching itself: some objected only to the compulsory scheme and some who broke the law had been or were engaged in voluntary fire-watching.

With regard to the detail of the law, some objectors were willing to register but not to perform compulsory duties. On the other hand, some objected to registration even though they were in classes exempted from compulsory duties. A pacifist of long experience, in an article published in 1941, described as follows some of the considerations involved.

"It is in the nature of conscience that it does not work to a single pattern... It is difficult to believe that anyone, except perhaps a fire worshipper, can object to fire prevention as such... A person might object to preventing fire in a particular kind of building, for example, in a distillery, slum property, or an armaments factory... Another would be glad to assist in fire prevention in peace time but will have nothing to do with it in war; his objection is to fire prevention for war purposes. A third is already doing the work voluntarily, but may still object to fire prevention under compulsion... The man that objects to fire prevention for war purposes will argue that the real reason why he is being asked to take part in it is for the more successful prosecution of the war effort – and in the utterances of government spokesmen and the phraseology of official documents he will find plenty of evidence to support this contention – and that on those grounds he must refuse. On the other side it can be said that whatever the motive behind the compulsion the effect will be the desirable one of saving lives, homes and places of employment, and from this it is difficult to stand aside."[101]

The following are examples of statements made in court by objectors prosecuted under the fire-watching regulations.

Ten members of a Christadelphian community said that they would not in any circumstances associate themselves with the Government's military machine. They pointed out that Mr Herbert Morrison had stated that fire-watching had become a military operation and they objected not to voluntary fire-watching as such but to registering under the Government Order. They declared that they did not vote or take part in political matters and did not interfere with the State in its wars. "There comes a time," they stated, "when human laws conflict with the laws of God."[102]

An objector prosecuted several times stated:

Fire-watching as an act is not wrong: it is the motive behind the act that is wrong – the motive of fire-watching being to assist the prosecution of the war even though it be indirectly. I am endeavouring to live a useful life within the dictates of my conscience, and if I were in any place where I could be of any help to my fellow-men, be it fire-fighting, first-aid or such like, I should do it in the capacity of a free citizen, but never as a member of any civil defence service.[103]

Another objector stated:

I believe in democracy quite as much as those taking part in this war but it seems to me that acquiescence in the claims of the State to conscript for war purposes will prove to be the first nail in the coffin of democracy. I hope I shall have the strength to resist it whether under democratic government or a Nazi government... Now that women under 20 have been prosecuted and boys under 18 are to be made liable for conscription I am more than ever convinced that conscription for war purposes is completely wrong: and that is one of the prime reasons why I refuse to fire-watch or undertake civil defence.[104]

The total number of prosecutions of conscientious objectors to fire-watching regulations was 555: of these prosecutions 475 were prosecutions of men and 80 were prosecutions of women.[105] (These and other figures in this account are of cases known to the Central Board for Conscientious Objectors.) These prosecutions occurred between March 1941 and February 1945,[106] especially in 1942 and 1943 in the case of men and in 1943 in the case of women.

These figures included prosecutions for various kinds of legal offence, and with regard to some offences the law was not uniform in detail over the whole period. The offences for which objectors were prosecuted were in four main groups. Under the Business Premises Orders a number of objectors were prosecuted for failing to fire-watch at their places of employment, and a few objectors who were occupiers of business premises were prosecuted for failing to make fire-watching arrangements at these premises. Under the Orders relating to fire-watching under local authority schemes objectors were prosecuted for refusing to register, or to supply particulars about themselves, or to report that they had not registered. Objectors were also prosecuted for failing to perform required duties under local authority schemes. For all these various offences the Defence Regulations provided that the maximum penalty which could be imposed on summary conviction was imprisonment for three months or a fine of £100 or both these penalties. [107]

In at least three cases of men these maximum penalties were imposed. In one of these cases the Recorder at Quarter Sessions, after hearing an appeal, reduced the penalty to one month's imprisonment and a fine of £10, remarking: "maximum penalties should not be imposed except for the gravest offences". It was the objector's first offence: he had refused to register but was doing voluntary fire-watching.[108]

There were several men and at least two women on whom a penalty of three months' imprisonment was imposed. One of these men served three sentences of three months' imprisonment for fire-watching offences and another served two such sentences.[109]

At the other end of the scale there were many cases in which penalties of fines only were imposed, sometimes as low as 10s (50p). A number of objectors in prison for fire-watching offences were imprisoned because they refused to pay the fines imposed.

Prosecutions for fire-watching offences shared with prosecutions for offences against military conscription and industrial conscription the general feature that they resulted in sentences differing greatly between different courts. But in the case of fire-watching offences there was an additional reason for local discrepancies: instead of one prosecuting body, the Ministry of Labour and National Service, there were many potential prosecuting bodies, namely all the local authorities concerned. There was considerable variation between local authorities in the rigour with which they enforced the fire-watching law and in their zeal or reluctance to prosecute offenders.

There were a considerable number of repeated prosecutions of men. Up to 8th June 1943 there were known to have been 291 prosecutions of 227 men, including 20 men who had been prosecuted 3 times or more,[110] and there were additional repeated prosecutions after this date. In the case of women, the total number of prosecutions was only 80, "this modest total being due in no small measure to the reasonableness of employers and the reluctance of local authorities to prosecute women."[111] But in at least 6 cases a woman was prosecuted 3 times.

There were two extreme cases of persistent prosecution by a local authority. In one case the local authority prosecuted the man eleven times before finally placing him in the Fire Guard Reserve, where he was not again posted for duty. In contrast with the attitude of the local authority, the magistrates imposed moderate fines and no sentence of imprisonment.[112] In the second case another local authority prosecuted the man nine times over a period of more than two and half years, despite the fact that after the third prosecution the Regional Commissioner had opined that no good purpose would be served by further prosecution. In this case the magistrates imposed one sentence of imprisonment and the objector went to prison on four other occasions for refusing to pay the fines imposed.[113]

On 6th September 1944 the Minister of Home Security announced that most fire-watching duties would be suspended from 12th September.[114] In May 1945 the Defence (Fire Guard) Regulations, 1943, were revoked.[115]

Compulsory Payments for Defence Purposes

In the twentieth century a very large proportion of the total expenditure on military and other Defence purposes has been financed from general taxation. Some of this expenditure has been originally financed from loans, but ultimately most of this loan-expenditure has been financed from taxation, as taxation has provided the sums expended on interest on these loans and towards repayment of them. There has been no specific allocation of the receipts from particular taxes to Defence purposes, and Defence expenditure has been financed both from income tax and other forms of direct taxation and from customs and excise duties and other forms of indirect taxation.

With regard to those Civil Defence services administered by local authorities a proportion of the expenditure has been financed from local rates, the remainder being financed from Government grants.

The War Damage Act, 1943,[116] imposed a compulsory scheme of contributions to insure against damage from air raids to buildings, land and other irremovable property. These compulsory contributions were paid by the owner of the property.

To the best of my knowledge, there has not been in this century any refusal by considerable numbers of people of payments for Defence purposes, such as the refusal which occurred in the resistance by Quakers in the seventeenth, eighteenth and early nineteenth centuries (described in Chapter 3). But there have been individual cases of refusal and the following are some examples.

In the years 1937, 1938 and 1940 an engineer was imprisoned five times (three times for 5 days, once for 7 days and once for 21 days) for refusing to pay a proportion of his income tax. On a later occasion of prosecution for an offence arising from his pacifism he stated in court: "I have been victimised for years. I believe in God only and the law which says 'Thou shalt not kill.' The law of England is not satisfied with that command.[117]

In 1943 two women appeared in court charged with failing to pay the compulsory war damage contribution on their house. One of the women stated that "she was unable to support any measure which put the country on a war basis". The court ordered payment within a month and the amount was paid anonymously on their behalf.[118]

In 1960 a Welsh Quaker was imprisoned for six weeks for non-payment of income tax after telling the magistrates that he would not pay income tax while conscription was in operation. In 1961 he was again imprisoned for six weeks for the same offence.[119]

In 1961 a woman general practitioner "refused to pay 1s 4d (7p) of her rates, the amount she calculated was due for civil defence." She told the Court that "civil defence against nuclear warfare was about as effective as trying to stop an avalanche with an umbrella." A distress warrant was issued.[120]

In 1961 a former Polish soldier, decorated for valour, refused to pay his rates and gave the money to charity because the rates included expenditure on the local technological college. He stated to the magistrates: "The college trains scientists to make rockets. We are equipping politicians with the means to destroy humanity." He was imprisoned for two weeks.[121]

In recent years, a Peace Tax campaign, pressed forward by Stanley Keable, aroused support from many Quakers and others. It led to some supporters withholding a proportion of their income tax on the grounds that this was being spent for military purposes. Various cases have reiterated the general legal principle that a taxpayer does not have the choice as to how to pay his taxes, nor upon what they should be spent. A bill introduced into the House of Commons to permit the diversion of a proportion of tax to some non-military purposes did not succeed.

References

Cmd. 7225 = Report of the Ministry of Labour and National Service for the Years 1939–1946
CBCO = Central Board for Conscientious Objectors
MLNS = Ministry of Labour and National Service

1   Cmd. 7225 pp. 53, 124–125, and 350–351
2   Ibid. p. 124
3   2 & 3 Geo. 6. c. 104
4   2 & 3 Geo.6.c.62
5   3 & 4 Geo. 6. c. 20
6   Bullock, Allan *The Life and Times of Ernest Bevin* Vol. II p. 15
7   S.R. & O. 1940. No. 781
8   S.R. & O. 1941. No. 2052
9   S.R. & O. 1941. No. 302
10   Cmd. 7225 p. 49
11   Ibid. p. 51
12   S.R. & O. 1942. No. 100
13   S.R. & O. 1942. No. 797
14   S.R. & O. 1943. No. 142
15   Defence Regulation 58A. Clause 3A
16   S.R. & O. 1943. No. 1173
17   Cmd. 7225 pp. 336–337
18   S.R. & O. 1941. No. 368
19   Cmd. 7225 p. 337
20   Ibid. p. 43
21   Ibid. p. 44
22   Ibid. p. 337
23   Ibid. p. 44
24   Bullock op. cit. Vol. II p. 127
25   Cmd. 7225 p. 41
26   Bullock op. cit. Vol. II p. 96
27   Ibid. Vol. II p. 16
28   Ibid. Vol. II p. 141
29   Ibid. Vol. II p. 142
30   Cmd. 7225 p. 48
31   Hayes, Denis *Challenge of Conscience. The Story of the Conscientious Objectors* of 1939–1949 p. 261
32   Home Security Circular No. 16211943
33   Letter 21.5.1942. Private information
34   Hayes op. cit. pp. 261–262
35   Ibid. p. 265
36   Ibid. pp. 266–267 and CBCO Bulletin. February 1942
37   Hayes op. cit. pp. 389–390
38   Ibid. p. 274
39   Ibid. pp. 274–275
40   Defence Regulation 92

41   CBCO Bulletin. March 1945
42   CBCO Bulletin. April 1942
43   CBCO Bulletin. May 1942
44   CBCO Bulletin. November 1943
45   CBCO Bulletin. October 1944
46   CBCO Bulletin. September 1943
47   Statement in court 18.1.1943. Private information
48   Letter 9.5.1942. Private information
49   2 & 3 Geo. 6. c. 62
50   3 & 4 Geo.6.c.20
51   8 & 9 Geo. 6. c. 31
52   S.R. & O. 1945. No. 1620
53   9 & 10 Geo.6.c.10
54   10 & 11 Geo.6.c.55
55   14 & 15 Geo. 6. c. 25
56   Cmd. 7225 pp. 173–175
57   MLNS Report for 1947. Cmd. 7559 p. 31
58   S.l. 1952. No. 2091
59   S.R. & O. 1947. No. 2409
60   MLNS Report for 1948. Cmd. 7822 pp. 19–20
61   S.I. 1952. No. 2091
62   Cmd. 7225 pp. 167–168
63   MLNS Report for 1947 pp. 30 and 34–35
      Ibid. Report for 1948. p. 20
      Ibid. Report for 1949. Cmd. 8017. p. 14
64   Ibid. Report for 1950. Cmd. 8338. p. 53
65   S.I. 1953. No. 1664
66   S.R. & O. 1943. No. 1173
67   S.R. & O. 1945. No. 579
68   S.R. & O. 1945. No. 1557
69   S.R. & O. 1947. No. 197
70   S.R. & O. 1947. No. 2021
71   S.I. 1950. No. 329
72   S.I. 1952. No. 136
73   S.I. 1952. No. 1402
74   MLNS Report for 1952. Cmd. 8893. p. 21
75   S.I. 1956. No. 649
76   S.I. 1956. No. 1005
77   S.R. & O. 1941. No. 2052
78   Police and Civil Defence (Tribunals) Order, 1942. S.R. & O. 1942.
      No.914
79   S.R. & O. 1945. No. 504
80   Cmd. 7225 pp. 30 and 35
81   CBCO Broadsheet No. 14
82   Hayes op. cit. p. 198
83   Ibid. pp. 197–198
84   Ibid. p. 199
85   CBCO Bulletin. August 1943

86   Hayes op. cit. pp. 199, 200, 389 and 390
87   Defence Regulation 92
88   Hayes op. cit. p. 199
89   S.R. & O. 1941. No. 69
90   Fire Prevention (Business Premises) No. 2 Order 1941, S.R. & O. 1941.
     No. 1411
91   Civil Defence Duties (Compulsory Enrolment) City of London Order
     1941. S.R. & O. 1941. No. 538
92   Fire Prevention (Business Premises) No. 3 Order 1942, S.R. & O. 1942.
     No. 1655
93   S.R. & O. 1943. No. 916
94   S.R. & O. 1943. No. 1044
95   S.R. & O. 1941. No. 70
96   Civil Defence Duties (Compulsory Enrolment) Order 1942. S.R. & O.
     1942. No. 1654
97   S.R. & O. 1943. No. 916
98   S.R. & O. 1943. No. 1043
99   CBCO Broadsheets Nos. 6 and 7
100 Hayes op. cit. pp. 300–301
101 Sutherland, G.A., in CBCO Bulletin. September 1941
102 CBCO Bulletin. September 1941
     Western Daily Press & Bristol Mirror. 26.8.1941
103 Hayes op. cit. pp. 318–319
104 CBCO Bulletin. December 1942
105 Hayes op. cit. pp. 389 and 390
106 Ibid. pp. 301 and 325
107 Defence Regulation 92
108 CBCO Bulletin. December 1942
109 CBCO Bulletins. April 1944 and August 1944
110 CBCO Bulletin. June 1943
111 Hayes op. cit. p. 308
112 Ibid. pp. 316–318
113 Ibid. pp. 318–324
114 Ibid. p. 324
115 S.R. & O. No. 504
116 (War Damage Act, 1943) 687 Geo. 6. c. 21
117 CBCO Bulletin. November 1944
118 CBCO Bulletin. February and May 1943
119 *Guardian* 6.9.1960
     The Friend 1961 Vol. 119 p. 272
120 *Guardian* 9.2.1961
121 *Guardian* 25.4.1961

Chronological Table of Acts Relating to Twentieth-Century Defence Compulsions (other than military service)

Date	Short Title	Page Refs
1939	Emergency Powers (Defence) Act	2 & 3 Geo. 6.c. 62
1939	Control of Employment Act	2 & 3 Geo. 6. c. 104
1940	Emergency Powers (Defence) Act	3 & 4 Geo. 6. c. 20
1943	War Damage Act	6 & 7 Geo. 6. c. 21
1945	Emergency Powers (Defence) Act	8 & 9 Geo. 6. c. 31
1945	Supplies and Services (Transitional Powers) Act	9 & 10 Geo. 6. c. 10
1947	Supplies and Services (Extended Purposes) Act	10 & 11 Geo. 6. c. 55
1951	Supplies and Services (Defence Purposes) Act	14 & 15 Geo. 6. c. 25

CHAPTER 8

Religion in Schools

Note:

The reader is referred to the Foreword on page iv. Notes made by the author indicate that this chapter was written circa 1974. Where relevant, it should be contrasted with the Education Reform Act, 1988 – see addendum on p. 278.

Introduction

In Chapter 1 of this book it was noted that compulsory oaths are one exception to the general state of affairs in present-day Great Britain in which the legal duties of the ordinary citizen do not include any religious activity or any statement of religious belief. The other exception is in the sphere of education: in this sphere the ordinary citizen has two duties which involve the support of religious activities. Firstly, if the citizen is the parent of a child of compulsory school age, it is his duty to cause the child "to receive efficient full-time education suitable to his age, ability, and aptitude, either by regular attendance at school or otherwise."[1&2] A parent can fulfil his duty by sending his child to an "independent" school which is entirely outside the public educational system or by arranging for him to receive approved education at home – in these cases the law is not concerned with whether the child's education includes any religious worship or any religious instruction. But in England and Wales, in schools under the public educational system, every school day must begin with collective worship on the part of all pupils in attendance at the school and religious instruction must be given in every school. In Scotland, religious worship and religious instruction are provided in the large majority of schools maintained or aided by public authorities. Thus it is fair to say that in Great Britain there is a general, though not universal, compulsion on children of compulsory school age to participate in religious activities at school, and a general, though not universal, compulsion on the parents of these children to cause them to attend schools which include these activities in their curricula. But this compulsion on the parent is subject to his right of legal conscientious objection: throughout the whole period during which education has been compulsory, the parent of a child attending a school maintained or assisted by public authorities has had the legal right to withdraw his child from religious worship or religious instruction or from both these activities at school. The history and nature of this legal right, usually known as the "conscience clause" for parents, will be described in this chapter.

The second duty of the ordinary citizen which involves his support of religious activities in schools is his duty to pay taxes and rates for the support of schools whose curricula include these activities. In England and Wales in the early twentieth century there were a considerable number of people who had conscientious objections to fulfilling this duty. The law has never made provision for any legal conscientious objection to the payment of taxes or rates to finance education. Thus the conscientious objectors who joined in what was known as the "passive resistance movement" were conscientious law-breakers. The passive resistance movement is also described in this chapter.

The general position of denominational religion in the public educational system in Scotland differs, both in its history and in its present features, from the general position in England and Wales. There is a completely separate series of Education Acts for Scotland. The principles of the conscience clause for parents have been similar in Scotland to those in England and Wales but there have been differences of detail. The passive resistance movement occurred only in England and Wales. For these reasons the following account covers England and Wales only and at the end of the chapter there is a short account of the history in Scotland.

The History in England and Wales

The history and significance of the conscience clause in relation to public education in England and Wales is intimately related to the way in which the public educational system has developed. Before 1870 there were (with a few minor exceptions) no schools

administered by public authorities, though there were many receiving public grants. The schools receiving grants were all providing
religious education and regarded this provision as an essential part
of their functions. But there was strong and sometimes bitter
disagreement as to the kind of religious education which should
be provided. The schools were in three main religious groups –
Anglican, Nonconformist and Catholic. The controversies with
regard to religious education between Anglicans and Nonconformists greatly affected the development of the public educational
system in the whole period up to the First World War. In more
recent times these controversies have been less important and much
less bitter. But the lack of agreement as to the content of religious
education has remained, and our present public educational system
includes both schools providing undenominational religious education and schools, mainly Anglican and Catholic, providing denominational worship and denominational religious instruction.

In the early nineteenth century two societies were formed for
the provision of schools and both societies provided or promoted
the provision of a large number of schools. The British and Foreign
Schools Society, dating from 1808, was supported by Nonconformists and gave Christian education of an undenominational
character in its schools, which came to be known as "British
schools". In 1811 a society was formed to promote schools providing
education according to the principles of the Church of England.
The original name of the society was "The National Society for
promoting the Education of the Poor in the Doctrine and Discipline
of the Established Church": the society became generally known as
"The National Society" and its schools as "National Schools".

In 1833 the first grants from taxation towards public education
were made in the form of grants to these two societies. From that
date public grants were made continuously and, at various dates,
groups of schools, other than those under these two societies, were
made eligible for public grants; Catholic schools, for example, were
included from 1847 onwards.

Figures produced in 1861[3] showed the very predominant position
of Anglican religious education in the system of popular education.
This predominance did not fairly represent the proportion of
practising Christians in the various denominations, if this is
assessed from the figures of attendance at public worship given
in the Census of 1851. These figures showed that out of 10,419,000

attendances at public worship on the selected day 3.5% were Catholic and the other attendances at Christian public worship were almost equally divided between the Church of England and the total attendances at the various Nonconformist churches.[4] The fact that many children of Nonconformists were attending Anglican schools and that in many cases, especially in rural areas, the Anglican school was the only available school was a very important reason for the institution of a conscience clause for parents.

The Elementary Education Act of 1870[5] instituted for the first time the provision of elementary education by public bodies. The Act provided in Section 14 that in any school provided by a School Board – School Boards were ad hoc local authorities for the provision of elementary education, elected by the local ratepayers or burgesses – "No religious catechism or religious formulary which is distinctive of any particular denomination shall be taught in the school." (This provision was generally known as the "Cowper-Temple Clause.") Thus the principle was established that in schools provided by local education authorities religious worship and religious instruction should be undenominational; this principle has been maintained ever since 1870. The Act included a conscience clause for parents which covered both these "Board" schools and voluntary schools.

Under the system established by the 1870 Act, religious instruction in schools was not made universally compulsory. With regard to voluntary schools, under the New Code of 1871, "For the first time secular schools became eligible for grants, as the condition making the reading of the Scriptures compulsory was withdrawn."[6] With regard to the new Board schools, School Boards were allowed to make such regulations as they thought fit for providing undenominational religious education. "The question of religious instruction in the new Board schools was fought out all over the country, and although a few Boards decided for secular schools, the vast majority followed the lead of the London School Board which resolved, by 38 votes to 3, that 'in the schools provided by the board, the Bible shall be read and there shall be given such explanations and such instruction therefrom in the principles of morality and religion as are suited to the capacity of the children.'"[7]

In 1902 the number of children receiving denominational religious education still exceeded those receiving undenominational religious education, or in the case of a few schools no religious education, in schools under the School Boards.[8]

The Education Act of 1902[9] changed the administrative system with regard to elementary education and allowed to local authorities important new responsibilities with regard to secondary education.

The School Boards were abolished and elementary education became the responsibility of Education Committees of the ordinary local authorities (Counties, County Boroughs and the larger Non-County Boroughs and Urban Districts). These new local education authorities became solely responsible for schools previously under School Boards and also jointly responsible for voluntary schools previously receiving Government grants. Under the new system the first group were termed "provided schools" and the second group "non-provided schools". A non-provided school came under the general control of the local education authority but the voluntary body which had established the school appointed the majority of the school managers and the school was allowed to provide denominational religious worship and denominational religious instruction and to discriminate in favour of the appointment of teachers who were members of its denomination.

Local education authorities financed the expenditure of non-provided schools with regard to the salaries of teachers and the general running expenses of the schools, but the voluntary bodies concerned were responsible for financing the provision, alteration and repair of the school buildings. Thus the denominational schools, which prior to 1902 had been assisted from taxation, now became financed from both taxation and rates. (It was this new provision for financing denominational education from rates which provoked the passive resistance movement.) "Few Bills in our history can have been more fiercely contested and yet passed substantially in their original form... With the advent of a Liberal Government in 1906, Bill after Bill was introduced by successive Presidents" (of the Board of Education)... "to undo the religious settlement of 1902. All failed".[10]

The legal position of non-provided elementary schools established by the 1902 Act remained substantially unchanged until the Education Act of 1944.[11]

The 1902 Act[12] empowered the major local authorities – Counties and County Boroughs – to provide and assist secondary education. (In England these powers were conferred for the first time: in Wales local public bodies had already powers under the Welsh Intermediate Education Act of 1889.)[13]

Section 4 of the Act provided that "no catechism or formulary distinctive of any particular religious denomination shall be taught" in any secondary school provided by the local education authority (except that some provision, not at the cost of the authority, could be made at the request of parents). The Section also provided that in aiding a voluntary school the local education authority should neither require nor forbid denominational religious education. A conscience clause for individual pupils was included in the Section and covered both schools provided by and schools aided by local education authorities. Thus the law regarding the public system of secondary education included three principles already adopted in the law regarding elementary education: (1) undenominational religious education in schools provided by the local education authority; (2) inclusion in the system of voluntary denominational schools; (3) a conscience clause regarding participation of the individual child in either undenominational or denominational religious activities.

By 1944, when the next reorganisation of the public educational system took place, the system was providing education for a much larger proportion of all children than in the first years after 1870. The provisions of the 1870 Act[14] were the first measures of compulsion applied to children in general, though compulsory part-time schooling had already been enacted with regard to children employed in factories (in 1833[15] and, more effectively, in 1844[16]). The 1870 Act empowered School Boards to make bye-laws compelling school attendance between the ages of 5 and 10 and between the ages of 10 and 13 if a certain standard of education had not been reached by the child concerned. The "compulsory school age" is, strictly speaking, the age of compulsory education, as such education can be provided outside school. The lower limit of this age has remained at 5 ever since 1870. The upper limit of age has been raised on several occasions. Up to 1918 there were two upper age limits at any particular time, one unconditional and the other affecting only children who had not already attained a certain standard of education; since 1918 the upper age limit has been unconditional. The Elementary Education Act of 1876[17] made it the duty of every parent of a child aged 5–14 to cause him "to receive efficient elementary instruction in reading, writing and arithmetic". The employment was prohibited of all children under 10 and of children under 14 who had not already attained a certain standard of education or record of school attendance. If the parent did not provide efficient elementary instruction for any child prohibited from employment a court could order such a child to attend school. In 1893[18] the unconditional upper age for compulsory education was raised to 11, in 1899[19] it was raised to 12, and in 1918[20] it was raised to 14. Under the Education Act of 1944[21] the upper age of compulsory education was raised in 1947 to 15 and in the school year 1973–74 to 16. (From 1918 compulsion applied until the end of the term in which the child attained the relevant age. Later there were only two leaving dates during the school year and the child had to attend school until the first leaving date after attaining the age of 16.)

The Education Act of 1944[22] reconstructed the public system of education, and established the present system. The Bill was promoted by R.A. Butler (later Lord Butler) as President of the Board of Education in the war-time Coalition Government. Butler and his Parliamentary Secretary, Chuter Ede, spent much time and effort in negotiations with the bodies concerned to try to find a satisfactory solution of the problem of the "dual system" of provided and non-provided schools. Butler stated in a 1971 book: "Since this issue was a particularly thorny one, I was to spend more time in trying to reach the settlement than on anything else."[23] Views presented to him varied between the views of several bodies which desired the abolition of denominational schools, to the views of Catholics who "argued that they had to pay rates and taxes for the upkeep of the local authority schools which their consciences would not let them use"[24] and that they were "saddled with extra and crushing financial burdens because of their definite religious convictions and because they cannot accept a syllabus of religious instruction agreeable to many."[25] The solution finally proposed by Butler, and embodied in the Act, was to offer to the voluntary schools the alternatives of becoming either "controlled" or "aided" schools.

The Act provided for three categories of "voluntary" primary and secondary schools within the public educational system. One category was that of "special agreement" schools, dating from the Education Act of 1936[26] – there were few of these schools. The other two categories were those of "controlled" and "aided" schools.

In the case of a controlled school the body owning the school appointed one third of the school managers (for a primary school) or school governors (for a secondary school). These were "foundation" managers or governors. The managers or governors were not responsible for any expenses: all expenditure was the responsibility of the local education authority. The local education authority was, in general, responsible for the appointment and dismissal of teachers. The religious education in the school was undenominational except that, on the request of the parents, their children received denominational religious instruction for not more than two periods a week. The teaching staff of the school included "reserved teachers", selected for their fitness and competence to give this denominational religious instruction, and the foundation managers or governors had to approve the selection.

In the case of an aided school, the body owning the school appointed two-thirds of the school managers or governors. With certain restrictions, the school managers or governors were responsible for the appointment of teachers. They were also responsible for the religious worship and religious instruction provided in the school. The voluntary bodies concerned were responsible for the expenses of building new aided schools and also for the expenses of alterations and of external repairs to the schools. But from 1944 to 1975, successive Education Acts provided for Government grants of 50% rising to 85% to be made towards the expenses of repairs and alterations of aided schools and, in certain types of circumstance, the cost of building new aided schools.

The choice between controlled and aided schools was very differently viewed by the two main churches concerned. "The Roman Catholics rejected 'controlled status' completely as being incompatible with fully denominational religious instruction in a denominational 'atmosphere'. To many Anglicans 'controlled status' seemed attractive; denominational teaching was to become possible in what were in effect state schools. To others it appeared very unattractive indeed, and was only to be accepted, if at all, because of the difficulty of raising large sums of money in a short time for building, repairs and alterations."[27]

In 1960 there were also a small number of "direct grant" grammar schools – schools not maintained by local education authorities but receiving grants direct from the Ministry of Education.[28] These schools were allowed to provide denominational religious education and a considerable number of them did so. The conscience clause for individual pupils included these schools.[29]

In 1960 there were also the "independent" primary and secondary schools, that is schools neither maintained by local education authorities nor receiving grants from the Ministry of Education. These were not affected by any legal requirements regarding religious education.[30]

The Education Act of 1944[31] for the first time made religious worship and religious instruction compulsory in all schools maintained by local education authorities. This provision made universal what had in fact previously existed in the large majority of schools.

The Act stated in Section 25 (1): "The school day in every county school and in every voluntary school shall begin with collective worship on the part of all pupils in attendance at the school." (This requirement is modified by the conscience clause included in the same Section.) There had to be a single act of worship attended by all pupils, unless the premises were such as to make this impracticable. Section 26 stated that the collective worship in a "county" school should not be distinctive of any particular religious denomination. The Education Act, 1946[32] (Section 7) provided that in county and controlled schools the collective worship at the beginning of the school day had to take place on the school premises. In aided and special agreement schools on special occasions the collective worship could be held elsewhere.

With regard to religious instruction the 1944 Act provided, in Section 25 (2), "religious instruction shall be given in every county school and in every voluntary school." The "Plowden Report" (1967) noted that: "At the moment Religious Education is the only subject which the law requires to be taught and the only subject from which both the individual child and the teacher may be excused."[33] There was no legal regulation as to the number of periods of instruction. Prior to this Act religious instruction had to be given at the beginning or end of a school session (to facilitate the withdrawal of individual children), but this restriction ceased, facilitating the provision of specialist teaching. Such specialist teaching was in secondary schools; in primary schools religious instruction was usually given by class teachers to their own classes.

The Act provided in Section 26 that in all county schools religious instruction "shall be given in accordance with an agreed syllabus" and "shall not include any catechism or formulary which is distinctive of any particular religious denomination." In controlled schools religious instruction was also according to an agreed syllabus, except for the limited amount of denominational religious instruction which was provided at the request of parents.

The Fifth Schedule of the Act laid down the procedure for bringing into operation an agreed syllabus.

Addendum

Section 6 of the Education Reform Act, 1988 requires all pupils in attendance at a maintained school to take part in an act of collective worship each day, generally on the school premises, and "wholly or mainly of a broadly Christian character". This has already raised certain problems and has been criticised for its divisive effects by some teachers and educationalists. Section 9, however, gives the parent of any pupil the right to have the pupil excused from such act of worship and from any other religious education being given in the school, but there are no provisions for pupils themselves to possess any right to choose to be excused from religious attendance.

The Conscience Clause for Parents

The principle of a conscience clause for parents had been much discussed and in some cases accepted before it was included in the Education Act of 1870. The schools under the British and Foreign Schools Society had from the beginning "accepted teachers and children of any denomination without question, merely hoping that they would attend a place of worship of their own choice on Sunday."[34]

But the National Society (formed in 1811 to promote schools providing education according to the principles of the Church of England) came to be responsible for a much larger number of schools. Its aim, as was stated by its Committee at its origin, was to teach the children in its schools "the doctrines of Religion according to the principles of the Established Church, and to train them in the performance of their religious duties by early discipline."[35] "This enforced conformity to the Established Church caused many difficulties all through the century. In most places the landowners and works managers would provide a National School, but not a British one; so that non-conformist parents were in a sad dilemma."[36]

But by 1870 "the Church of England was modifying its attitude of exclusion. Since 1863, when the Education Department received an application for a building grant for a Church school in a parish too small to support two schools, it has insisted on a conscience clause which prevented any discrimination against children who were not members of the Church. At first this clause had been resisted; but by 1867 'the agitation against it was assuming its proper proportions' and the Archbishop of Canterbury said that he approved of it."[37]

In introducing the motion for the First Reading of the Elementary Education Bill of 1870, W.E. Forster, the Vice-President of the Committee of the Privy Council for Education, spoke about the conscience clause proposed to be included in the Bill. He proposed "that after a limited period we attach what is called a Conscience Clause as a condition to the receipt by any elementary school of public money. It seems to me quite clear, if we approach the subject without any prejudice, that in taking money from the taxpayer to give his children a secular education, we have no right to interfere with his feelings as a parent, or to oblige him to accept for his children religious education to which he objects. Therefore, in voting money or making public provision for elementary schools, we hold that they ought not to be schools from which the public would be excluded. The principle of that condition is so clear, and the violation of it has been so mischievous, that I am glad to find the opposition to the proposed change has almost disappeared. The proposed clause will apply to all schools, secular as well as denominational, and will give to the parent the power of withdrawing his child from instruction if, on religious grounds, he thinks that instruction to be such as the child ought not to hear."[38]

The Elementary Education Act of 1870[39] in Section 7 made the following provisions with regard to every "public elementary school." (Such a school was either a school provided by a School Board or a voluntary elementary school receiving a Government grant.)

"It shall not be required, as a condition of any child being admitted into or continuing in the school, that he shall attend or abstain from attending, any Sunday School, or any place of religious worship, or that he shall attend any religious observance or any instruction in religious subjects in the school or elsewhere, from which observance or instruction he may be withdrawn by his parent, or that he shall if withdrawn by his parent, attend the school on any day exclusively set apart for religious observance by the religious body to which his parent belongs."

The time of any religious observance or religious instruction must be at the beginning or end of a school session and "any scholar may be withdrawn by his parent from such observance or instruction without forfeiting any of the other benefits of the school."

The Education Act of 1902[40] continued unaltered with regard to elementary schools the provisions of the conscience clause as stated in the Act of 1870.

With regard to the new responsibilities for secondary education and various forms of education other than elementary education which were allowed to local education authorities under the Act, the provisions of the conscience clause were as follows:

"No pupil shall, on the ground of religious belief, be excluded from or placed in an inferior position in any school, college or hostel provided by the council."

"In a school or college receiving a grant from, or maintained by, a council a scholar attending as a day or evening scholar shall not be required, as a condition of being admitted into or remaining in the school or college, to attend or abstain from attending any Sunday school, place of religious worship, religious observance or instruction in religious subjects in the school or college or elsewhere."

"The times for religious worship or for any lesson on a religious subject shall be conveniently arranged for the purpose of allowing the withdrawal of any such scholar therefrom."

It is interesting to note that in these provisions there is no mention of the parent.

The provisions of the conscience clause were continued unaltered in the consolidating Education Act of 1921.[41]

The legal provisions regarding the conscience clause as stated in Section 25 of the Education Act of 1944[42] cover all primary and secondary schools administered by local education authorities, namely "county schools", undenominational schools administered entirely by the local education authorities, and "voluntary schools" of which the large majority are denominational, administered jointly by the local education authorities and voluntary bodies. The provisions are as follows.

"It shall not be required, as a condition of any pupil attending any county school or any voluntary school, that he shall attend or abstain from attending any Sunday school or any place of religious worship."

"If the parent of any pupil in attendance at any county school or any voluntary school requests that he be wholly or partly excused from attendance at religious worship in the school, or from attendance at religious instruction in the school, or from attendance at both religious worship and religious instruction in the school, then, until the request is withdrawn, the pupil shall be excused from such attendance accordingly."

Section 25 also provides that, with regard to any pupil wholly or partly excused from attendance at religious worship or instruction, if the parent desires him to receive religious instruction of a kind not provided in the school during the periods which he is excused from such attendance, then certain arrangements may be made for his withdrawal from the school to receive such religious instruction.

The Section also provides for a boarder at a school, at the request of the parent, to attend the worship of a particular religious denomination and to receive denominational religious instruction.

There is very little statistical information with regard to the number of parents making use of the conscience clause. In connection with the Education Bill of 1902 the Church of England submitted a tabulated sheet by bishoprics. This showed that out of a total attendance of 1,748,722 at Anglican Schools (not a complete figure) 12,743 children (0.73%) were wholly or partially withdrawn from religious activities in the school. (5,147 were wholly withdrawn and 7,596 were partially withdrawn.)[43]

It has been common for parents of Jewish religion to withdraw their children from Christian worship and Christian religious instruction. It has also been common in the past for Catholic parents to withdraw their children from religious activities in schools other than Catholic schools. It is possible that the new ecumenical tendencies in the Catholic Church have made this less common in recent years.

A new phenomenon in the period since the Second World War is the presence in some schools of considerable numbers of children of immigrant parents who are adherents of non-Christian faiths – Muslim, Hindu and Sikh. It seems that some of these parents do not withdraw their children from Christian religious activities. A survey conducted by the Institute of Education of the University of Leeds in 1967 speaks of the parents' desire that the child should "fit in" at school and states that most parents "seem to tell their children that while at school they are to do whatever is required of them and behave as the other children do. Consequently the children often take part quite happily in morning assembly and join in the spirit of

Christmas celebrations, and may participate in religious knowledge lessons too."[44]

It is interesting to note that the wording of British legislation on public education refers to "religious" observance or worship and "religious" instruction, not to "Christian" worship or instruction. Public grants have been made to Jewish schools since the middle of the nineteenth century. Apart from the few Jewish schools in the public educational system, "It has long been common for special provision to be made in some schools for Jewish children."[45] The "Plowden Report" gives an example of a school with many Muslims which encourages them to bring their prayer-mats to school and to use them in a special room instead of going elsewhere in the town.[46] The provisions of Section 25 of the Education Act, 1944, allowing a pupil at the desire of his parent, to be withdrawn from school to receive religious instruction, cover non-Christian religious instruction as well as particular forms of Christian religious instruction. There is also no legal reason why the undenominational religious worship and religious instruction in "county" schools should not include material from non-Christian religions and in some cases it does so.

The 1967 Report of the Central Advisory Council for Education in England on "Children and their Primary Schools" (the Plowden Report) makes two references to the conscience clause. The Report states: "For the non-Christian parent there is a difficult choice: either he must acquiesce in his child being taught beliefs which he holds to be untrue and harmful, or he must take the initiative and ask for his child to be excused from religious education, thus setting him apart from the rest of the school. He may not be prepared to do this because he does not wish to make the child appear different."[47] The Report recommends that more information should be given to parents. "We believe that... to carry out the spirit of the 1944 Act all parents should be told, when children are admitted to school, of their rights of excusal from the Act of Worship and from religious education. They should be told how both these forms of religious education are conducted in the school and what provision, if any, is made for the children who are withdrawn from them."[48]

In a "Reservation on Religious Education" six members of the Council producing the Report make further comments on the conscience clause. These members state: "There is a minority of parents who for one reason or another, but most often because of their own religious beliefs or disbeliefs, would prefer their children not to receive the kind of religious teaching which the primary schools now give. These parents have the right to withdraw their children from religious instruction, but in many cases do not exercise it either because they do not know that they possess it or because they fear that it will prejudice the children's standing in the school. Moreover, the children themselves do not like to be put in a position which sets them apart from their fellows."[49] These members do not consider religious instruction as a suitable subject to be taken in primary schools.[50] But "We agree that if religious instruction is to remain a subject in primary schools it should be left to the parents to enrol their children for it and left also to the teachers to volunteer to give it; in other words, that opting in should be substituted for the present system of opting out."[51]

Two other members of the Council, in a separate "Reservation on Religious Education", comment as follows on the conscience clause. "We are concerned about the difficulty which at present faces parents who wish to exercise their right under the Act of 1944 to withdraw their children from religious education. The difficulty is that withdrawal generally means withdrawal into an empty room or corridor. No alternative programme of moral or ethical education exists for such parents to choose for their children. The admittedly difficult problem of drawing up such a programme should surely be faced. One would welcome the setting up of committees of interested teachers, lecturers (and parents) within local education authorities and institutes of education to devise an alternative 'Agreed Syllabus' of ethical teaching which does not rely on the sanction of religious belief."[52]

The Passive Resistance Movement

The so-called "passive resistance movement" in the early years of this century was provoked by certain changes made by the Education Act of 1902.[53] Before 1902, elementary schools managed by voluntary bodies, most of them providing denominational religious education, received grants from the central government but no financial assistance from local authorities (except sometimes in the payment of school fees for certain children). The 1902 Act placed these voluntary schools, along with the undenominational schools previously managed by School Boards, under the general control of the larger ordinary local authorities (Counties, County Boroughs, and the larger Non-County Boroughs and Urban Districts). As already mentioned, these new local education authorities were to finance the expenditure of voluntary or "non-provided schools" with regard to the salaries of teachers and the general running expenses of the schools, while voluntary bodies concerned were to be responsible for financing the provision, alteration and repair of school buildings. Thus local education authorities were obliged in future to provide a large proportion of the expenditure of the voluntary schools: this provision was to be made from local rates, assisted by grants from the central government, financed from taxation.

At the time of the passing of the 1902 Act there were a much larger number of denominational elementary schools than of undenominational Board schools. As compared with 5,943 schools under School Boards, there were 11,711 Church of England schools, 1,056 Catholic schools, 458 Wesleyan or Methodist schools, and 1,039 other voluntary schools. Of the total accommodation in public elementary schools more than half was in voluntary schools, including nearly 42% in Church of England schools and 6% in Catholic schools.[54] Thus the local education authorities' new responsibility for voluntary schools involved a large increase in their expenditure on education.

Under the system instituted by the 1902 Act the voluntary schools continued to provide denominational worship and denominational religious instruction. Each voluntary school had six managers, of whom two were appointed by the local authority or authorities and four were "foundation managers" representing the particular religious denomination concerned. The consent of the local authority was required for the appointment of teachers but the managers were allowed to discriminate in favour of teachers who were members of the religious denomination to which the school was attached.

In December 1902 the National Passive Resistance League was organised under the chairmanship of Dr. John Clifford.[55] Clifford, the Baptist minister of a large London chapel, became a leader of the movement and personally persisted in his resistance for nearly twenty years. In a letter to the "Daily News" about the 1902 Education Bill, Clifford wrote: "If Englishmen have any conscience and pluck left they will start, organise, and sustain such a resistance as will defeat a policy which threatens to kill democratic control of education, increase educational inefficiency, add to the State endowments of sectarianism, and fix more securely than ever the tyrannies of the State Church over the life of the land."[56]

The fact that religious discrimination could be applied to such a considerable proportion of teachers was greatly resented by Clifford. He stated: "Here is a member of the teaching profession, but who is not an Anglican, and for that reason, and that only, he cannot obtain any other than a subordinate position in State Schools, except by the special favour of private and sectarian managers, and cannot become a headmaster in any of them. It is a re-imposition of the Test Act in the Civil Service of the country in the most flagrant way. It is a direct bribe to the Free Churchmen to enter the Anglican Church, and I, as a Free Churchman, am asked to share in this act of bribery. It is putting a premium on hypocrisy, and I, as an honest man, am to join in the creation of hypocrites."[57]

The passive resistance movement was essentially a movement of Non-conformists. Many Anglicans were also dissatisfied with the system, for they were compelled to pay rates and taxes to support, in the undenominational elementary schools, a kind of religion of which they disapproved,[58] but they did not become passive resisters. Though there were resisters from nearly all the Nonconformist denominations,[59] not all Nonconformists supported or approved of the movement. For example, the Quakers at their annual meeting in 1903 refused to endorse passive resistance, considering that it was a matter for private judgment.[60] It was difficult to make a strictly logical distinction between paying taxes towards Government grants to denominational schools, which had been acquiesced in by Nonconformists, and paying rates for the support of these schools. "No new principle was involved, but the whole transaction was easier to observe and therefore raised greater passion."[61] Moreover, while expenditure on elementary education from Government grants was financed from general taxation, the education rate was collected for a specific purpose, so that the ratepayer might feel more directly involved in the purposes for which his money was spent.

The active campaign started in May 1903. "The plan was to form local councils, raise a central fund to help victims and provide legal aid. Where all schools under the local authority were council schools, no resistance would be offered to the school rate. But if there were one Anglican or Roman Catholic school in a district, then participants would be asked to deduct from their rate payments the amount estimated to go to the voluntary school. The constabulary should be allowed to attach personal belongings and sell them at auction for the amount deducted by the passive resister in paying his rates. The dictates of conscience would be served and, perhaps more importantly, lead to the removal of Nonconformist grievances."[62]

Non-payment of rates was not an offence under the criminal law. If a rate was duly demanded and remained unpaid the rating authority might apply by summons to the Justices in Petty Sessions for the issue of a warrant of "distress" or "distraint" on the defaulter's goods, and the Justices were then legally obliged to issue such a warrant.

The following account of the proceedings at Cambridge Magistrates Court on a day in September 1903 exemplifies the conflict of passive resisters with the law. Twenty persons were summoned before the court for non-payment of the rate; they included a well known Congregational minister and a Quaker scholar. The assistant overseer, on behalf of the overseers, expressing regret that they had to continue to trouble the magistrates, stated that there were still many further summonses with which the magistrates would have to deal. All the defendants were allowed to address the magistrates briefly: in each case an order for a distress warrant was made.

The Quaker scholar objected to 12s (60p) of the rate. He said that he was sensible of the courtesy with which his friends had been treated. "He endorsed the objections which had been made with regard to the rate, especially those which affected conscience peculiarly – the objections to the payment of money for the propagation of religious beliefs which they not only disbelieved themselves, but which they thought they were constitutionally entitled to object to. He would like to add one other objection. He thought he appeared for the State against itself on this ground. Lord Bacon, in giving the causes of sedition, enumerated taxes, changes and innovations in religion, and so on; but he closed the catalogue by saying that the climax of the whole was the promotion of unworthy persons. He held that the exclusion of worthy persons from the civil service – and the teaching profession was a branch of the civil service – meant the promotion of unworthy persons. The State could never be rightly served in educational matters as long as from a large number of schools one-half of the community were excluded from the service of the State."[63]

By the close of 1903 there had been 37,296 summonses of passive resisters for non-payment of rates, 1,504 sales under distraint, and 80 imprisonments.[64] By the close of 1904 there had been 66,234 summonses, 2,274 sales under distraint, and 250 imprisonments.[65] By April 1906 there had been 73,816 summonses, 2,382 sales under distraint and 280 imprisonments.[66]

It will be seen from the figures cited that the large majority of resisters on whom summonses were served paid the amounts due in rates, either before or after the issue of a warrant of distraint. "Usually, after the formal protest of a first refusal, the recalcitrant gave way. But he sometimes preferred to allow his goods to be distrained and sold by auction in the street until a sufficient sum had been obtained to discharge the rate."[67] By April 1906 there had been nearly 2,400 sales under distraint. An example of the amounts involved is the £600–17–4 (£600.87) deducted from rates and the £929–15–11 (£929.80) recovered from passive resisters in Norwich between 1904 and 1911.[68] "Goods were taken in undue proportion to the amount claimed, and many had to suffer loss of trade in various ways, and even loss of employment."[69]

The following is an example of distraint on an individual, as recorded by the son of a Congregational minister at Hereford. "Each year Father and the other resisters all over the country refused to pay their rates for the upkeep of Church Schools:... the passive resisters thought the issue of principle paramount and annually surrendered their goods instead of paying their rates. I well remember how each year one or two of our chairs and a silver teapot and jug were put out on the hall table for the local officers to take away. They were auctioned in the Market Place and brought back to us." At neighbouring village auctions "Father would explain the nature of passive resistance before the sale began."[70]

Occasionally the power of the local authority to obtain the money due to it by distraint was hindered by a local boycott on sales of distrained property. For example, it was reported in June 1903 that all the auctioneers in the Belper neighbourhood of Derbyshire had refused to act as sellers of the distrained goods of local passive resisters.[71]

The cases of imprisonment – 280 up to April 1906 – arose from the legal power (not obligation) of the Justices to order the imprisonment of the defaulter for up to three calendar months if he possessed insufficient property to satisfy the default claim. Some resisters deliberately put themselves in this position by transferring their property to their wives.[72] The biographer of Clifford recorded: "Nearly all the Free Churches have had their representatives in jail, and a few ministers were treated as common felons. For the sum of eightpence (3p) withheld, a fortnight in prison was imposed; because a young Christian Endeavour would not pay four-and-sixpence (22l/2p) he was committed to jail for a month; when a certain elderman withheld half a crown (12l/2p), one of those who were supposed to administer the law called out 'Give him three months' and told the worthy elderman to 'put his conscience in his pocket.'"[73] The same author recorded cases of one resister imprisoned sixteen times, another eight times, and another six times and added that they "were not the least bit nearer to submitting to the injustice of the Act."[74]

The passive resistance movement in Wales had some special features, as in Wales the new law was resisted not only by individuals but also by public bodies. "The vast majority of the population was Nonconformist, five-sixths of the Welsh members had voted against the Bill. In fact, the body of Nonconformist sects constituted the national religion of Wales, and the Church of England could be regarded as a foreign church."[75] (The position of the Anglican Church as a minority church led to its disestablishment in Wales under an Act of 1914.)[76] "In Wales – opposition took the form of a serious national campaign in which some Welsh local education authorities refused to carry out their statutory duties in respect of denominational elementary schools."[77] These authorities decided "not to make payments to any school over which they did not possess entire control, or in which the teachers were obliged to belong to a particular denomination."[78] The Board of Education postponed till 1 February 1904 the date when the 1902 Act came into operation. Then in 1904 an Act[79] was passed under which the costs of maintenance of voluntary schools (other than those payable by school managers) were met by the Board of Education and recovered from the defaulting local education authorities by deductions from the grants payable to them. The conflict continued until the introduction of the Education Bill of 1906.

The passive resistance movement and other opposition to the 1902 Act were among the causes of the replacement of the Conservative

Government by a Liberal Government as the result of the General Election of 1906. The Education Bill, introduced by the Government in 1906, provided for the transfer of all voluntary elementary schools to the local education authorities and would have much diminished the denominational element in the public educational system. This Bill was passed in the House of Commons but was greatly altered in the House of Lords and was subsequently abandoned by the Government.[80] The religious position established by the 1902 Act remained substantially unchanged until the Education Act of 1944.[81]

Passive resistance to the law continued. "In 1910 there were groups of resisters of 30,26,22,75,37, brought up at one time."[82] Clifford himself was still resisting the law in 1922 (he died in 1923). He wrote in December 1922: "I have received my 57th summons to meet the Magistrates on Friday morning next at 10 o'clock."[83]

Religion in Scottish Schools

Public education in Scotland has a much longer history than in England and Wales. In 1696 the Scottish Parliament enacted that there should be a school established in every parish where one was not already provided and that the expenses of the school and the salary of the schoolmaster should be defrayed by a compulsory levy on the local landowner.[84] The first provisions concerning compulsory education were enacted, at about the same time as the first provisions in England and Wales, in the Education (Scotland) Act, 1872.[85]

The Act of 1872 provided for compulsory education for children aged between five and thirteen but exemption was granted to children with ability to read and write and a knowledge of elementary arithmetic. The Education (Scotland) Act, 1883[86] raised the school-leaving age to fourteen with the same exemptions. The Education (Scotland) Act, 1901[87] retained the school-leaving age at fourteen but allowed no exemptions. Under the Education (Scotland) Act, 1946[88] the upper age of compulsory education was raised to fifteen in 1947 and to sixteen in the school year 1973–74. The Act provided that an education authority could grant exemption to a child aged fourteen and over to assist at home if his attendance at school would cause exceptional hardship.

Since the Reformation the religious history of Scotland has differed greatly from that of England and Wales: "In religion

Scotland has been for the last four hundred years a predominantly Protestant Presbyterian country and the smallness of the numbers of the other denominations made them relatively unimportant. Even today (1966) the 760,000 Roman Catholics and the 56,000 members of the Scottish Episcopal Church constitute only 17 per cent of the total population of the country: in the past they were proportionately fewer and their position correspondingly weaker. Denominationalism in education, while it may sometimes have been an irritant in Scotland, has never been a deep-seated malady and today it does not exist."[89]

At the time of the passing of the Education (Scotland), Act 1872[90] the superintendence of the parish schools was in the hands of the Established (Presbyterian) Church of Scotland and every headmaster "undertook that he would never endeavour to teach or inculcate any opinions opposed to the Divine Authority of the Holy Scriptures or to the doctrines contained in the Shorter Catechism" and "that he would faithfully conform thereto in his teaching of the school." It was the custom in the parish schools to give instruction in religion to children whose parents did not object and there were similar arrangements for religious instruction in the "burgh schools" in towns.[91] In 1864 there was a total of 1,220 schools in these two groups. The Act of 1872 transferred these schools to the control of School Boards which were elected in every parish and burgh. Schools under School Boards were termed "public schools."[92] The preamble to the Act declared that it was expedient that the managers of public schools should be at liberty to continue the custom of religious instruction and the School Boards nearly all did so. "With only two or three exceptions they resolved to make the Holy Scriptures and the Shorter Catechism the basis of their instruction."[93]

In 1864 there were in Scotland 3,310 other schools. Of these 910 were "private adventure schools"; of the other 2,400 more than half were managed by denominational bodies. Under the 1872 Act, voluntary schools were left free to continue and they might receive Government grants if the Scottish Education Department were satisfied that they were efficiently contributing to the secular education of their localities. A voluntary school established or maintained by contributions or donations might apply for transfer to the School Board and, if accepted, it became a public school. The terms of transfer were not advantageous to the former owners and only about a quarter of these schools were transferred between 1872 and 1915; in the case of Catholic and Episcopalian schools only nine were transferred. In 1880 there were 618 voluntary schools receiving Government grants: in 1910 this total had decreased to 347, though one group, Catholic schools, had increased from 126 to 220.[94]

Section 18 of the Education (Scotland) Act, 1918[95] greatly changed this position. It covered efficient voluntary day schools providing free or nearly free education for children aged between five and fourteen or fifteen. Such schools could be transferred to the local education authorities under terms agreed with them by the managers of the schools and the authorities had to accept such transfers. After a period of two years no Government grant might be paid to such schools unless they had been transferred. The transferred schools would become public schools with the local education authority responsible for all their expenditure and for the appointment of their teachers. But the transferred schools could maintain their previous type of religious worship and religious instruction and various legal provisions safeguarded this position. New public schools could also be provided under these provisions.[96]

The provisions of the 1918 Act satisfied the needs of the Catholic and Episcopalian voluntary schools and during the two years after the passing of the Act 226 Catholic schools and 50 Episcopalian schools as well as 25 other voluntary schools were transferred. At the beginning of 1943, out of 3,211 public schools in Scotland 273 were Catholic or Episcopalian transferred schools.[97]

"The concordat which was established between the churches and the state in 1918 gave Scotland a single unified system of state education which has worked ever since without change and to everybody's satisfaction: no one would now lightly seek to have it changed. There is to-day (1966) no discernible difference between the public and the 'transferred' schools, whether primary or secondary, in buildings, staffing, equipment, educational standards and achievement, or status, and as a result the bitterness of religious acrimony is wholly absent from Scottish education."[98]

Since 1872 there have been two changes in the framework of local control of public education. The Education (Scotland) Act, 1918[99] abolished the School Boards, numbering about 1,000, and substituted for them 38 directly elected education authorities. The Local Government (Scotland) Act, 1929[100] abolished these *ad hoc* education authorities and put public education under the control of the major general local authorities. The education committee of a local authority must include at least two persons nominated by representatives of the churches or denominational bodies in the area and at least one person to represent any denominational schools managed by the education authority.'[101]

In the consolidating Education (Scotland) Act of 1946,[102] it is stated in Section 8 that "it has been the custom in the public schools of Scotland for religious observance to be practised and for instruction in religion to be given" and that education authorities shall be at liberty to continue this custom. An education authority could not discontinue religious observance or instruction unless a resolution to this effect had been approved by a poll of electors.

An official document stated in 1958 that, except in "transferred" and similar schools, education authorities were free to provide in any school the form of denominational instruction acceptable to the parents. At that time all the education authorities set apart one or more periods for religious instruction; this generally followed the lines laid down by the syllabus on religious education prepared by a Joint Committee on Religious Education.[103] An official report in 1943 stated: "Except in a few areas the use of the Shorter Catechism has been discontinued, but the Bible has retained its place in the schools."[104]

The 1946 Act continued the provisions of the 1918 Act[105] with regard to the transfer of voluntary schools to education authorities and the setting up of new public schools to meet the religious requirements of parents. With regard to "transferred" and similar schools, Section 18 of the Act provided that the teachers appointed should be approved, "as regards their religious belief and character" by representatives of the church or denominational body in whose interest the school had been conducted; that, subject to similar approval, the education authority should appoint an unpaid supervisor of religious instruction for each school; and that the time set apart for religious instruction or observance should be not less than that so set apart by the former management of the school.

The principle of the conscience clause for parents was well established in Scotland before it was included in the Education (Scotland) Act of 1872.[106] In the preamble to that Act it was stated that it had been the custom in the public schools of Scotland to give instruction in religion to children whose parents did not object to the instruction so given, but with liberty to parents, without forfeiting any of the other advantages of the schools, to elect that their children should not receive such instruction.

The conscience clause was contained in Section 68 of the Education (Scotland) Act of 1872 and the main part of that Section was repeated almost word for word in Section 9 of the Education (Scotland) Act of 1946.[107] The wording of the main part of Section 9 is as follows. "Every public school and every grant-aided school shall be open to pupils of all denominations, and any pupil may be withdrawn by his parents from any instruction in religious subjects and from any religious observance in any such school; and no pupil shall in any such school be placed at any disadvantage with respect to the secular instruction given therein by reason of the denomination to which such pupil or his parents belong, or by reason of his being withdrawn from any instruction in religious subjects."

An official report in 1943 stated: "The number of cases in which parents have availed themselves in recent years of their rights under the Conscience Clause is negligible."[108]

Section 10 of the 1946 Act applied the same principle to special schools. The section also provided, with regard to any boarder at a school or other educational establishment under an education authority, that, at the request of his parent, he should be allowed to attend outside working hours religious worship or religious instruction according to the tenets of a particular religious denomination.

References

Plowden Report = Central Advisory Council for Education (England). Children and their Primary Schools. Vol. I Report. 1967

Cmd. 6426 = Scottish Education Department Memorandum with regard to the provision made for Religious Instruction in the Schools in Scotland. 1943.

1   7 & 8 Geo. 6. c. 31 (England)
2   9 & 10 Geo. 6. c. 72 (Scotland)
3   Royal Commission on the state of Popular Education in England. Vol. I pp. 55 and 592
4   Census of England and Wales 1851. Volume on Religious Worship
5   33 & 34 Vic. c. 75

6   Birchenough, Charles, *History of Elementary Education in England and Wales from 1800 to the Present Day* 2nd Edition 1932 p. 146

7   Smith, Frank *A History of English Elementary Education 1760–1902* p. 294

8   Statistics of Public Education 1925 – 26
Birchenough op. cit. pp. 149, 150, 483

9   2 Edw.7.c.42

10   Report of the Ministry of Education for 1950. Cmd. 8244 pp. 4 and 5

11   7 & 8 Geo. 6c. 31

12   2 Edw. 7. c. 42

13   52 & 53 Vic. c. 40

14   33 & 34 Vic. c. 75. Sect. 74

15   Factories Regulation Act, 1833. 3 & 4 Will. 4. c. 103. Sect. 21

16   Factory Act, 1844. 7 Vic. c. 15. Sects. 31 and 38

17   39 & 40 Vic. c. 79. Sects 4,5, and 11

18   Elementary Education (School Attendance) Act, 1983. 56 & 57 Vic. c. 51. Sect. 1

19   Elementary Education (School Attendance) Act (1893) Amendment Act, 1899. 62 & 63 Vic. c. 13

20   Education Act, 1918

21   7 & 8 Geo. 6. c. 31 Sect. 35

22   7 & 8 Geo. 6. c. 31

23   Butler, R.A. *The Art of the Possible* 1971. p. 96

24   Ibid. pp. 98–99

25   Hinsley, Cardinal. Letter to The Times 31.11.1942

26   26 Geo. 5 & 1 Edw. 8. c. 41

27   Murphy, James, Report in *The World Year Book of Education 1966* pp. 29–30

28   Education in 1960. Cmd. 1439 p. 178

29   Murphy op. cit. p. 33

30   Education in 1960. Cmd. 1439 p. 147

31   7 & 8 Geo. 6. c. 31

32   9 &10 Geo. 6. c. 50

33   Plowden Report p. 204

34   Sturt, Mary *The Education of the People. A History of Primary Education in England and Wales in the Nineteenth Century.*, p.30

35   Quoted Ibid. p. 28

36   Ibid. p. 29

37   Ibid. p. 299

38   Hansard Vol. 199. Cols. 447–449

39   33 & 34 Vic. c. 75

40   2 Edw. 7. c. 42

41   11 & 12 Geo. 5. c. 51

42   7 & 8 Geo.6.c.31

43   Sacks, Benjamin *The Religious Issue in the State Schools of England and Wales 1902–1914. A Nation's Quest for Human Dignity* p. 32 note

44   Kinnibrugh, A.D. and Butterworth, Eric. *The Social Background of Immigrant Children from Asia and Cyprus*. Institute of Education, University of Leeds. Occasional Paper No. 1 1967

45   Plowden Report p. 206
46   Ibid. p. 206
47   Ibid. p. 205
48   Ibid. p. 206
49   Ibid. p. 491
50   Ibid. p. 492
51   Ibid. p. 491
52   Ibid. p. 492
53   2 Edw. 7. c. 42
54   Statistics of Public Education 1925 – 26
55   Sacks op. cit. p. 42
56   Marchant, Sir James *Dr. John Clifford C.H. Life, Letters and Reminiscences* 1924 p. 122
57   Ibid. p. 126
58   Sacks op. cit. p. 50
59   Marchant op. cit. p. 141
60   *The Friend* 29.5.1903
61   Peterson, A.D.C. *A Hundred Years of Education.* 1952. p. 39
62   Sacks op. cit. p. 42
63   *The Friend* 25.9.1903
64   *Annual Register* 1904 pp. 203 – 4*
65   *New Age* January 1905
66   *Liberator* April 1906*
67   Halévy, Elie *A History of the English People in the Nineteenth Century* Vol. V pp. 375 – 6
68   Marchant op. cit. p. 141
69   Ibid. p. 141
70   Martin, Kingsley *Father Figures. A First Volume of Autobiography* 1897–1931 1966
71   *The Friend* 12.6.1903
72   Sacks op. cit. p. 43
73   Marchant op. cit. p. 141
74   Ibid.
75   Halévy op. cit. p. 376
76   Welsh Church Act 1914. 4 & 5 Geo. 5. c. 91 ss. 1,2
77   Cmd. 8244 p. 114
78   Halevy op. cit. p. 376
79   Education (Local Authorities Default) Act, 1904 4 Edw. 7. c. 18
80   Marchant op. cit. p. 127
81   7 & 8 Geo. 6. c. 31
82   Marchant op. cit. p. 141
83   Ibid. p. 144
84   Cmd. 6426 p. 3
85   35 & 36 Vic. c. 62
86   46 & 47 Vic. c. 56

---

* All quoted in Sacks, p. 43

87   1 Edw. 7. c. 9
88   9 & 10 Geo. 6. c. 72
89   Craigie, James, *Report in the World Year Book of Education* 1966 p. 323
90   35 & 36 Vic. c. 62
91   Cmd. 6426 p. 3
92   Ibid. p. 4
93   Ibid. p. 6
94   Ibid. pp. 4–5
95   8 & 9 Geo. 5. c. 48
96   Cmd. 6426 pp. 7–8
97   Ibid. p. 9
98   Craigie op. cit. pp. 324– 5
99   8 & 9 Geo.5.c.48
100   19 & 20 Geo. 5. c. 25
101   Scottish Education Dept. Public Education in Scotland. 1958 p. 15
102   9 & 10 Geo. 6. c. 72
103   Public Education in Scotland. 1958 p. 20
104   Cmd. 6426 p. 12
105   8 & 9 Geo. 5. c. 48
106   35 & 36 Vic. c. 62
107   9 & 10 Geo. 6. c. 72
108   Cmd. 6426 p. 7

Chronological Table of Education Acts

Date

1696	Establishment of Schools (Scotland)	Scot. Parl. 1696. c. 26
1833	Factories Regulation Act	3 & 4 Will. 4. c. 103
1844	Factory Act	7 Vic. c. 15
1870	Elementary Education Act	33 & 34 Vic. c. 75
1872	Education (Scotland) Act	35 & 36 Vic. c. 62
1876	Elementary Education Act	39 & 40 Vic. c. 79
1883	Education (Scotland) Act	46 & 47 Vic. c. 56
1889	Welsh Intermediate Education Act	52 & 53 Vic. c. 40
1893	Elementary Education (School Attendance) Act	56 & 57 Vic. c. 51
1899	Elementary Education (School Attendance) Act (1893) Amendment Act	62 & 63 Vic. c. 13
1901	Education (Scotland) Act	1 Edw. 7. c. 9
1902	Education Act	2 Edw. 7. c. 42
1904	Education (Local Authorities Default) Act	4 Edw. 7. c. 18
1918	Education Act	Geo. 5. c. 39
1918	Education (Scotland) Act	8 & 9 Geo. 5. c. 48
1921	Education Act	11 & 12 Geo. 5. c. 51
1929	Local Government (Scotland) Act	19 & 20 Geo. 5. c. 25

1936	Education Act	26 Geo. 5 & 1 Edw. 8. c. 41
1944	Education Act	7 & 8 Geo. 6. c. 31
1946	Education Act	9 & 10 Geo. 6. c. 50
1946	Education (Scotland) Act	9 & 10 Geo. 6. c. 72
1959	Education Act	7 & 8 Eliz. 2. c. 60
1967	Education Act	Eliz. 2. 1967. c. 3

CHAPTER 9

The Medical Care of Children

Introduction

In general, British law allows an adult to make his own decisions with regard to his own medical care. If an adult does not consult a doctor when ill, or, after consulting a doctor, does not follow the doctor's advice or take the prescribed medicines or, having been medically advised to have an operation, refuses to do so, the law is not concerned with his actions, nor is it usually concerned if he chooses to be treated by persons outside the legally recognised medical profession. Among adults who act in some of these unorthodox ways are those who do so because of their religious beliefs, but these beliefs lead to no conflict with the law when they concern the decisions of adults with regard to their own lives.

When, however, parents make these kinds of unorthodox decisions with regard to their children they may find themselves in conflict with the law. Parents have certain legal duties with regard to the medical care of their children and these will be described in this chapter. When parents have not fulfilled these legal duties for conscientious reasons they have been illegal conscientious objectors, as in this sphere of law there has been no provision for legal conscientious objection. Thus the legal position of conscientious objectors in this sphere of law has been in contrast with their position in the two other spheres of law described in this book in which conscientious objectors have acted in a parental capacity: with regard to religious activities in schools parents have had, since the introduction of compulsory education, the statutory right of conscientious objection and with regard to compulsory vaccination they had this statutory right from 1898 onwards.

The whole of this chapter covers England and Wales only.

The Legal Duties of Parents

In 1906 in the course of a trial of a parent for the manslaughter of his child, who had died without medical attendance, the judge stated that, apart from the then-existing legislative provisions on the matter, "a person is guilty of manslaughter if he is (a) under a duty to supply food or medicine; (b) to a child or person who is unable to provide it for himself; and (c) wilfully neglects to do so; and (d) the person dies in consequence."[1] But under the common law there was sometimes a difficulty in securing a conviction because of the common law maxim that there could not be a criminal act without a criminal intent. The first legislative provision on the matter removed this difficulty by making parental neglect a statutory offence.[2]

Section 37 of the Poor Law Amendment Act of 1868[3] stated: "When any parent shall wilfully neglect to provide adequate food, clothing, medical aid, or lodging for his child, being in his custody, under the age of fourteen years, whereby the health of such child shall have been or shall be likely to be seriously injured, he shall be guilty of an offence." It was assumed that if the parent could not provide these necessities for his children from his own resources, it was his duty to apply for relief under the Poor Law. The Act made it the duty of the local Board of Guardians (the authority under the Poor Law) to prosecute in cases of neglect. On summary conviction the parent could be imprisoned for up to six months, with or without hard labour, and the justices might suspend the sentence on his own recognisances.

The next piece of legislation on the matter was not a Poor Law Act but an Act of which the title was the Prevention of Cruelty to and Protection of Children Act, 1889.[4] This was the first Act concerned with this purpose and its passing was, to a considerable extent, the result of the efforts of the London Society for the Prevention of Cruelty to Children. A society for this purpose was founded in Liverpool in 1883; the London Society was founded in 1884; and in 1889 the National Society for the Prevention of Cruelty to Children, commonly known as the N.S.P.C.C., was founded.[5] From 1889 onwards there were both a series of Acts concerned with the protection of children and a national society for this purpose. The N.S.P.C.C. had branches in many parts of the country and built up its own staff of inspectors whose work was to advise parents and to help them to obey the law, to assist in the enforcement of the law, and generally to protect children in their own homes.

The Act of 1889[6] repealed the provision in the Poor Law Amendment Act of 1868[7] and replaced it by its own provision. Section 1 of the Act did not specifically mention neglect to provide medical aid but made it an offence wilfully to neglect a child "in a manner likely to cause such child unnecessary suffering or injury to its health." The two subsequent Prevention of Cruelty to Children Acts of 1894[8] and 1904[9] (which, in turn, repealed the whole of the previous Act) also did not specifically mention neglect to provide medical aid. In a trial for manslaughter in 1898 this point was raised. The trial judge told the jury that the question was whether the defendant's failure to procure medical aid could be called "wilfully neglecting the child in a manner likely to cause serious injury to its health" but that the jury must be satisfied that medical aid and medicine were such essential things for the child that reasonably careful parents would have provided them in this case. The jury convicted the defendant and he was sentenced to four months' imprisonment with hard labour. (The defendant was a member of the Peculiar People and his case is referred to later in this chapter – Example (6) on p309.) The case was referred to the Court for Consideration of Crown Cases Reserved which held that the trial judge's direction to the jury was right in point of law.[10]

The provisions were very similar in the three Prevention of Cruelty to Children Acts of 1889,[11] 1894,[12] and 1904.[13] All the Acts made potentially responsible for neglect "any person over sixteen years of age having the custody, control, or charge of a child". The age of the children covered was, in the Act of 1889, under fourteen for boys and under sixteen for girls: the two later Acts covered all children under sixteen. Under the act of 1889 the penalties for neglect were: on indictment, a fine up to £100 and/or imprisonment, with or without hard labour, up to two years; on summary conviction, a fine up to £25 and/or imprisonment, with or without hard labour, up to three months. The Act of 1894 increased the maximum length of imprisonment on summary conviction to six months. This Act added, after the phrase "injury to its health", the phrase "(including injury to or loss of sight, or hearing, or limb, or organ of the body, and any mental derangement)". The Act of 1904 stated that a defendant indicted for manslaughter could be found by the jury guilty of an offence under the Act.

The Children Act of 1908[14] repealed the provision in the Prevention of Cruelty to Children Act of 1904[15] and replaced that provision by its own very similar provision in Section 12. But the Act restored to statutory law the explicit offence of neglect to provide medical aid: "a parent or other person liable to maintain a child or young person shall be deemed to have neglected him in a manner likely to cause injury to his health if he fails to provide adequate food, clothing, medical aid, or lodging for the child or young person, or if, being unable otherwise to provide such food, clothing, medical aid, or lodging, he fails to take steps to procure the same to be provided under the Acts relating to the relief of the poor."

Under the Act the ages covered by the provision remained as before but a child was defined as being under the age of fourteen and a young person as being between the ages of fourteen and sixteen. A person could be convicted notwithstanding that actual suffering or injury to health, or the likelihood of this, was obviated by the action of another person. The penalties remained as before and it was provided that imprisonment with the same maximum lengths could be imposed in default of payment of a fine.

The Children and Young Persons Act of 1933[16] repealed Section 12 of the Children Act of 1908[17] and reproduced that Section (and Section 13 which dealt with the negligent suffocation of infants) almost verbatim in its own Section 1.

Since 1933 the Children and Young Persons Act of 1963[18] has raised the maximum fine on summary conviction for negligence from £25 to £100 and has repealed the provision that imprisonment up to the maximum lengths specified could be imposed in default of payment of a fine. Changes in other branches of law have also affected the provisions of the Act of 1933 – the Poor Law has been abolished, the National Health Service has provided a free medical service available to all, and "hard labour" as a condition of imprisonment no longer exists. But the law is still substantially as stated in Section 1 of the Act of 1933. The following is a summary of the statutory law in so far as it concerns the duty of parents (and some other persons) to provide medical aid for a child or young person and the possible legal penalties for failure to fulfil this duty.

A parent or other person legally liable to maintain a child (aged under fourteen) or a young person (aged between fourteen and sixteen) shall be deemed to have neglected him in a manner likely to cause injury to his health if he fails to provide adequate medical aid for him. If he has the custody, charge or care of the child or young person and wilfully neglects him in a manner likely to cause him unnecessary suffering or injury to health (including injury to or loss of sight, or hearing, or limb, or organ of the body, and any mental derangement) he is guilty of an offence. He may be convicted of the offence notwithstanding that actual suffering or injury to health, or the likelihood of this, was obviated by the action of another person. The possible penalties for the offence of neglect are: on conviction on indictment a fine up to £100 and/or imprisonment for up to two years; on summary conviction a fine up to £100 and/or imprisonment for up to six months. If he is indicted for infanticide or manslaughter the jury may find him guilty of the offence of neglect.

Besides defining the duties of parents and providing for legal penalties for the non-fulfilment of these duties, legislation has provided for the legal removal of a child or young person, in certain circumstances, from the care of his parents.

Since the Act of 1889[19] the various statutes for the protection of children have provided for the temporary removal of a child or young person to "a place of safety". For the purposes of this chapter it is unnecessary to describe these provisions in detail: the provisions are stated in Section 28 of the Children and Young Persons Act of 1969.[20]

Since the Act of 1889 the various statutes for the protection of children have also provided that, by order of a court, a child or young person may be removed from his home and committed to the care of a "fit person". The kinds of circumstance in which a committal order could be made were originally limited and it is only since 1952 that they have included the circumstance of parental failure to provide medical care, unless the parent had been prosecuted for this offence.

The Prevention of Cruelty to and Protection of Children Act of 1889[21] covered broadly cases in which a parent or guardian had been convicted of an offence against the child, or was awaiting trial for such an offence, or had been bound over to keep the peace towards the child. In such a case a petty sessional court, "if

302

satisfied on inquiry that it is expedient so to deal with the child", might remove him from the custody of his parent or guardian and commit him to the charge of "a relation of the child, or some other fit person named by the court, such relation or other person being willing to undertake such charge."

While the committal order was in force the "fit person" assumed parental rights and duties with regard to the child.

The Children Act of 1908[22] repealed previous provisions on the matter and made substantially the same provision in Section 21. It also provided, in Section 58, that children in a number of other kinds of circumstance might be committed to Industrial Schools. The Act also made an important change by enacting that a court of summary jurisdiction, when dealing with offences of children or young persons or with orders concerning them, should sit separately from the ordinary sittings of the court: this was the beginning of a general system of Juvenile Courts.

The Children and Young Persons Act of 1933[23] replaced the previous provisions by provisions dealing with "children and young persons in need of care or protection." For the purpose of these provisions a young person was one between the ages of fourteen and seventeen. A child or young person was defined in Section 61 as "in need of care or protection" if he was in certain circumstances, including those covered in previous legal provisions, or if he was "a child or young person who, having no parent or guardian or a parent or guardian unfit to exercise care and guardianship or not exercising proper care and guardianship, is either falling into bad associations, or exposed to moral danger, or beyond control." This definition was amended in the Children and Young Persons (Amendment) Act of 1952[24] by adding the words "or is ill-treated or neglected in a manner likely to cause him unnecessary suffering or injury to health." This was an important amendment as it meant that a child or young person could now be brought before a Juvenile Court as being in need of care or protection because he had suffered from parental ill-treatment or neglect, including neglect to provide adequate medical aid, without the need to prosecute the parent in a senior court.[25]

Under the Act of 1933 if a Juvenile Court was satisfied that a child or young person brought before the court was in need of care or protection it could deal with him in various ways. He could be sent to an Approved School (the successor of an Industrial School), he could be placed under the supervision of a probation officer, his parent or guardian could be ordered to enter into a recognisance to exercise proper care and guardianship, or he could be committed to the care of a fit person (Section 62). The local authority should be deemed to be a fit person and a child or young person could be committed to its care (Section 76). This was an important new provision. Under this Act a local authority was not compelled to undertake the care of a child committed by the court. But this position was changed by the Children Act of 1948[26] which stated that, with some exceptions, the local authority must undertake the care of a child or young person committed to it as a fit person.

The Children and Young Persons Act of 1963[27] repealed the amended Section 61 of the Act of 1933[28] and replaced it by its own Section 2, which defined the circumstances in which children and young persons were regarded as being "in need of care, protection or control". A child or young person lacking adequate medical care was covered by the following provision. "A child or young person is in need of care, protection or control within the meaning of this Act if he is not receiving such care, protection and guidance as a good parent may reasonably be expected to give" and "the lack of care, protection or guidance is likely to cause him unnecessary suffering or seriously to affect his health or proper development."

The Children and Young Persons Act of 1969[29] repealed the previous legal provisions regarding the definition of a child or young person in need of care, protection or control, and the powers of a juvenile court to remove such a child or young person from the care of his parents and to commit him to the care of some other person or body. The legal provisions on these matters are the provisions in so far as they affect the position of a child or young person deprived of adequate medical care by his parents.

A child (aged under fourteen) or a young person (aged between fourteen and seventeen) may be brought before a juvenile court by any local authority, constable, or authorised person who reasonably believes that he is in need of care or control (Section 1 (1)). With some exceptions, it is the duty of the local authority to bring such a child or young person before the court (Section 2(2)). The court may, if it thinks fit, make an order in respect of him if "his health is being avoidably impaired or neglected" and he is also "in need of care or control which he is unlikely to receive unless the court makes an order". The court may, with the consent of his parent or guardian, make an order requiring his parent or guardian to enter into a recognisance to take proper care of him. Alternatively, the court may make a "care order" in respect of him (Section 1). A court may make an order in respect of a child aged under five without the presence of the child in court provided that his parent or guardian is present (Section 2 (9)).

A "care order" is an order committing the child or young person to the care of the local authority for the area in which he resides (Section 20 (1) and (2)). (The court can no longer commit to the care of a "fit person" other than the local authority.) The local authority must receive into its care such a child or young person. Subject to certain conditions, the local authority has the same powers and duties with respect to a child or young person committed to its care as his parent or guardian would have (Section 24 (1) and (2)). A child or young person may appeal to quarter sessions against a care order made in respect of him (Section 2 (12)). A care order ceases to have effect when the young person attains the age of eighteen or, if he is aged sixteen when the order is made, when he attains the age of nineteen (Section 20 (3)).

Application to the juvenile court for the discharge of a care order may be made by the local authority to whose care a child or young person has been committed, or by the child or young person himself, or by his parent or guardian on his behalf. If it appears to the court "that it is appropriate to discharge the order" the court may discharge it (Sections 21 (2) and 70 (2)).

In relation to conscientious objection to medical care it is interesting that there seems to be some uncertainty as to whether the legal position just described applies to young persons aged between sixteen and seventeen. The Act exempts from liability to have an order made in respect of him a young person aged sixteen who is or has been married (Section 1(5)). But with regard to medical care the legal position may be affected also by the Family Law Reform Act of 1969.[30] This Act states in Section 8: "The consent of a minor who has attained the age of sixteen years to any surgical, medical or dental treatment which, in the absence of consent, would constitute a trespass to his person, shall be as effective as it would be if he were of full age; and where a minor has by virtue of this section given an effective consent to any treatment it shall not be necessary to obtain any consent for it from his parent or guardian." This implies that a young person aged sixteen can accept medical care or consent to an operation against the conscientious views of his parents, whose consent is not necessary. But if a young person aged sixteen himself refuses, for conscientious reasons, to have necessary medical care or to undergo a necessary operation, can he be made subject to a "care order" so that the local authority shall give the consent which he refuses to give? (This uncertainty regarding young persons aged sixteen does not occur in relation to the legal position with regard to the criminal offence of parental neglect, because that offence concerns only children and young persons under the age of sixteen.)

Conscientious Objections to Parental Legal Duties

With the information at my disposal it is impossible to cover adequately the whole subject of the possible types of conscientious objection to the fulfilment of parental duties concerning the medical care of children. Such objection can relate to medical care in general or to particular forms of treatment: it can be based on general principles or on disagreement with the medical authorities on the right treatment of a particular case.

An example of objection to the kind of treatment of a particular case occurred in 1971. "A mother with a young daughter suffering from diabetes did not believe insulin, the normal medical treatment, would cure her. Conscientiously, she believed the condition of her daughter could be controlled by diet alone. So she reduced the daily dose of insulin. But after the girl twice had to go into hospital, Somerset County Council took proceedings against the mother, on the grounds that the child was in need of care and protection." Yeovil juvenile magistrates agreed and sent the girl to a Home. The mother appealed to the Queen's Bench Divisional Court, which refused to interfere with the magistrates' decision.[31]

The remainder of this account will describe the conscientious objections of two groups of parents whose objections were based on religious principles – members of the Peculiar People who objected to all medical care and members of Jehovah's Witnesses who objected to blood transfusions.

The Peculiar People

The Christian sect known as the Peculiar People, and originally known as the Plumstead Peculiars, was founded in London in 1838. The founder was William Bridges, a hat-block maker; his companion John Banyard of Romford spread the teaching in Essex. It was estimated that in 1934 there were some 6,000 members and in 1962 some 200 members, mainly in East London, Essex and Thames-side Kent.[32]

The Peculiar People accepted the whole Bible as literally true and their conscientious objection to consulting doctors arose from their obedience to the instructions of the Apostle James in his Epistle. James wrote as follows: "Is any sick among you? Let him call for the elders of the church; and let them pray over him, anointing him with oil in the name of the Lord: And the prayer of faith shall save the sick, and the Lord shall raise him up; and if he has committed sins, they shall be forgiven him." (James Ch. 5 w. 14 – 15 A.V.).

In the late nineteenth century and early twentieth century there were a number of prosecutions of parents who were members of the Peculiar People. In the preface to Bernard Shaw's play The Doctor's Dilemma, published in 1911, the author wrote: "The calling in of the doctor is now compulsory except in cases where the patient is an adult and not too ill to decide the steps to be taken. We are subject to prosecution for manslaughter or for criminal neglect if the patient dies without the consolations of the medical profession. This menace is kept before the public by the Peculiar People. The Peculiars, as they are called, have gained their name by believing that the Bible is infallible, and taking their belief quite seriously. The Bible is very clear as to the treatment of illness." The author then quoted the passage from the Epistle of James quoted above: "The Peculiars obey these instructions and dispense with doctors. They are therefore prosecuted for manslaughter when their children die." Shaw then wrote scathingly about the increasing claims of doctors to be omniscient and ended his account by the statement: "The Peculiar goes unpitied to his cell, though nothing whatever has been proved except that his child died without the interference of a doctor as effectually as any of the hundreds of children who die every day of the same disease in the doctor's care."[33]

The following descriptions of examples (except the last example) are based on accounts given in *The British Medical Journal* and *The Lancet*. All the examples concern members of the Peculiar People.

In 1868 two parents were tried for manslaughter at the Central Criminal Court on account of their child who had died from pneumonia. The judge called attention to the uncertainty of medical opinions as to the treatment of this class of disease and the parents escaped with severe censure.[34]

In 1875 at the Central Criminal Court a father was tried for the manslaughter by criminal neglect of his son aged two. Evidence was given that the child, who suffered from pleurisy and pneumonia, had no medical assistance. There was anointing with oil, the laying on of hands and prayer. The child was also given nourishing food and port wine. The jury found the father guilty, adding that they believed that he considered that he was acting for the best, according to his religious notions, and that what he did was intended for the benefit of the child. The case was referred to the Court for Consideration of Crown Cases Reserved which affirmed the conviction for manslaughter. One of the judges observed that the jury had found that the man thought that to fulfil the duty imposed by statute was wrong. The law, however, did not excuse a man on that account.[35]

In 1882 the Court for the Consideration of Crown Cases Reserved quashed the conviction of a parent for the manslaughter of his son, who suffered from smallpox, by neglecting to provide proper medical assistance. The five judges stated that, in order to sustain a conviction for manslaughter, it was not enough to show a neglect of the legal duty: there must also be evidence to show that the neglect to take reasonable means to prolong life had the effect of shortening it. In this case the evidence of a responsible and competent witness was that "probably" this "might" have been so, and on such evidence it would be dangerous to allow the conviction for manslaughter to be sustained.[36]

In 1898 a husband and wife were convicted at the Central Criminal Court of the manslaughter of their daughter, aged twenty months, who died from whooping-cough. No doctor was called in but an elder of the Peculiar People prayed over the child and anointed her with oil. The father gave evidence that he and his wife trusted in the Lord. At a previous trial of the same defendants the jury had disagreed, but at this trial the jury found both defendants guilty. The judge, addressing the defendants, impressed upon them their duty to reconsider carefully whether they were following a right course in neglecting those worldly means which God had provided. They should remember that He intended man to use the assistance which science and skill undoubtedly afforded. Taking into consideration his belief that they thought they were acting rightly, he would discharge them upon their own recognisances to come up for judgment at some future time if called upon to do so.[37]

In 1906 the same father was sentenced at the Central Criminal Court to nine months' imprisonment with hard labour for the manslaughter of two of his children by refusing to call medical attendance. The father did not dispute the facts but showed that he had acted in accordance with his beliefs, habitually took good care of his children, taught them the Bible and took them to chapel. He said that he himself had been cured of an attack of rheumatism by the prayers of his brethren. At a previous inquest he had admitted that doctors were God's creatures but had said that he would not take advantage of their knowledge "because it was got from colleges". The jury, after finding him guilty, recommended him to mercy on the ground of his religious views. When passing sentence the judge reminded him that he had been tried in 1898 on a similar charge and discharged: he must not be allowed to escape a second time.[38]

In 1898, in the trial of another father who was a member of the Peculiar People, the defendant was sentenced to four months' imprisonment with hard labour. This sentence led to an unsuccessful request in the House of Commons for the remission of part of the sentence.[39] An opposing view was taken by The Lancet which stated that seven out of the twelve children of the defendant had died at various times without receiving medical aid, and opined that the sentence was a light one.[40]

In 1901, in the preliminary hearing at the Magistrates' Court of his prosecution for manslaughter by neglect of his son, aged six months, a member of the Peculiar People made the following statement. "I wish to say that, proving the Word of God as I have done for nearly thirty years, God having saved me for that period, my reason for taking this course is wholly and solely to obey the Word of God. He has answered prayers and taken pains away from myself, my wife, and my children many times in less time than I could walk a quarter of a mile to fetch a doctor. I am not despising doctors, but having proved God's power above their power, I desire to obey His Word, and thus doing so I honour Him."[41]

At the Chelmsford Assizes in 1907, the father of a child who had died from diphtheria was charged with manslaughter and with neglect under the Prevention of Cruelty to Children Act, 1904.[42] The father was a member of the Peculiar People and had refused to summon medical aid. The jury found him guilty of neglect under the Act and added a recommendation to mercy. The judge said that at the previous assizes a sentence of one month's imprisonment had been passed for a similar offence. As this had not acted as a sufficient deterrent, it was the duty of judges to increase from time to time the sentences passed in such cases until persons such as the prisoner learned to comply with the law. The sentence, therefore, would be one of two months' imprisonment in the second division.[43]

In 1923, at the Central Criminal Court, a husband and wife were charged with the manslaughter of their son, aged three years, who died from diphtheria without the attendance of a doctor. The jury found the defendants guilty but recommended them to mercy. The husband was sentenced to six months' imprisonment: the wife was bound over and discharged. The wife stated: "I didn't call in a doctor because I trusted in the Lord. I have been a member of the Peculiar People sect all my life. Had I known my child was seriously ill I should not have called a doctor." The assistant clerk of the sect, a J.P., stated that he had known many cases of healing through prayer, laying on of hands and anointing, including his daughter when a child. When asked by the Recorder: "Suppose you had a child obviously dying with diphtheria, would you call a doctor?" he replied: "No, my lord. When a child dies we are satisfied it was beyond human skill."[44]

It was reported in the press in 1904 that some members of the Peculiar People were taking the view that they should call in medical assistance in the case of children, thus obeying the law and avoiding prosecution. This view was strongly resented by the strict members.[45] In 1906 it was reported that younger members held the view that the question of whether to call in medical assistance should be left to the conscience of the individual member.[46]

Jehovah's Witnesses

The Christian sect now generally known as Jehovah's Witnesses was founded in the United States of America about 1880. In 1900 a branch office was established in London[47] and in 1914 a British corporation was formed under the name of International Bible Students Association.[48] In 1931 the sect decided to be known as Jehovah's Witnesses.[49] The main headquarters of the sect are in the United States: its membership in the British Isles was about 42,000 in 1960 (and about 113,000 in 1988).[50]

The Witnesses are one of the bodies which believe in the imminent Second Coming of Christ. (They have been mentioned a number of times in this book as conscientious objectors to military service and other Defence compulsions and a brief description of their view on these matters was given in Chapter 5.) There seems to be no direct connection between the eschatological views of the Witnesses and their religious objection to blood transfusion except that both arise from their attitude to the Bible. In an official publication of the sect this attitude is expressed as follows. "The Bible is Jehovah God's written word to mankind, revealing himself and expressing his purpose. Jehovah, as the Author, inspired at least thirty-five different faithful men to write."[51]

The Witnesses (who have no objection to medical care in general) object to blood transfusion on the ground that God prohibited the eating of blood, as is shown by various texts in the Old Testament, and that this prohibition was confirmed for Christians by the Apostles. Some of the biblical texts quoted as authorities for this view are the following.

"And God blessed Noah and his sons, and said unto them,... Every moving thing that liveth shall be food for you; as the green herb have I given you all. But flesh with the life thereof, which is the blood thereof, shall ye not eat. And surely your blood, the blood of your lives, will I require; at the hand of every beast will I require it: and at the hand of man, even at the hand of every man's brother, will I require the life of man" (Genesis Ch. 9 w. 1 and 3–5 RV). The Witnesses regard this as a "Prohibition upon All Nations".[52]

"And the Lord spake unto Moses, saying,... And whatsoever man there be of the house of Israel, or of the strangers that sojourn among them, that eateth any manner of blood; I will set my face against that soul that eateth blood, and will cut him off from among his people. For the life of the flesh is in the blood: and I have given it to you upon the altar to make atonement for your souls: for it is the blood that maketh atonement by reason of the life. Therefore I said unto the children of Israel, No soul of you shall eat blood, neither shall any stranger that sojourneth among you eat blood." (Leviticus Ch. 17 w. 1 and 10– 12 RV).

"When the Lord thy God shall enlarge thy border, as he hath promised thee,... thou mayest eat flesh after all the desire of thy soul. Only be sure that thou eat not the blood: for the blood is the life: and thou shalt not eat the life with the flesh. Thou shalt not eat it; thou shalt pour it out upon the earth as water." (Deuteronomy Ch. 12 w. 20 and 23– 24 RV).

The Witnesses regard this and certain other texts as commanding that blood should not be stored.[53]

In The Acts of the Apostles there is a description of a controversy and a decision concerning the extent to which Gentile Christians should be bound by Jewish religious law. "Then it seemed good to the apostles and elders, with the whole church, to choose men out of their company, and send them to Antioch with Paul and Barnabas; and they wrote thus by them, The apostles and the elder brethren unto the brethren which are of the Gentiles in Antioch and Syria and Alicia, greeting; For it seemed good to the Holy Ghost, and to us, to lay upon you no greater burden than these necessary things; that ye abstain from things sacrificed to idols, and from blood, and from things strangled and from fornication; from which if ye keep yourselves, it shall be well with you." (Acts Ch. 15 w. 22 – 23 and 28 – 29 RV). The Witnesses regard this as a "Prohibition Enjoined upon Christians".[54]

The definition of blood transfusion in an official publication of the Witnesses is as follows. "Transferring blood from the veins or arteries of one person to another. As in intravenous feeding, it is feeding upon blood. An unscriptural practice."[55]

At the beginning of the twentieth century two discoveries made it possible for blood transfusion to become "a valuable tool in the hands of the medical profession. One was the finding of a harmless substance which could be mixed with blood to prevent clotting, and

the other was the discovery of the blood groups".[56] But the use
of blood transfusion in large numbers of civilian cases throughout
the whole country dates only from the Second World War, when
regional blood transfusion services were established. Large panels
of voluntary unpaid donors were organised in each region: at the
end of 1944 there were a million donors on these panels and up
to that date there had been nearly two million "blood gifts".[57]
Under the National Health Service each regional hospital board
became responsible for the National Blood Transfusion Service in
its area, including collecting blood, maintaining blood banks, and
making blood available to hospitals, nursing homes and general
practitioners.[58] In the last three decades blood transfusion has
become accepted as desirable in the treatment not only of accidents
but of certain conditions of illness, including haemolytic disease
of the new-born, and blood transfusions have become generally
available. It is in this period that the objection of Jehovah's
Witnesses to blood transfusions for their children has led them
into conflict with the law. The following are some examples.

At a coroner's inquest in November 1957 evidence was given
that the parents, who were Jehovah's Witnesses, refused to allow
a blood transfusion for their baby, who died at the age of five
days. A doctor stated that the ideal treatment was to give a blood
transfusion at the first sign of jaundice: with a transfusion there
would have been a possibility of saving the child's life. The father
told the coroner that he and his wife refused the transfusion on
scriptural grounds. It was one of the tenets of their faith that they
should not allow blood to be spilt. The Coroner asked the father:
"Irrespective of whether it meant the saving or destroying of life?"
He replied: "There will be a resurrection and, by our carrying
out God's will, that child can be brought back to us in a better
world."[59] In February 1958 the husband and wife were charged
with manslaughter at the Nottinghamshire Assizes. The family
doctor stated that he had not warned the parents that failure
to give a transfusion would cause the child's death. The judge
therefore stopped the case and the parents were acquitted. But
the judge warned the parents with regard to any future action
of the same kind.[60]

In September 1964, a diabetic girl aged fourteen had been
admitted to hospital suffering from internal bleeding. Doctors
agreed that another haemorrhage could prove fatal and that the

only chance was to give her a blood transfusion. The parents, who were both Jehovah's Witnesses, refused to allow the transfusion. The Norwich Juvenile Court held an emergency sitting to consider the case put to it by the hospital. The court then adjourned to the girl's bedside because by law the circumstances had to be placed before her. The court then made an order placing the girl, as being in need of care and protection, in the care of the Norfolk County Council. The council's deputy children's officer immediately agreed to the transfusion. He stated: "It was the only thing that could be done in the circumstances. We did not like to take this action, but it was the only way to save the girl's life." The girl's father said that as the blood had been given without consent it would not affect his daughter's plans to enter the ministry.[61]

In February 1968 parents, who were Jehovah's Witnesses, refused to allow a blood transfusion for their son, aged ten years, who suffered from anaemia. A Derby juvenile court placed him in the care of the local authority and the transfusion was then given.[62]

In September 1968 parents, who were Jehovah's Witnesses, refused permission for a blood transfusion for their three-day old daughter, which was needed because of danger of brain damage or deafness from jaundice. A court placed the child in the care of the Bromley council and the transfusion was then given. The chairman of the children's committee of the council said that it had been "a heart-tearing decision" to ask magistrates to rule that the parents of the child were harming her by following their religious beliefs. He stated: "It is a matter of conscience. I respect the parents' beliefs but somebody had to take the responsibility for them." A minister of the sect commented: "The court took away parental control and that is an attack on personal freedom."[63]

References

BMJ = British Medical Journal
1   BMJ 1906 Vo. II p. 1610
2   BMJ 1923 Vol. II. p. 1230
3   31 & 32 Vic. c. 122
4   52 & 53 Vic. c. 44
5   Allen, Anne and Morton, Arthur *This is Your Child. The Story of the National Society for the Prevention of Cruelty to Children* Paperback edition 1962 pp. 17, 19 – 20, 26, 29 – 30
6   52 & 53 Vic. c. 44

7   31 & 32 Vic. c. 122
8   57 & 58 Vic. c. 41
9   4 Edw. 7. c. 15
10   BMJ 1898 Vol. II pp. 1831 and 1916
11   52 & 53 Vic. c. 44
12   57 & 58 Vic. c. 41
13   4 Edw. 7. c. 15
14   8 Edw. 7. c. 67
15   4 Edw. 7. c. 15
16   23 Geo. 5. c. 12
17   8 Edw. 7. c. 67
18   11 & 12 Eliz. 2. c. 37 Sect. 31 and Schedules 3 and 4
19   Prevention of Cruelty to and Protection of Children Act, 1889 52 & 53 Vic. c. 44 Sect. 44
20   Eliz. 2. 1969 c. 54
21   52 & 53 Vic. c. 44 Sect. 5 & 6
22   8 Edw. 7. c. 67
23   23 Geo. 5. c. 12
24   15 & 16 Geo. 6 & 1 Eliz. 2. c. 50
25   Allen and Morton op. cit. p. 47
26   11 & 12 Geo. 6. c. 43 Sect. 5
27   11 & 12 Eliz. 2. c. 37
28   23 Geo. 5. c. 12 amended by 15 & 16 Geo. 6. & 1 Eliz. 2. c. 50
29   Eliz. 2. 1969. c. 54
30   Eliz. 2. 1969. c. 46
31   *Guardian* 29.6.1971
32   Montgomery, John *Abodes of Love* pp. 121,130,131
33   Shaw, Bernard *The Doctor's Dilemma. A Tragedy* 1911. Penguin Edition pp. 11 – 12
34   *Lancet* 1868 Vol. I p. 103
35   BMJ 1875 Vol. I p. 791 and Vol. II p. 649
36   BMJ 1882 Vol. I p. 470
37   BMJ 1898 Vol. I p. 1378
38   BMJ 1906 Vol. I pp. 1256 and 1566
39   BMJ 1898 Vol. II p. 1916 and 1899 Vol. I pp. 809 – 810
40   *Lancet* 1898 Vol. II p. 1716
41   BMJ 1901 Vol. I p. 992
42   4 Edw. 7. c. 15
43   BMJ 1907 Vol. 1 1574
44   Montgomery op. cit. pp. 129– 130
45   BMJ 1904 Vol. I p. 409
46   BMJ 1906 Vol. II p. 710
47   Stevenson, W.C. Year of Doom, 1975. *The Inside Story of Jehovah's Witnesses.* 1967 pp. 136 and 139
48   Hoekema, Anthony A. *The Four Major Cults. Christian Science, Iehovah's Witnesses, Mormonism, Seventh-day Adventism* . British paperback edition 1969. p. 226 note

49 Ibid. p. 230
50 Daily Mail Year Book, 1960
51 International Bible Students Association *Make Sure of All Things* 1957 p. 36
52 Ibid. p. 47
53 Ibid.
54 Ibid.
55 Ibid.
56 Central Office of Information. Pamphlet: The Blood Groups
57 Ministry of Health: On the State of the Public Health during Six Years of War. 1946 pp. 161 and 162
58 Central Office of Information: Health Services in Britain 1959 p. 18
59 *Times* 23.11.1957
60 *Guardian* 1.3. 1958
   Lancet 15.3.1958
61 *Daily Telegraph* 19.9.1964
   Guardian 19.9. and 21.9.1964
62 *Guardian* 19.2.1968
63 *Guardian* 30.9.1968

Chronological Table of Acts Relating to the Protection of Children and Young Persons

Date		
1868	Poor Law Amendment Act	31 & 32 Vic. c. 122
1889	Prevention of Cruelty to & Protection of Children Act	52 & 53 Vic. c. 44
1894	Prevention of Cruelty to Children Act	57 & 58 Vic. c. 41
1904	Prevention of Cruelty to Children Act	4 Edw. 7. c. 15
1908	Children Act	8 Edw. 7. c. 67
1933	Children and Young Persons Act	23 Geo. 5. c. 12
1948	Children Act	11 & 12 Geo. 6. c. 43
1952	Children and Young Persons (Amendment) Act	15 & 16 Geo. 6 & 1 Eliz. 2. c.50
1963	Children and Young Persons Act	11 & 12 Eliz. 2. c.37
1969	Family Law Reform Act	Eliz. 2. 1969. c. 46
1969	Children and Young Persons Act	Eliz. 2. 1969. c. 54

PART II

Analysis and Evaluation

CHAPTER 10

Problems of Illegal
Conscientious Objection

Introduction

In the spheres of law covered in the histories in this book
illegal conscientious objection – conscientious lawbreaking – has
occurred in three kinds of circumstance. Firstly, it has occurred in
resistance to compulsions with regard to which there has never been
statutory provision for legal exemption of conscientious objectors.
There have been six such legal compulsions: the compulsion on
parents to provide or allow necessary medical care for their
children; the three war-time compulsions of industrial conscription,
compulsory part-time Civil Defence, and compulsory fire-watching;
compulsory payments for military and other Defence purposes; and
compulsory payments for religious education. Secondly, illegal
objection occurred in spheres of law in which ultimately provision
was made for legal conscientious objection. This illegal objection
occurred in periods before provision was made for the legal
exemption of any objectors, or before such provision covered
all occasions of objection and all groups of objectors. There
were three such spheres of law: compulsory military service
before this century; compulsory oaths; and compulsory vaccination.
Thirdly, illegal objection to vaccination occurred in England and
Wales during the first nine and a half years in which legal
conscientious objection was allowed; and illegal objection occurred
under the twentieth-century law of compulsory military service,
which provided for legal conscientious objection. In both these
cases the legal exemption of objectors depended on a judicial
decision in each individual case. While this provision satisfied
the consciences of many objectors, other objectors either received

no exemption from courts or tribunals, or received types of exemption which did not satisfy their consciences, and in both these circumstances some such objectors became conscientious law-breakers.

The enforcement of the law in cases of illegal conscientious objection has included three types of sanction: (1) Legal disabilities; (2) Direct constraint; (3) Punishment under the criminal law. These three types of sanction will be discussed in turn.

Legal Disabilities

It was shown in Chapter 1 that conscientious objectors to oath-taking suffered from legal disabilities on many occasions when oaths were required by law. These occasions were numerous in the seventeenth, eighteenth and early nineteenth centuries. The Statutory Declarations Act of 1835[1] greatly reduced the number of these occasions and they were further reduced by the Promissory Oaths Act of 1868.[2] But there remained a number of important occasions on which an oath was obligatory. The disabilities of objectors were removed only when the objectors were allowed to affirm instead of taking an oath. Rights of affirmation were granted piecemeal over a period of nearly two hundred years: their scope was originally limited both with regard to the groups of objectors covered and with regard to the occasions when affirmations were allowed. At various times the scope was enlarged in both these respects until under the Oaths Act of 1888[3] all occasions of oath-taking and substantially all conscientious objectors who claimed the right were included.

The occasions of oath-taking were in two main classes. The first class included the occasions when assertory oaths – oaths swearing to the truth of factual statements – were required, for example, in evidence in court in civil and criminal proceedings, in the proving of wills, and in connection with customs and excise duties. In the eighteenth and early nineteenth centuries a considerable number of objectors would have suffered severe inconvenience because of the oaths necessary in civil legal procedures, had it not been for the fact that the main group of objectors, the Quakers, had since 1696[4] been allowed to affirm in these procedures and that since 1749[5] the same right had been granted to the Moravian Brethren, in which many members were objectors. Except for the inclusion of Separatists in

1833,[6] there was no extension of rights to other objectors until the inclusion of all religious objectors in 1854.[7]

With regard to the oaths necessary in giving evidence in criminal proceedings, even Quakers and Moravians had no right to affirm until 1828[8] and the exclusion of the evidence of objectors in such proceedings could be harmful to the community. The harm caused by the then-existing law of oaths to both the objectors and the community was recognised in 1833 in the preamble to the Act[9] giving Separatists rights of affirmation. The Separatists "from conscientious scruples, refuse to take an oath in courts of justice and other places, and in consequence thereof are exposed to great losses and inconveniences in their trades and concerns, and are subject to fines and to imprisonment for contempt of court, and the community at large are deprived of the benefit of their testimony." In addition to objectors who excluded themselves from giving evidence by refusing to take the oath, there were in the nineteenth century a number of cases in which witnesses who did not believe in God, or who did not believe in a future state of rewards and punishments, were refused by the court permission to take the oath. A striking example of the harm to the community caused by such refusal was cited in Parliament in 1869: a witness as to the identity of the murderer was not allowed to take the oath and his evidence was therefore excluded.

The second class of occasions of oath-taking was concerned with promissory oaths, including the oath of allegiance and various other oaths required as a condition of holding certain offices. Objectors to oaths could not hold these offices, which included membership of both Houses of Parliament, the office of Justice of the Peace and the office of member of a jury. The motives for maintaining this state of law were more mixed than the motives with regard to assertory oaths. Long after British law-makers had ceased to approve of legal religious persecution they continued to approve of legal religious discrimination. Legislation discriminating against objectors to oaths was only one of the types of legislation which discriminated against all those outside the Established Church throughout the eighteenth and early nineteenth centuries.[10] Nonconformists and Catholics were discriminated against by the Corporation Act of 1661[11] and the Test Act of 1673,[12] which excluded from many offices (though not from Parliament) all those who did not communicate according to the rites of the Church of England: these Acts were not repealed until 1828.[13] Catholics were discriminated against by various other legal measures, including the oath of supremacy, which had to be taken by members of Parliament and to the content of which they objected: their disqualification from public offices and from Parliament was ended by the Roman Catholic Relief Act of 1829.[14] In the 1830s, Separatists and present and former Quakers and Moravians were granted rights of affirmation on all occasions so that in future they could become members of juries and members of Parliament and could hold various other offices which required promissory oaths. In the 1860s, all religious objectors were granted the right of affirmation as jurors. But, except for the three religious bodies just mentioned, before 1888 no affirmations were allowed as alternatives to most types of promissory oath, including the parliamentary oaths. Membership of Parliament was one of the last citadels of legal religious discrimination and the weapon used to defend it was enforcement of the parliamentary oaths: The eleven years' struggle (from 1847 to 1858) of Rothschild to hold his seat as a Jew and the nearly six years' struggle (from 1880 to 1886) of Bradlaugh to hold his seat as an atheist were essentially fights against religious discrimination.

Direct Constraint

I am using the term "direct constraint" to mean coercion which attains the object of the law without involving the co-operation or consent of the person coerced. This method of coercion has a number of advantages but the possible scope for its use is limited. Many kinds of action can be prevented by direct constraint: for example, a person can be prevented by imprisonment from engaging in activities as a burglar, an offence under the present law, or from hearing Mass, a legal offence in some past periods. But very few kinds of action can be compelled by direct constraint: in fact no "actions" in a narrow sense can be compelled by this method. Physical brutality or severe mental pressure can be used in an attempt to compel a person to perform some action, for example, to conform with the law in future, to confess his crime, or to inform on his acquaintances. But if such coercion is successful, it succeeds by changing the will of the person coerced and obtaining his consent to the action and is thus not a case of direct constraint. However, the method of direct constraint can be used successfully to enforce claims on property and to perform certain medical operations, and there are examples of both these uses in the history of conscientious objection.

Distraint on the property of the defaulter was the normal method of enforcing the law in the case of non-payment of rates and of certain other legally compulsory payments. This method of law-enforcement had the result that the authority concerned eventually received the money due to it except in two circumstances. The first exceptional circumstance was that the defaulter possessed no or insufficient distrainable property to meet the claim. The second circumstance which sometimes occurred, for example in some cases of distraints for tithes and for rates for education, was that a local boycott prevented or hindered the authority from selling the distrained property. Except in these two circumstances, the method of distraint enabled the purpose of the law to be achieved with regard to every defaulter to whom it was applied.

Thus, in one sense, the conscientious objector was usually defeated by the use of this method of law-enforcement – he could not prevent the authorities from taking his property as he could prevent them from using his personal services. Nevertheless, it has been shown in this book that, in addition to individual isolated cases, there were two spheres of law in which considerable numbers of conscientious objectors refused to make legally due payments, although they knew that this refusal would be countered by distraint on their property. These two spheres of law were the compulsory payments for the militia and allied purposes resisted by Quakers for some two hundred years (described in Chapter 3) and the compulsory rates for denominational schools resisted in the passive resistance movement from 1903 onwards (described in Chapter 8). There were also, in a sphere of law not described in this book, a considerable number of conscientious objectors to tithes, whose resistance over a long period was countered by the method of distraint. What could such objectors hope to achieve by their resistance?

In my view there were two types of motive involved, though probably some individuals acted from only one or other of these motives. One motive was a strongly felt conscientious objection to making payments for specific purposes which the objector considered to be immoral. Thus the Society of Friends collectively stated in the eighteenth century in relation to certain demands under a Militia Act: "It is our sense and judgment, that we cannot, consistent with our well known principles, actively pay the rate or assessment."[15] To conscientious objectors who felt in this way, their moral duty to refuse active co-operation with the law was not nullified by the fact that the authorities could take their property without their consent.

The second motive was to use resistance to the law as a form of protest or propaganda. Though the resisters could not prevent the ultimate taking of their property by the authorities, they could delay the enforcement of the law and involve the authorities in the expenditure of considerable effort in this enforcement. The resisters could also, in the course of their resistance, give considerable publicity to their views. This motive was important in the passive resistance movement: a large majority of the resisters paid the amounts due after either a summons or a warrant of distraint by a court had been issued and therefore in their cases actual distraint was not necessary.

The medical operation of vaccination against smallpox, when performed on babies or young children, has usually involved the use of direct constraint on these children. But (except for children in institutions) these children have normally been under the care of a parent during the conduct of the operation. In the last half of the nineteenth century, when vaccination was compulsory and there was no legal exemption of the children of parents with conscientious objections, it would have been physically possible to vaccinate children without the consent of their parents, when necessary restraining the parents by force. Such action would have involved great difficulties and would have caused great resentment: it was never legally sanctioned in Britain. Instead, the law was enforced by prosecuting or by threatening to prosecute those parents who refused to have their children vaccinated. Sometimes this action resulted in the vaccination of the child concerned: sometimes it did not achieve this purpose.

During the Second World War and the period of post-war National Service a considerable number of objectors to military service refused to take their medical examinations (the examination being a necessary preliminary to enlistment in the army). After April 1941[16] the enforcing procedure was as follows. When a court had convicted an objector for this offence it then usually applied direct constraint to him by ordering that he be detained in custody and taken by a constable before the medical board. But at that point direct constraint ceased. Presumably it would have been possible to conduct some sort of medical examination against the will of the objector and with no co-operation from him. But such action was not attempted: if the objector refused to submit to medical examination under the court order he was prosecuted for this offence.

In contrast with these two spheres of law in which direct constraint was not used, the method was used in recent years in a few cases in which parents refused to allow their children to have blood transfusions because, as Jehovah's Witnesses, they had conscientious objections to the operation. In these cases (some of which were described in Chapter 9) a court made an order placing the child under the care of the local authority, the officer of the local authority then gave his consent for the blood transfusion, and the operation was then performed without the consent of the parents. In these cases there was immediate and serious danger to the life or health of the child and enforcement of the law by direct constraint was the only way to avert this danger. Even if the parents could have been influenced by persuasion or by the threat of legal punishment, there was not time to try these alternative methods. In my view these facts made the method of direct constraint appropriate.

As compared with law-enforcement by the threat or infliction of legal penalties, law-enforcement by direct constraint has advantages both to the enforcing authority and to the conscientious objector concerned. The advantage to the enforcing authority is that the object of the law is attained in the individual case – the money legally due is obtained or the desired medical operation is performed – whereas enforcement by legal penalties is uncertain of attaining this result. The advantage to the conscientious objector is that, when he has done all that is possible to obey his conscience, the matter is then taken out of his hands. He is neither induced by fear of penalties to act against his conscience nor, if he refuses to do this, subjected to punishment.

Legal Penalties

Penalties liable to be imposed on conscientious objectors under the criminal law have varied in severity from the maximum penalty of a fine of twenty shillings (£1) and costs under the Vaccination Acts, to the sentences of imprisonment for life or at the King's pleasure incurred by some seventeenth-century oath-refusers and the death sentences pronounced, but not executed, on some objectors to military service during the First World War. There have been in Britain no executions of conscientious objectors to the compulsions described in this book. But there have been cases of objectors whose deaths were caused or partly caused by conditions of imprisonment, both among resisters to oaths in the seventeenth century and among resisters to military service in the twentieth century.

Information about the numbers of prosecutions is not available with regard to some of the spheres of law in which prosecutions of conscientious objectors have occurred. But, from figures already cited in this book, examples can be given of the number of prosecutions in each of the three kinds of circumstance of illegal objection described at the beginning of this chapter. Firstly, there are available figures of prosecutions in three spheres of law in which there has never been statutory provision for legal conscientious objection. Between March 1941 and the end of 1948 there were a total of 1608 known prosecutions of objectors (1,186 of men and 422 of women) for offences relating to industrial conscription, compulsory part-time Civil Defence, and compulsory fire-watching. Secondly, under the Vaccination Acts, which later allowed legal conscientious objection, there were in England and Wales in the 1880s, before such legal objection was allowed, a total of 11,408 cases of fines imposed over a period of about ten years. Thirdly, under the twentieth-century law of compulsory military service, which provided for legal conscientious objection there were, during the First World War and the few months succeeding it, 8,608 court-martial sentences imposed on 5,739 men objectors, and there were, during the Second World War, 931 court-martial trials of 613 men who had provisionally registered as objectors. During the Second World War there were also a total of 2,756 known civilian prosecutions of objectors (of which 84 were of women) for refusal of medical examination under court order, for non-compliance with the condition of exemption, and for offences against Home Guard regulations.

The number of prosecutions is not necessarily an adequate measure of the extent of conscientious law-breaking. It is probably a good measure of the amount of illegal objection to twentieth-century compulsory military service. But with regard to illegal objection to compulsory vaccination it is a most inadequate measure: some of the local authorities concerned did not enforce the law, while others did not use their full powers of enforcement. With regard to the war-time measures compelling personal services other than military service, my opinion is that the law was not enforced against a considerable number of law-breakers.

With the exception of the seventeenth-century period of persecution of Nonconformists, I think it is fair to say that the motives for punishing the conscientious objector have not normally been vindictive. The purpose of punishment has been to enforce the law, both by coercing the law-breaker himself and by deterring others from taking his line of action. In considering the enforcement of the law against conscientious law-breakers, the effects of successful deterrence or coercion must be distinguished from the effects of unsuccessful deterrence or coercion.

Legal deterrence of the conscientious objector has probably been successful in the case of many individuals. It must be remembered that for some people the deterrent effect of the law depends not only on the legal penalties but also on the uncertainties involved in awaiting possible prosecution and on the publicity and other disagreeable features of the prosecution itself. On the matter of the numbers successfully deterred, one would not expect to find any conclusive evidence, but the two following sets of figures show a strong probability that many objectors were successfully deterred. This conclusion must, however, be modified by the consideration that probably some of these objectors held that their general moral duty to be law-abiding overrode their objection to a particular law, and obeyed the law for this reason and not because of their fear of prosecution.

In England and Wales in the 1880s, when there was no legal exemption from vaccination, there were about 11,400 cases of fines inflicted on parents breaking the law over a period of about ten years. In the nine years 1899 to 1907 nearly 400,000 legal exemptions were granted to parents claiming as conscientious objectors. It is true that the number of fines inflicted would have been considerably greater had all the local authorities concerned rigorously enforced the law – there were many law-breakers unpunished. It is also true that the annual number of births was larger in the later period. It is also likely that the number of parents opposed to vaccination had increased in the interval between the two periods. But the difference between the two figures is so great as to convince me that many parents in the 1880s did not disobey the law but would have applied for legal exemption had it been available.

Another convincing set of figures concerns objectors to military service in the Second World War. Out of about 12,200 men refused any exemption by tribunals, probably not more than a quarter proceeded to resist military service by breaking the law (though a considerable number among the others were able to work in Civil Defence or other civilian employments). There were also some objectors who were successfully coerced after starting illegal resistance: probably about 8 per cent of those prosecuted for refusing medical examination then submitted to examination (though a number did so for the purpose of entering Civil Defence).

The effect of successful deterrence or coercion of the conscientious objector is that the object of the law is attained by forcing the individual to act against his conscience. In my opinion this is, in itself, a very harmful result, and in any particular sphere of law the question should always be asked whether it is too high a price to pay for the advantages of enforcing conformity with the law.

Public opinion and the authorities have usually been much more worried about the effects of unsuccessful deterrence than about the unseen effects of successful deterrence. Fines and, to a greater extent, imprisonment cause suffering to the objector and his family. This has often roused the sympathy not only of people agreeing with his views but of many disagreeing. Most objectors have been generally law-abiding people, often respected by their neighbours and acquaintances, and their treatment as criminals has been resented by those who have known them. It has also shocked many Christians to find fellow-Christians punished for acting according to their interpretation of Christian principles.

With regard to civilians, the severity of the law has often been mitigated by two circumstances. The first circumstance has been that prosecution has not invariably followed an offence: the authorities have had to decide whether to prosecute the offender and they have sometimes decided not to do so. To enforce the law rigorously against all recalcitrants may seem to the enforcing authority not to be worthwhile. The offences committed by conscientious objectors have usually not involved the enforcing authorities in great expenditure of effort in detection and legal proof of the offence, but there have been other disadvantages of enforcement. A prosecution inevitably leads to a trial which is held in public and the authorities may be reluctant to give publicity to the fact that the law is being broken and to the reasons for this. If there is considerable opposition to the law, as was the case, particularly in some localities, with regard to compulsory vaccination, prosecutions may increase this opposition.

The second mitigating circumstance has been that usually the law has specified not actual but maximum penalties. Magistrates or judges have been able to impose a penalty much below the maximum or, in some cases, no penalty. Moreover, while conscientious objection has not been a legal excuse for the offence, nothing in the law has prevented magistrates or judges from taking it into account when deciding on the penalty to be imposed. A countervailing circumstance has been that a considerable number of objectors have suffered a heavier penalty than that originally imposed by the court because they have refused, usually on principle, to pay the fine imposed and have therefore suffered the imprisonment imposed in lieu of the fine.

From the point of view of society, a disadvantage of imposing sentences of imprisonment is that imprisonment causes waste – waste of the services of the prison staff and waste of the services of the imprisoned objector. This waste has been regarded as particularly harmful in war-time and the wish to avoid it has influenced the treatment of law-breaking objectors to military service, particularly during the Second World War. In that war the Ministry of Labour and National Service often refrained from using its power to proceed further against an objector who refused to take his medical examination, if the objector had already served a substantial sentence of imprisonment for this offence: instead it tried to fit the objector into some form of useful civilian work which he was willing to undertake.

In recent times it has been officially recognised as undesirable to send young adult offenders to prison and the Criminal Justice Act of 1948[17] enacted that "No court shall impose imprisonment on a person under twenty-one years of age unless the court is of the opinion that no other method of dealing with him is appropriate." This policy conflicted with the duty of courts to impose adequate penalties on young men who were illegal conscientious objectors to post-war National Service. In two cases courts solved the dilemma by sentencing the objector to Borstal treatment but in both cases the

Court of Criminal Appeal overruled this decision and substituted a sentence of imprisonment.[18] In some cases courts imposed fines and in some cases young objectors were committed to detention centres.[19] But a considerable number of young men were sent to prison. The following comment was made about some of them by a prison governor in 1952. "These youths are, in the main, non-delinquents and possessed of strong religious beliefs. Many of them are Jehovah's Witnesses. The effect of imprisonment on these young men seems to be to strengthen rather than shake their convictions. Fortunately there is no evidence to suggest that any of them are contaminated by their criminal comrades, who tend either to laugh at them or ignore them."[20]

Objectors in prison have been unusual prisoners: the puzzlement sometimes caused by them to their fellow-prisoners is illustrated by two incidents during the Second World War. An objector was conversing at exercise with a man who was in prison for assaulting a policeman, not for the first time. This man remarked: "Funny, ain't it? I'm in here because I will fight and you're in here because you won't! It do seem as if whatever you do or don't do doesn't do, doesn't it?"[21] Another objector in prison, a Jehovah's Witness, used to read his Bible at associated meals. His neighbour, becoming tired of this, remarked to him: "You seem to read your Bible the whole time. I don't think I've looked at mine for twenty years. But we've both come to the same place in the end!"

From the point of view of society, the imprisonment of objectors has not been a complete waste. Some former prisoners have used their experiences constructively in work for the welfare of prisoners and other offenders and in propaganda for penal reform. The presence in British prisons at various times of idealistic and intelligent prisoners – conscientious objectors, Suffragettes, and others in prison for conscientious reasons – who in their normal lives have been respectable citizens, has helped to lessen the widespread ignorance and unconcern with regard to prison life which is one of the obstacles to prison reform.

One of the difficult problems in the treatment of conscientious law-breakers is how to regard the repeated prosecution of the same individual. The possibility of repeated prosecutions has occurred whenever the law has created a continuing obligation and the objector has not been induced to obey the law by being punished once. The histories in this book have shown many instances of repeated prosecutions. For example, two extreme cases, cited before the Royal Commission on Vaccination, were those of one parent prosecuted sixty times in respect of nine children and another parent prosecuted seventy-nine times in respect of two children. During the First World War 1,548 objectors to military service were sentenced by court-martial more than once and of these 372 were sentenced more than three times.

The position of conscientious objectors in the army (and of some cases in the other Armed Forces) has been especially unfortunate. In the First World War, though the matter was not dealt with by legislation, the cases of several thousand army objectors who were in prison were referred to the Central Tribunal for consideration and consequently 3,750 objectors were released from prison and seconded from the army to work under the "Home Office Scheme". During the Second World War and the period of post-war National Service, the objector in the Forces, who had originally registered provisionally as a conscientious objector, had the statutory right[22] to apply to the Appellate Tribunal if he had been sentenced, on account of an offence committed for conscientious reasons, to imprisonment for three months or more (extended from 1949[23] onwards to include military detention for three months or more). By an administrative concession the same right was given to members of the Forces who had become objectors while in the Forces. Decisions of the tribunal, on a first or subsequent application, resulted in the discharge from the Forces of several hundred objectors. A number of other objectors were also eventually discharged.

In 1941[24] legislation gave the same right to objectors who resisted military service by refusing to take their medical examinations under court order. Under this provision, during the War and in the post-war period, the Appellate Tribunal gave decisions which freed more than a thousand objectors from future liability for military service.

These two pieces of legislation tackled the problem of repeated prosecutions by giving to the law-breaking objector a further opportunity to have his objection legally recognised. In another sphere of law – compulsory vaccination – legislation directly limited the number of possible convictions of the same individual. After an attempt by the House of Commons to limit this number in 1871, unsuccessful because defeated in the House of Lords, Parliament achieved this purpose twenty-seven years later. The Vaccination Act of 1898,[25] (which covered England and Wales) provided that no parent could be convicted more than twice on account of the same child.

There was no other case of legal limitation of the number of prosecutions, but the authorities often refrained from using their powers to continue indefinitely the prosecution of the same offender. The Government Department concerned sometimes pursued a definite policy which took into account not only the number of previous prosecutions of the offender but also the severity of the sentences imposed. When local authorities were the enforcing authorities, as in the case of vaccination and fire-watching regulations, they pursued differing policies and the central government, while it sometimes tried to persuade them, was unable to compel them.

In my opinion, the case in favour of repeated prosecutions of an individual conscientious law-breaker is usually much weaker than the case in favour of his first prosecution. The original prosecution may serve to distinguish the conscientious law-breaker from the person who breaks the law from the motive of self-interest or from indolence. It can be argued that a first prosecution may successfully deter both the objector himself and others from future law-breaking. In contrast, an objector who has not been successfully coerced by one punishment is not very likely to be successfully coerced by further punishments (though in some cases his resistance may be worn down by them). The public are likely to respect a determined resister, even while disagreeing with him, and may regard his repeated punishment as persecution and a discredit to the authorities which inflict it.

The argument against repeated prosecutions was well expressed during the Second World War by the Chairman of the Magistrates on the occasion of the ninth prosecution of an objector for a fire-watching offence. "We do feel that his case has been before us quite often enough, and we cannot see any useful purpose is served by further prosecution. The law cannot make a man do things – it can only punish him for not doing them."[26] This case, and many other cases of repeated prosecutions, have demonstrated the impotence of the State to enforce its will on the determined and persistent conscientious resister.

References

CBCO = Central Board for Conscientious Objectors

1   5 & 6 Will. 4. c. 62
2   31 & 32 Vic. c. 72
3   51 & 52 Vic. c. 46
4   7 & 8 Will. 3. c. 34
5   22 Geo. 2. c. 30
6   3 & 4 Will.4.c.82
7   17 & 18 Vic. c. 125
8   9 Geo. 4. c. 32
9   3 & 4 Will. 4. c. 82
10   See Addison, William George *Religious Equality in Modern England
     1 714 – 1914*
11   13 Car. 2. St. 2. c. 1
12   25 Car. 2. c. 2
13   9 Geo. 4. c. 17
14   10 Geo. 4. c. 7
15   Friends, Society of *Extracts from Minutes and Advices of Yearly Meeting*
     1783
16   4 & 5 Geo. 6. c. 15 Sect. 4 Temporary Migration of Children (Guard-
     ianship) Act, 1941
17   11 & 12 Geo. 6. c. 58 Sect. 17 (2)
18   CBCO Annual Report 1948–49
     The Objector June 1952 and February 1953
19   CBCO Annual Reports 1949 – 50 and 1954 – 55
20   Report of the Commissioners of Prisons for 1952
21   CBCO Bulletin. April 1942
22   2 & 3 Geo. 6. c. 81 Sect. 13
23   11 & 12 Geo. 6. c. 64 Sect. 21
24   5 & 6 Geo. 6c. 3Sect. 5
25   61 & 62 Vic. c. 49 Sects. 3 & 4
26   Hayes, Denis *Challenge of Conscience. The Story of the Conscientious
     Objectors of 1939–1949* pp. 323–324

CHAPTER 11

Tests of Legal Conscientious Objection

Introduction

Regarded logically, provision for legal conscientious objection is a queer phenomenon. When Parliament has decided, rightly or wrongly, to make a particular type of action compulsory, it can be presumed that Parliament has also decided that the advantages to be gained from the universal performance of the action outweigh the expense of effort and other disadvantages involved in enforcing compulsion on the recalcitrant. Why then, should Parliament make concessions based on the motives for recalcitrance of some of those unwilling to obey the law?

It was shown in Chapters 1, 2 and 3 that, in three out of the four spheres of law in which legislation made provision for legal conscientious objection, this legislation was preceded by a considerable amount of conscientious law-breaking over considerable periods. The granting of the first legal right of affirmation in 1689 was preceded by thirty years of illegal refusal of oath-taking by Quakers and Baptists. The first concession made to Quakers in the Militia Acts, in 1757, was preceded by a hundred years of Quaker resistance to military service. Compulsory vaccination of children against smallpox existed for forty-five years – from 1853 to 1898 – before legal conscientious objection was allowed, and in the last thirty years of this period there were a considerable number of conscientious law-breakers. The fourth sphere of law – the "conscience clause" in the Education Acts, described in Chapter 8 – seems to show a contrast, as the legal right of parents to withdraw their children from religious worship and religious instruction in schools has existed as long as there has been compulsory education, that is since 1870. But, if this right is regarded as part of the wider right of religious freedom, then it can be said that the enactment of the conscience clause was preceded by much conscientious law-breaking in the sixteenth and seventeenth centuries. Thus it is clear that one motive for the enactment of provisions allowing legal conscientious objection was the wish to avoid a state of law under which a considerable amount of illegal conscientious objection occurred. But there was also another motive – a desire to respect conscience and a reluctance to coerce it.

British law has wisely not attempted to define conscience but, in conceding the right of legal conscientious objection, it has had to decide how to distinguish between the conscientious objector and the objector for other reasons. Three main alternative methods of identifying the conscientious objector have been used: (1) to confine the right of legal conscientious objection (2) to give the right substantially to all who claim it by making some form of statement; (3) to make the right dependent on the decision of a judicial body in each case. These three methods will be discussed in turn.

Rights Confined to Members of Specified Religious Bodies

The two spheres of legislation which confined the right of legal conscientious objection to members of specified religious bodies were the early law of affirmations and the law concerning the militia.

Except for the right of affirmation on very limited occasions provided by the Toleration Act of 1689,[1] legal rights of affirmation prior to 1854 were confined to members of three religious bodies – Quakers, Moravians and Separatists: in the case of Quakers and Moravians former members were also included. Quakers were covered by legislation from 1696 onwards, Moravians were covered from 1749 onwards, and Separatists were covered in 1833.

The law concerning the militia first made special concessions to Quakers in 1757 and from 1786 onwards they were protected from compulsory enrolment in the militia. From 1803 onwards these concessions were extended to Moravians. In practice there was no compulsory military service between the 1830s and 1916. In 1916 a proposal was made during the parliamentary debates on the Military Service Bill that the grounds for legal conscientious objection should be that the applicant was "a member of the

Society of Friends or of any other recognised religious body one of whose fundamental tenets is an objection to all war". But this proposal was not adopted and the twentieth-century law of military conscription has not confined legal conscientious objection to members of specified religious bodies nor exempted such members solely on account of their membership.

There are some considerations in favour of confining the right of legal conscientious objection to members of specified religious bodies. Probably a historical reason for the use of this method was that concessions to religious bodies, whose objection to oaths or military service was well known, were regarded as logical corollaries of religious toleration of these bodies. During the Second World War Professor G.C. Field, a former member of a Conscientious Objectors' Tribunal, wrote as follows in favour of toleration of the established tenets of certain religious bodies (though he did not believe in confinement of rights to members of these bodies). "There are some people who, during the war, have adopted a very hostile attitude to all conscientious objectors and expressed the view that they should not be tolerated. Yet those people knew very well that there were religious bodies which included Pacifism as part of their system of belief, and yet they never objected to the toleration of these bodies in time of peace. What right have they, then, to object to the members of these bodies being allowed to act, when war came, as they have always said they were going to act?"[2]

A second consideration in favour of this method of exemption was that it was easy for the administrators. The objectors were in well defined groups, and proof of membership of the religious body concerned could be secured by a statement from the member himself[3] or by the evidence of fellow-members.[4] The authorities also knew that the membership of the bodies concerned was small, and they had not to contemplate the possibility of a large number of people being exempted from the normal requirements of the law.

A third argument in favour of this method of exemption is that it involves little risk of pretended conscientious objections. For example, few people would become Quakers or Christadelphians or Jehovah's Witnesses only in order to avoid military service: they would be deterred by the other obligations of membership of these bodies.

But there are two strong arguments against this method of exemption. One argument is that the method excludes a considerable number of conscientious objectors. This consideration, in relation to rights of affirmation, led in the second half of the nineteenth century to the extension of these rights first to all religious objectors and then also to unbelievers. In relation to military service a statistical example can be given. During two years of the Second World War, out of 3,353 applicants to the South Western Tribunal only some 40 per cent were members of religious denominations with collective views against military service.[5] (See pp.193–6.)

The second strong argument against this method of exemption is that it shows insufficient respect for the conscience of the individual. Consciences should not be classified tidily in groups. Though the conscience of an individual has been affected by many influences, including those of any religious body of which he may be a member, yet the decisions of his conscience are his individual decisions. Any satisfactory form of provision for legal conscientious objection must treat the objector as an individual and must respect his individual conscience.

Rights available to All Who Claim Them

There have been three spheres of British law in which legislation has given the right of legal conscientious objection substantially to all who claim it. In two spheres of law this legal right exists at the present time: the Education Acts give parents the right to withdraw their children from religious worship andlor religious instruction in schools, and under the Oaths Act of 1888[6] individuals can claim the right to make an affirmation instead of taking an oath. In the third sphere of law the legal right of conscientious objection to vaccination was available substantially to all parents who claimed it during the last forty years of compulsory vaccination: this right ceased to have effect with the ending of compulsory vaccination in 1948.

The Conscience Clause under the Present Education Acts

In both England and Wales and Scotland (as was shown in detail in Chapter 8) throughout the whole period during which education has been compulsory, the parent of a child attending a school maintained or assisted by public authorities has had the legal right to withdraw his child from religious worship or religious instruction or from both these activities at school. The principles of this "conscience clause" have been similar in the two countries. In England and Wales the first legislative provision was made in the Elementary Education Act of 1870[7] and the present law is stated in the Education Reform Act of 1988.[8] In Scotland, legislative provision was made in the Education (Scotland) Act of 1872[9] and the present law is stated in the Education (Scotland) Act of 1946.[10]

The law gives to the parent the unconditional right to withdraw his child, wholly or partially, from religious worship or from religious instruction or from both these activities at school. There are no legal restrictions on the exercise of this right and the request of the parent to the school must be complied with. It is perhaps strange that nowhere in the past or present legislation is there any mention in the text of the statutes of conscientious or religious objections as reasons for the parent's withdrawal of his child. (In some statutes the term "conscience clause" is used as a marginal heading.) A parent can legally withdraw his child for any reason whatever. But the intention of the law has obviously been to provide for parents whose objections arise from their religious views. Parents may have such objections because, for example, they have no religious beliefs, or because their religious beliefs are different from those inculcated at the school, or because they object to the nature of the school's religious worship, or because they object to the kind of religious instruction given by a particular teacher. Such kinds of objection would all be conscientious objections and it seems likely that hardly any withdrawals are made for unconscientious reasons.

The second legal point to be noted is that the legal right is the right of the parent: the pupil himself has no legal right to be excused from religious worship or religious instruction at his own request though in practice this is sometimes allowed. The law has remained substantially the same for a hundred years while there has been a radical change in the age-distribution of the school pupils affected by the law. In England and Wales, between 1870 and 1902 the conscience clause covered only elementary schools whose pupils were all aged under fourteen. The conscience clause now covers both primary and secondary schools and affects pupils who cannot leave school until they are aged between sixteen and seventeen and many of whom continue voluntarily at school at later ages. It seems to me that there is a good case for giving to older pupils the legal right to be excused at their own request from religious worship and/or religious instruction at school. Such a legal right could be given either instead of or in addition to the right of parents on their behalf. My opinion as to the age at which this right should be given is uncertain: I think it might be desirable to give the right to pupils aged fourteen and over. At the age of sixteen a young person has now the right to make his own decisions about his medical care[11] and it seems to me inconsistent to allow him this right and not to consider him responsible enough to make his own decision with regard to participation in religious worship and religious education. (The National Union of Teachers recommended in 1969 that attendance at religious worship and religious education should be voluntary for pupils aged sixteen and over.)[12]

Although the legal right available to parents is wide and unconditional, there are, in practice, several kinds of circumstance which may deter some parents, who object to the participation of their children in the school's religious activities, from claiming the right.

The first circumstance is that some parents are ignorant with regard to their rights. There seems to be no legal obligation for either the school or the local education authority to inform parents of their rights. The "Plowden" Report (covering primary schools in England) recommended in 1967 that all parents should be informed of their rights when their children were admitted to school.[13]

The second circumstance is that some parents do not withdraw their children for fear that the children, if withdrawn, would feel uncomfortably conspicuous. A minority statement in the "Plowden" Report speaks of parents who do not exercise their right "because they fear that it will prejudice the children's standing in the school. Moreover, the children themselves do not like to be put in a position which sets them apart from their fellows."[14] The embarrassment of the withdrawn child is likely to be greater in a school where there are very few withdrawals than in a school where there are more cases. The child may also be affected by the reason for his withdrawal: he is likely to find it easier to defend his position if he is a Catholic or a Jew or a member of some other widely recognised religious group than if he is the child of unbelieving parents. Of course, some children like to be exceptional and conspicuous, but many fear it.

The third circumstance is that in many cases there is inadequate provision of accommodation or alternative activities for children who are withdrawn. There are large variations in the adequacy of provision in different schools. For example, a child may have to wait in the school corridor; or he may remain in his own place in his classroom, expected to disregard the religious instruction being given to his class; or he may work on his own in the school library; or, at the request of his parent, he may attend religious worship or religious instruction of a kind different from that normally provided by the school. A minority statement in the "Plowden" Report says that the difficulty which faces parents who wish to exercise their right "is that withdrawal generally means withdrawal into an empty room or corridor. No alternative programme of moral or ethical education exists for such parents to choose for their children."[15] The Report itself recommends that all parents should be informed, when their children are admitted to school, not only of their rights but also of how religious worship and religious education are conducted in the school and of what provision, if any, is made for the children who are withdrawn from them.[16]

Though no collected figures are available, it seems clear that, in general, only a small minority of parents withdraw their children, though there may be some schools where this is not the case. The defects of the conscience clause for parents consist not in any legal limitations of the right but in the disadvantages to some children involved in the exercise of this right by their parents. Of those who criticise the present position, some would urge administrative action by schools within the present law, while others would urge the more radical remedy of making attendance at religious worship and religious instruction subject to voluntary enrolment.

Affirmations under the Present Law

Since 1888, the law relating to affirmations has been uniform throughout Great Britain. In Chapter 1 a description was given of the history of the law from 1689. The present law is contained in the Oaths Act of 1978 which repealed the whole of the Oaths Acts 1838, 1888, 1909 and 1961 together with relevant sections of the Administration of Justice Act, 1977 and Circuit Courts

(Scotland) Act, 1828.[17] (The Oaths Act of 1961,[18] described in Chapter 1, allowed an affirmation in the case of "a person to whom it is not reasonably practicable to administer an oath in the manner appropriate to his religious belief". This occasion for affirmation does not arise from conscientious objection to oath-taking and it will not be included in this discussion. As the Quakers and Moravians Acts of 1833[19] and 1837[20] are still in force, present or former Quakers or Moravians, instead of claiming their right under the Oaths Act, can claim the right to affirm on the basis of their membership of these religious bodies. This test of conscientious objection has been discussed in a previous Section of this chapter and will not be further discussed here.)

Section 6 of the Oaths Act of 1978[21] states: "Any person who objects to being sworn shall be permitted to make his solemn affirmation instead of taking an oath", and "A solemn affirmation shall be of the same force and effect as an oath." The wording of the affirmation contains no religious reference.

Certain legal points should be noted. Firstly, the right of affirmation exists on all occasions of legal oath-taking: prior to 1888 this was not the case with regard to objectors other than Separatists or present or former Quakers or Moravians. The 1888 Act ended all the complications and uncertainties arising from the granting of rights of affirmation available only on certain occasions. Under the present law the objector to oaths can affirm not only in all criminal and civil legal procedures but also on occasions when he would normally have to take a promissory oath. Thus his objection no longer disqualifies him from any office or appointment.

Secondly, the right to affirm has to be claimed. On an occasion when an oath is required, the person concerned is not normally asked whether he wishes to affirm: he must take the initiative to claim his right. Taking an oath remains the normal procedure and, though there are no figures available, there is little doubt that this normal procedure is followed by the large majority of those concerned: persons claiming the right to affirm are a small minority.

Thirdly, there is no legal or other material advantage to be obtained by affirming. Throughout the whole history of the law relating to affirmations the statutes have enacted that the offence of perjury shall relate to an affirmation in the same way as it relates

341

to an oath. Thus there is no risk of persons pretending to have conscientious objections to oath-taking from motives of material self-interest.

To what extent does the present law provide for all conscientious objectors to oaths? There are two distinct points to be considered: first, to what extent objectors claim their right; second, to what extent those who claim the right are granted it.

There are certain non-legal deterrents to claiming the right of affirmation when this has to be done in courts of justice or otherwise in public. Many people dislike making themselves conspicuous and this is particularly likely to be true with regard to witnesses in court who are often in a nervous condition. In the case of unbelievers, there is an additional deterrent in that, in some cases, it is probably still a social disadvantage to the person concerned to make a public statement of unbelief, although he is no longer required to state his grounds for his request to affirm. In a report of the Criminal Law Revision Committee in 1972, some members stated the opinion: "It is probable that many witnesses who in fact have no religious belief take the oath because they do not wish to call attention to themselves or because they fear that the impact of their evidence will be weakened if they depart from the customary oath."[22] It can be argued that, if individuals are deterred by the considerations just mentioned, they cannot have strong conscientious objections to oath-taking. This seems to me to be true and, in my opinion, the importance of these deterrents is not their effect on the objector with strong convictions. Their importance is that they induce a considerable number of people to make the solemn religious statement in an oath not from sincere belief but purely as a matter of legal and conventional requirement.

Before 1978 the Oaths Acts did not include a general category of conscientious objection but instead allowed a claim to affirm on one of two alternative grounds: either that the taking of an oath was contrary to the objector's religious belief or that the objector had no religious belief. It was in these two categories that conscientious objection to oath-taking had occurred in the past. There could possibly be conscientious objections which did not come under either of these categories (for example, a strong moral but not religious objection held by a religious believer) but I think it unlikely that there are any considerable numbers of these.

However, some members of the Criminal Law Revision Committee stated in their 1972 report that cases had occurred in which persons who could not bring themselves within either of the requirements for affirmation of the Oaths Act, nor state what form of oath was binding on them, had their evidence rejected altogether.[23]

An undesirable result of the pre-1978 law was that an objector who was an unbeliever or sceptical about Christian beliefs was sometimes subjected to considerable questioning by the court. In a letter to the press in 1963 an anonymous "court officer", describing the position in magistrates' courts, said that sometimes the exchange of question and answer "extends into a full dress theological inquisition in which the unfortunate witness is forced to define in open court his exact brand of agnosticism or unbelief." Such proceedings "will very often put a witness into an unsuitable frame of mind for the examination, and there is also the suspicion that he has antagonised the magistrate where the latter has orthodox views,"[24]

At the London Sessions in November 1961 there was a striking example of the possible difficulties of an agnostic wishing to affirm. A witness for the defence asked to affirm and the following conversation then took place.

Chairman of the Sessions (a Queen's Counsel): "Why?"

Witness: "I don't believe that the Bible tells the whole truth, and would rather affirm."

Chairman: "Do you believe in the New Testament? Do you think that it tells the truth?"

Witness: "Parts of it, yes."

Chairman: "Which parts?"

Witness: "Well, I think the synoptic gospels mainly are true."

Chairman (to the court usher): "Give him the New Testament and he can take the oath."

Witness: "Can I not affirm?"

Chairman: "No, you cannot. Take the oath."

Witness: "I am an agnostic, you see."

Chairman: "You have told us you believe in some of the Bible. You can take the Bible and take the oath."

Witness: "I am not sure I agree."

Chairman: "Don't argue. Take the oath."

Witness: "I am not willing to take the oath."

Chairman: "Very well. Stand down."[25]

The defendant in this case was convicted and he appealed against conviction on the ground that a defence witness had not been allowed to affirm. The Court of Criminal Appeal in January 1962 allowed the appeal.

The Lord Chief Justice, giving the judgment of the Court, said that it was important for a Judge to satisfy himself that a witness was within Section 1 of the Oaths Act, 1888, and to ask whether a witness objected to being sworn because he had no religious belief or because it would be contrary to his religious belief. In most cases, if the answer was 'Yes' to one of those questions, a Judge would be satisfied and allow the witness to affirm; but it would be going too far to say that a Judge must be satisfied by the answer and should not question the witness further if there were any doubts about his answer. Unfortunately, the proper course had not been taken in this case, and it was important to see what the witness was really saying. The true effect was that the witness was an agnostic, and that although he accepted part of the New Testament as fact he did not accept that the central figure was divine. The witness was entitled to affirm, and the evidence of that witness was wrongly excluded.[26]

During the parliamentary debates on the Bill which became the 1888 Oaths Act an M.P. stated: "There were many people who would be slow to speak falsely, if they thought they would have to take God to witness that they were speaking the truth; whereas they would think it a much less heinous offence to speak untruly if they were allowed to make a mere affirmation."[27] Is there a temptation for an individual to claim the right to affirm because, if he makes an affirmation, he treats less seriously his obligation to tell the truth or to fulfil his promises than he would do if he took an oath?

There have probably been great changes in people's views on this matter since 1888. On the one hand, the purely superstitious element in the respect for an oath probably exists for a much smaller proportion of religious believers. On the other hand, partly because of the large increase in the number of unbelievers, much fewer people now hold the view that atheists cannot hold or act on moral principles.

In a report of the Criminal Law Revision Committee, the majority of the committee, in stating their opinion that the oath of witnesses in criminal proceedings should be replaced by a declaration undertaking to tell the truth, gave the following as one reason for this opinion. "There would be a good case for keeping the oath if there were a real probability that it increases the amount of truth told. The majority do not think that it does this very much. For a person who has a firm religious belief, it is unlikely that taking the oath will act as any additional incentive to tell the truth. For a person without any religious belief, by hypothesis the oath can make no difference. There is value in having a witness 'solemnly and sincerely' promise that he will tell the truth, and from this point of view the words of the affirmation are, to many at least, more impressive than the customary oath. The oath has not prevented an enormous amount of perjury in the courts. A witness who wishes to lie and who feels that the oath may be an impediment can easily say that taking an oath is contrary to his religious belief."[28] On the other hand, in the opinion of the minority of the committee, "there are many persons to whom the oath, administered properly and in complete silence, serves to bring home most strongly the solemnity of their obligation to tell the truth and to be careful about what they say in giving their evidence."[29]

Since 1888 the right of affirmation has been available substantially to all conscientious objectors to oaths who have claimed it. But this has not meant that these objectors have been in conflict with the general purpose of the law of oaths. That purpose was, and still is, to attach to certain important statements and promises as strong a moral sanction as possible, but there is now a wider conception of the means to this end. It is now realised that the seriousness with which an individual regards his statements and promises is not necessarily dependent on an explicit religious reference or on any religious sanction. It is now recognised that not only unorthodox Christians but also unbelievers can have high standards with regard to truth-speaking and the fulfilment of promises. It is now accepted that those who conscientiously take an oath and those who conscientiously make an affirmation are equally fulfilling the purpose of the law.

Exemption from Vaccination 1908 –1948

In both England and Wales and Scotland from 1908 to 1948 the right of legal conscientious objection to vaccination was available to all parents (or other persons responsible for the child) who made a statutory declaration. In England and Wales this provision was contained in the Vaccination Act, 1907[30] and came into force at the beginning of 1908: the declaration had to be made within four months from the birth of the child. In Scotland the provision was contained in the Vaccination (Scotland) Act, 1907,[31] and came into force on 28th August 1907: the declaration had to be made within six months from the birth of the child. In Scotland this provision was the first provision of any kind for legal conscientious objection to vaccination. In England and Wales the provision took the place of a provision in the Vaccination Act, 1898,[32] which gave the right of legal conscientious objection to parents who satisfied magistrates in court that they conscientiously believed that vaccination would be prejudicial to the health of the child. (Conscientious objection from 1898 to 1907 under this provision will be discussed later in this chapter.) In both England and Wales and Scotland the law with regard to conscientious objection remained the same until it ceased to have effect with the ending of compulsory vaccination in 1948 under the provisions of the National Health Service Act, 1946,[33] and the National Health Service (Scotland) Act, 1947.[34]

The following discussion relates to England and Wales only. (Further details on several matters mentioned were given in Chapter 2.) In 1908, the first year of the new law, the proportion of babies exempted was 17% – double the proportion in the previous year. In the years prior to 1939, from 1913 onwards the proportion was over 35%; from 1925 onwards the proportion was over 40%; and in each of the years 1935 to 1938 the proportion was slightly above 50%. The actual number of exemptions was large: its average was 259,000 a year in the decade 1908–1917 and 295,000 a year in the decade 1928–1937. In the other spheres of law covered in this book, legal conscientious objectors have been only a small minority of all those affected by the law. In contrast, legal conscientious objectors to vaccination were from 1908 onwards a substantial minority, and from 1913 onwards a large minority. This exceptional position with regard to the numbers of objectors raises two interesting questions. The first question is whether exemptions were obtained by some parents whose objections were not conscientious. The second question is whether the effects of this system of exemptions defeated the purpose of the Vaccination Acts to obtain universal or near-universal vaccination of children. These two questions will be discussed in turn.

The majority of the Royal Commission on Vaccination, reporting in 1896, recommended some method to protect from prosecution those who were "honestly opposed" to vaccination. "When we speak of our honest opposition to the practice we intend to confine ourselves to cases in which the objection is to the operation itself, and to exclude cases in which the objection arises merely from an indisposition to take the trouble involved."[35] In the law as established by the act of 1907 there were two tests intended to distinguish the "honest" or conscientious objector from others unwilling to obey the law: one test was the wording of the declaration and the other test was the action which must be taken by the objector to obtain exemption.

The wording of the declaration was as follows.[36] "I... being the parent... of a child named... do hereby solemnly and sincerely declare that I conscientiously believe that vaccination would be prejudicial to the health of the child, and I make this solemn declaration conscientiously believing the same to be true, and by virtue of the Statutory Declarations Act, 1835."[37] This was signed by the person making the declaration and also by the Justice of the Peace or other officers authorised to receive a statutory declaration.

In order to obtain exemption from vaccination for his child the parent had to make this declaration before a Justice of the Peace or other authorised officer within four months from the birth of the child and then had to deliver or send the signed declarations within seven days to the vaccination officer of the district.[38] If the parent did not obtain exemption, the child had to be vaccinated within six months from its birth[39] (with the possibility of postponement in some circumstances). If the child was vaccinated under the public vaccinations service the operation was free and normally performed at the child's home.

Thus the parent claiming exemption had to be willing to sign the prescribed declaration and had to visit a magistrate (or other authorised officer) and state his position, and this had to be done at least two months before he would be compelled to have his child vaccinated. The amount of effort and, in some cases, moral courage involved in taking this course would obviously vary with the personal characters of parents. It might also vary with other circumstances, for example, the ease with which the parent could find an approachable or sympathetic magistrate. Probably the parents' action was easiest in areas with a strong body of anti-vaccination opinion than in areas where there was little opposition to vaccination.

Was this test sufficient to deter a parent not "honestly opposed" to vaccination? A selfish or lazy parent or a parent unwilling to consider the long-period interests of his child, as distinct from its temporary comfort, might wish to avoid the operation and, to an overworked mother, particularly if not in good health, any extra strain might seem intolerable. My guess would be that some parents not "honestly opposed" to vaccination did obtain exemption, but there is not and could not be any evidence of the numbers of such parents. However, it seems fair to say that the law, in providing for all conscientious objectors willing to make the prescribed declaration, took the risk of providing also for some unconscientious objectors.

There could be good reasons, not provided for in the law, for wishing to avoid the vaccination of a child: I will give an example from my personal acquaintance. The father involved told me that during the First World War he obtained exemption for his twin babies: he was in favour of vaccination but he was concerned for the health of his wife, which had been badly affected by the bearing and rearing of twins under war-time conditions. The law did not provide for the postponement of a vaccination on account of the health of the mother.

Between 1919 and 1934 there were a total of 81,000 notified cases of a mild form of smallpox (variola minor). The Ministry of Health Report for 1923–24 stated: "In consequence of local epidemics of smallpox in many parts of the country there was a considerable increase in the amount of vaccination performed, and many of those who sought the protection of vaccination for themselves and their families, when smallpox threatened, were persons who had previously made declarations of conscientious objection to vaccination."[40] This fact might be regarded by some people as evidence that these former objectors were not genuine conscientious objectors at the time when they obtained their exemptions. In my opinion this view is not valid. Probably the large majority of objectors had objections based not on general principles but on their assessments of the facts of the situation at the time when their decisions were made. The objecting parent acted on his views, whether true or false, regarding the comparative risks involved for his child in being vaccinated or being left unvaccinated. The number of cases of smallpox at the time of his decision was an obvious fact to be taken into account in his assessment of these comparative risks: if this number increased, his conscientious decision might be different from his conscientious decision taken previously in different circumstances.

The wording of the declaration was intended to exclude those not "honestly opposed" to vaccination. But did it also exclude some parents who had conscientious objections? In 1904 the Lord Chief Justice in a speech stated his view that in order to conscientiously believe that vaccination would be prejudicial to the health of the child, the objector must believe this with regard to the particular child in question. It was not sufficient that the objector believed generally that vaccination was an improper thing or that he objected on the ground of interference with the subject or the question of parental control. (For more details of this speech see p.354.) On this strict interpretation some reasons for conscientious objection would be excluded, for example, that vaccination was ineffective, or that it involved cruelty to animals in the preparation of the lymph, or that it was against a religious principle of the objectors. But, of course, an objector, in addition to some other reason for objection, could also believe that vaccination would be prejudicial to the health of his child, at least temporarily. It seems to me unlikely that any considerable numbers of parents with conscientious objections to vaccination were excluded by feeling themselves unable to subscribe to the words of the declaration.

The second interesting question raised by the facts of conscientious objection during the period 1908 – 1948 is whether the effects of the system of exemptions existing during that period defeated the purpose of the Vaccination Acts to obtain the universal or near-universal vaccination of children. My answer to this question is that the rise in the proportion of parents obtaining exemption was not caused merely by the change in the law regarding exemptions.

In my opinion this proportion would have risen even if the previous system of discretionary exemption by magistrates' courts had continued, though the figures would not have been so high. The rise in the proportion of exemptions reflected the rise in the proportion of parents opposed to vaccination and this opposition certainly did defeat the purpose of the Vaccination Acts to obtain the near-universal vaccination of children. In 1905 the proportion of all infants successfully vaccinated was 75.8% (the highest figure since 1891); in 1908 the proportion was 63.2%; in 1918 it was 41.5%; in 1928 it was 42.6%; and in 1938 it was 34.0%. The law had given to all parents opposed to vaccination the opportunity to obtain exemption and by the 1930s such a large proportion of parents were using this opportunity that the logical sequel was to make vaccination voluntary.

Rights Dependent on Decisions of a Judicial Body

There were two spheres of legislation which made the right of legal conscientious objection dependent on the decision of a judicial body in each individual case. From 1898 to 1907 the right of an individual parent to his child's exemption from compulsory vaccination was dependent on the decision of a magistrates' court. During the First World War, and again from 1939 to 1960, the right of an individual to exemption from compulsory military service was dependent on the decision of a tribunal.

Exemption from Vaccination by Magistrates' Courts 1898–1907

The Vaccination Act of 1898[41] provided for the first time for legal conscientious objection to vaccination, the test being that the applicant should satisfy magistrates in court as to his objection. This system lasted for nine and a half years until it was superseded by the provisions of the Vaccination Act of 1907.[42] The Act of 1898 covered England and Wales only: objectors in Scotland never came under the system now to be described.

The Act of 1898 stated in Section 2 (1): "No parent or other person shall be liable to any penalty under Section 29 or Section 31 of the Vaccination Act of 1867,[43] if within four months from the birth of the child he satisfies two Justices, or a Stipendiary or Metropolitan

Police Magistrate in petty sessions, that he conscientiously believes that vaccination would be prejudicial to the health of the child and within seven days thereafter delivers to the Vaccination Officer for the district a certificate by such justice or magistrate of such conscientious objection." With regard to children born before the passing of the Act, exemptions could be obtained within four months from 12th August 1898, when the Act came into force.

A large number of parents immediately took advantage of the provisions of the Act. During the remainder of 1898, 203,413 certificates of exemption were received by Vaccination Officers relating to 230,147 children.[44] A large number of these certificates were for children born before the passing of the Act. During the next nine years, up to the end of 1907 when this system of exemptions ended, the numbers and proportions of births were as follows.[45]

	Number of Exemptions	Percentage of Total Births
1899	33,573	3.6
1900	39,699	4.3
1901	39,925	4.5
1902	33,759	3.6
1903	37,675	4.0
1904	40,461	4.3
1905	44,369	4.8
1906	53,828	5.8
1907	76,709	8.4

Thus, over the whole period covered by this system of exemption, parents obtained certificates of exemption for more than 630,000 children. To a considerable extent, the purpose was attained of giving the objecting parent the opportunity to obey his conscience without breaking the law.

The Act of 1898 gave the power to grant or withhold exemptions to the magistrates in Petty Sessions: outside London and certain large towns this meant to two or more Justices of the Peace. Magistrates (of whom there were 17–18,000 in 1907) were given no initial guidance as to how their powers should be exercised in the completely new type of judgments which they now had to make. The applicant had no right of appeal against the decision of his local magistrates and moreover, if subsequently prosecuted, would often have his case judged by the same Bench which had judged his application for exemption. The President of the Local Government Board stated in the House of Commons, on a number of occasions, that he had no power to remedy defects in the working of the machinery of exemption, which the law had made subject to the judiciary. It is not surprising that in these circumstances there was great variation between the policies and judgments of different Benches of Magistrates. These differences were increased by the fact that the subject of vaccination was highly controversial and that magistrates, like other citizens, often had strongly held opinions for or against it. Opinions on the merits of vaccination were very differently distributed in different localities, and this fact tended to widen the gap between the policies of local Benches of Magistrates.

Contemporary comments and criticisms provide evidence of the kinds of differences which existed. Some courts insisted on the application for exemption being made by the father, if available; other courts accepted the mother as applicant. Attendance at courts held at the ordinary times often involved absence from work by the applicant and therefore loss of wages; on the other hand, some courts held special evening sessions for the convenience of applicants. Some courts charged more than the required fee of one shilling for certificates of exemption. Some courts insisted on the production of birth certificates costing two shillings and sixpence. With regard to these differences affecting the amount of trouble and expense involved for the applicant, some commentators favoured stringency, on the ground that it was intended that an applicant for exemption should have to take as much trouble to obtain his certificate as would be required to procure the vaccination of his child. the opposite point of view is illustrated by the argument of the Mayor of Oldham in defending the holding of special evening sessions of the court. "If it is right to make it easy and cheap for pro-vaccinators to get vaccinated it is equally right to make it easy and cheap for anti-vaccinators to obtain certificates of exemption from vaccination."[46]

But the differences in the treatment of applicants were not confined to these matters of incidental costs and trouble for the applicant: there were wide differences in the interpretation of the requirement that the applicant should "satisfy" the magistrates. At one extreme were magistrates who granted exemption with no examination of the case. A Blackpool Justice of the Peace stated in

December 1898: "In the large manufacturing towns of Lancashire and Yorkshire the magistrates have had sittings lasting all day, where 800 to 900 objectors have had certificates of exemption granted. It is a mere farce asking for reasons, a mere waste of time; the 'reasons' are always forthcoming, such as they are."[47]

The British Medical Association in February 1899 passed a resolution: "That the manner in which Section 2 of the Vaccination Act, 1898, had been administered by various benches of magistrates proves that the section does not necessarily provide any test whatever of the reality or strength of objection to vaccination."[48]

On the other hand, there were criticisms of some magistrates for acting with undue severity. In 1902 attention was called in the House of Commons to a rule of Norwich by which the justices asked for a medical certificate showing that vaccination would be injurious before granting an exemption, though the Home Secretary replied that he understood that action was not governed by the rule referred to.[49] In the same year an M.P. objected to the cross-examination of applicants by magistrates.[50] Magistrates sometimes urged their own views on applicants: for example, the Liverpool Stipendiary Magistrate was reported to have stated his intention to read extracts from a pro-vaccination pamphlet to every objector appearing before him.[51]

In a debate in the House of Commons in 1906, E.H. Pickersgill, M.P. for Bethnal Green, stated that poor applicants were bullied, insulted, and humiliated, whereas a Peer who had recently applied for exemption was treated with the utmost courtesy and consideration. In the same debate, John Burns called attention to the fact that the poor workman was often very nervous at a court and unable to express his objections as well as the objector in a higher social class.[52]

There was no information available as to the number of applications refused: a Home Office circular in 1906 stated that the Home Secretary "receives frequent complaints" of the refusal of certificates.[53] The following examples were cited in the House of Commons. In 1902 a Norfolk objector was fined, although he had on two occasions applied to the same Bench for a certificate of exemption.[54] In 1905 a Warwickshire objector made four unsuccessful applications for exemption.[55] In 1906 an objector was refused exemption after he had obtained certificates from another magistrate on similar grounds for two other children.[56] In the same year, at

Dorchester Petty Sessions, the Chairman dismissed an application with the remark that he knew the benefits of vaccination, for he had seen them all over the world, and he would never grant a certificate of exemption.[57]

In July 1904 the Lord Chief Justice, addressing the Grand Jury at the Warwickshire Assizes, stated certain principles with regard to the duty of magistrates regarding exemptions, and his statement gives further evidence of the kind of problems which had arisen. The statement, as quoted in a Home Office Circular to Magistrates, was as follows: "Some Magistrates appeared to think that they ought to be satisfied that vaccination would be harmful to the child, others seemed to think that they were entitled to have medical evidence before them that such vaccination would be prejudicial. He desired to point out that this was not the question which Magistrates had to decide. The section, as he read it, laid down two conditions – one, that the person who applied 'conscientiously believed', and the other that he 'believed that vaccination would be prejudicial to the health of the child'. The only question which the Magistrates had to entertain was: Did the applicant conscientiously believe that vaccination would be prejudicial to the health of the child? With regard to the conscientious belief, of course, there were many occasions upon which there could be no doubt about it, but it was not sufficient that a man believed generally that vaccination was an improper thing, or that he had been led to form that belief without considering the particular case of the child in point. It must be an honest conscientious belief on the part of the applicant that vaccination would be prejudicial to the child in question.... Applicants must not hold a general objection to it either on the ground of interference with the rights of the subject or the question of parental control. It must be the conscientious belief that vaccination would be prejudicial to the health of the child."[58]

The Home Office in September 1904 sent a circular to magistrates with a copy of this statement and in May 1906 a further circular was issued: the latter circular included the Lord Chief Justice's statement and made some further observations, including the following. "The question for Magistrates is not whether the applicant's belief is well-founded or ill-founded: the Act does not require that the belief should be reasonably founded. In order to satisfy themselves that the applicant's belief is conscientious, the Justices may think it desirable to ask him the origin and grounds of his opinion, but if that belief is genuinely entertained, any ignorance on medical or sanitary or statistical questions which he may display is no ground for the refusal of a certificate. Applicants frequently state to the Home Office that they have made long journeys to the Court and have lost a day's wage by so doing, but yet have not succeeded in satisfying the Bench; and they urge that the trouble they have taken and the loss they have undergone ought to be regarded as a practical testimony to the conscientious nature of their objection. Mr. Gladstone [J.J. Gladstone, Home Secretary at the time] would not attempt to define the grounds on which he thinks Magistrates ought to be satisfied that an applicant's belief is sincere, though it seems to him that such considerations as the above might properly be taken into account."[59]

The system of exemption at the discretion of Magistrates' Courts ceased at the end of 1907 and was never used again in this sphere of law. The most fundamental problem of this kind of system of exemption was already apparent – the problem of determining what is a conscientious objection and what is adequate evidence of it. The Lord Chief Justice stated that, under the Act of 1898, a conscientious objection must relate to the actual action in question and must not be merely a general opinion. The Home Secretary in 1906 suggested that the applicant's ignorance or the ill-founded nature of his belief was irrelevant, and that the efforts and sacrifices that he had made were relevant. But John Burns who, as President of the Local Government Board, introduced the amending Bill of 1907, thought that the system itself had been shown to be unsatisfactory and spoke of "requiring the applicant to satisfy the Bench of the reality of his conscientious conviction – that is, to satisfy others of the state of his own conscience – an impossible task".[60]

The Tribunal System in the First World War

The Military Service Act, 1916,[61] made the right of legal conscientious objection subject to the judicial decision of tribunals. The Second Schedule of the Act laid down the main principles as to the constitution of tribunals and also gave power to make, by order in council, regulations as to the constitution, functions and procedure of tribunals. Any order in council could be revoked or varied by a subsequent order, and all regulations had to be presented to

Parliament. The Minister responsible was the President of the Local Government Board with regard to England and Wales and the Secretary for Scotland with regard to that country.

Local tribunals were established for each local registration district under the National Registration Act, that is for the area of each local authority, or in some cases for divisions of this district. There were at first a total of 2,086 local tribunals in Great Britain – 1,805 in England and Wales and 281 in Scotland.[62] The number of members of the tribunal could not be less than five or more than twenty-five: the tribunal could act through a committee of its members and five was recommended as a suitable number to hear cases. The members of the tribunal were appointed by the councils of the local authorities – Boroughs or Districts – and generally members of the council formed a majority of the members of the tribunal. After the passing of the Military Service Act it was suggested to local authorities that the tribunals already existing under the "Derby Scheme" should be reappointed. But the Local Government Board also advised the inclusion on tribunals of persons not members of the local council and the inclusion of women. Regulations required the adequate representation of labour in the area. Men of military age could be appointed as tribunal members only if attested or unfit for military service. In April 1918 the existing members of tribunals were re-appointed by the Government Departments concerned and future members were appointed by these Departments. In 1918 the number of tribunals was somewhat reduced by amalgamations of areas and in many cases the number of members of tribunals was reduced.

There was a right of appeal against the decision of the local tribunal: such appeals were heard by Appeal Tribunals appointed for county areas. There were 68 appeal tribunals in England and Wales, with a total membership of 814, and 15 in Scotland, with a total membership of 190. These members were appointed by the Crown after consultation with the Chairmen of County Councils.

There was also a Central Appeal Tribunal with members appointed by the Crown: sixteen individuals were at some time members. It was intended that appeals to the Central Tribunal should be restricted to cases involving matters of principle or other important questions.

Applications to local tribunals had to be heard by not less than three persons and decisions were made by majority vote with an additional casting vote for the chairman where opinion was equally divided. Hearings had to be in public unless the tribunal decided otherwise in any particular case: both the public and the parties concerned could be excluded while the members of the tribunal were conferring. In general, the application had to be made to the tribunal for the area where the applicant resided: it could be made either by, or on behalf of, the man concerned. One "military representative" had the right to appear as a party to each application heard by a local tribunal: the military representative was defined in the regulations as a "recruiting officer or other representative of military interests" authorised for this function on behalf of the Army Council. This was a very important provision: it meant that there was always present someone who had the duty, if he thought it wise, to oppose any application for exemption.

The applicant for exemption could make a written statement and could conduct his own application or be represented for this purpose by someone chosen by him. Both the applicant and the military representative had the right, if present, to be heard by the local tribunal, who might also hear such other witnesses as they thought fit. The applicant or his representative could be questioned, not only by the members of the tribunal, but also by the military representative. If the military representative assented in writing to the application, the tribunal had the power to grant an exemption without hearing the case. The decision on the application was communicated in writing to both the applicant and the military representative. A register of applications and decisions had to be kept by the tribunal but, to the best of my knowledge, no total figures of the applications to, and decisions of, all local tribunals were assembled or published.

Both the applicant and the military representative had the right of appeal to an appeal tribunal against the decision of the local tribunal, and both could ask for leave to appeal to the Central Tribunal against the decision of an appeal tribunal, the appeal tribunal deciding whether such leave should be granted. An appeal tribunal could dismiss an appeal without hearing the case if it considered that the notice of appeal did not give the required particulars or did not disclose *prima facie* grounds for reviewing the decision of the local tribunal, but before doing so it had to warn the appellant and give him time to supply further and better particulars or grounds. On any appeal an appeal tribunal had power to grant or withdraw a certificate of exemption or to vary the conditions attached to it.

With regard to an application on conscientious grounds, the tribunal could make one of four decisions – no exemption, exemption from combatant service only, exemption conditional on the applicant engaging in work of national importance, and absolute exemption – that is exemption with no conditions. It could also make an exemption temporary. A certificate of exemption could be reviewed or renewed at any time on the application either of the holder or of a person authorised by the Army Council, and it could be withdrawn or varied by the reviewing authority.

The description just given covers the main points in the law concerning the constitution and powers of tribunals. These tribunals dealt with many applications for exemption on grounds other than conscientious objection but the following account and comment are concerned only with their dealing with men who applied for exemption as conscientious objectors.

It was shown in Chapter 4 that the decisions of the tribunals gave to over 9,000 conscientious objectors types of exemption which they were willing to accept; refused any exemption or gave unacceptable types of exemption to about 6,250 men who subsequently disobeyed the law and were arrested; and refused exemption on conscientious grounds to an unknown number of men who subsequently complied with the law. Excluding the last group, about whom there is no information, and assuming that the men who were arrested showed by their actions that their objections to military service were strongly held, the figures show that for every three objectors to whom acceptable types of exemption were granted, there were two to whom such exemptions were refused.

It seems clear that the Government, in providing for legal conscientious objection, did not foresee that the decisions of tribunals would exclude so many men from its benefits and force them to become law-breakers: it was intended that genuine conscientious objectors should be exempted. There is good evidence of this intention in the wording used in the circular sent by Walter Long, the President of the Local Government Board, to the local authorities responsible for the appointment of tribunals. "The man who honestly and as a matter of conscience objects to combatant service is entitled to exemption. While care must be taken that the man who shirks his duty to his country does not find unworthy shelter behind this provision, every consideration should be given to the man whose objection genuinely rests on religious or moral conviction. Whatever may be the views of the tribunal, they must interpret the act in an impartial and tolerant spirit. Differences of conviction must not bias judgment." The circular went on to mention the three types of exemption in "exceptional cases", and stated that "The exemption should be the minimum required to meet the conscientious scruples of the applicant."[63]

In any account of the working of the tribunal system it must be remembered that there were over two thousand tribunals in Great Britain so that very few statements about tribunals are universally true. In any criticism it must also be remembered that tribunals did fulfil the intentions of the law in providing acceptable exemptions for over nine thousand men. A further consideration, in my opinion, is that it is unreasonable to expect infallible judgments from any judicial body, and that to judge of the state of another man's conscience is particularly difficult. But, when these allowances are made, there is still need to explain why the tribunals failed to give acceptable exemptions to such a large number of men.

One explanation lies in the personnel of tribunals. Members of local tribunals were (until 1918) appointed by local authorities; most of them were not selected on account of any special qualification for, or interest in, judging matters of conscience, and many had been appointed to deal with applications under the "Derby Scheme", in which matters of conscience did not arise. Many tribunals had no members with legal training, though probably a considerable number of tribunal members were Justices of the Peace. In the larger places, where stipendiary magistrates and county court judges were made chairmen, "Their judicial experience was a real check on the zeal of their amateur colleagues."[64] In John W. Graham's experience, tribunals "consisted of elderly local magnates or tradesmen, often with a Labour man, known to be in favour of the war, added." There were "a few women, who were generally fiercer than the men." The members of tribunals tended to be elderly both because of the absence of many men of military age on war service and because regulations forbade the appointment of men of military age unless attested or unfit. As members were appointed by local authorities they were likely to be local notabilities and in fact the majority were members of the appointing Borough or District Council. They were not paid for their service and were not expected to require any special qualifications for it. In the words of a contemporary article, the members of tribunals "are the average men, with the average opinions, the average ethics and wisdom, and the average notions of how to deal with fellow-men."[65]

These average men had to deal, often very hurriedly, not only with claims for exemption as conscientious objectors, but also with claims for exemption for other reasons. They had no precedents to guide them and they had not the opportunity, given to members of tribunals in the Second World War, of enlarging their experience of conscientious objectors by dealing with considerable numbers of them over a long period. Their ordinary experience of life, which might equip them well for judging as to the national importance of a man's work or the degree of exceptional hardship which his call-up would involve, often did not include any understanding of the exceptional views and attitudes of conscientious objectors, and their public work had not, before the introduction of conscription, necessitated any knowledge of these kinds of minority opinions. Thus many tribunal members, in order to fulfil the intentions of the law, had to make a great effort of sympathetic understanding, and this would have been true even if the views of objectors had appeared to them to be strange but harmless. But the views of objectors, far from appearing harmless, seemed to many tribunal members to be dangerous to a country engaged in a great war, and selfishly indifferent to its needs, so that, in order to judge as required by the law, they had to make a great effort to act impartially despite their own strong feelings.

The following are judgments from two people who observed many proceedings of tribunals. Adrian Stephen, who as a press representative attended several hundred hearings, wrote as follows: "The judges were, like most of us, men untrained to stand aside from their own prejudice, and hold their judgments in suspense while they considered difficult evidence, untrained entirely in the delicate task of psychological discrimination that was imposed upon them; and had they been the best trained men in the world, with twenty or thirty applicants to be dealt with between lunch and tea-time, what nicety of judgment could have been expected of them?... I do not know that there is any need for special indignation against the tribunals. I felt some myself while I watched them, but it would have been asking much of half a dozen grocers, haberdashers and retired colonels, to rise above the general body of mankind to such a height as to behave with reasonable forbearance."[66] Ruth Fry, the Secretary of the Friends' War Victims Relief Committee, who often attended tribunals to support the applications of the Committee's workers abroad, wrote about "an experience which gave an interesting, if sometimes painful, insight into the sensations of a religious pacifist in the hands of frequently untrained judges of conscience during war-fever. The courtesy and understanding of some tribunals were delightful, while in others one realised that one was speaking in a language of different thought, which it was impossible to make understood. It must be admitted that it would be most difficult even for a body of highly trained and sympathetic investigators to ascertain the springs of a decision of such an intimate nature in an unknown fellow-creature, and for it to be attempted in a few minutes by a body of people such as usually comprised a tribunal would have been ludicrous had it not been tragic."[67]

The position of the "military representative", whose legal status and powers have already been described, was a great disadvantage to applicants. John W. Graham stated: "he was an emissary of the War Office, a standing counsel against every application. Through being always there, often sitting at the same table with members of the Tribunal, and being akin in sympathies, these men dominated weak Tribunals. They were treated with a deference not granted to their opponents. With conspicuous unfairness, they were not, in any case known to me, sent out of the room when the appellant withdrew for the Tribunal to consult. They were generally in khaki, and often used their position to browbeat and intimidate applicants."[68] Adrian Stephen wrote of his experience of applications on various grounds that, though according to the official rules of procedure the applicant and the military representative were two parties to a case. "In war time things did not work out so." He continued: "Many times, I have been present when the applicant has stated his case, brought his evidence and been duly examined and then sent from the room while the tribunal has considered its award. While he has been out of the room I have known the Military Representative – who was as a rule allowed to remain and even to take part in the deliberations of the tribunal – I have known him turn to the tribunal and say: 'Now I will tell you the truth about this man' and I have heard him bring up fresh evidence which the applicant had no chance of refuting and which he was probably never aware had been given against him."[69] The opposition of the military representative was not necessarily overcome even when the objector had received an acceptable decision from the local tribunal. The military representative often exercised his right to appeal against the decision and he sometimes exercised his right to apply later for the removal or revision of a certificate of exemption.

Quite a number of tribunals misunderstood or disregarded the law. One breach of the law was that a number of tribunals held sessions not open to the public. The most important breach was with regard to types of exemption. A number of tribunals stated that they had power to exempt only from combatant service so that all those whom they exempted were registered for non-combatant service in the army. The President of the Local Government Board, in a circular to tribunals in March 1916,[70] pointed out that these tribunals were in error in their interpretation of the law, but some tribunals continued to mis-understand or ignore the law in this respect. A number of objectors applied for revision of their certificates on the ground of this misunderstanding of the law and some were successful.[71] Some tribunals were in doubt as to their power to grant absolute exemption to conscientious objectors and the amending Military Service Act, 1916 (Session 2),[72] made it clear that they had power to do so, stating: "It is hereby declared that the power to grant special certificates of exemption in the case of an application on conscientious grounds... is additional to and not in derogation of the general power conferred to grant an absolute, conditional or temporary certificate in such cases."

The duty of acting with impartiality and fairness was flagrantly disregarded by some members of tribunals, who used their position to abuse applicants. In a letter to *The Times* the Bishop of Lincoln (who supported the war) wrote that in reading the reports of some local tribunals "I am set thinking of the rough treatment of Faithful by the Courts of Vanity Fair, as described by John Bunyan, or of the trial of heretics by agents of the inquisition."[73] A letter to the press signed by the Bishop of Oxford and ten other well-known men stated: "There is considerable evidence of brow-beating and of a disposition to treat with scorn the very idea of conscientious objection. Conscience, however mistaken, ought not to be a subject for public ridicule."[74] Such conduct was not only objectionable in itself but was likely to hinder a nervous or inarticulate applicant from explaining his position and to prevent the tribunal from considering the case dispassionately.

The tribunals tended to regard certain types of objection with more favour, or less disfavour, than others. The views of the Society of Friends were comparatively well known to the public and Quakers often received favourable treatment, especially if they were willing to join the Friends' Ambulance Unit. Objections not based on religious grounds were often rejected on the ground that only a religious objection could be conscientious. The Central Tribunal circularised its opinion that non-religious objectors should receive exemption if the objectors "have a genuine belief that the taking of human life in any circumstances is morally wrong." But objections "based on opposition to the present war" or "on disapproval of the present organisation of society, which the man considers not worthy of defence, though he would fight in defence of a State organised in a way he approves" were held by the Central Tribunal not to constitute conscientious objections within the meaning of the Act. The same Circular stated "The Central Tribunal regard the age of the man alleging conscientious objection as an important factor in the consideration of the question whether his objection is so deliberate and settled as to entitle him to exemption or to the widest form of exemption."[75] In agreement with this view, young men, conscripted at eighteen, were sometimes told by tribunals that they were too young to have consciences.

There is evidence that many tribunals had more sympathy with an objection to actual participation in killing than with a wider objection to military service. This fact, along with the misunderstanding of the law already described, led them, even when convinced of the sincerity of the objector, to limit the exemption in many cases to exemption from combatant service. For example, the Birmingham Tribunal up to June 1916 had given exemption to 241 out of 397 applicants on conscientious grounds and of these 199 were exempted from combatant service only.[76] In quite a number of cases Appeal Tribunals substituted this type of exemption for other types given by the local tribunal. The result of this attitude of the tribunals was that, in addition to over 3,000 men who were called up for the Non-Combatant Corps and who were willing to serve in it, a large number of objectors who objected to non-combatant military service, and who had often stated clearly that they objected, were made liable for this service.

Over 6,000 men were exempted on condition that they performed various forms of civilian work of national importance and accepted this condition. A description of the main forms of work performed by objectors was given in Chapter 4. In deciding on the precise conditions which they would impose, tribunals were influenced by two considerations which often conflicted. On the one hand, an objector might be employed to the greatest social advantage by remaining in his existing job or in another job in his own occupation. On the other hand, it was felt that to allow an objector to go on doing his normal work was to make life much too easy for him, so conditions were often imposed obliging an objector to make some obvious sacrifice such as changing his job, changing his place of residence, or working for lower remuneration. The tribunals often respected the wishes of many objectors to engage in various forms of humanitarian work which were concerned with needs resulting from the war. But they usually had little sympathy with the convictions of objectors who held that they had vocations for other types of work.

The position of "absolutists", whose views were described in Chapter 4, met with little sympathy from tribunals. Relatively few objectors were given absolute exemption and in a number of cases objectors given such exemptions by local tribunals had the decision reversed by appeal tribunals to which the military representative had applied. Some tribunals continued to state that they had no power to give absolute exemption even after an explicit provision that such exemption was legal was made in the amending Military Service Act of May 1916.

There were great differences between the preponderant types of decisions made by individual tribunals. This was true not only of local tribunals but also of the eighty-three appeal tribunals. For example, "The Appeal Tribunal at Manchester was being held one day in two divisions. All the men in one court got non-combatant service, all in the other had no exemption at all."[77] John W. Graham opined that the Appeal Tribunals "consisting of county instead of municipal magnates" did not fulfil the hope that they would redress the "impulsive irregularities" of the local tribunals: they were sometimes better, sometimes worse than the local tribunals; on the average they were about the same.[78]

The Central Tribunal, to which appeals were made only by leave of the Appeal Tribunals, "concerned itself with doubtful issues and the interpretation of facts, and did not always see the applicant."[79] It had no power to direct other tribunals but it circulated from time to time notes of some of its more important decisions for the guidance of local and appeal tribunals. It compiled a questionnaire to which it required answers in writing from appellants and it recommended the use of this questionnaire by other tribunals. The Central Tribunal's special work with regard to objectors under arrest was described in Chapter 4.

The Tribunal System 1939–1960

An account of the tribunal system and its decisions during the Second World War was given in Chapter 5 (pp181–2 and 185–191) and an account of the system for the post-war period of National Service, 1945–1960, was given in Chapter 6 (pp227–232). These accounts should be referred to in relation to the following discussion. The system established in 1939 continued, with only minor modifications, over the whole period 1939–1960. The following account will describe some features of the system in greater detail than the previous accounts and will discuss the system with particular reference to its effectiveness in testing the validity of the conscientious objections of the individuals with whom it dealt.

There is no doubt that the system over this period was administered with much greater efficiency and generosity than the system of the First World War. This fact was due in part to a different climate of public opinion, which was far more tolerant towards conscientious objectors. But the difference was also due to a number of differences in the system itself, as compared with the system of the First World War: the most important of these differences were as follows.

(1) The tribunals of this period were specialist bodies concerned only with decisions as to the exemption of conscientious objectors: they had no functions with regard to the other kinds of exemption dealt with by the tribunals of the First World War. Tribunal members, who often served for long periods, acquired much specialist experience.

(2) The local tribunals covered large regions instead of the areas of local authorities: they were therefore much fewer in

number – a maximum of nineteen during the War period and only seven in the later post-war period, as compared with over two thousand in the First War.

(3) The members of local tribunals were appointed by the Minister of Labour and National Service instead of by local authorities. All chairmen of local tribunals were required to have specified legal qualifications. With regard to both local tribunals and the Appellate Tribunal, the law required that the Minister, in making appointments, should "have regard to the necessity of selecting impartial persons."

(4) The Armed Forces were not represented at tribunal sessions, as they were by the "Military representatives" at the tribunal sessions of the First War. There was no one present at the tribunal session whose function it was to oppose the granting of exemptions, and the officials of the Ministry of Labour and National Service, who acted as a secretariat for the tribunals, were entirely impartial.

Over the whole period between July 1939 and the end of 1960, local tribunals considered 69,582 original applications from men under the Military Training Act, 1939, and the National Service Acts and in relation to legal obligations for service in the Home Guard. Of these applications, 59,192 were considered just before and during the War (up to the end of June 1945) and 10,390 were considered during the post-war period.

The total decisions over the whole period were as follows.

	Number	Per Cent
Registered unconditionally as Conscientious Objectors	3,073	4.4
Registered conditionally as Conscientious Objectors	26,305	37 8
Registered for non-combatant duties in the Forces	18,843	27.1
Total registered as Conscientious Objectors	48,221	69.3
Name removed from register of Conscientious Objectors	21,361	30.7

Local tribunals also considered 1,074 original applications from women up to the end of 1945 – there were no applications after that date (see Chapter 5 pp190–191). Local tribunals acting in an advisory capacity, considered (in 1951 and 1952) 942 applications from reservists liable to be recalled for training (see Chapter 6 p 232) . The figures for these latter applications are not included in any of the figures discussed in this Section.[80]

Under the tribunal system, the application of a conscientious objector was always considered first by the local tribunal covering the area of the objector's residence, and one feature of the system in practice, a feature not previously described in this book, was the large variation between the decisions of individual local tribunals.

The following account is based on two sets of official figures. The first set of figures covers 91/2 years from the meeting of the first tribunal in July 1939 to the end of 1948.[81] In that first period there were 19 local tribunals (12 in England, 5 in Scotland and 2 in Wales) but most of these tribunals did not function for the whole period. The tribunals dealt with a total of 62,301 original applications of which 1,074 were applications from women.

The second set of figures covers 11 years from the beginning of 1949, when the National Service Act of 1948 came into operation, to the end of 1959.[82] (There were some applications dealt with after that date and not included in the figures.) In that second period there were 7 local tribunals (5 in England, 1 in Scotland and 1 in Wales), all functioning for the whole period. The tribunals dealt with a total of 8,106 original applications: all were applications from men.

The total number registered as conscientious objectors by local tribunals collectively was 70.3% of all applicants in the first period: the variation was between about 85% registered by two English tribunals and about 45% registered by two Scottish tribunals. In the second period the proportion registered collectively was 62.0%, considerably lower than in the first period: the variation between tribunals was between 89.7% and 52.3%. (A possible reason why the collective percentage was lower in the second period was discussed in Chapter 6, p.230) Thus, in both periods, the likelihood that an applicant would have this application totally rejected was much greater at some tribunals than at others.

There was also a large variation between tribunals with regard to the comparative importance of the classes to which they assigned those applicants whom they registered as conscientious objectors.

In the first period, local tribunals collectively registered unconditionally 4.7% of applicants (6.7% of all registered as objectors). In the second period tribunals collectively registered unconditionally 2.4% of applicants (3.9% of all registered as objectors). Thus only a small minority of applicants were given "unconditional exemption", though the total number given this exemption over the whole period 1939 – 1959 was 3,128.

Every local tribunal in both periods assigned fewer applicants to this class than to the two other classes of exemption, but there was a large difference between tribunals with regard to the proportion of applicants so assigned. In the first period, three tribunals registered unconditionally more than 10% of applicants while five tribunals so registered less than 2%: the extreme variation was between 14.7% and 0.2%. In the second period, the Scottish tribunal registered 14.4%, the Welsh tribunal registered 9.3% and the five English tribunals all registered less than 3.5%, the lowest figure being 0.4%.

There was not a numerical correspondence between the number of applicants registered unconditionally and the number who claimed to have conscientious objections to accepting any conditions of exemption. On the one hand, the law gave no legal right of objection to civilian work. On the other hand, for various reasons, tribunals registered unconditionally some applicants who had no absolute objection to accepting any condition of exemption. (There are no statistics regarding the class of exemption claimed or requested by applicants.)

If a tribunal decided to register an applicant as a conscientious objector and to impose conditions of registration its choice was between two alternatives – to register him for non-combatant duties in the Forces or to register him for special civilian work. But a tribunal had not complete freedom of choice between these alternatives. The Acts provided that, on his application form, an applicant could state that he objected to performing combatant military duties. If it was clear from this form or from subsequent statements to the tribunal that he had no objection to performing non-combatant military duties, a tribunal might feel obliged to register him for these. Professor G.C. Field, a former tribunal member, wrote in 1944: "No one who has seen the work of the Non-Combatant Corps would put it very high in the ranks of valuable services. It is a great pity that, once a valid objection to combatant service had been established, more latitude was not given to Tribunals or to objectors with regard to this particular Choice."[83]

In the first period, five local tribunals registered more objectors for non-combatant military service than for civilian work: the other fourteen tribunals made the opposite decision. In the second period, all tribunals except the Scottish Tribunal registered more objectors for civilian work.

In the first period, local tribunals collectively registered for non-combatant military service 27.7% of applicants (39.4% of all registered as objectors). The total proportion of applicants registered for military service, either combatant or non-combatant, was 57.4%. (This is the preceding figure plus the proportion refused any exemption.) In the second period, tribunals collectively registered for non-combatant military service 20.1% of applicants (32.4% of all registered as objectors). The total proportion of applicants registered for military service, either combatant or non-combatant was 58.1%.

In the first period, the highest proportion of applicants registered for non-combatant military service was 47.2% (by a tribunal with comparatively few applicants): the second highest proportion was 36.7%. The third highest proportion was 36.4% (by a tribunal with a large number of applicants): this tribunal registered a total proportion of 75.7% for military service, either combatant or non-combatant. The lowest proportion registered for non-combatant military service was 12.3%, but this tribunal totally rejected more than half its applicants and registered a total proportion of 66.7% for military service, either combatant or non-combatant. In the second period, the proportion of applicants registered for non-combatant military service varied between 38.6% and 10.9% and the tribunal with the highest proportion also had the highest total proportion – 70.2% – registered for military service, either combatant or non-combatant.

A considerable number of applicants registered for non-combatant military service had their class of exemption varied as the result of appeal to the Appellate Tribunal. The large majority of objectors who were registered for non-combatant military service by either the local or the Appellate Tribunal found that they could conscientiously perform this service. But a considerable number of objectors registered in this class had conscientious objections to all military service and broke the law either by disobeying orders in the army or by refusing to take their medical examinations.

Exemption with a condition of civilian work was given by local tribunals collectively in the first period to 37.9% of applicants (53.9% of all registered as objectors). The proportion of applicants so exempted varied between four tribunals with over 50%, the highest being 65.1%, and two tribunals with under 20%, the lowest being 15.3% (this tribunal had only a small total number of applicants) and the next lowest being 18.6%. In the second period, tribunals collectively gave this class of exemption to 39.5% of applicants (63.7% of all registered as objectors). Five tribunals gave this exemption to over 40% of applicants, the highest proportion being 71.2%: the other two tribunals gave this exemption respectively to 33.6% and 15.4% of applicants.

Unless a tribunal exempted an applicant on the condition that he remained in his existing occupation, it very often imposed not one condition but a number of alternative conditions. Alternative conditions often imposed were agricultural work, forestry work, hospital or other medical work and (during part of the war period) Civil Defence work.

Professor Field wrote in 1944 with regard to his experience as a member of a local tribunal: "If... the Pacifist feels that he cannot take an active part in war-like activities, what can he do when his country is actually at war? This is a question which, as a rule, does not receive much attention in the general discussions of Pacifism. Yet it is obviously of vital practical importance, and on the Tribunal by far the greater part of our time was taken up by its consideration."[84]

Professor Field argued that "other people, beside the man himself, are concerned in the work he proposes to do" and that "both sides should have some say, and the final decision should be a matter of mutual adjustment and agreement." He then stated that the great majority of tribunals "consult with the applicant about the kind of work that he feels drawn to, and formulate their conditions in general terms, leaving the applicant a considerable range of freedom of choice. The great majority of objectors, fortunately, are reasonable enough to recognise this and are glad to co-operate with the Tribunals and come half-way to meet them."[85]

The figures which have been cited in this account show strikingly some of the contrasts between the decisions of individual local tribunals. There is no doubt that the chance of many applicants to obtain any exemption from their local tribunal, and also their chance of being allocated by it to one or other of the three possible classes of exemption, depended considerably on the irrelevant circumstances of their areas of residence. The following example of an extreme contrast between two tribunals with regard to their decisions as a whole, supports this conclusion. In the first period, the London No. 1 Tribunal (which considered 13,319 applications, far more than any other tribunal) refused any exemption to 39.3% of applicants and registered 36.4% for non-combatant military duties, 23.2% for civilian work, and 1.1% without conditions. In the same period the (English) South Western Tribunal (with 5,130 applications) refused any exemption to 11.5% of applicants and registered 23.5% for non-combatant military duties, 53.9% for civilian work, and 11.1% without conditions.

The injustices arising from the differences between the decisions of different local tribunals would have been far more serious but for the legal provision of a right of appeal to the Appellate Tribunal. This right was unconditional both for applicants and for the Ministry of Labour and National Service. The Ministry seldom exercised its right but the right was widely exercised by applicants. In the years 1939–1959 over 21,900 male applicants (about 31.5% of all male applicants) appealed to the Appellate Tribunal against the original decisions of their local tribunals and in these cases it was the decision of the Appellate Tribunal which determined the applicant's legal status. There were also 430 women applicants who appealed.[86] (On pages 188, 190 and 231 figures were given showing the legal status of all applicants as determined by either the local or the Appellate Tribunal.)

There were several divisions of the Appellate Tribunal (the number varying at different periods). Members of the Appellate Tribunal were, of course, like members of local tribunals, not infallible in their decisions, but the appeal system ensured that a second group of adjudicators should consider the cases of dissatisfied applicants. The system also gave to the appellant a second chance to present his case and to present it more adequately. For example, sometimes an appellant had, at his local tribunal, failed to give adequate verbal expression to his convictions, or to produce adequate evidence regarding his relevant past conduct, or to show that he had adequately considered his attitude to non-combatant military duties or to various forms of civilian work. When appealing, he benefited from having had further time to consider his position with experience of the kind of matters with which a tribunal was concerned.

The Appellate Tribunal could give any of the decisions possible for local tribunals. (It could reject completely a previously recognised conscientious objector and it did so, in 1939–1959, in the cases of 182 men.) It could vary the appellant's status as between the four possible classes or, within the class of exemption with conditions of civilian work, it could vary the conditions. In the period 1939 – 1959 slightly over half of the men who appeared before it had their status changed in some way.

In this period there were two numerically important groups of decisions. The first decreased by a net number of 5,716 the number of men whose objection was totally unrecognised – in other words 5,716 additional men became legally recognised as conscientious objectors. The gross number recognised for the first time was 5,898, of whom 2,279 were registered for non-combatant duties in the army. The second important group of decisions transferred a net number of 3,595 men from registration for non-combatant duties in the army to registration for civilian work. There is little doubt that, had it not been for these decisions, a considerably larger number of men would have felt it morally necessary to break the law.

The Appellate Tribunal also did important work with regard to some of those who broke the law for conscientious reasons. Men sentenced by court-martial to imprisonment (or, from 1949 onwards, to military detention) for three months or more, and men sentenced to imprisonment for three months or more for refusal of medical examination under court order, had the statutory right to apply to the Appellate Tribunal. (There were no women in either of these groups.)

In the years 1939–1959 there were, under these statutory provisions, 2,888 applications to the Appellate Tribunal. (It was possible to apply more than once and the number of men involved was smaller than this figure.) These applications resulted in 1,820 decisions which changed the status of the applicant – in the large majority of cases the applicant became free from obligation for military service of any kind: in 96 cases he became free from obligation for combatant military service. Thus over 1,800 men who had previously failed to convince tribunals of the sincerity of their objections to combatant service or to all military service had their objections legally recognised.[87]

In addition, members of the Appellate Tribunal, acting as an "Advisory Tribunal", adjudicated on a number of cases of men who had not originally applied for registration as conscientious objectors but had become objectors while full-time members of the Forces or reservists. These men had no statutory rights but, by administrative concessions, they were allowed to apply to the Advisory Tribunal if sentenced by court-martial to imprisonment (or, from 1949 onwards, to military detention) for three months or more. The tribunal could recommend the discharge of an applicant from the Forces. A number of full-time members of the Forces and reservists were discharged on the recommendation of the tribunal. (There are no published official figures regarding applications to the "Advisory Tribunal" or regarding the tribunal's decisions.)

The following are some written comments made in retrospect by Alfred W. Braithwaite, who on more than 200 occasions represented objectors before tribunals, mainly before divisions of the Appellate Tribunal meeting in London.[88]

"Frequently it was clear that the decision of the local tribunal appealed against had been based on its doubts on some particular point, due mostly to insufficient evidence, and if it could be shown that this defect had now been remedied, the case was often plain sailing. "

"The most difficult problem for the tribunals was to know what to do with the objectors who objected to undertaking any form of compulsory service, civilian as much as military. The belief held by many people was that they were entitled, as of right, to be given unconditional exemption, but this was not the case. There was no right under the Act for anyone to object to civilian service, and therefore no right for the tribunal to recognise such an objection, or to base its decision on it. What then was the purpose of the provision for unconditional registration which was certainly one of the alternatives allowed under the Act? The answer of the tribunals was that this had nothing to do with objections to civilian service at all, but was an alternative available for us in a very small number of quite exceptional cases, as, for example, where the objector was precluded by physical disability from doing any

373

civilian war-work, or, at the other end of the scale, where he could clearly be trusted himself to find useful and acceptable work, and any condition imposed by a tribunal was therefore unnecessary, but this interpretation was not altogether satisfactory, and it did leave many objectors to all forms of compulsion with the feeling that they had not been fairly dealt with. This always seemed to me one of the points on which the Act might have been more explicit."

"It is generally agreed that these tribunals functioned as well as could reasonably have been expected, granted that their task, of judging conscience, was in the last resort an impossible one. It is not surprising that they made many errors. The wonder really is that the system on the whole worked so well."

In addition to the "unconditionalists", I think that at least two types of objector were sometimes at a disadvantage. The first type was the objector who did not base his objection on religious grounds. Members of Christian churches had the advantage of being regarded as following, or as trying to follow, a generally known and respected ideal of conduct. In many cases the churches to which they belonged had collective principles against military service: in other cases conscientious objection was often recognised by their churches as a permissible interpretation of Christian principles. In contrast, the objection of an atheist or agnostic was not regarded as part of a recognised system of beliefs and values. He had to defend his individual beliefs and values and he was sometimes expected to be able to answer very difficult questions of fundamental ethics.

Secondly, I think that the tribunal system sometimes put at a disadvantage the verbally inarticulate applicant. The degree of an applicant's verbal articulateness affected both his written statement to a tribunal and his oral statements at the tribunal-hearing, though his oral statements could be supplemented by the statements of his witnesses and of his representative (if he had one) and by evidence of his past actions, including, in some cases, experience in the Forces or experience of imprisonment. There is no necessary connection between the sincerity and depth of a conscientious conviction and the power to express this conviction in words. This was sometimes recognised by tribunal members; for example, Professor Field wrote: "When at the Tribunal we had before us a simple, unlettered applicant who has had little more to say than 'I just couldn't do it,' I often felt more certain of the reality of the moral conviction than when listening to some of the most skilful and elaborate arguments of the more sophisticated intellectuals."[89] I remember with admiration the trouble taken by the first Chairman of the Midlands Tribunal to encourage inarticulate applicants to express themselves, but tribunal members were not all so helpful to the inarticulate. I also remember appearing unsuccessfully before the Appellate Tribunal as a witness on behalf of an objector applying from prison, whose sincerity was not doubted by those who knew him but who was both extremely verbally inarticulate and a non-religious objector.

No one who observed the tribunal system working would claim that tribunals made no mistaken decisions. Tribunal members were fallible and sometimes prejudiced. Objectors did not always make the best of their case. But, in my opinion, the system had great achievements to its credit. It did not eliminate conscientious law-breaking but it did enable the large majority of objectors to obey their consciences without breaking the law. Though the decision of the tribunal had a coercive sanction, in practice the decision was often one agreed on between the tribunal and the objector. The system gave to all objectors the right to two tribunal-hearings and to some law-breaking objectors the right to additional hearings. Both by its existence and by much of its administration the system was striking evidence of the community's respect for individual conscience, even in a period of great national danger.

In relation to possible future problems it is worth considering to what extent the mistaken decisions of tribunals could have been avoided. The large statistical differences between the decisions of different tribunals suggest that some of the personnel of tribunals could have been better. But I think that any system of this kind will make some mistakes. All adjudicating bodies are composed of fallible and sometimes prejudiced human beings: I have served on two such bodies and I am well aware of this in my own case, and the matters on which I helped to judge were less difficult to assess than the matters of conscience on which tribunals had to adjudicate. In my opinion it is impossible to make a completely sure judgment with regard to the conscience of another person: I should be loath to try to do so even with regard to someone whom I knew intimately. Tribunals were required to judge on a very small knowledge of the applicant concerned: it seems to me to be greatly to their credit that the applicant was so often satisfied with the decisions.

Problems of Future Public Policy

The discussions in this chapter and in the previous chapter throw some light on the nature of future problems of conscientious objection. I see no likelihood that these problems will cease to exist: they will remain as long as there are legal compulsions which some individuals feel that they cannot conscientiously obey. The list of compulsions which provoke conscientious objection changes from time to time and in some cases provision has been made in legislation. The Abortion Act of 1967[90] made some provision with regard to persons having conscientious objections to participating in conducting abortions under the Act; the Industrial Relations Act of 1971[91] made some provision with regard to workers having conscientious objections to being members of trade unions and to making financial contributions to them. Under the law concerning unemployment, though the legislation itself has not mentioned conscientious objection, the independent statutory authorities adjudicating with regard to the receipt of unemployment benefit have decided in some cases that a job shall not be considered as "suitable employment" for a worker who has a conscientious objection to the work or its conditions (for example, an objection to working on Sunday or on the Jewish Sabbath).

There are also occasions of conscientious objection for which no legal provision has been made: the following are some examples. A few individuals have refused on conscientious grounds to make compulsory National Insurance contributions or to pay the portion of their personal taxation which relates to military or other Defence purposes. Some individuals have refused to answer some or all of the questions asked by the Census. In the public educational system, some parents have objected to the sex education given to their children at school and some Muslim parents have objected to the attendance of their adolescent daughters at schools attended also by boys. Under a Road Traffic Act[92] a legal compulsion requiring all motor cyclists to wear crash-helmets conflicted with the religious duty of Sikhs to wear their hair long. It is impossible to foretell what other new occasions of conscientious objection may occur in the future.

In my opinion future public policy with regard to conscientious objection should be guided by the principle that individual conscience should be respected as valuable in itself, though its expression in particular cases may seem mistaken and though it is likely to be regarded as a nuisance by those who place a high value on tidy administration. The coercion of conscience by law is, in itself, harmful: if the coercion is unsuccessful it causes suffering and waste; if it is successful it violates the moral integrity of the individual by forcing him to act against his conscience. When the law makes any kind of personal action generally compulsory and some adult individuals have conscientious objections to performing that action, then the desirability of making provision for legal conscientious objection should be seriously considered. When conscientious objectors are acting as parents on behalf of their children, or when conscientious objection is objection to the payment of taxes or other compulsory financial contributions, then the considerations involved are somewhat different and there is some discussion of these considerations in the following chapter.

If it is decided that a legal right of conscientious objection should be granted in relation to a particular legal compulsion, what is the best method of identifying the conscientious objector? The discussion of the three main methods used in the past has shown the advantages and disadvantages of each method. In my view, a future legal right confined to members of specified religious bodies would be unsatisfactory in most cases though it might be suitable in exceptional cases when an objection was confined to members of one religious group. If the legal right is made dependent on the decision of a judicial body in each individual case then, as no members of a judicial body are infallible, some genuine conscientious objectors are likely to be refused the right and, of these, some are likely to become law-breakers. If the legal right is available to all who claim it then there is the risk that the right will be claimed by some unconscientious objectors. The temptation to claim the right for unconscientious reasons and the harm to the State if such a claim is granted will vary according to the sphere of law concerned: in my view both are small in relation to the right of affirmation and in relation to the right of withdrawal of children from religious activities at school. But the position is quite different with regard to military conscription. Some people would be greatly tempted to claim falsely that they were conscientious objectors and, if exemption were granted to all who made a statement of conscientious objection, with no further test, this legal position would be regarded by many people as grossly unfair to other citizens compelled by conscription. Thus the kind of legal test which will give the best balance of advantages over disadvantages is likely to vary according to the sphere of law concerned.

Our views on what is a desirable public policy towards conscientious objectors are influenced not only by the kind of legal and administrative considerations discussed in this chapter and the previous chapter. Our views are influenced also by considerations concerning the importance or unimportance of individual conscience, the kind of State which is desirable, and the principles which should govern the relations between the State and its citizens. The following chapter, which is in the form of a dialogue, introduces these wider considerations and discusses some ethical and political problems of conscientious objection.

References

BMJ = British Medical Journal
The Tribunal = Periodical of the No Conscription Fellowship 1916 – 1920
CBCO = Central Board for Conscientious Objectors

1   Will. & Mar. c. 18
2   Field, G.C. *Pacifism and Conscientious Objection* p. 112
3   See e.g. Quakers and Moravians Act, 1833. 3 & 4 Will. 4. c. 48
4   See e.g. Militia Act, 1802. 42 Geo. 3. c. 90 Sect. 51
5   Hayes, Denis *Challenge of Conscience. The Story of the Conscientious Objectors of 1939–1949* Table p. 26
6   51 & 52 Vic. c. 46
7   33 & 34 Vic. c. 75 Sect. 7
8   Eliz. 2. 1988. c. 40
9   35 & 36 Vic. c. 62 Sect. 68
10 9 & 10 Geo. 6 c. 72 Sect. 9
11 Family Law Reform Act, 1969. Eliz. 2. 1969. c. 46 Sect. 8
12 Guardian 9.12.1969
13 Central Advisory Council for Education (England) "Children and their Primary Schools". Vol. I Report 1967 p. 206
14 Ibid. p. 491
15 Ibid. p. 492
16 Ibid. p. 206
17 Eliz. 2. c. 19
18 9 & 10 Eliz. 2. c. 21
19 3 & 4 Will. 4. c. 48
20 1 &2 Vic. c. 77
21 Eliz. 2. c. 19
22 Criminal Law Revision Committee. Eleventh Report. Evidence (General) 1972. Cmd. 4991 p. 165
23 Ibid. p. 164
24 Letter to New Statesman 13.12.1963
25 Court Transcript. Quoted in Peace News 19.1.1962
26 Times 13.1.1962
27 W.A. Macdonald. Hansard Vol. 323 Cols. 1222–1223
28 Cmd. 4991 p. 165
29 Ibid. p. 166
30 7 Edw. 7. c. 31
31 7 Edw. 7. c. 49
32 61 & 62 Vic. c. 49
33 9 & 10 Geo. 6. c. 81
34 10 & 11 Geo. 6. c. 27
35 Final Report of the Royal Commission on Vaccination. Par. 524
36 Vaccination Act, 1907. 7 Edw. 7. c. 31. Schedule
37 5 & 6 Will. 4. c. 62
38 Vaccination Act, 1907. 7 Edw. 7 c. 31 Sect. 2 (1)
39 Vaccination Act, 1898. 61 & 62 Vic. c. 49 Sect. 1 (1)

40   Ministry of Health Report for 1923–24 p. 12
41   61 & 62 Vic. c. 49
42   7 Edw. 7. c. 31
43   30 & 31 Vic. c. 84
44   Parliamentary Return No. 89. H.C. Session 1899
45   Ministry of Health Report for 1919 – 20 Part I p. 148
46   BMJ 10.12.1898 p. 1773
47   Letter to BMJ 17.12.1898 p. 1848
48   BMJ 11.2.1899 p. 353
49   BMJ 1.3.1902 p. 544
50   BMJ 31.5.1902 p. 1364
51   BMJ 15.2.1902 p. 411
52   BMJ 28.4.1906 pp. 1003–4
53   Home Office Circular 18.5.1906. Quoted in BMJ 1906 I p. 1322
54   BMJ 9.8.1902 p. 414
55   BMJ 3.6.1905 p. 1247
56   BMJ 17.11.1906 p. 1424
57   Debate on 22.5.1907. Hansard Vol. 174 p. 1278
58   Home Office Circular 18.5.1906. Quoted in BMJ 1906 I p. 1322
59   Ibid.
60   23.5.1907 BMJ 1.6.1907 p. 1318
61   5 & 6 Geo. 5. c. 104
62   Report of Local Government Board 1918 – 19 p. 116
63   Local Government Board Circular 3.2.1916
64   Graham, John W. *Conscription and Conscience. A History 1916 –1919* p. 65
65   The Tribunal 21.12.1916
66   Bell, Julian (edited) *We Did Not Fight. 1914–18 Experiences of War Resisters* pp. 381 – 382 and 384
67   Fry, A. Ruth *A Quaker Adventure. The Story of Nine Years' Relief and Reconstruction* pp. xxiv–xxv. Nisbet. 1926
68   Graham op. cit. p. 66
69   Bell op. cit. p. 379
70   Local Government Board Circular 23.3.1916
71   Fellowship of Reconciliation News Sheet 25.6.1916
72   6 & 7 Geo. 5. c. 15 Sect. 4 (3)
73   Letter to Times 4.4.1916
74   Letter to Daily News, Daily Chronicle & Manchester Guardian 30.3.1916
75   Local Government Board Circular R. 96. 23.8.1916. Case No. 55
76   Statement by Chairman of Birmingham Tribunal. The Friend 16.6.1916
77   Graham op. cit. p. 88
78   Ibid. p. 85
79   Ibid.
80   Hayes op. cit. p. 383
      Ministry of Labour and National Service: figures supplied to CBCO
      Cmd 1364 p. 10
      Cmd. 8640 p. 15

Cmd. 8893 pp. 15 – 16
81   Hayes op. cit. p. 383
82   Ministry of Labour & National Service: figures supplied to CBCO
83   Field op. cit. p. 104
84   Ibid. p. 79
85   Ibid. pp. 98–99
86   Hayes op. cit. table opposite p. 386
     Ministry of Labour and National Service: figures supplied to CBCO
87   Hayes op. cit. p. 386
     Ministry of Labour & National Service: figures supplied to CBCO
88   Private information
89   Field op. cit. p. 56
90   Eliz. 2. 1967 c. 87 Sect. 4
91   Eliz. 2. 1971 c. 72 Sect. 9
92   Eliz. 2. 1972 c. 20

See also: Department of Education Circular No. 3189 of 20th January 1989, 'The Education Reform Act, 1988: Religious Education and Collective Worship'.

CHAPTER 12

A Dialogue on Some Ethical and Political Problems of Conscientious Objection

C = A Critic. A = The Author

C: Are you claiming that the conscientious objector should be allowed to do as he likes while other people must do as they are told?

A: Obeying one's conscience is not the same thing as doing what one likes.

C: But isn't the distinction difficult for the objector to make?

A: The distinction can be made by the objector, in some circumstances more easily than in others. In the case of illegal objection there are legal penalties to be faced and the worries and uncertainties arising from actual or possible prosecution: these circumstances help the objector to make the distinction. In the case of legal objection the objector may find his action easy. But in some kinds of legal objection, such as objection to military service in war-time, there is the pervasive pressure of war-supporting opinion to be resisted and this circumstance may help to make the distinction clear.

C: But, even if the objector is not exactly doing what he likes, isn't he simply acting on a personal taste or preference?

A: My own experience as an objector may throw some light on this question. On one matter I persistently disobeyed the law and I had no doubt that I was acting conscientiously in doing so. I felt both that I was acting completely freely and that I could not possibly act otherwise; that I was expressing my essential self and that I was bearing an impersonal witness. I did not feel that I was acting merely on a personal taste or preference.

C: But what was the impersonal element in your feeling?

A: I acted under a sense of moral obligation. I have no doubt about the reality of this sense, both from my own experience and from what I have observed in the actions and statements of others. But I find it very difficult to describe the sense of moral obligation in general terms.

C: Does it imply that you think that all others in similar circumstances should act as you should act?

A: No. If I believe, as I do, that acting according to one's own sense of moral obligation is intrinsically valuable, I can hardly think that others should act as I do unless their own consciences prescribe such action. The authority of my conscience covers   my actions, not the actions of others.

C: But surely you would like others to act as you do?

A: Certainly, because what for me is "subjectively right" is so because I consider such action to be also "objectively right", that is to say right in general, right quite independently of any reference to myself. (In contrast, I do not make a general reference of this kind with regard to a personal taste).

C: In order to be right in general does the action have to be based on some general principle?

A: I'm inclined to think that some general principles are involved, explicitly or implicitly, in all action which is determined by a deliberate moral decision. But as all action is action in particular circumstances, there is always also some judgment with regard to the facts of the situation.

383

The history of conscientious objection shows some interesting contrasts with regard to the relative importance in particular controversies of conflicts of principles and conflicts of judgments of facts. For example, the controversy about oaths was almost entirely a controversy of principles – whether or not a religious reference was necessary in a statement, as a sanction to ensure truth-speaking or the fulfilment of a promise. In contrast, the controversy about vaccination was mainly a conflict of judgments of facts: both sides recognised that smallpox was a serious evil and wished to reduce its incidence, but they differed as to whether vaccination was an efficient and desirable means to this end. But, with regard to compulsion to submit to vaccination, there was a conflict of principles – whether the judgment of facts which determined action should be the judgment of the State or the judgment of the parents of the child concerned.

C: I don't consider that objection to vaccination was really conscientious objection, though that term was often used to describe it. I am willing to respect and to make concessions for objectors who act according to the requirements of their religion (or what they consider to be those requirements) because such objectors are appealing to an authority outside themselves and are trying to live by standards other than their own wishes. But objection to vaccination was merely a difference of opinion, similar to many other differences of opinion in public affairs, and we don't consider these differences to be matters of conscience.

A: The distinction you make has often been made and objectors on religious grounds have often found it easier to get their objections recognised than have other objectors. (This was often the case in the treatment by tribunals of applicants for exemption from military service.) There have been at least three reasons for the preferential treatment of religious objectors. Firstly, the struggle for freedom of conscience occurred earliest with regard to matters of religion or matters arising from religious beliefs and, as religious toleration was achieved, it was thought logical to include in it toleration on matters of conduct controlled by the tenets of a tolerated religious group. (An example is the concessions made to Quakers with

384

regard to affirmations and under the Militia Acts.) Secondly, many Christians had some sympathy with Christian objectors with whom they disagreed: they shared with the objectors the acceptance of the same authority for conduct, though they disagreed with the objectors' interpretations of the requirements of that authority. Thirdly, in the case of an objector who practises a religion, it is obvious that he is not just "doing as he likes" and that he is trying to obey his conscience on many matters of conduct, not only on the particular matter on which he disagrees with the law.

C: You seem to be making my case for me.

A: No: I am agreeing that many religious objectors have been obviously sincere conscientious objectors. What I am not admitting is that genuine conscientious objection has been confined to objection on religious grounds. I would include both non-religious objections on grounds of general moral principles and at least some objections based partly on judgments of the facts of particular situations.

There have been numerous cases of conscientious objections based on general moral principles not associated with religious belief. The nineteenth-century unbelievers who objected to taking oaths had a high standard with regard to their obligation to speak the truth, and it was this very standard which made them object to invoking a religious sanction in which they did not believe. Pacifists have considered all war to be wrong, and the moral obligation to refuse to participate in war has been felt as strongly by many pacifist unbelievers as by religious pacifists. Nowadays, when unbelievers have become numerous in this country, probably few people hold the fairly common nineteenth-century view that atheists cannot have moral principles. But a non-religious objector is more likely to be expected to give reasons for his views and a personal defence of them because his standards are not related to a generally known system of beliefs and values.

C: Yes, and because we do not necessarily know anything about his standards on other matters, and in some cases we may suspect that he is claiming to have a high standard on the matter of his objection just for his personal convenience. But, of course, I recognise that many unbelievers hold and act on moral principles. However, you have not answered my criticism of objection to conscientious objection to vaccination, where the question at issue was not a disagreement on principles but a disagreement on judgments of facts.

A: I do not accept the argument that a decision cannot be a matter of conscience because it is based on a judgment of facts. Many of our decisions in ordinary life are decisions of this kind. Some of them are not matters of conscience because they involve no moral considerations, or because they are comparatively unimportant, or because we do not feel strongly enough about them. But, in the case of objectors to vaccination, many of the parents concerned thought that vaccination was harmful, felt very strongly with regard to a matter affecting their children, and regarded the health of their children as their moral responsibility. In refusing to have their children vaccinated they were acting as conscientious parents. It was this moral element of disinterested concern for their children which distinguished the so-called "honest" objectors from parents who merely wished to avoid the trouble and discomfort to themselves involved in the vaccination of their children.

Objection to vaccination has not been the only case of objection based partly on a judgment of facts. There have been objectors to military service who have not been pacifists but who have objected to participation in a particular war. (In Britain some objectors of this type were granted exemption by tribunals.) In the United States of America many "draft-resisters" were non-pacifist objectors to the war in Vietnam. It would be absurd to consider that such objections were mere matters of opinion. The objector was refusing to assist in what he considered an evil action-an unjustified war. He had to make a judgment of facts, in addition to a judgment of principles, to decide that the war was unjustified but, if he did so decide, his further decision not to participate was an exercise of moral responsibility.

C: You have claimed that a wide variety of kinds of objection to the law can be based on conscientious grounds. But the decisions of those with views opposed to the objectors' views have often also been made on conscientious grounds. Surely objectors should recognise this fact, and yet some objectors have been very intolerant of their opponents. Why should the objector think that he knows better than the Government or has better moral principles than the majority of his fellow-citizens?

A: Some objectors have certainly been undesirably intolerant. The combination of intense conviction with tolerance is a difficult one. It is easy to confuse the view that one should act according to one's conscience with the view that one's conscience is infallible. I'm quite clear that my conscience is not infallible. All I can be sure about is that it is right for me (not other people) to act in a particular way at a particular time. I cannot even be sure that I shall not change my views in the future and I regard it as a moral duty not to shut my mind to this possibility. But the fact that my conscience is not infallible, with regard to either principles or judgments of acts, does not worry me unduly as it is a condition I share with everyone else, including Governments and Parliaments and the enforcers of laws. This universal human fallibility seems to me to be a strong argument in favour of rights of conscientious objection, as it has long been recognised to be a strong argument in favour of freedom of speech.

C: You have made fairly clear to me what you conceive as the essential features of conscientious objection. I now want to challenge your view, stated in the Introduction to this book, that conscientious objection is an important matter. The actions of conscientious objectors described in your histories seem to me to be interesting but not important. In the spheres of law which you have covered conscientious objectors have always been an insignificant minority, with the sole exception of objectors to vaccination. They have had little influence on public opinion and their actions have been remarkably ineffective. With the sole exception of compulsory vaccination, the compulsions which objectors have resisted have either remained part of the law or have been ended for quite other reasons. For example, it was not the actions of conscientious objectors that ended military conscription nor did their actions have any effect in preventing or shortening wars.

A: I agree with you that compulsory vaccination is the only clear case in which the existence of a body of conscientious objectors was one important reason for the ending of compulsion. But success in removing the compulsion objected to is not my criterion of the effectiveness of conscientious objection. The objector is claiming moral autonomy on a matter of personal action on which he has strong convictions: he is resisting the power of the State, not trying to capture that power. The effectiveness of his action lies in the action itself: he refuses to accept the State as the ultimate moral authority and instead acts on the authority of his own conscience, or, if he is a religious believer, on what his conscience shows to be the will of God for him. This is an important contribution to morality.

C: It could be a self-righteous protection of his own scruples with no concern for social morality. The objector is granted exemption or exempts himself from a general legal obligation, that is from what is generally regarded as his duty as a citizen. The law is the guardian of social morality and in disregarding the law he is a bad citizen: he is weakening social morality, a far more important thing than his own views of right and wrong, which are not only fallible but often the result of ignorance or prejudice.

A: Very few objectors have been anarchists. Most objectors have been generally law-abiding people: the laws which they have felt it necessary to resist have been exceptional. Moreover, in many cases the very standards which have made them resist particular laws have made them scrupulous in their observance of the law in general. You say that the law is the guardian of social morality and I agree that this is true of good law. But the sanction behind good law is not only its coercive sanction but the fact that its provisions are respected by the consciences of individual citizens. Any State which is not ruling merely by force must appeal to the moral standards of its citizens: it depends on a social morality which it has influenced but not created. The citizen obeying his conscience is the basis of social morality and of moral support for the law; he should be valued by the State even though, on exceptional occasions, that same conscience leads him to resist the law.

C: Is there any guarantee that conscientious resistance to the law will occur only on exceptional occasions? There are quite a number of present laws of which I disapprove: do you want me to break them all with no consideration for the democratic principle of respect for majority decisions? I have the legal right of a citizen in a democracy to try to alter laws by persuading others to share my views and by co-operating in propaganda activities with those who agree with me, in the hope that my views will become the views of the majority. I expect other people to obey laws of which I approve, even when they disagree with these laws: surely I ought to do the same for them.

A: This raises the question of whether the position of the conscientious objector is essentially affected by the type of government under which he lives. Conscientious objection has occurred, and will probably continue to occur, under a variety of types of government and its ethics are fundamentally the same under all systems of government because any system of government can make legal demands on the individual which he cannot conscientiously fulfil. But there are certain features of our democratic system which tend to limit the occasions of conscientious resistance to the law. One of these features you yourself have just emphasised – the fact that citizens who object to particular laws can hope to change them by legal political methods. This fact seems to me to provide a strong argument against methods of illegal "non-violent resistance" or "civil disobedience", when these methods are used as attempts to change the law or Government policy, the argument being that by such methods a minority are trying to overrule the decisions of the representatives of the majority. But the action of the conscientious objector is not an attempt to overrule the majority; it is a defence of his individual rights against the majority. The fact that in Britain the Government normally represents majority opinion is not in itself an adequate defence of the rights of the individual. It is quite possible for an individual citizen to think that a law represents the views of a large majority of his fellow-citizens (for example, military conscription during the Second World War) and still feel that it is wrong for him to obey that law. He can approve of political democracy without accepting the views of the majority as the moral authority for his own actions.

C: From what you have just said I might assume that you think that there are as many possible occasions for conscientious resistance to the law in democratic Britain as there are in Soviet Russia or as there were in Nazi Germany.

A: That is certainly not my view. I think that in a democratic State, as we have come to understand it in Britain, conscientious resistance to the law is likely to be very exceptional. The mere fact of democratic majority rule is not an adequate protection of rights of conscience. But our present British system and conventions of government include a strong respect for individual liberty and for the rights of minorities. Some important results of this respect are freedom of speech, freedom of association, and freedom of religious worship and other religious activities. Thus, several very important kinds of activity are now free from legal control and no longer provide occasions for conscientious conflict with the law.

Conscientious objection is likely to occur when there is a combination of two conditions, first, that there is legal control on a matter on which citizens have strong and divergent moral views; second, that the law imposes a compulsion on citizens directly affecting their personal actions or the actions of their dependent children. (Laws which are morally controversial but do not compel personal actions, for #xample, laws permitting divorce or facilitating contraception, do not normally cause ordinary citizens to become conscientious objectors.) To the extent that the State can avoid compelling the actions of individuals in types of activity which are morally controversial, to the same extent it can avoid problems of conscientious objection. Except in war-time, and with regard to post-war National Service, Britain in recent times has been fairly successful in avoiding such legal personal compulsions. It is interesting to note that compulsory vaccination against small-pox has been the only case in Britain of general legal compulsion regarding any form of vaccination or immunisation and I think it unlikely that the unhappy experience of compulsion under the Vaccination Acts will ever be repeated.

C: Do you think that the State ought to refrain from imposing any legal compulsions to which there is likely to be conscientious objection?

A: I wish I could answer a straight "Yes" to that question as I think that in itself the coercion of conscience by law is always undesirable. This coercion is, of course, avoided in the cases of objectors who are granted legal exemption, and respect for rights of conscience has been very apparent in the provisions of British law allowing legal conscientious objection. But such provisions may not entirely prevent the coercion of conscience. With regard to military conscription, in addition to those whose applications for legal exemption were refused and who then obeyed the law, there were probably a considerable number of others who were morally troubled about performing military service but were not sufficiently sure about their views to apply for exemption. I consider that military conscription, even with generous provisions for legal exemption of conscientious objectors, is morally wrong. In a matter as serious as personal participation in war, the ultimate decision should be left to the individual: the actions necessary in war should be performed only by those who consider them morally justified.

With regard to compulsory oaths, the legal right to affirm is available to all who claim it. But the present law shares a bad feature of other legal compulsions in religious matters – the encouragement of insincerity. On just those occasions when it is especially important that people should speak truthfully, they are normally required to preface their statements by invoking "Almighty God" in whom they may or may not believe. Under present conditions compulsory oath-taking is an anachronism which does not serve the interests of either truth-speaking or religion. I should like the law changed so that affirmations were made on all occasions on which, at present, oaths are taken or, alternatively, so that affirmations were normally made, with the right for the person concerned to take an oath if he asked to do so.

C: You have just said that you think legal compulsion is undesirable in two spheres of law in which conscientious objection has occurred. Do you extend this view to the other spheres of law described in this book?

A: I extend the view to some other spheres of law: for example, I would include as undesirable legal provisions compelling personal services, other than military service, for war or Defence purposes. But I do not advocate the ending of the present compulsion on parents to provide or allow necessary medical care for their children.

There is an important distinction between a decision taken by an adult with regard to his own actions and a decision taken by him on behalf of his children. Children under a certain age, which varies with the kind of decision and with the individual child, are not yet responsible enough to make their own decisions. Therefore it is not a violation of their personalities for these decisions to be made by others and the question at issue is whether those who make the decisions should be their parents or the State. It has been found necessary in some cases to give children legal protection against the unconscientious cruelty or neglect of their parents. But it may also be necessary to protect children against the conscientious actions of their parents. I think that a clear example of this necessity is shown in the cases of Jehovah's Witnesses who refuse to allow blood-transfusions for their children. The assumption of temporary control of the child by a public body in some of these cases has been, in my view, the best solution of the problem: the object of the law is attained, punishment is avoided, and there is no violation of the conscience of the objecting parent because his consent is not involved. However, the assumption of merely temporary control of the child would not solve the problem of parents with conscientious objections to all medical care for their children, as was the case with members of the Peculiar People. In this kind of case I think that a careful assessment would have to be made with regard to the family concerned, comparing the risks involved for the child because of his parents' conscientious objection to medical care with the disadvantages of removing him from the care of otherwise good and responsible parents.

British law allows an adult (with some exceptions) to make his own decisions with regard to his own medical care. If he acts in an unorthodox manner for conscientious reasons it is he himself who suffers from the results of his actions. But a child suffers from the results of the actions of his parents and he should sometimes have legal protection against these actions, even though they are conscientious. In my view the authority of a parent's conscience covers those actions of his children which are under his control but, as the children also have rights, his conscience when he acts in a parental capacity has not such a high degree of authority as it has with regard to his personal actions.

C: Are there any other spheres of law in which you think that the coercion of conscience by legal compulsions may be justified?

A: Yes: having distinguished between personal actions and decisions in a parental capacity, I want to make a further distinction between personal "actions" in a narrower sense and the disposal of a person's property. This brings me to the subject of taxation.

I am using the term "taxation" to include rates and other kinds of legally compulsory financial contributions. The question at issue is whether it is desirable for the State to avoid imposing taxation for a particular purpose when there is likely to be conscientious objection to that taxation. In British experience there have been conscientious objectors to two kinds of taxation which no longer exist – church rates and tithes. With regard to present compulsions there have been conscientious objectors to taxation for Defence purposes and for religious education, and there have been a few cases of conscientious refusal to pay National Insurance contributions. Taxation is also imposed at present to finance various other types of expenditure for morally controversial purposes, for example, operations for abortion and instruction on methods of contraception. While I do not know of any cases of conscientious refusal to pay taxes for either of these purposes, there may have been such cases and there could be such cases in the future. I do not doubt the sincerity of individuals who refuse to pay a tax, or the relevant proportion of a tax, because it will be spent on purposes to which they have strong moral objections. But I think that there are important distinctions between conscientious refusal of taxation and conscientious refusal to perform personal actions.

From the point of view of the objector, or potential objector, one distinction is the fact that refusal of property cannot be made effective in the same way as refusal of personal action. Some forms of indirect taxation cannot be avoided and refusal to pay income tax is often possible only with the co-operation of the objector's employer or of the body from which the objector receives investment income. When payment of a tax can be refused, the State can often, as in the case of distraint for rates, eventually enforce its claim without the consent of the objector, so that his refusal has some effect as a protest but no effect in depriving the State of his property. Even if the objector does successfully withhold the amount due from him, this will not reduce the resources available for the type of expenditure to which he objects unless the tax is collected for, and allotted to, a specific purpose, and such taxes are now exceptional. However, the conscientious objector to taxation may feel that these limitations on the effectiveness of his action do not nullify his moral duty to refuse to co-operate actively with the law.

In addition to these practical distinctions, there is a moral distinction made by some potential objectors between the right of the State to their property and its right to compel their actions. For some Christians the question has been authoritatively settled by the reported words of Christ who, when asked whether it was lawful to pay tribute to Caesar, referred to the image of Caesar on the tribute money and said: "Render therefore unto Caesar the things that are Caesar's; and unto God the things that are God's." (Matt. 22. v. 21. R.V.) My own view is that my right to my property is so dependent on laws and other social factors that I am not justified in resisting legal claims on it.

It seems to me that in a modern democratic State it would be not only very difficult in practice but also undesirable to refrain from financing a particular service from taxation simply because a minority of citizens had moral objections to that service. Many services which are regarded as desirable by the majority cannot be adequately financed except by taxation, and, if they are not so financed, it is the minority views which are in fact effective. However, though I think that the coercion of the conscientious refuser of taxes is sometimes justified, I should like the authorities to be content with the forcible collection of the amount due to them. The number of future conscientious tax-refusers in Britain is likely to be so small that punishment seems unnecessary as a deterrent, and to refrain from punishment would show that conscience, though coerced, is still respected.

C: Your arguments have become involved with very general questions of the respective rights of the State and the individual citizen.

A: This is because my views on rights of conscientious objection are related to my general views concerning the kind of State which should be not only obeyed but loyally supported. I believe in the conception of the "democratic" or "pluralistic" State as contrasted with the "totalitarian" State. To put it briefly, I believe that it is the individual that matters and that every individual matters. This belief implies that the actions of the State should be judged according to the extent to which they further or hinder the welfare (in the widest sense) of individuals, including individuals in the future and individuals who live under other States.

C: I would criticise this conception of the State as valuing individual welfare too much in comparison with the national interest. The individual should be expected to make some sacrifices for the public good.

A: I am not arguing that the individual should never sacrifice his interests for those of other individuals – there are many occasions when he rightly does so. There are also many occasions when he rightly sacrifices his interests for the "national interest" or the "public good" but only, in my view, when these conceptions represent the welfare of individuals.

Moreover, an individual may rightly make voluntary sacrifices for the welfare of others which it would be unjustified for the State to compel, and there may be elements in the life of an individual which he should not sacrifice for the welfare of others even if such sacrifice would be voluntary.

C: Your last statement seems to imply that the rights of the individual, in comparison with the welfare of others, are greater with regard to certain aspects of his life than with regard to other aspects.

A: Certainly. We all make distinctions as to the more and less important elements in our lives. The problem of rights of individual liberty is not just a problem of the rights of the individual versus the rights of the State: it is also the problem of what elements in individual life should or should not be compulsorily sacrificed for the welfare of others, or for what the State considers to be their welfare. In sixteenth-century England it was considered justified to prohibit freedom of religious worship in the interests of good order in the State: in later times this view was gradually changed, until the individual was left in complete freedom with regard to this very important aspect of his life. In recent times general freedom of speech has been regarded as a fundamental liberty of the individual which the State must not forbid, however inconvenient it may find it. These two types of freedom are concerned with the intellectual, moral and emotional life of the individual, that is with his essential self. We rightly feel that to restrict his freedom in these matters is a far more serious injury to him than, for example, to make him obey traffic regulations. In my view the aspects of life with which conscientious objection has been concerned are of the same kind of importance in the life of the individual: to enforce personal action which is against the conscience of the individual is to injure his essential self.

C: But should the State be concerned with the individual's "essential self," as you term it?

A: It cannot avoid such concern in the education of children, for which it is now responsible solely or jointly, in the large majority of cases. With regard to adults I think that its concern should be shown mainly indirectly – by removing hindrances to the achievement of a good life by individuals and by helping to provide favourable conditions for its achievement.

C: Please define what you mean by a "good life".

A: I cannot define it but I can say certain things about it which are relevant to this discussion. The meaning of a good life varies in detail with each individual and I welcome this variation. Because individuals have different as well as similar needs they should be treated similarly only in certain respects. Most individuals do not achieve a good life in isolation. Normally the individual finds valuable elements in his life in his relations and associations with others, but many of these relations and associations are and should remain completely voluntary. A large degree of liberty is desirable for the individual as a human being: a State under which "everything that is not forbidden is compulsory" is treating individuals as if they were merely citizens and is refusing to recognise some of their needs, rights and duties as human beings.

C: Do you think that there is an inevitable conflict between the duties of an individual as a citizen and as a human being?

A: I think that there will inevitably be some conflicts. Probably the most important occasion of conflict is when the State is at war. On this occasion the conflict occurs partly because the duties of an individual as a citizen are to a State covering only a limited geographical area, while as a human being an individual has potentially conflicting duties to human beings outside this area.

In peace-time, in the kind of State that I have described as desirable, I think that conflicts between human duties and citizen duties will be exceptional and that normally the individual who is achieving a good life will also be a good citizen.

C: Your last statement is very optimistic. It is also a rather strange conclusion to result from a study of conscientious objection.

397

A: The statement implies that, when conscientious objectors find a conflict between their duties as citizens and their duties as human beings, the conflict arises not only from the views of the objector but also from the nature and laws of the State of which he is a citizen.

The State should recognise that the individual is not merely a citizen and that his human rights and duties are wider than his citizen rights and duties. The State should also recognise that, though it is the ultimate legal authority, it is not the ultimate moral authority. These general principles are accepted to a large extent by the present British State and I would claim that conscientious objectors have helped to achieve this acceptance.

Birth and Death Dates of Prominent Individuals

Albert, Prince Consort 1819 – 1861
Allen, Clifford 1889 – 1939
Beveridge, W.H. 1879 – 1963
Bevin, Ernest 1881 – 1951
Booth, Charles 1840 – 1916
Bradlaugh, Charles 1833 – 1891
Bright, John 1811 – 1889
Burn, W.L. (No Univ) 1904 – 1966
Burns, John (E.) 1858 – 1943
Clifford, John 1836 – 1923
Cole, G.D.H. 1889 – 1959
Cromwell, Oliver 1599 – 1658
Edward VII 1841 – 1910
Forster, W.E. 1818 – 1886
Gladstone, W.E. 1809 – 1898
Hardie, J. Keir 1856 – 1915
Henderson, Arthur 1863 – 1935
Keynes, J .M. 1883 – 1946
Knox, John 1505 – 1572
Lansbury, George 1859 – 1940
Marx, Karl 1818 – 1883
Masterman, C.F.G. 1874 – 1927
Mill, John Stuart 1806 – 1873
Orwell, George 1903 – 1950
Pease, Joseph M.P. 1799 – 1872
Shaw, G Bernard 1856 – 1950
Trevelyan, G.M. 1876 –1962
Webb, Sidney 1859 – 1947
Webb, Beatric 1858 – 1943
Wesley, John 1703 – 1791
Wilberforce, Bishop Samuel 1805 – 1873

Bibliography

Addison, William George, *Religious Equality in Modern England 1714–1914*, 1944.
Allen, Anne and Morton, Arthur *This is Your Child: The Story of the National Society for the Prevention of Cruelty to Children* 1961; Paperback Edition, 1962.
Arnstein, Walter L., *The Bradlaugh Case: A Study in Late Victorian Opinion and Politics*, Oxford, 1965.
Bell, Julian (edited), *We Did Not Fight 1914 – 1918 Experiences of War Resisters*, 1935.
Bentham, Jeremy, (1) *Swear Not at All*, Works. 1962 Edition. Vol. V.
(2) *Theory of Legislation.*
Birchenough, Charles, *History of Elementary Education in England and Wales from 1800 to the Present Day*, 2nd Edition. 1925.
Bonner, Hypatia Bradlaugh and Robertson, John M., *Charles Bradlaugh*, 2 Vols. 1894.
Bost, Ami, *History of the Bohemian and Moravian Brethren...* 1834.
Bradlaugh, Charles, *Champion of Liberty: Charles Bradlaugh*, Centenary Volume, 1933.
Braithwaite, William C. (1) *The Beginnings of Quakerism*, 1912.
(2) *The Second Period of Quakerism*, 1919.
Bullock, Allan, *The Life and Times of Ernest Bevin*, Vol. 11, 1967.
Butler, Lord, *The Art of the Possible*, 1971.
Chalkley, Thomas A., *Journal or Historical Account of the Life, Travels and Christian Experiences of... Thomas Chalkley*, 1751 Edition.
Clode, Charles M., *The Military Forces of the Crown*, 2 Vols. 1869.
Coulton, G.G., *The Case for Compulsory Military Service*, 1917.
Creighton, Charles, *A History of Epidemics in Britain*, Vol. II, Cambridge, 1894.
Davies, A. Tegla, *Friends Ambulance Unit*, 1947.
Dixon, C.W., *Smallpox*, 1962.
Field, G.C., *Pacifism and Conscientious Objection*, Cambridge, 1945.
Fox, George, *Journal*, Cambridge Edition 1911, Vol. I Everyman Edition.
Foxe, John, *Actes and Monuments (The Book of Martyrs)*, 1563.
Friends, Society of, (1) *Extracts from Minutes and Advices of Yearly Meeting*, 1783.
(2) *Extracts Relating to Christian Doctrine, Practice and Discipline*, 1861.
(3) *Christian Faith and Practice in the Experience of the Society of Friends*, 1960.
Fry, A. Ruth, *A Quaker Adventure. The Story of Nine Years' Relief and Reconstruction*, Nisbet, 1926.
Graham, John W., *Conscription and Conscience. A History 1916–1919*, 1922.
Halévy, Elie, *A History of the English People in the Nineteenth Century*, Vol. V. London, 1924–34.
Hayes, Denis, (1) *Challenge of Conscience. The Story of the Conscientious Objectors of 1939–1949*, 1949.
(2) *Conscription Conflict. The Struggle For and Against Military Conscription in Britain between 1901 and 1939*, 1949.

Hirst, Margaret E., *The Quakers in Peace and War: An Account of their Peace Principles and Practice*, New York, 1923.

Hoekema, Anthony A., *The Four Major Cults: Christian Science, Jehovah's Witnesses, Mormonism, Seventh-Day Adventism*, Exeter, 1964.

Holmes, John, *History of the Protestant Church of the United Brethren*, Vol. 1, Bradford, 1825.

Hooke, Ellis, *Record of Sufferings*, 1679.

International Bible Students Association, *Make Sure of All Things*, 1957.

Jones, Rufus M., (1) *Studies in Mystical Religion*, 1909.

(2) *The Later Periods of Quakerism* Vol. 1, 1921.

Knox, Ronald, *Enthusiasm: A Chapter in the History of Religion, With Special Reference to the XVII and XVIII Centuries*, Oxford, 1950.

Lewis, Michael, *The Navy of Britain: A Historical Portrait*, 1948.

Livingstone, Adelaide, *The Peace Ballot: The Official History*, 1935.

Locke, John, *First Letter Concerning Toleration Works*, 1824 Edition, Vol. V.

McCallum, R.B., *Public Opinion and the Last Peace*, 1944.

Manwaring, G.E. and Dobree, Bonamy, *The Floating Republic*, 1935.

Marchant, Sir James. *Dr. John Clifford C.H. Life Letters and Reminiscences*, 1924.

Martin, Kingsley, *Father Figures. A First Volume of Autobiography 1897–1931*, 1966.

Mellanby, Kenneth, *Human Guinea Pigs*, 1945.

Mill, John Stuart, *On Liberty*, 1859.

Montgomery, John, *Abodes of Love*, 1962.

Nelson, John, *An Extract of J. Nelson's Journal. . .* Bristol, 1767.

New English Bible: New Testament, Oxford and Cambridge, 1961.

New English Dictionary, Oxford, 1905 Edition.

Paul, Hugh, *The Control of Communicable Diseases*, 1952.

Penn, William and Richardson, Richard, *A Treatise of Oaths*, 1675.

Peterson, A.D.C., *A Hundred Years of Education*, 1952.

Rideman, Peter of the Hutterian Brothers, *Account of our Religion Doctrine and Faith...* 1950 Edition.

Roth, Cecil, *A History of the Jews in England*, Oxford, 1941.

Sacks, Benjamin, *The Religious Issue in the State Schools of England and Wales 1902–1914. A Nation's Quest of Human Dignity*, Albuquerque, 1961.

Shaw, Bernard, *The Doctor's Dilemma: A Tragedy*, 1913.

Smith, Frank, *A History of English Elementary Education 1760–1902*, 1931.

Stephens, Tom (edited), *Problem Families: An Experiment in Social Rehabilitation*, 1945.

Stevenson, W.C., *Year of Doom, 1975. The Inside Story of Jehovah's Witnesses*, 1967.

Sturt, Mary, *The Education of the People. A History of Primary Education in England and Wales in the Nineteenth Century*, 1967.

Taylor, A.J.P., *English History 1914–1945*, Oxford, 1965.

Taylor, Jeremy, *Works*, Vol. II 1854 Edition.

Taylor, Stephen, *Battle for Health. A Primer of Social Medicine*, 1944.

Trevelyan, G.M., *England under the Stuarts*, 1904.

Underwood, A.C., *A History of the English Baptists*, 1947.

Wesley, John, *The Journal of the Rev. John Wesley*, Everyman Edition Vol. 1, 1906.

Westermarck, Edward, *The Origin and Development of the Moral Ideas*, 2 Vols., 1906–1908.

World Year Book of Education, 1966, *Church and State in Education*.

Index